Presented To:

_____

_____

By:

_____

_____

On the _____ Day of _____
In the Year of Our Lord _____

On the Occasion of:

_____

_____

A BOOK
OF
PRAYER

For Baptists

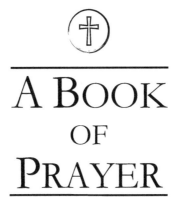

A BOOK
OF
PRAYER

For Baptists

With Resources for Ministry in the Church

Compiled and Edited by:

Rev. Patrick S. Morrow, M.Div.
Rev. W. David Stone, M.Div.

2021

1st Edition

ISBN:
978-1-7349607-0-9 (Paperback)
978-1-7349607-1-6 (Hardcover)

orare est laborare

Table of Contents

INTRODUCTION

Preface

by Patrick Morrow

Although I am a "cradle Baptist," I remain a Baptist today as a matter of conviction. I believe the Baptist witness deserves its place as an equal among all the churches of orthodox (Nicene) confession, because it contributes in its own vocationally unique way to the preservation of important elements of the New Testament church. There is much to be proud of about our Baptist heritage. In some seasons, the Baptist witness has even been a first among equals in bold evangelism and the faithful preaching of God's Word. Even so, we have not been without our own unique challenges and mistakes. Too often, we have ignored or over-individualized spiritual disciplines and the process of spiritual formation. The consequences of these deficiencies are becoming increasingly apparent.

I first became aware of spiritual disciplines during my time in seminary, but my first genuine *experience* of these practices came during the final months of my theological education. I was given permission to fulfill my seminary's mentoring requirement in an Anglican church planting context. As part of that process, my mentor, Fr. Lee Nelson of Christ Church in Waco, Texas, asked that I join a small but dedicated group of believers in common prayer at least once a week. In this way, I was introduced to the Episcopal Book of Common Prayer. Even as a seminarian, I was humbled by these Anglican brothers and sisters that believed in the testimony and truth of Holy Scripture, in the power of prayer, and in the formative power of daily worship. Through them, I discovered how the Daily Office effectively combined and incorporated these commitments into the rhythms of daily life to form the human spirit.

The Lord used this season to bring about a process of deep spiritual formation that permanently changed my walk of faith. Perhaps even more importantly, it has profoundly changed our *family's* private life of worship. As a "good Baptist," I do not and cannot make the claim that *all* will have a similar experience with common prayer. And yet, I do believe that there are *many* who are hungry for this type of spiritual formation but don't know how to begin. I know there are many who are looking for a way to maintain the core and the best of what it means to be a Baptist, even as we long to learn and incorporate ancient rhythms of church life into our families and worshiping communities. While there appears to be a general uptick in the number of discipleship resources available that touch on these subjects, I have found there are few written specifically to our "tribe" (Southern Baptists). And so, for some time, it has been on my heart to write, or at least compile and edit, a Prayer Book that could help remedy this oversight in one small way. This book represents our humble attempt at the effort.

This project has been unapologetically influenced by my mentoring experience. Its current form seeks to draw on the best of the tradition of common prayer as I learned it, while making it a little more accessible to Baptists and more consistent with core Baptist convictions, especially as they are rooted in the theological commitments of the Reformation.

While there are many commonalities between this book and the 1979 Episcopal Church (ECUSA) Book of Common Prayer, there are also several differences of note. The rhythm of the annual Church Year has been simplified, with the observances of Saints' Days and feasts entirely eliminated. All apocryphal readings have been omitted from the schedule of readings. Some prayer services or orders have been slightly altered in a way we feel may be beneficial to Baptists or to those who have no specific religious tradition. At various places in this volume, directions, helps, and prompts have been added and are usually italicized. Examples include explanations of when church seasons begin and end and how to introduce or move from one part of a service to another. Some of these helps do not appear in an Anglican book of prayer because the reader's knowledge is assumed. Finally, some theological revision has been necessary in certain elements such as written prayers, and the descriptive language of the liturgy. We have, however, avoided theological revision in ancient elements like the *Kyrie Eleison* or *Te Deum Laudamus* (an ancient hymn entitled "You, oh God, we Praise!") that hover chronologically around the great ecumenical councils of the early church. These are the heritage of *all* Christians. Even so, while the orthodox continue to share a great body of common belief, there are some differences that one cannot and should not simply paper over. The goal of Christian unity is not well served by concluding that distinctives do not really matter. And, in any case, such conclusions are inevitably patronizing.

Allow me, if you will, a few thoughts about why I think common prayer can and should be part of the overall work of renewal in Baptist life in general and Southern Baptist life in particular. It is my belief that nothing about common prayer contributes to our justification. That is the Lord's work — totally and completely free, bought by Jesus Christ alone, and given according to God's sovereign grace. And yet, I am also reminded of how many times Paul uses athletic metaphors to convey deep truths about life and spiritual formation. Here I must admit another deep debt of gratitude to my good friend Fr. Lee Nelson for introducing me to the writings of Fr. Martin Thornton. Fr. Thornton helped me think about common prayer not as an empty or legalistic ritual, nor yet as a kind of self-righteous striving, but rather as *preparation and training*. For me, common prayer has functioned as the spiritual equivalent of running laps, doing push-ups, and lifting weights before competing. In the practice of common prayer, we immerse ourselves in Scripture and in the whole worldview of the Bible. We confess sins and are reminded of God's forgiveness of sinners in Christ. We confess the historic faith of the Church and look with anticipation toward the day when Christ will return. In all of these, the Spirit of God shapes our spirits and prepares us for the day when we face unexpected sorrow, doubt, or temptation.

Seemingly everyone admits that the Christian Church is in a time of crisis in the Western World (and has been for some time). There are no silver bullets that will solve all the problems we face. And yet, I cannot shake the nagging suspicion that much of our current crisis, at least in Southern Baptist circles, has a direct connection to an impoverished understanding and practice of the disciplines of spiritual formation. We know how to put on a great show, but we have lost something of the quiet dignity that accompanies a deep and daily commitment to be formed into the image of Christ. While common prayer is not a one size fits all solution, I do believe it can help to create the foundation for real renewal in our witness and denominational vitality.

Why a Prayer Book?

Perhaps it is best to begin by answering the question, "Why a *Baptist* Prayer Book?" There are many good prayer books already, not least the 1979 Episcopal Book of Common Prayer that has been so influential in the compilation of this work. Is there really a need for *another* denominationally distinct prayer book? We believe the answer to that question is *yes*, for several reasons.

Baptists have unique theological commitments. Baptists have a distinctively Protestant understanding of the authority of Scripture and of the canon of Scripture. Southern Baptists also have a distinct spectrum of understanding of theological concepts like the Ordinances ("sacraments" to many of our Protestant brothers and sisters) and the means of the presence of God's grace in the life of believers. Thus, uncritically appropriating the *forms* of Anglican Prayer (or of any other tradition) without a serious and thorough review of their theological content will invariably give rise to theological confusion, or even conflict, in the performance of the Daily Office. This is far from the heart and aim of any truly Christian liturgy. Some confusion, it must be admitted, is unavoidable, especially for those who have never been exposed to this ancient Christian practice. Even so, a distinct prayer book with appropriate theological revision can help minimize such unnecessary theological distractions.

From a liturgical perspective, Baptists have their own "heart language" when it comes to the ordering of worship and ministry and the expression of prayer. Some of this will benefit from the reforming effect of ancient practices, but much of it is good and helpful. Most Southern Baptist Sunday morning gatherings proceed along one of several basic templates. Typically, Baptist Sunday gatherings begin with worship music followed by Scripture and prayer. The service usually climaxes with a sermon or with the Lord's Supper, and sometimes there is a time of prayerful response. With respect to prayer, many Baptists will have grown up knowing and using acronyms like ACTS (Adoration, Confession, Thanksgiving, Supplication) as a basic structure for individual prayer. So, for many Baptists, it makes sense for Morning Prayer to begin with adoration before moving on to the penitential act (confession). Learning the Daily Office is hard enough by itself; there is no need to disrupt every rhythm of Baptist spirituality for the sake of a shallow appreciation of old, traditional elements.

In compiling the first Book of Common prayer, Thomas Cranmer sought to make the full benefit of worship available to *all* English-speaking people by translating its forms from Latin into the English language. In just such a way, our intent is to make the benefit of liturgy available to Baptists by translating some of its structures and forms, as best as we are able, into the tongue of our tribe. Thus, we believe this project to be in perfect accord with Thomas Cranmer's basic intent *and* with Baptist notions of freedom. Not surprisingly, this project also inherits all the basic tensions and difficulties that accompany any other translation project. When do we stick with tradition? When do we adapt for the sake of comprehensibility? When do we insist on literalism? When do we allow the freedom to explore idiomatic correspondence? We believe writing a new book of prayer, by Baptists *and for* Baptists, even one that seeks as much liturgical beauty and antiquity as possible, can help to answer these questions in a way that best promotes spiritual formation in a Baptist context.

The basic function of *this* Baptist prayer book is to help believers walk daily with Jesus outside of the Sunday morning gathering. Of course, many of us who grew up Baptist heard regularly that we needed to be "in the Word" and needed to cultivate a personal "quiet time." But there were and are several serious problems with this as a model for spiritual formation. The first problem is practical; most of us never spring forward from the starting blocks. Of the few that do, almost all quit a couple of weeks after church camp. These failures are canaries in the coal mine of modern spirituality.

Theologically, the most glaring defect in an overly individualistic devotional model is that we are *not* personally and individually at the center of the story. The Gospel is the victory and Lordship of Jesus and the *overflow* of that victory to sinners. We do not appropriate that overflow by our own devices. God, by his own sovereign grace, calls sinners from darkness into light, purchases them, and adopts them into his family. He alone pays the price for sin, and he alone makes the human heart of stone into a heart of flesh. And so, the Christian life is the story of *Christ*, and it is always a story already in progress when we join it. Thus, the Christian life is always a life in and through his body, the Church.

Growing in grace through daily worship, prayer, and exposure to the Word of God is not and can never be simply a personal or individual matter. We should never reduce it to this! Maturity in the Christian life is God's work. And, it is a work he invariably does in and through *the Church*. That is not to say there is no place for individual or "secret" devotion. It is to say, quite simply, that for all but a few of the most extraordinarily gifted prayers,[1] such individualized devotion is simply not sustainable nor was it ever meant to be! Most people get stuck at the starting line. Almost everyone else will stumble from a lack of method or accountability. People don't need to become Christian "Supermen." This kind of bootstrap spirituality nearly always leads to self-righteousness, hypocrisy, and spiritual narcissism. A better choice is to humbly acknowledge the weakness common to all flesh and seek the remedy for that weakness where God has provided it: *in the community of the Church*.

In the beginning, God said it was not good for people to be alone. Should it surprise us that these words still inform the life of

---

1 Like the anchoritic monks!

Christian discipleship? God created people to *need* the Church's help in sustaining a life of worship. Most people need a guide or help laid down by the Church that grounds them in Holy Scripture, which is itself the supreme and final rule of faith. Indeed, this is the very purpose of traditional Southern Baptist Sunday School curriculums. People also need the accountability that comes from the community of the Church, through the regular reading of Scripture in that community. In and with his Church, God equips believers to live godly, righteous, and sober lives to the glory of Christ. The practice of prayer book spirituality and common prayer provides that rule and accountability.

A Brief Survey of the Book

This edition of *A Book of Prayer for Baptists* includes: Orders for Morning Prayer, Individual or Midday Devotions, Orders for Evening Prayer, and Prayers at the End of the Day. The Episcopal Book of Common Prayer (1979) lists the abbreviated orders under a separate devotional section *after* the regular services. We have reversed this and placed shorter orders for prayer *first* as a way of helping Baptist folk "stick their toe in the water," so to speak. Those who do so and perceive spiritual value in the discipline may go further and incorporate the elements that occur in the full orders. So, do not feel guilty about starting small! The reality is that life gets busy, children get squirmy, and longer services do not better Christians make (at least automatically). The key for this kind of prayer is to find a sustainable way of incorporating it into the rhythm of your family's daily life.

After the orders for daily prayer, you will find a section of Written Prayers. These prayers are traditionally called "collects" and many were originally translations of ancient Latin prayers. We have taken these traditional, seasonal "collects" from the Book of Common prayer and revised them to enhance readability and, to some extent, for theological compatibility with broadly Baptist commitments. Also, we have reduced the overall number and thematic complexity of the written prayers. For example, we have omitted written prayers for various special occasions in national or civic life because Baptists will almost always prefer to pray extemporaneously on those occasions.

The next section includes the entire book of Psalms, as you will use Psalms regularly in the practice of common prayer. The Psalms in this book are drawn from the New Living Translation (NLT) and are bolded for responsive reading. Reading the book of Psalms in this way is both deeply formative and profoundly authentic.

Next, the prayer book contains a section titled "The Journey of Discipleship." This section includes ministry aids, in a rough order of life occurrence, for the various seasons in the journey toward and through a life of discipleship. New ministers in particular may find these resources helpful as they begin to practice the craft of their calling. However, these practices are not only for ordained ministers. Since the Reformation, Baptists have believed in the "priesthood of all believers." When Martin Luther asserted that all believers are priests, it was not because he disliked priests or the priesthood but rather because he disliked the exclusion of believers from their priestly birthright and responsibility. It is not that Baptist churches do not have priests; it is rather that they do not have laypersons. Of course, some practices like Baptism (or anointing with oil) will continue to be performed primarily by ordained ministers, elders, and deacons. Even so, we hope these resources will encourage our Baptist "laypersons" to reflect upon their own calling to minister and will give them some practical guides for the practice of that calling.

For many, the journey toward discipleship begins with infant dedication, so we have included a guide to help order these types of services. Infant dedication is followed by a catechism for the instruction of unconverted persons or those preparing for baptism.

We believe that proper catechesis is indispensable for laying a healthy foundation for discipleship. Some Baptists will be unfamiliar with this method of instruction, but it is not new in Christian history or in Southern Baptist practice. The English word "catechesis" comes from the Greek word, κατήχησις, and quite simply means "instruction." In a church context, this idea refers specifically to theological instruction that takes the form of question and answer. Southern Baptists have been writing catechisms since 1864 when The Sunday School Board of the Southern Baptist Convention published its first catechism by J.P. Boyce titled *A Brief Catechism of Bible Doctrine*. A subsequent work was written in 1892 by John A. Broadus titled *A Catechism of Bible Teaching*. "The New Baptist Catechism" is based primarily on the 1963 and 2000 versions of the Baptist Faith and Message, but it contains additional material that seeks to add clarity and to reflect the current situation and diversity of Southern Baptist witness while remaining faithful to historic Baptist commitments. However, there are some nuances in the answers. Teachers should review it carefully and consult with their church leadership before using it.

After the New Baptist Catechism, there are guides for baptism and communion services, as well as for reading and studying the Bible. We have also included a guide for what is commonly called "Confession" and, in the Book of Common Prayer, called "Reconciliation of the Penitent." In Baptist practice, the emphasis should be *pastoral*, depriving sin of the power it maintains through silence and on assuring the believer of pardon, so we have titled this ministry Confession and Consolation. After "The Ministry of Confession and Consolation," there are resources to help prepare couples for holy matrimony and for planning marriage ceremonies. There are also resources for ministry to the sick and to those who are dying, as well as resources for conducting funerals.

After the Journey of Discipleship, we have included guides for worship on selected holy days. These are not intended as legalistic mandates, but as guides to help Baptists critically reflect on and appropriate historical elements of worship into the lives of local churches.

The worship orders are followed by an entirely new schedule of scripture readings. We briefly considered using a schedule based on the Daily Office Lectionary for the 1979 Edition of the ECUSA Book of Common Prayer, but we eventually decided for several reasons that a new schedule would be better fitted to Baptist life. Most lifelong Baptists have a very limited familiarity with the Church Year. For such believers, a table of readings based on the Church Year would be very difficult to simply pick up and use. Thus, the schedule we have created is entirely new and is primarily based on our modern-day calendar. The "Schedule of Readings" walks through the entire Old Testament every four years, the book of Psalms twice a year, and the New Testament yearly. During the four year Old Testament cycle, readers will proceed along four different alternating "tracks" each quarter: The Pentateuch, Histories, Wisdom Literature, and Prophets. This schedule has kept the readings intentionally short. Anyone who has tried to shepherd their cranky and restless children through a time of family prayer will appreciate that brevity has its own beauty! Even so, there are many other schedules that walk through the Bible in one, two, four, or even five years. You should feel free to use the one that works best in your family or church setting. The important thing is for the voice of God in Scripture to be part of the "warp and woof" of your everyday life. This is how the children come to know the tenor of the Father's voice!

A Word of Encouragement

As you get started on your own journey into this brand-new world of ancient customs, please allow me (Patrick) to express a borrowed word of encouragement. As my friend and mentor, Lee Nelson, once observed, the key with this type of prayer is to simply jump right in! I would extend this same ethic to the whole tradition of the ancient Church. As Southern Baptists, we are children of the Western Tradition. Yes, we are Protestant, but the whole majestic (and sometimes ugly) history of the Church is our history as well. We should not be afraid to draw on the best of that history as a resource.

In the beginning, common prayer will seem foreign and even a little confusing or downright weird for many Baptists. In time, however common prayer will become like the background music of your life, coloring every season with the rich tenor of God's grace and goodness. In due course, its rhythms will become like second nature. In fact, this reality points to the whole underlying theological process of spiritual formation. In the course of time, you will find yourself memorizing Scripture and prayers, and you will be delighted when friends and family members are able to recite these by memory as well! This is another of the many blessings of a commitment to the Daily Office! Common prayer helps "the word of Christ to dwell in you richly." So persevere in it, friend, and you will be formed by the Spirit of God.

How to Use This Prayer Book

Most Baptists are not taught from childhood how to pray the Daily Office, so here are some pointers to help get you started:

1. First of all, **do not be intimidated**! Once you have learned the rhythm for this kind of prayer, you will realize a great deal of spiritual "work" can be done in a relatively brief time. The key is to learn by immersion, so jump in.

2. After arriving at the place of prayer **decide who will lead**. As Baptists, we believe this shared leadership is grounded in a deep theological truth! The Body of Christ is a kingdom of priests, and that means *all* have the privilege and responsibility of leading in the Daily Office along with the other spiritual disciplines of the Church. Don't hesitate to allow a young person or child to lead; this is a great way to pass down the faith (Deut. 6: 7–8)!

3. Before starting **make sure that everyone is utilizing the same *edition.*** This can be done quickly because each printing uses the same color for its cover (1st Edition is blue, 2nd Edition is green, etc.)

4. Next, **decide which Service or "Order" you will use**. Then, if you do not already know the current season of the Church Year, use your phone to determine the season. (For example, type "When is Ash Wednesday [or Easter, etc.]?" into your browser's search engine.)

5. Then look at the section titled "Schedule of Readings" to **determine the appointed scripture readings and Psalm** for the day. Mark the Psalm in your prayer book with a ribbon or bookmark.

6. **Decide who will be a reader** (or two, if two are necessary), and have this person use a ribbon or piece of paper to keep that Scripture reference marked.

7. **Look up the appropriate Written Prayer** for whatever week it is. This is when it is especially important to know where you are in the Church Year. Have everyone mark that prayer with a ribbon or bookmark.

8. Before the office begins, in a spirit of love, the one leading may wish to **inquire whether there are any present whose conscience objects to the reading of the Creeds**. (Historically, many Baptists have had an aversion to the recitation of creeds.) If any object, the one who is leading may choose to substitute a free prayer at that part of the office normally reserved for the recitation of the Apostles Creed or Nicene Creed.

9. After deciding the matter of creeds, all those who have gathered should keep silence and **wait for the leader to begin**.

10. As you work your way through the prayer service, **pay close attention to the prompts and helps in italics**. If you make a mistake, don't worry too much, and whatever you do, don't stop! Everything will become more natural in time. However, it does take time to learn how to read together in unison, and to feel the rhythms of the prayer service, so be patient with yourself (and others!).

Introduction to the Church Year

The Holy Days and Seasons

In this section you will find simplified explanations and a timeline for observing the Church Year. Colors can be reflected in cloths for the altar, banners, the color of flowers, or other simple church and home decorations (or even in a pastor's tie!).

Brief Explanation of Holy Days and Seasons

Advent

Advent is the season of preparation for Christmas. The Sundays of Advent are always the four Sundays before Christmas Day. Traditionally each Sunday focuses on a distinct theme of Advent (for example, in order: Hope, Love, Joy, and Peace). Advent begins the first Sunday after Christ the King Sunday and ends on Christmas Eve. The color for Advent is blue.

The Twelve Days of Christmas (Christmastide)

The Twelves Days of Christmas, or Christmastide, commemorate the birth and infancy of Jesus before the visitation of the Magi. Christmastide begins on Christmas Day (or at sundown on Christmas Eve) and ends on January 5th of the following year. The color for Christmastide is gold.

The Season of Epiphany (Epiphanytide)

The Season of Epiphany commemorates the first appearance, or manifestation, of Jesus to the Gentiles. Epiphanytide begins on the Day of Epiphany which is always January the 6th. This season of the manifestation of Jesus includes the celebration of the Lord's Baptism on the Sunday after Epiphany. Epiphany Season ends on different days according to different traditions. In the timeline that follows, it ends on the Tuesday before Ash Wednesday. The color for Epiphanytide is green.

Lent

Lent is a season in which Christians prepare for Holy Week by recalling and demonstrating sorrow for sin. Traditionally this remembrance is accompanied by signs of repentance including various types of fasts (which, for Baptists, should be considered a matter of conscience). Lent begins on Ash Wednesday which is always 46 days before Easter. Lent ends on the Saturday before Palm Sunday. The color for Lent is purple.

Holy Week

Holy Week commemorates the Passion of Christ. It begins on Palm Sunday (the Sunday before Easter Sunday) and ends on Easter Eve. Holy Week includes solemn observances of Maundy Thursday, Good Friday, and The Great Vigil of Easter (held after sundown on Easter Eve). Maundy Thursday commemorates the Last Supper. Good Friday commemorates the crucifixion and death of Jesus. The color for Holy Week is red or crimson before Maundy Thursday. On Maundy Thursday the color is Black. After M aundy Thursday there is no color until Easter.

The Season of Easter (Eastertide)

The Season of Easter, or Eastertide, lasts 49 days and commemorates the time between the resurrection of Jesus and the birth of the Church at Pentecost. Traditionally this has been a season of feasting and celebration. Eastertide begins with the Great Vigil of Easter and ends the Saturday before Pentecost. It includes the celebration of the Ascension of Jesus on the Sunday before Pentecost. The color for Eastertide is white.

Ordinary (Proper) Time

Ordinary Time begins with Pentecost and ends with Christ the King Sunday (the last Sunday before Advent). This season includes Trinity Sunday and Reformation Sunday. The color for Ordinary Time is green.

The Church Year

The First Sunday of Advent to Easter Sunday

Days and Their Colors:
Above the timeline

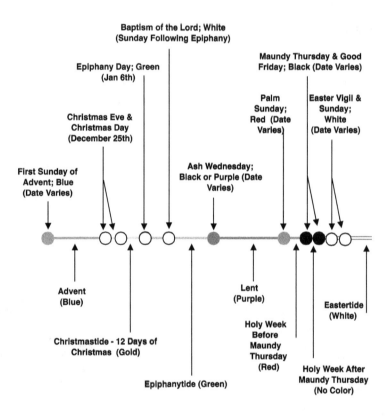

Seasons and Their Colors:
Below the timeline

The Church Year

Eastertide through Christ The King Sunday

Days and Their Colors:

Above the timeline

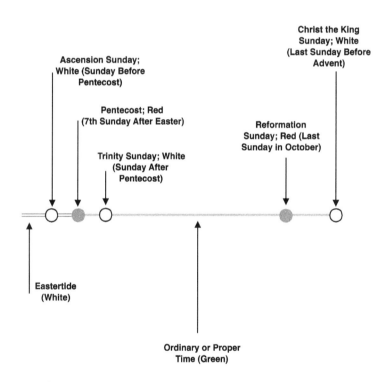

Seasons and Their Colors:

Below the timeline

DAILY PRAYER

A Brief Order for Morning Prayer

Morning Prayers should be observed around 6:00 a.m. but may be observed anytime between 5:00 and 8:30 a.m.

The Greeting

The leader will begin the Office by greeting everyone with the following scripture:

"Since you have been raised to new life with Christ, set your sights on the realities of heaven, where Christ sits in the place of honor at God's right hand" (Col. 3:1 NLT).

The Opening Praise

The leader will ask all gathered to stand, and will continue by saying:

Leader: O Lord, open thou our lips.
People: **And our mouths shall show forth thy praise.**

Then all will say the following praise in unison:

Glory to the Father, and to the Son, and to the Holy Spirit, as it was in the beginning, is now, and will be forever. Amen.

Confession and Consolation

Then all will be seated, and the leader will say this invitation to confession:
Let us keep silence and humbly confess our sins to almighty God.

Silence is kept, and after a due allowance of time, the leader says these words:

In the mercy of almighty God, Jesus Christ was given to die for you, and for his sake, God is faithful to forgive all your sins. To those who believe in Jesus Christ he gives the power to become the children of God and bestows on them the Holy Spirit. May the Lord, who has begun this good work in us, bring it to completion in the day of our Lord Jesus Christ. Amen.

Then all will say the following prayer in unison (Kyrie Elesion[2]):

Lord have mercy.
Christ have mercy.
Lord have mercy.

The Psalm

Psalm 118: 1–4; 22–29 (NLT)

Then all will say the following selection from Psalm 118 (or the appointed Psalm for the day) either in unison or responsively.

Oh give thanks to the LORD, for he is good;
for his steadfast love endures forever!
  Let Israel say,
  "His steadfast love endures forever."

2This is one of the earliest prayers used in Christian worship. It is known to have been used as early as the fourth century AD. For its New Testament origins see Matthew 15:22, 17:15, and 20:30.

Let the house of Aaron say,
"His steadfast love endures forever."
  Let those who fear the LORD **say,**
  "His steadfast love endures forever."
Out of my distress I called on the LORD;
  the LORD **answered me and set me free.**
Open to me the gates of righteousness,
  that I may enter through them
  and give thanks to the LORD.
This is the gate of the LORD;
  the righteous shall enter through it.
I thank you that you have answered me
and have become my salvation.
  The stone that the builders rejected
  has become the cornerstone.
This is the LORD's doing;
  it is marvelous in our eyes.
This is the day that the LORD has made;
  let us rejoice and be glad in it.
Save us, we pray, O LORD!
  O LORD**, we pray, give us success!**
Blessed is he who comes in the name of the LORD!
  We bless you from the house of the LORD.
The LORD is God,
  and he has made his light to shine upon us.
Bind the festal sacrifice with cords,
  up to the horns of the altar!
You are my God, and I will give thanks to you;
  you are my God; I will extol you.
Oh give thanks to the LORD, for he is good;
  for his steadfast love endures forever!

Glory to the Father, and to the Son, and to the Holy Spirit, as it was in the beginning, is now, and will be forever. Amen.[3]

---

3 This short prayer is called the Gloria Patri (Glory to the Father). The Gloria Patri is an ancient Christian prayer, traditionally read after the reading of a Psalm; it is not part of the book of Psalms

The Scripture Reading

Then someone will read an appointed passage for the day. Before reading the appointed passage, the reader may begin by saying:

A reading from [a citation giving book and chapter]. *Or the reader may say:* Hear the word of the Lord from [a citation giving book and chapter].

Depending on where the appointed reading begins, it may be necessary to provide some context.

For example: "This is from the reply of the Lord to Job," *or:* "This is while Jesus was teaching on the mount."

The scripture reading ends as follows:

Reader: The word of the Lord.
Or the reader may say: May God bless the reading of his word.

People: **Thanks be to God.**

The Profession of Faith

If conscience permits, all gathered will stand and recite the Apostles Creed. If there are any who object, then the leader may say a free-form prayer derived from the scripture reading.

**I believe in God, the Father Almighty,
creator of heaven and earth.
I believe in Jesus Christ, his only Son, our Lord.
He was conceived by the power of the Holy Spirit
and born of the Virgin Mary.
He suffered under Pontius Pilate,
was crucified, died, and was buried.
He descended to the dead.
On the third day he rose again.**

He ascended into heaven
and is seated at the right hand of the Father.
He will come again to judge the living and the dead.
I believe in the Holy Spirit,
the one holy universal Church,
the communion of saints,
the forgiveness of sins,
the resurrection of the body,
and the life everlasting. Amen.

Free Prayer

Then all will be seated, and the leader will continue by saying:

Let us pray for ourselves and for others.

All may pray aloud or silently as the Spirit of God leads them.

The Lord's Prayer

After due allowance of time for free prayer, the leader will say:

And now, Lord, we pray as you taught us.

Then all gathered will say the Lord's Prayer (Matt. 6:9–13 ESV) in unison:

9"Our Father in heaven,
hallowed be your name.
10 Your kingdom come,
your will be done,
   on earth as it is in heaven.
11 Give us this day our daily bread,
12 and forgive us our debts,
   as we also have forgiven our debtors.
13 And lead us not into temptation,
   but deliver us from evil.

For thine is the kingdom, and the power, and the glory,
for ever and ever. Amen[4]

---

[4] This postscript to the Lord's Prayer is drawn from the 1979 version of the Book of
Common Prayer. Most modern biblical scholars are in agreement that these words are not

The Benediction

The following elements of the Benediction are omitted if the Shorter Order for Morning Prayer is used as the Service of the Word before a Last Communion.

Then the leader will say: Let us bless the Lord.
The people respond: **Thanks be to God.**

Then the leader will conclude the service with one of the following benedictions.

"May the grace of the Lord Jesus Christ, the love of God, and the fellowship of the Holy Spirit be with you all." Amen. (2 Cor 13:14 NLT).

Or this:

"Now all glory to God, who is able, through his mighty power at work within us, to accomplish infinitely more than we might ask or think. Glory to him in the church and in Christ Jesus through all generations forever and ever! Amen." (Eph 3:20–21 NLT)

---

an original part of the Lord's Prayer in Matthew's gospel account. The ending is included, but set it apart, to be said as a theologically fitting praise to conclude the words that Jesus gave his disciples.

The Full Order for Morning Prayer

Morning Prayers should be observed around 6:00 a.m. but may be observed anytime between 5:00 and 8:30a.m.

The Greeting

The leader will begin the office by greeting everyone with one of the following Scriptures:

<u>During the Season of Advent</u>

Beginning with the First Sunday of Advent until Christmas Eve, any one of the following verses may be used as a greeting:

"You, too, must keep watch! For you don't know when the master of the household will return — in the evening, at midnight, before dawn, or at daybreak. Don't let him find you sleeping when he arrives without warning." Mark 13:35, 36 (NLT)

"Listen! It's the voice of someone shouting, 'Clear the way through the wilderness for the Lord! Make a straight highway through the wasteland for our God!'" Isaiah 40:3 (NLT)

"O Zion, messenger of good news, shout from the mountaintops! Shout it louder, O Jerusalem. Shout, and do not be afraid. Tell the towns of Judah, 'Your God is coming!'" Isaiah 40:9 (NLT)

"For a child is born to us, a son is given to us. The government will rest on his shoulders. And he will be called: Wonderful Counselor, Mighty God, Everlasting Father, Prince of Peace." Isaiah 9:6, 7 (NLT)

On Christmas Day and during Christmastide

During Christmastide or the Twelve Days of Christmas (from Dec. 25–January 5), any one of the following verses may be used as a greeting:

"I bring you good news that will bring great joy to all people. The Savior — yes, the Messiah, the Lord — has been born today in Bethlehem, the city of David!" Luke 2:10,11 (NLT)

"I heard a loud shout from the throne, saying, 'Look, God's home is now among his people! He will live with them, and they will be his people. God himself will be with them." Revelation 21:3 (NLT)

On Epiphany Day and through the night before Ash Wednesday

Beginning on Epiphany (always January 6) until the Tuesday before Ash Wednesday, any one of the following verses may be used as a greeting:

"All nations will come to your light; mighty kings will come to see your radiance." Isaiah 60:3 (NLT)

"I will make you a light to the Gentiles, and you will bring my salvation to the ends of the earth." Isaiah 49:6b (NLT)

"'My name is honored by people of other nations from morning till night. All around the world they offer sweet incense and pure offerings in honor of my name. For my name is great among the nations,' says the Lord of Heaven's Armies." Malachi 1:11 (NLT)

On Ash Wednesday and during the Season of Lent

Beginning on Ash Wednesday (always exactly 46 days before Easter Sunday) and throughout the Season of Lent, any one of the following verses may be used as a greeting:

"If we claim we have no sin, we are only fooling ourselves and not living in the truth. But if we confess our sins to him, he is faithful and just to forgive us our sins and to cleanse us from all wickedness."
1 John1:8–9 (NLT)

"Don't tear your clothing in your grief, but tear your hearts instead. Return to the Lord your God, for he is merciful and compassionate, slow to get angry and filled with unfailing love. He is eager to relent and not punish." Joel 2:13 (NLT)

"I will go home to my father and say, 'Father, I have sinned against both heaven and you, and I am no longer worthy of being called your son. Please take me on as a hired servant.'" Luke 15:18–19 (NLT)

"The Lord our God is merciful and forgiving, even though we have rebelled against him. We have not obeyed the Lord our God, for we have not followed the instructions he gave us through his servants the prophets." Daniel 9:9, 10 (NLT)

"Calling the crowd to join his disciples, [Jesus] said, 'If any of you wants to be my follower, you must give up your own way, take up your cross, and follow me.'" Mark 8:34 (NLT)

During Holy Week

Beginning on Palm Sunday and through Good Friday any one of the following verses may be used as a greeting:

"All we like sheep have gone astray; we have turned every one to his own way; and the Lord has laid on him the iniquity of us all." Isaiah 53:6 (ESV)

"Is it nothing to you, all you who pass by? Look and see if there is any sorrow like my sorrow, which was brought upon me, which the Lord inflicted on the day of his fierce anger." Lamentations 1:12 (ESV)

During Eastertide, Ascension Day, and the Day of Pentecost

During Easter Season the leader may use the traditional Paschal Greeting:

Leader: Alleluia! Christ is risen.
People: **The Lord is risen indeed. Alleluia!**

Or the leader may use any one of these verses as a greeting:

"This is the day the Lord has made. We will rejoice and be glad in it." Psalm 118:24 (NLT)

"Thank God! He gives us victory over sin and death through our Lord Jesus Christ." 1 Corinthians 15:57 (NLT)

"Since you have been raised to new life with Christ, set your sights on the realities of heaven, where Christ sits in the place of honor at God's right hand." Colossians 3:1 (NLT)

"Christ did not enter into a holy place made with human hands, which was only a copy of the true one in heaven. He entered into heaven itself to appear now before God on our behalf." Hebrews 9:24 (NLT)

"You will receive power when the Holy Spirit comes upon you. And you will be my witnesses, telling people about me everywhere — in Jerusalem, throughout Judea, in Samaria, and to the ends of the earth." Acts 1:8 (NLT)

During Ordinary Time

Beginning on the day after Pentecost and through Christ the King Sunday (the last Sunday before Advent) any of the following may be used as a greeting:

"Holy, holy, holy is the Lord God, the Almighty — the one who always was, who is, and who is still to come." Revelation 4:8b (NLT)

"May you be filled with joy, always thanking the Father. He has enabled you to share in the inheritance that belongs to his people, who live in the light." Colossians 1:11–12 (NLT)

"So now you Gentiles are no longer strangers and foreigners. You are citizens along with all of God's holy people. You are members of God's family." Ephesians 2:19 (NLT)

"Give thanks to the Lord and proclaim his greatness. Let the whole world know what he has done." Psalm 105:1 (NLT)

"May God our Father and the Lord Jesus Christ give you grace and peace." Philippians 1:2 (NLT)

"I was glad when they said to me, 'Let us go to the house of the Lord.'" Psalm 122:1 (NLT)

"May the words of my mouth and the meditation of my heart be pleasing to you, O Lord, my rock and my redeemer." Psalm 19:14 (NLT)

"Send out your light and your truth; let them guide me. Let them lead me to your holy mountain, to the place where you live." Psalm 43:3 (NLT)

"The Lord is in his holy Temple. Let all the earth be silent before him." Habakkuk 2:20 (NLT)

"The time is coming — indeed it's here now — when true worshipers will worship the Father in spirit and in truth." John 4:23 (NLT)

"The high and lofty one who lives in eternity, the Holy One, says this: 'I live in the high and holy place with those whose spirits are contrite and humble. I restore the crushed spirit of the humble and revive the courage of those with repentant hearts." Isaiah 57:15 (NLT)

The Opening Praise

<u>Glory to God!</u>

After the greeting, the leader will ask all gathered to stand and will continue by saying an invitation to praise:

Leader: O Lord, open thou our lips.
People: **And our mouth shall show forth thy praise.**

Then everyone will say the following praise[5] in unison:

---

[5]This short prayer is called the Gloria Patri (Glory to the Father). The Gloria Patri is an ancient Christian rayer, traditionally read after the reading of a Psalm; it is not a part of the book of Psalms.

Glory to the Father, and to the Son, and to the Holy Spirit, as it was in the beginning, is now, and will be forever. Amen.

Call to Worship

Then the time of praise continues with one of the following Antiphons:[6]

In Advent:

    Leader: Our King and Savior now draws near.
    People: **O come, let us adore him.**

On the Twelve Days of Christmas (December 25–January 5)

    Leader: Alleluia. Unto us a child is born.
    People: **O come, let us adore him. Alleluia.**

From Epiphany (Jan 6) until Ash Wednesday

    Leader: The Lord has manifested his glory to all peoples.
    People: **O come, let us adore him.**

On Ash Wednesday, During Lent and Through Holy Week

    Leader: The Lord is full of compassion and mercy.
    People: **O come, let us adore him.**

From Easter Day until the Ascension

    Leader: Alleluia. The Lord is risen indeed.
    People: **O come, let us adore him. Alleluia.**

---

[6]An 'antiphon' is a short sentence sung or recited before or after a psalm or canticle.

From Ascension Day until the Day of Pentecost

> *Leader:* Alleluia. Christ the Lord ascends into heaven.
> *People:* **O come, let us adore him. Alleluia.**

On the Day of Pentecost

> *Leader:* Alleluia. The Spirit of the Lord fills the world.
> *People:* **O come, let us adore him. Alleluia.**

On Trinity Sunday (The Sunday After Pentecost Sunday)

> *Leader:* Father, Son, and Holy Spirit, one God.
> *People:* **O come, let us adore him.**

During Ordinary Time

> *Leader:* The earth is the Lord's for he made it.
> *People:* **O come, let us adore him.**

> *Leader:* Worship the Lord in the beauty of holiness.
> *People:* **O come, let us adore him.**

> *Leader:* The mercy of the Lord is everlasting.
> *People:* **O come, let us adore him.**

The Hymn

Then all gathered will say one of the following hymns in unison or responsively with the leader reading the normal font and all others reading the bold font.

Glory be to God

> *The following may be said at any time, but especially during Advent Season.*

> Glory to God in the highest,
> **and peace to his people on earth.**

Lord God, heavenly King,
almighty God and Father,
we worship you; we give you thanks;
we praise you for your glory.
Lord Jesus Christ, only Son of the Father,
Lord God, Lamb of God,
you take away the sin of the world;
have mercy on us;
you are seated at the right hand of the Father;
receive our prayer.
For you alone are the Holy One;
you alone are the Lord;
you alone are the Most High,
Jesus Christ,
with the Holy Spirit,
in the glory of God the Father. Amen.

A Song of Praise

Glory to you, Lord God of our fathers;
you are worthy of praise; glory to you.
Glory to you for the radiance of your holy name;
we will praise you and highly exalt you forever.
Glory to you in the splendor of your temple;
on the throne of your majesty, glory to you.
Glory to you, seated between the cherubim;
we will praise you and highly exalt you forever.
Glory to you, beholding the depths;
in the high vault of heaven, glory to you.
Glory to you, Father, Son, and Holy Spirit;
we will praise you and highly exalt you forever.

A Song of Creation

This song may be said in full, or any stanza may be said as a standalone reading.

I. Invocation

Glorify the Lord, all you works of the Lord,
  praise him and highly exalt him forever.
In the firmament of his power, glorify the Lord,
  praise him and highly exalt him forever.

II. The Cosmic Order

Glorify the Lord, you angels and all powers of the Lord,
  O heavens and all waters above the heavens.
Sun and moon and stars of the sky, glorify the Lord,
  praise him and highly exalt him forever.
Glorify the Lord, every shower of rain and fall of dew,
  all winds and fire and heat.
Winter and summer, glorify the Lord,
  praise him and highly exalt him forever.
Glorify the Lord, O chill and cold,
  drops of dew and flakes of snow.
Frost and cold, ice and sleet, glorify the Lord;
  praise him and highly exalt him forever.
Glorify the Lord, O nights and days,
  O shining light and enfolding dark.
Storm clouds and thunderbolts, glorify the Lord;
  praise him and highly exalt him forever.

III. The Earth and its Creatures

Let the earth glorify the Lord,
  praise him and highly exalt him forever.
Glorify the Lord, O mountains and hills,
and all that grows upon the earth;
  praise him and highly exalt him forever.
Glorify the Lord, O springs of water, seas, and streams,
  O whales and all that move in the waters.
All birds of the air, glorify the Lord;
  praise him and highly exalt him forever.

Glorify the Lord, O beasts of the wild,
and all you flocks and herds.
O men and women everywhere, glorify the Lord;
praise him and highly exalt him forever.

IV. The People of God

Let the people of God glorify the Lord;
praise him and highly exalt him forever.
Glorify the Lord, O priests and servants of the Lord;
praise him and highly exalt him forever.
Glorify the Lord, O spirits and souls of the righteous;
praise him and highly exalt him forever.
You that are holy and humble of heart, glorify the Lord;
praise him and highly exalt him forever.

V. Doxology

Let us glorify the Lord: Father, Son, and Holy Spirit;
praise him and highly exalt him forever.
In the firmament of his power, glorify the Lord;
praise him and highly exalt him forever.

The Summary of the Law

Then all will be seated. The leader will then give the Summary of the Law:

Now hear how Christ summarized the holy Law of God: "You shall love the Lord your God with all your heart and with all your soul and with all your mind. This is the great and first commandment. And a second is like it: You shall love your neighbor as yourself. On these two commandments depend all the Law and the Prophets." Matthew 22:37–40 (ESV)

Confession and Consolation

Then the leader says an invitation to confession:

[Brothers and/or sisters], we have come together this morning in the presence of almighty God, our heavenly Father, to give him thanks for the great blessings we have received from his hands, to offer him praise, to hear his holy Word, and to intercede for ourselves and others, that all may have those things necessary for life and for salvation. And so, in light of God's holy Law, let us prepare ourselves in heart and mind to worship him. Let us kneel in silence, with humble and obedient hearts, and confess our sins that we may obtain forgiveness by his infinite goodness and mercy.

All will kneel and keep silence, and, after due allowance of time, the leader will begin reading the following prayer. All gathered will join in unison while continuing to kneel:

> **Most merciful God,**
>   **we confess that we have sinned against you**
>   **in thought, word, and deed,**
>   **by what we have done**
>   **and by what we have left undone.**
> **We have not loved you with our whole heart;**
>   **we have not loved our neighbors as ourselves.**
> **We are truly sorry, and we humbly repent.**
>   **For the sake of your Son, Jesus Christ,**
>   **have mercy on us and forgive us;**
>   **give us grace to delight in your will**
>   **and to walk in your ways**
>   **for the glory of your name.**
> **Amen.**

Leader:

In the mercy of almighty God, Jesus Christ was given to die for you, and for his sake, God is faithful to forgive all your sins. To those who believe in Jesus Christ he gives the power to become the children of God and bestows on them the Holy Spirit. May the Lord, who has begun this good work in us, bring it to completion in the day of our Lord Jesus Christ. Amen.

Then all will say the following prayer (Kyrie Elesion)[7] in unison:

Lord have Mercy.
Christ have Mercy.
Lord have Mercy.

Response of Thanksgiving

Then all will respond to the Words of Assurance with gratitude through one of the following hymns:

Rejoice! (*Gaudete*)

The following may be said at any time, but especially during Advent Season.

Rejoice, Rejoice!
  Christ is born of the virgin Mary.
Rejoice!
  Now is the time of grace that we have desired.
Let us sing songs of joy.
  Let us give devotion.

God was made man,
  And nature marvels;
The world was renewed
  By Christ who is King.

---

7 This is one of the earliest prayers used in Christian worship. It is known to have been used as early as the fourth century AD but may, in some forms, even predate Christ. For its New Testament origins see Matthew 15:22, 17:15, and 20:30.

The closed gate of Ezekiel
  Has been passed through;
From where the light rises,
  Salvation is found.
Therefore, let our assembly now sing.
  Now sing in brightness.
Let it praise the Lord,
  And greet our king.

Make a Joyful Noise! (*Jubilate*) Psalm 100 (NLT)

Shout with joy to the Lord, all the earth!
  Worship the Lord with gladness.
Come before him, singing with joy.
  Acknowledge that the Lord is God!
He made us, and we are his.
  We are his people, the sheep of his pasture.
Enter his gates with thanksgiving;
  go into his courts with praise.
Give thanks to him and praise his name.
  For the Lord is good.
His unfailing love continues forever,
  and his faithfulness continues to each generation.

Glory to the Father, and to the Son, and to the Holy Spirit, as it was in the beginning, is now, and will be forever. Amen.

A Song of Triumph (*Venite*) Psalm 95:1–7, Psalm 96:9,13 (NLT)

Come, let us sing to the Lord!
  Let us shout joyfully to the Rock of our salvation.
Let us come to him with thanksgiving.
  Let us sing psalms of praise to him.

For the Lord is a great God,
a great King above all gods.
He holds in his hands the depths of the earth
and the mightiest mountains.
The sea belongs to him, for he made it.
His hands formed the dry land, too.
Come, let us worship and bow down.
Let us kneel before the Lord our maker,
for he is our God.
We are the people he watches over,
the flock under his care.
If only you would listen to his voice today!
Worship the Lord in all his holy splendor.
Let all the earth tremble before him.
… before the Lord, for he is coming!
He is coming to judge the earth.
He will judge the world with justice,
and the nations with his truth.

Glory to the Father, and to the Son, and to the Holy Spirit, as it was in the beginning, is now, and will be forever. Amen.

The Song of Zechariah, Luke 1:68–79 (NLT)

Praise the Lord, the God of Israel,
because he has visited and redeemed his people.
He has sent us a mighty Savior
from the royal line of his servant David,
just as he promised
through his holy prophets long ago.
Now we will be saved from our enemies
and from all who hate us.
He has been merciful to our ancestors
by remembering his sacred covenant —
the covenant he swore with an oath
to our ancestor Abraham.

We have been rescued from our enemies
so we can serve God without fear,
   in holiness and righteousness
   for as long as we live.
And you, my little son,
will be called the prophet of the Most High,
because you will prepare the way for the Lord.
   You will tell his people how to find salvation
   through forgiveness of their sins.
Because of God's tender mercy,
the morning light from heaven is about to break upon us,
to give light to those who sit in darkness and in the
shadow of death, and to guide us to the path of peace.

Glory to the Father, and to the Son, and to the Holy Spirit,
as it was in the beginning, is now, and will be forever.
Amen.

Christ our Passover, 1 Cor. 5:7–8; Rm. 6:9–11; 1 Cor. 15:20–22 (NLT)

The following may be said at any time, but especially during Easter Season.

Alleluia.

Christ, our Passover Lamb, has been sacrificed for us.
So let us celebrate the festival,
   not with the old bread of wickedness and evil,
   but with the new bread of sincerity and truth.
   Alleluia.

Christ was raised from the dead, and he will never die again.
   Death no longer has any power over him.
When he died, he died once to break the power of sin.
   But now that he lives, he lives for the glory of God.

So also, consider yourselves to be dead to the power of sin
  and alive to God through Christ Jesus.
  Alleluia.

But Christ has indeed been raised from the dead,
the first-fruits of those who have fallen asleep.
  For since death came through a man,
  the resurrection of the dead comes also through a man.

For as in Adam all die,
so in Christ all will be made alive.
  Alleluia.

**Glory to the Father, and to the Son, and to the Holy Spirit,
as it was in the beginning, is now, and will be forever.
Amen.**

We Praise You (*Te Deum Laudamus*)

You are God; we praise you.
  you are the Lord; we acclaim you.
You are the eternal Father;
  all creation worships you.
To you all angels, all the powers of heaven,
  cherubim and seraphim, sing in endless praise:
Holy, holy, holy, Lord, God of power and might,
  heaven and earth are full of your glory.
The glorious company of apostles praise you.
  The noble fellowship of prophets praises you.
The white-robed army of martyrs praise you.
  Throughout the world, the holy Church acclaims you:
Father, of majesty unbounded,
  your true and only Son, worthy of all worship,
and the Holy Spirit, advocate and guide.
  You, Christ, are the king of glory,
the eternal Son of the Father.

When you became man to set us free
you did not spurn the Virgin's womb.
You overcame the sting of death,
and opened the kingdom of heaven to all believers.
You are seated at God's right hand in glory.

Glory to the Father, and to the Son, and to the Holy Spirit, as it was in the beginning, is now, and will be forever. Amen.

The Old Testament Reading

Then someone will read an appointed Old Testament passage. Before reading the appointed passage, the reader may begin by saying:

A reading from [a citation giving book and chapter]. *Or the reader may say:* Hear the word of the Lord from [a citation giving book and chapter].

Depending on where the appointed reading begins, it may be necessary to provide some context.

For example: "This is from the reply of the Lord to Job," *or:* "This is while Jesus was teaching on the mount."

The scripture reading ends as follows:

Reader: The word of the Lord.
Or the reader may say: May God bless the reading of his word.

People: **Thanks be to God.**

The Psalm

Then the appointed psalm(s) for the morning will be read. The leader may decide whether it is said in unison or responsively.

At the end of the psalm(s) all say the Gloria Patri in unison:

Glory to the Father, and to the Son, and to the Holy Spirit, as it was in the beginning, is now, and will be forever. Amen.

The New Testament Reading

Then someone will read the appointed New Testament passage.

The scripture reading ends as follows:

Reader: The word of the Lord.
Or the reader may say: May God bless the reading of his word.

People: **Thanks be to God.**

The Profession of Faith

If conscience permits, all gathered will stand and recite the Nicene Creed. If there are any who object, then the leader will say a freeform prayer derived from one of the scripture readings.

We believe in one God, the Father, the Almighty,
    maker of heaven and earth,
    of all that is, seen and unseen.

We believe in one Lord, Jesus Christ,
    the only Son of God,
    eternally begotten of the Father,
    God from God, Light from Light,
    true God from true God,
    begotten, not made,
    of one Being with the Father.

Through him all things were made.
For us and for our salvation he came down from heaven;

by the power of the Holy Spirit he became incarnate from the Virgin Mary, and was made man.

For our sake he was crucified under Pontius Pilate;
he suffered death and was buried.

On the third day he rose again in accordance with the Scriptures;
he ascended into heaven and is seated at the right hand of the Father.

He will come again in glory
to judge the living and the dead,
and his kingdom will have no end.

We believe in the Holy Spirit,
the Lord, the giver of life,
who proceeds from the Father and the Son.

With the Father and the Son
he is worshiped and glorified.
He has spoken through the Prophets.

We believe in one holy universal and apostolic Church.

We acknowledge one baptism for the forgiveness of sins.[8]

We look for the resurrection of the dead,
and the life of the world to come.

Amen.

---

[8] See *A New Baptist Catechism*, Question 25, p. 336.

The Prayers

The Lord's Prayer

Then the leader will continue with the following words:

Leader: The Lord be with you.
People: **And with your spirit.**
Leader: Let us pray.

Then all gathered will say the Lord's Prayer (Matt. 6:9–13 ESV) in unison:

**[9]"Our Father in heaven,
hallowed be your name.
[10] Your kingdom come,
your will be done,
   on earth as it is in heaven.
[11] Give us this day our daily bread,
[12] and forgive us our debts,
   as we also have forgiven our debtors.
[13] And lead us not into temptation,
   but deliver us from evil.**

**For thine is the kingdom, and the power, and the glory,
for ever and ever. Amen**[9]

An Intercessory Prayer

*Then follows one of these sets of Suffrages (a 'suffrage' is an intercessory prayer).
The leader will choose which will be read.*

Show us your mercy, O Lord,
and grant us your salvation.

---

[9] This postscript to the Lord's Prayer is drawn from the 1979 version of the Book of Common Prayer. Most modern biblical scholars are in agreement that these words are not an original part of the Lord's Prayer in Matthew's gospel account. The ending is included, but set it apart, to be said as a theologically fitting praise to conclude the words that Jesus gave his disciples.

51

Clothe your ministers with righteousness;
let your people sing with joy.
Give peace, O Lord, in all the world,
for only in you can we live in safety.
Lord, keep this nation under your care,
and guide us in the way of justice and truth.
Let your way be known upon earth,
your saving health among all nations.
Let not the needy, O Lord, be forgotten
nor the hope of the poor be taken away.
Create in us clean hearts, O God,
and sustain us with your Holy Spirit.

or this:

Save your people, Lord, and bless your inheritance;
govern and uphold them, now and always.
Day by day we bless you;
we praise your name forever.
Lord, keep us from all sin today;
O Lord, have mercy upon us, have mercy upon us.
Lord, let your mercy be upon us,
for we have put our trust in you.
And only in you, have we trusted;
let us never be put to shame.

The Written Prayer

Then all gathered will say the Written Prayer for the Day in unison.

The Invitation to Free Prayer

Then the leader will say this invitation to free prayer:

Almighty and everlasting God, by whose Spirit the whole body of Christ is governed and sanctified: receive the requests and praises we offer to you for all the members of your holy Church. Grant that in their vocations and ministries they may serve you in truth and godliness, through our Lord and Savior Jesus Christ. Amen.

Free Prayer

Then the leader will say:

Now let us offer up thanksgivings and prayers for ourselves and for others.

And people may pray aloud or silently as they feel led by the Spirit of God.

A Shared Prayer For the Church

Then, before the close of the Office, the leader should say:

Now let us gather all our prayers together in one prayer for the whole church:

**Lord, remember your Church;
to rescue her by your love.**

**And gather the ones you have made holy
from the four winds and into your kingdom,
which you have prepared for her,
for yours is the power and the glory forever.**

Let grace come, and let this world pass away.

Hosanna to the God of David!

**If anyone is holy, let him come;
if anyone is not, let him repent.
Oh Lord, come!
Amen.**[10]

---

[10] This is an excerpt of a prayer in Didache X.VIII meant to be said after the Lord's Supper. The Didache is a first century Christian document.

The Benediction

Leader: Let us bless the Lord.
People: **Thanks be to God.**

Then the leader will conclude the service with one of the following benedictions:

"May the grace of the Lord Jesus Christ, the love of God, and the fellowship of the Holy Spirit be with you all." Amen. (2 Cor 13:14 NLT)

Or this:

"Let the message about Christ, in all its richness, fill your lives. Teach and counsel each other with all the wisdom he gives. Sing psalms and hymns and spiritual songs to God with thankful hearts. And whatever you do or say, do it as a representative of the Lord Jesus, giving thanks through him to God the Father." Amen. (Col 3:16–17 NLT)

Or this:

"May you experience the love of Christ, though it is too great to understand fully. Then you will be made complete with all the fullness of life and power that comes from God. Now all glory to God, who is able, through his mighty power at work within us, to accomplish infinitely more than we might ask or think. Glory to him in the church and in Christ Jesus through all generations forever and ever! Amen." (Eph 3:19–21 NLT)

Midday Devotion

Midday Prayers should be observed around noon but may be observed between 11:00 a.m. and 2:00 p.m.

This Order is intended primarily for group use at midday, but it is suitable for use at any time of day and may be used as a template for any personal devotion.

Invocation

Leader: The Lord has manifested his glory to all peoples.
People: **O come, let us adore him.**

Or the leader may say:

Therefore, if anyone is in Christ, he is a new creation.
   Glory to the Father, and to the Son, and to the Holy Spirit.
The old has passed away; behold, the new has come,
   As it was in the beginning, is now, and will be forever. Amen.

Praise

O Lord of Might

If this devotion is observed at midday, either corporately or personally, the following hymn is most suitable:

O God our king, you are powerful and true.
You ordain the turning of all seasons and times.
You illuminate the morning with splendor,
And you establish the midday with fire.
Even so, extinguish the fires of contention in our spirits,
And break the harmful fever of our sin.
Grant us health in our bodies,
And let your peace dwell in our hearts.
All this we ask Father, in your holy name,
Through Jesus, your incomparable Son,
Who lives with you, in the unity of the Holy Spirit
And reigns eternally in the glory of heaven;
Three in One,
And One in Three. Amen.[11]

The Breastplate of Patrick of Ireland

If this Order is observed as a personal devotion in place of the Order for Morning Prayer, the following hymn is suitable:

I arise today through a mighty strength,
the invocation of the Trinity,[12]
Through a belief in the Threeness,
Through confession of the Oneness,
Of the Creator of creation.

I bind unto myself this day,
The strength of Christ's birth and his baptism,
The strength of his crucifixion and his burial,
The strength of his resurrection and his ascension,
The strength of his descent for the judgment of doom.

---

[11] This is an original translation of the hymn *Rector Potens,* that may have been written by Ambrose of Milan and date from the 4th century.
[12] This hymn is a form of the Breastplate of St. Patrick that has been modified for compatibility with broadly Baptist theological commitments.

I bind unto myself this day
God's strength to pilot me,
  God's might to uphold me,
God's wisdom to guide me,
  God's eye to look before me,
God's ear to hear me,
  God's word to speak for me,
God's hand to guard me,
  God's way to lie before me,
God's shield to protect me,
  God's hosts to save me
  From snares of the devil,
From temptations of vices,
  From everyone who desires me ill,
Both afar and near,
  Alone or in a multitude.

I arise today through the might of God's power,
  To guard me against every form of evil.
Against every cruel, merciless power
that opposes my body and soul,
  Against teachings of false prophets and heretics,
Against every craft of idolatry,
  Against every ill wish and ill spoken word,
Against every dark and nameless power that opposes Christ,
  Against every knowledge
  that corrupts the human body and soul,
Against poison, against burning,
  Against drowning, against wounding,
  Christ shield me today.

Christ with me, Christ before me, Christ behind me,
  Christ in me, Christ beneath me, Christ above me,
Christ on my right, Christ on my left,
  Christ when I lie down, Christ when I sit down,
Christ in the heart of every man who thinks of me,
  Christ in the mouth of every man who speaks of me,

Christ in the eye that sees me,
Christ in the ear that hears me.
I arise today through a mighty strength,
the invocation of the Trinity,
Through a belief in the Threeness,
Through confession of the Oneness,
Of the Creator of creation.

My Soul Magnifies the Lord (Luke 1:46–55, NLT)

If this Order is observed as a personal devotion in place of the Order for Evening Prayer or for Prayers at the End of the Day, the following hymn is suitable:

Oh, how my soul praises the Lord.
How my spirit rejoices in God my Savior!
For he took notice of his lowly servant girl,
and from now on all generations will call me blessed.
For the Mighty One is holy,
and he has done great things for me.
He shows mercy from generation to generation
to all who fear him.
His mighty arm has done tremendous things!
He has scattered the proud and haughty ones.
He has brought down princes from their thrones
and exalted the humble.
He has filled the hungry with good things
and sent the rich away with empty hands.
He has helped his servant Israel
and remembered to be merciful.
For he made this promise to our ancestors,
to Abraham and his children forever.

After one of these hymns, you may add other praises, songs, or choruses as you feel led by the Spirit of God.

Confession and Consolation

If this is the only devotional you observe in the day, then you should continue with this Confession of Sins to God. If, however, you plan to pray three or four Offices (Morning, Evening, Midday, and End of Day), you may pass over Confession and move on to the scripture reading.

Whether alone or in a group, begin by saying this prayer aloud (the Jesus Prayer):

Lord Jesus Christ,
Son of God,
Have mercy on me, a sinner.

Then, if you are in a group, keep silence or, if alone, you may say this (or something similar in your own words) as many times as is necessary:

Almighty God, I confess to you that I have sinned in many ways, but especially by_____. I am truly sorry for this sin/these sins and for all others which I cannot recall. I ask you, Lord, to have mercy on me, to forgive me according to the riches of your grace in Christ Jesus. With all my heart, I intend to go and sin no more, as you give me grace to live a godly life.

Then you should conclude your confession with this prayer, said aloud (the Kyrie Eleison):

Lord Have mercy.
Christ have mercy.
Lord have mercy.

Scripture Reading

Then you should continue by reading one or more of the appointed texts for the day.

The Lord's Prayer

*When you are done reading the scripture, you should continue by saying the
Lord's Prayer. If in a group, the leader may wish to introduce the Lord's
Prayer by saying:* And now, Lord, we pray as you taught us.
Then all gathered will say the Lord's Prayer (Matt. 6:9–13 ESV) in unison:

9"Our Father in heaven,
hallowed be your name.
10 Your kingdom come,
your will be done,
   on earth as it is in heaven.
11 Give us this day our daily bread,
12 and forgive us our debts,
   as we also have forgiven our debtors.
13 And lead us not into temptation,
   but deliver us from evil.

For thine is the kingdom, and the power, and the glory,
for ever and ever. Amen[13]

Intercessory Prayer

*Conclude your time of devotion by giving thanks to God for his manifold
blessings and by making intercessions for others and for yourself.*

The Benediction

*If Midday Prayer has been observed in common (with others), then the one
leading should say a brief benediction to conclude the service.*

---

[13] This postscript to the Lord's Prayer is drawn from the 1979 version of the Book of
Common Prayer. Most modern biblical scholars are in agreement that these words are not
an original part of the Lord's Prayer in Matthew's gospel account. The ending is included,
but set it apart, to be said as a theologically fitting praise to conclude the words that Jesus
gave his disciples.

60

"The Lord bless you and keep you; the Lord make his face to shine upon you and be gracious to you; the Lord lift up his countenance upon you and give you peace." Amen. (Numbers 6:22–26 ESV)

A Brief Order for Evening Prayer

Evening Prayers should be observed around 6:00 p.m. but may be observed anytime between 5:00 and 7:00 p.m.

This order is intended for an evening devotional model for families with children. It is intentionally simple and brief; however, there are both positive and negative consequences to this approach. Brevity requires the removal of some important elements of the ancient orders for evening worship, some traditional written prayers, and responsive readings. Even so, as any parent of a nine-year-old knows, attention spans are very short, and parents must capitalize on whatever precious time they are able to carve out at the end of a busy day. The bottom line is that parents should feel free to use their own discretion as they lead their families in evening prayer. Over time, they can gradually add elements back into the shorter order as the family grows together in the practice of the Daily Office.

The Call to Prayer

The one leading will begin the time of silence and reflection by saying the following verse:

Be still, and know that I am God.
I will be exalted among the nations,
I will be exalted in the earth!
(Psalm 46:10 ESV)

As attention spans allow, take a few seconds to reflect on God's blessings this day.

Confession and Consolation

Then the leader will say: Now let us confess our sins to almighty God.

Then silence is kept. After a due allowance of time, the leader says these words:

In the mercy of almighty God, Jesus Christ was given to die for you, and for his sake, God is faithful to forgive all your sins. To those who believe in Jesus Christ he gives the power to become the children of God and bestows on them the Holy Spirit. May the Lord, who has begun this good work in us, bring it to completion in the day of our Lord Jesus Christ. Amen.

Then all will say the following prayer (Kyrie Elesion[14]) in unison:

Lord Have Mercy.
Christ have Mercy.
Lord Have Mercy.

The Evening Praise

Then a candle may be lit, and the following hymn is said in unison.

O gracious light,
pure brightness of the ever-living Father in heaven,
O Jesus Christ, holy and blessed!

Now as we come to the setting of the sun,
and our eyes behold the vesper light,
we sing your praises, O God: Father, Son, and Holy Spirit.

---

[14]This is one of the earliest prayers used in Christian worship. It is known to have been in use as early as the fourth century but may, in some forms, even predate Christ. For its New Testament origins see Matthew 15:22, 17:15, and 20:30.

You are worthy at all times to be praised by happy voices,
O Son of God, O Giver of Life,
and to be glorified through all the worlds.

The Psalm

*Then all will say a Psalm for the evening; either an appointed psalm or the
following:*

Psalm 134:1–3 (NLT)

Oh, praise the Lord, all you servants of the Lord,
  you who serve at night in the house of the Lord.
Lift your hands toward the sanctuary,
  and praise the Lord.
May the Lord, who made heaven and earth,
  bless you from Jerusalem.

The Psalm is always followed by the Gloria Patri[15], spoken in unison:

Glory to the Father, and to the Son, and to the Holy Spirit, as
it was in the beginning, is now, and will be forever. Amen.

The Reading

*Then someone will read an appointed passage for the evening. Before reading
the appointed passage, the reader may begin by saying:*

A reading from [a citation giving book and chapter]. *Or the reader
may say:* Hear the word of the Lord from [a citation giving book
and chapter].

---

[15] This short prayer is called the *Gloria Patri* (Glory to the Father). The Gloria Patri is an
ancient Christian prayer traditionally read after the reading of a Psalm; it is not a part of the
book of Psalms.

Depending on where the appointed reading begins, it may be necessary to provide some context.

For example: "This is from the reply of the Lord to Job," *or:* "This is while Jesus was teaching on the mount."

The scripture reading ends as follows:

Reader: The word of the Lord.
Or the reader may say: May God bless the reading of his word.

People: **Thanks be to God.**

Or, the leader may choose to read one of the following suggested passages:

A Reading from Jeremiah 14:7–9 (ESV)

> Though our iniquities testify against us,
> act, O LORD, for your name's sake;
> for our backslidings are many;
> we have sinned against you.
> O you hope of Israel,
> its savior in time of trouble,
> why should you be like a stranger in the land,
> like a traveler who turns aside to tarry for a night?
> Why should you be like a man confused,
> like a mighty warrior who cannot save?
> Yet you, O LORD, are in the midst of us,
> and we are called by your name;
> do not leave us.

A Reading from Matthew 11:25–30 (ESV)

> At that time Jesus declared, "I thank you, Father, Lord of heaven and earth, that you have hidden these things from the wise and understanding and revealed them to little children; yes, Father,

for such was your gracious will. All things have been handed over to me by my Father, and no one knows the Son except the Father, and no one knows the Father except the Son and anyone to whom the Son chooses to reveal him. Come to me, all who labor and are heavy laden, and I will give you rest. Take my yoke upon you, and learn from me, for I am gentle and lowly in heart, and you will find rest for your souls. For my yoke is easy, and my burden is light."

The Prayers

<u>Free Intercession</u>

The leader will say: Now let us offer up prayers for ourselves and for others.

After this, all gathered may pray as led by the Holy Spirit.

<u>The Lord's Prayer</u>

After due allowance of time for free intercession, the leader will say:
And now, let us gather all our prayers together in the Lord's prayer.

Then all gathered will say the Lord's Prayer (Matt. 6:9–13 ESV) in unison:

9"Our Father in heaven,
hallowed be your name.
10 Your kingdom come,
your will be done,
on earth as it is in heaven.
11 Give us this day our daily bread,
12 and forgive us our debts,
as we also have forgiven our debtors.
13 And lead us not into temptation,
but deliver us from evil.

For thine is the kingdom, and the power, and the glory,
for ever and ever. Amen

The Benediction

Leader: Let us bless the Lord.
People: **Thanks be to God.**

Then the leader will end evening prayer with the following words of benediction:

"The Lord bless you and keep you; the Lord make his face to shine upon you and be gracious to you; the Lord lift up his countenance upon you and give you peace." Amen. (Numbers 6:22–26 ESV)

Then the candle is reverently extinguished.

The Full Order for Evening Prayer

Evening Prayers should be observed around 6:00 p.m. but may be observed anytime between 5:00 and 7:00 p.m.

Greeting

As all gather, let the room be dim, but with sufficient light to read. A candle or candles may be lit.[16] During the candle-lighting silence is kept.

The one leading will begin the time of silence and reflection by saying one or more of the following verses:

The LORD will fight for you, and you have only to be silent. (Exodus 14:14 ESV)

It is good that one should wait quietly for the salvation of the LORD. (Lamentations 3:26 ESV)

The LORD is in his holy temple; let all the earth keep silence before him. (Habakkuk 2:20 ESV)

Be still, and know that I am God.
I will be exalted among the nations,
I will be exalted in the earth! (Psalm 46:10 ESV)

---

16 Traditional Christian worship settings have often used incense to symbolize prayers rising toward heaven, and to engage the sense of smell in the act of worship. Baptists should feel free, if conscience permits, to use incense to enhance this worship experience.

Silence and Reflection

And then the leader should say:

Let us keep silence and reflect on the day the Lord has made.

Then all gathered will keep one or two moments of silence and will reflect on the day. Try reflecting on the presence of God, gratitude for the day's events, and one's emotions. During this time, thoughts may also be focused on a specific feature of the day or on the coming day. The leader should decide the length of silence. The silence is broken with the Call to Prayer.

Here are some further suggestions to guide the time of silence and reflection:

Take a few deep breaths at the beginning to aid in focusing.

Begin with a simple prayer expressing your desire to connect with God such as: Speak, Lord, your servant is listening (1 Sam. 3:10).

If your mind wanders, return to your simple prayer or to another traditional prayer such as the Kyrie Elesion:

> Lord have mercy.
> Christ have mercy.
> Lord have mercy.

> *Or the Jesus Prayer:*

> Lord Jesus Christ, Son of God, have mercy on me, a sinner.

The Call to Prayer

The leader will break the silence by saying:

Leader: There is light and peace in Jesus Christ our Lord.
People: **Thanks be to God.**

Leader: Alleluia. Christ is risen.
People: **The Lord is risen indeed. Alleluia.**

Confession and Consolation

The leader begins the time of confession with one of the following short, responsive readings:

Leader: Our help is in the name of the Lord.
People: **The maker of heaven and earth.**

Or this:

Leader: O God, make speed to save us.
People: **O Lord, make haste to help us.**

Then the leader will continue with an invitation to confession:

[Brothers and/or sisters], we have come together this evening in the presence of almighty God, our heavenly Father, to give him thanks for the great blessings we have received from his hands, to offer him praise, to hear his holy Word, and to intercede for ourselves and for others, that all may have those things necessary for life and for salvation. So that me may do this with a clean heart and focused mind, let us kneel in silence, with humble and obedient hearts, and confess our sins that we may obtain forgiveness by his infinite goodness and mercy.

Then all will kneel and keep silence. After due allowance of time, the leader will begin reading the following prayer, and all gathered will join in unison while continuing to kneel:

Most merciful God,
  we confess that we have sinned against you
  in thought, word, and deed
  by what we have done
  and by what we have left undone.
We have not loved you with our whole heart;
  we have not loved our neighbors as ourselves.
We are truly sorry and we humbly repent.
For the sake of your Son Jesus Christ,
  have mercy on us and forgive us;
  give us grace to delight in your will,
  and to walk in your ways,
  for the glory of your name.
Amen.

Then the leader will say the following words of assurance:

In the mercy of almighty God, Jesus Christ was given to die for you, and for his sake, God is faithful to forgive all your sins. To those who believe in Jesus Christ he gives the power to become the children of God and bestows on them the Holy Spirit. May the Lord, who has begun this good work in us, bring it to completion in the day of our Lord Jesus Christ.

Leader: Bless the Lord who forgives all our sins.
People: His mercy endures forever.

The Prayer for Light

Then all will return to their seats, and the leader will continue with a Prayer for Light, using any one of the following, first saying:

Let us pray.

Almighty God, we give you thanks for surrounding us, as daylight fades, with the warmth of the vesper light. Just as you have shown us mercy and have surrounded us with the radiance of your light, so also let the brightness of the Holy Spirit shine new hope into our hearts this night, through Jesus Christ our Lord. Amen.

Grant us, Lord, the light of a love which never fails. Let it burn in us and shed its light on those around us, that by its brightness all may have a vision of the holy city, where the true and never-failing Light dwells, Jesus Christ our Lord. Amen.

Lord God Almighty, you have taught us to call the evening, the morning, and the noonday one day. You have caused the sun to rise on each day, bringing warmth and the hope of new mercies. So also let the light of your Son rise in our hearts to dispel every darkness and fear. Help us by this light to learn trust, to walk in faithfulness, and to know you as the true God, living and reigning forever and ever. Amen.

Lighten our darkness, O Lord; by your great mercy, defend us from all perils and dangers of this night, for the love of your only Son, our Savior, Jesus Christ. Amen.

Be our light in the darkness, O Lord, and in your great mercy defend us from all perils and dangers of this night, for the love of your only Son, our Savior Jesus Christ. Amen.

Look down, O Lord, from your heavenly throne, and illumine this night with your celestial brightness, that by night as by day your people may glorify your holy name, through Jesus Christ our Lord. Amen.

The Evening Praise

A candle may be lit if none have been already.

The following hymn is said in unison, or some other suitable song or songs may be sung:

O gracious light,
  pure brightness of the ever-living Father in heaven,
  O Jesus Christ, holy and blessed!
Now as we come to the setting of the sun,
  and our eyes behold the vesper light,
  we sing your praises, O God: Father, Son, and Holy Spirit.
You are worthy at all times to be praised by happy voices,
O Son of God, O Giver of Life,
and to be glorified through all the worlds.

The Psalm

Then, if there will be no Prayers at the End of the Day, all gathered will say one or all of the following psalms. Or, if there will be Prayers at the End of the Day, then those gathered may say the appointed Psalm for the evening out of the Schedule of Readings.

Psalm 4:1–8 (NLT)

Answer me when I call to you,
  O God who declares me innocent.
Free me from my troubles.
  Have mercy on me and hear my prayer.
How long will you people ruin my reputation?
  How long will you make groundless accusations?
How long will you continue your lies?
  You can be sure of this: the Lord set apart the godly for himself.
The Lord will answer when I call to him.
  Don't sin by letting anger control you.
Think about it overnight and remain silent.
  Offer sacrifices in the right spirit,
  and trust the Lord.
Many people say, "Who will show us better times?"
Let your face smile on us, Lord.

You have given me greater joy
than those who have abundant harvests of grain and new wine.
In peace I will lie down and sleep,
for you alone, O Lord, will keep me safe.

The Psalm is always followed by the Gloria Patri,[17] *spoken in unison:*

Glory to the Father, and to the Son, and to the Holy Spirit, as
it was in the beginning, is now, and will be forever. Amen.

Psalm 31:1–5 (NLT)

O Lord, I have come to you for protection; don't let me be
disgraced.
  Save me, for you do what is right.
Turn your ear to listen to me;
  rescue me quickly.
Be my rock of protection,
  a fortress where I will be safe.
You are my rock and my fortress.
  For the honor of your name, lead me out of this danger.
Pull me from the trap my enemies set for me,
  for I find protection in you alone.
I entrust my spirit into your hand.
  Rescue me, Lord, for you are a faithful God.

The Psalm is always followed by the Gloria Patri, spoken in unison:

Glory to the Father, and to the Son, and to the Holy Spirit, as
it was in the beginning, is now, and will be forever. Amen.

Psalm 91:1–16 (NLT)

---

17 This short prayer is called the Gloria Patri (Glory to the Father). The Gloria
Patri is an ancient Christian prayer traditionally read after the reading of a
Psalm; it is not a part of the book of Psalms.

Those who live in the shelter of the Most High will find rest in the shadow of the Almighty.

This I declare about the Lord:
He alone is my refuge, my place of safety;
he is my God, and I trust him.
For he will rescue you from every trap and protect you from deadly disease.
He will cover you with his feathers.
He will shelter you with his wings.
His faithful promises are your armor and protection.
Do not be afraid of the terrors of the night,
nor the arrow that flies in the day.
Do not dread the disease that stalks in darkness,
nor the disaster that strikes at midday.
Though a thousand fall at your side,
though ten thousand are dying around you,
these evils will not touch you.
Just open your eyes,
and see how the wicked are punished.
If you make the Lord your refuge,
if you make the Most High your shelter,
no evil will conquer you;
no plague will come near your home.
For he will order his angels to protect you wherever you go.
They will hold you up with their hands so you won't even hurt your foot on a stone.
You will trample upon lions and cobras;
you will crush fierce lions and serpents under your feet!
The Lord says, "I will rescue those who love me.
I will protect those who trust in my name.
When they call on me, I will answer;
I will be with them in trouble.
I will rescue and honor them.
I will reward them with a long life and give them my salvation.

The Psalm is always followed by the Gloria Patri, spoken in unison:

Glory to the Father, and to the Son, and to the Holy Spirit, as it was in the beginning, is now, and will be forever. Amen.

<u>Psalm 134:1–3 *(NLT)*</u>

Oh, praise the Lord, all you servants of the Lord,
  you who serve at night in the house of the Lord.
Lift your hands toward the sanctuary,
  and praise the Lord.
May the Lord, who made heaven and earth,
  bless you from Jerusalem.

The Psalm is always followed by the Gloria Patri, spoken in unison:

Glory to the Father, and to the Son, and to the Holy Spirit, as it was in the beginning, is now, and will be forever. Amen.

The Reading

Then someone will read an appointed passage for the evening. Before reading the appointed passage, the reader may begin by saying:

A reading from [a citation giving book and chapter]. *Or the reader may say:* Hear the word of the Lord from [a citation giving book and chapter].

Depending on where the appointed reading begins, it may be necessary to provide some context.

For example: "This is from the reply of the Lord to Job," *or:* "This is while Jesus was teaching on the mount."

The scripture reading ends as follows:

Reader: The word of the Lord.
Or the reader may say: May God bless the reading of his word.

People: **Thanks be to God.**

The Profession of Faith

If conscience permits, all gathered will stand and recite the Nicene Creed. If there are any who object, then the leader will say a freeform prayer derived from one of the scripture readings.

We believe in one God, the Father, the Almighty,
   maker of heaven and earth,
   of all that is, seen and unseen.

We believe in one Lord, Jesus Christ,
   the only Son of God,
   eternally begotten of the Father,
   God from God, Light from Light,
   true God from true God,
   begotten, not made,
   of one Being with the Father.

Through him all things were made.

For us and for our salvation he came down from heaven;
   by the power of the Holy Spirit he became incarnate from
   the Virgin Mary, and was made man.

For our sake he was crucified under Pontius Pilate;
   he suffered death and was buried.

On the third day he rose again in accordance with the
Scriptures;
   he ascended into heaven and is seated at the right hand of
   the Father.

He will come again in glory
   to judge the living and the dead,
   and his kingdom will have no end.

We believe in the Holy Spirit,
   the Lord, the giver of life,
   who proceeds from the Father and the Son.

With the Father and the Son
  he is worshiped and glorified.
  He has spoken through the Prophets.

We believe in one holy, universal, and apostolic Church.

We acknowledge one baptism for the forgiveness of sins.[18]

We look for the resurrection of the dead,
  and the life of the world to come.
Amen.

The Prayers

<u>The Seasonal Prayer for Evening</u>

Then all gathered will say the collect for the Evening Office in unison. (A collect is a short, written prayer.)

<u>*During Advent*</u>

Almighty God, give us the grace to reject every work of darkness. Clothe us with the armor of light in this life — the same mortal life Jesus chose to live in humility and obedience. We pray this so that in the last day, when he comes again in glory and majesty to judge both the living and the dead, we may rise to life immortal, through him who lives and reigns with you and the Holy Spirit, one God, now and forever. Amen.

<u>*During Christmastide and the Season of Epiphany*</u>

Almighty God, who has poured upon us the new light of your incarnate Word: grant that the same light, kindled in our hearts, may shine brightly in our lives and may light for others the path

---

[18] See *A New Baptist Catechism*, Question 25.

of Christ, our Lord, through him, who lives and reigns with you, in the unity of the Holy Spirit, one God, now and forever. Amen.

During the Season of Lent

Almighty and most merciful God, kindle within us the enduring fire of your love, that its flame may purify all we do and say and that we might worship you in spirit and in truth through Jesus Christ our Lord. Amen.

During the Easter Season

Eternal God, you led your ancient people into freedom by a pillar of cloud by day and a pillar of fire by night: grant that we who walk in the light of your presence may rejoice in the liberty of the children of God through Jesus Christ our Lord. Amen.

During Ordinary Time

Almighty and everlasting God, you have given your servants grace to know and confess the true faith, to acknowledge the glory of the eternal Trinity, and to worship the Divine Majesty of Your eternal Unity. We ask that you would preserve in us this faith and protect us against all the flaming arrows of the enemy. Heavenly Father, bring us at last to be with you in eternal glory, where with the Son and the Holy Spirit you live and reign, one God, now and forevermore. Amen.

Free Intercession

Then all will be seated, and the leader will say: Now let us offer up prayers for ourselves and for others.

After this, all gathered may pray as led by the Holy Spirit.

<u>The Lord's Prayer</u>

After due allowance of time for free intercession, the leader will say: And now, Lord, we pray as you taught us.

Then all gathered will say the Lord's Prayer in unison (Matt. 6:9–13 KJV):

Our Father, who art in heaven,
  hallowed be thy name,
  thy kingdom come,
  thy will be done,
  on earth as it is in heaven.
Give us this day our daily bread.
And forgive us our trespasses,
  as we forgive those who trespass against us.
And lead us not into temptation,
  but deliver us from evil.

For thine is the kingdom, and the power, and the glory,
  forever and ever. Amen.

The Final Praise

Then the one leading may say: Let us gather all our prayers together in the words of Holy Scripture.

Then, the following song from Scripture (Lk. 1:46–56 NLT) may be said responsively or in unison:

Oh, how my soul praises the Lord.
  How my spirit rejoices in God my Savior!
For he took notice of his lowly servant girl,
  and from now on, all generations will call me blessed.
For the Mighty One is holy,
  and he has done great things for me.
He shows mercy from generation to generation
  to all who fear him.

His mighty arm has done tremendous things!
He has scattered the proud and haughty ones.
He has brought down princes from their thrones
and exalted the humble.
He has filled the hungry with good things
and sent the rich away with empty hands.
He has helped his servant Israel
and remembered to be merciful.
For he made this promise to our ancestors,
to Abraham and his children forever.

Glory to the Father, and to the Son, and to the Holy Spirit, as
it was in the beginning, is now, and will be forever. Amen.

Or, if Prayers at the End of the Day are not said, then the Song of Simeon
(Lk. 2:29–32 ESV) may be said responsively or in unison:

Lord, now you are letting your servant depart in peace,
according to your word;
for my eyes have seen your salvation
that you have prepared in the presence of all peoples,
a light for revelation to the Gentiles,
and for glory to your people Israel.

Glory to the Father, and to the Son, and to the Holy Spirit, as
it was in the beginning, is now, and will be forever. Amen.

Leader: Let us bless the Lord.
People: **Thanks be to God.**

The Benediction

Then the leader will offer one of the following benedictions.

"Blessed are you, O Lord, the God of our fathers, creator of the
changes of day and night, giving rest to the weary, renewing the
strength of those who are spent, bestowing upon us occasions of

song in the evening. As you have protected us this day, so be with us in the coming night; keep us from every sin, every evil, and every fear; for you are our light and salvation, and the strength of our life. To you be glory for endless ages." Amen.

Or this:

Almighty, everlasting God, let our prayer in your sight be as incense, the lifting up of our hearts as the evening sacrifice. Give us grace to be strengthened and nourished in faith by your word and by the ordinances you have given the Church. Stir up in us the flame of love which burned in the heart of your Son as he suffered, so we can look with compassion on all we encounter. Let this passion burn in us to eternal life and to the ages of ages. Amen.

Or this:

"The Lord bless you and keep you; the Lord make his face to shine upon you and be gracious to you; the Lord lift up his countenance upon you and give you peace." Amen. (Numbers 6:22–26 ESV)

Then the candle is reverently extinguished.

Prayers at the End of the Day

Prayers at the End of the Day should be observed around 8:00 p.m., but may be observed anytime between 8:00 and 10:00 p.m.

Silence and Reflection

As all gather, let the room be dim, but with sufficient light to read. The one leading may begin a time of silence and reflection by saying:

The Lord will fight for you, and you have only to be silent.
Exodus 14:14 (ESV)

And then the leader should say:

Let us keep silence and reflect on the day the Lord has made.

Then all gathered will keep one or two moments of silence and will reflect on the day. Try reflecting on the presence of God, gratitude for the day's events, and one's emotions. During this time, thoughts may also be focused on a specific feature of the day or on the coming day. The leader should decide the length of silence. The silence is broken with the Call to Prayer.

Here are some further suggestions to guide the time of silence and reflection:

Take a few deep breaths at the beginning to aid in focusing.

Begin with a simple prayer expressing your desire to connect with God such as: Speak, Lord, your servant is listening (1 Sam. 3:10).

If your mind wanders, return to your simple prayer or to another traditional prayer such as the Kyrie Elesion:

> Lord have mercy.
> Christ have mercy.
> Lord have mercy.

> *Or the Jesus Prayer:*

> Lord Jesus Christ, Son of God, have mercy on me, a sinner.

The Call to Prayer

The leader will break the silence by saying: May the Lord grant us a peaceful night and a perfect end.

People: **Amen**

Leader: Our help is in the name of the Lord.
People: **The maker of heaven and earth.**

Confession and Consolation

Then the leader will say: Therefore, let us humbly confess our sins to almighty God.

Then silent prayers of confession are offered to God.

After a due allowance of time, the leader says these words:

In the mercy of almighty God, Jesus Christ was given to die for you, and for his sake, God is faithful to forgive all your sins. To those who believe in Jesus Christ he gives the power to become the children of God and bestows on them the Holy Spirit. May the Lord, who has begun this good work in us, bring it to completion in the day of our Lord Jesus Christ. Amen.

Then the following Antiphon[19] is said.

Leader: Oh God, make speed to save us.
People: **Oh Lord, make haste to help us.**

All those gathered say the following praise in unison:

Glory to the Father, and to the Son, and to the Holy Spirit, as it was in the beginning, is now, and will be forever. Amen.

The Psalm

Then all those gathered will say the appointed Psalm for the evening from the Schedule of Readings. Or, the following Psalm may be said.

Psalm 4:1–8 *(NLT)*

Answer me when I call to you,
  O God who declares me innocent.
Free me from my troubles.
  Have mercy on me and hear my prayer.
How long will you people ruin my reputation?
  How long will you make groundless accusations?
How long will you continue your lies?
  You can be sure of this: the Lord set apart the godly for himself.
The Lord will answer when I call to him.
  Don't sin by letting anger control you.
Think about it overnight and remain silent.
  Offer sacrifices in the right spirit,
  and trust the Lord.

---

19 An 'antiphon' is a short sentence sung or recited before or after a psalm or canticle.

Many people say, "Who will show us better times?"
Let your face smile on us, Lord.
You have given me greater joy
than those who have abundant harvests of grain and new wine.
In peace I will lie down and sleep,
for you alone, O Lord, will keep me safe.

The Psalm is followed by the Gloria Patri, spoken in unison:

**Glory to the Father, and to the Son, and to the Holy Spirit, as
it was in the beginning, is now, and will be forever. Amen.**

The Reading

*Then someone will read an appointed passage. Before reading the appointed
passage, the reader may begin by saying:*

A reading from [a citation giving book and chapter]. *Or the reader
may say:* Hear the word of the Lord from [a citation giving book
and chapter].

*Depending on where the appointed reading begins, it may be necessary to
provide some context.*

For example: "This is from the reply of the Lord to Job," *or:* "This
is while Jesus was teaching on the mount."

The scripture reading ends as follows:

Reader: The word of the Lord.
Or the reader may say: May God bless the reading of his word.

People: **Thanks be to God.**

Or, the leader may choose to read the following suggested passage:

<u>A Reading from Matthew 11:25–30 (ESV)</u>

At that time Jesus declared, "I thank you, Father, Lord of heaven and earth, that you have hidden these things from the wise and understanding and revealed them to little children; yes, Father, for such was your gracious will. All things have been handed over to me by my Father, and no one knows the Son except the Father, and no one knows the Father except the Son and anyone to whom the Son chooses to reveal him. Come to me, all who labor and are heavy laden, and I will give you rest. Take my yoke upon you, and learn from me, for I am gentle and lowly in heart, and you will find rest for your souls. For my yoke is easy, and my burden is light."

The Prayers

<u>Prayers for Mercy and Protection</u>

Then the leader will continue by saying the following responsive prayer (Ps. 31:5; Ps. 17:8):

Into your hands, O Lord, I commend my spirit;
  For You have redeemed me, O Lord, O God of truth.
Keep us, O Lord, as the apple of your eye.
  Hide us under the shadow of your wings.

Then all will say the following prayer (Kyrie Elesion[20]) in unison:

Lord Have Mercy.
Christ have Mercy.
Lord Have Mercy.

---

[20] This is one of the earliest prayers used in Christian worship. It is known to have been used as early as the fourth century AD but may, in some forms, even predate Christ. For its New Testament origins see Matthew 15:22, 17:15, and 20:30.

The Written Prayers

Then all say the following responsive:

Lord, hear our prayer;
And let our cry come to you.
Let us pray.

Then, in uison all will say the Written Prayer *for the season.*

After the written prayer, the leader will continue by saying one of the following written prayers:

Visit this place, O Lord, and drive far from it all snares of the enemy; let your holy angels dwell with us to preserve us in peace; and let your blessing be upon us always, through Jesus Christ our Lord. Amen.

Be present, O merciful God, and protect us through the hours of this night, so that we who are wearied by the changes and chances of this life may rest in your eternal changelessness, through Jesus Christ our Lord. Amen.

Keep watch, dear Lord, with those who work, or watch, or weep this night, and give your angels charge over those who sleep. Tend the sick, Lord Christ; give rest to the weary, bless the dying, soothe the suffering, pity the afflicted, shield the joyous; and all for your love's sake. *Amen.*

O God, your unfailing providence sustains the world we live in and the life we live: Watch over those, both night and day, who work while others sleep, and grant that we may never forget that our common life depends upon each other's toil; through Jesus Christ our Lord. *Amen.*

Free Intercession

Then the leader will say: Now let us offer up prayers for ourselves and for others.

After this, all gathered may pray as led by the Holy Spirit.

The Lord's Prayer

The leader will say: And now, let us gather our prayers together in the words of the Lord's prayer.

Then all gathered will say the Lord's Prayer in unison (Matt. 6:9–13 KJV):

> **Our Father, who art in heaven,**
>   **hallowed be thy name,**
>   **thy kingdom come,**
>   **thy will be done,**
>   **on earth as it is in heaven.**
> **Give us this day our daily bread.**
> **And forgive us our trespasses,**
>   **as we forgive those who trespass against us.**
> **And lead us not into temptation,**
>   **but deliver us from evil.**
> **For thine is the kingdom, and the power, and the glory,**
>   **forever and ever. Amen.**

The Benediction

Then all will say the following in unison:

Guide us waking, O Lord, and guard us sleeping, that awake we may watch with Christ and asleep we may rest in peace.

During Eastertide add "Alleluia!"

Then the Song of Simeon (Lk. 2:29–32 ESV) is said responsively or in unison:

Lord, now you are letting your servant depart in peace,
  according to your word;
for my eyes have seen your salvation
  that you have prepared in the presence of all peoples,
a light for revelation to the Gentiles,
  and for glory to your people Israel.

Then all will repeat the following in unison:

Guide us waking, O Lord, and guard us sleeping, that awake we may watch with Christ and asleep we may rest in peace.

During Eastertide add "Alleluia!"

Then the leader will offer the following benediction:

Blessed are you, O Lord, the God of our fathers, creator of the changes of day and night, giving rest to the weary, renewing the strength of those who are spent, bestowing upon us occasions of song in the evening. As you have protected us this day, so be with us in the coming night; keep us from every sin, every evil, and every fear; for you are our light and salvation, and the strength of our life. To you be glory for endless ages. Amen.

Written Prayers

Advent

<u>First Sunday of Advent and the week following:</u>

Almighty God, give us the grace to reject the works and the kingdom of darkness. Surround us, Holy Spirit, with the armor of light and the truth of your word, now in this mortal life when our need is greatest, just as it was for Jesus when he came to live among us in great humility. We ask this so that on the last day, when Christ comes again in glory and majesty to judge both the living and the dead, we might be among those who rise to the glory of eternal life, through the same Jesus Christ, who lives and reigns with you and the Holy Spirit, one God, now and forever. Amen.

Or this prayer that emphasizes hope:

Everlasting God, it is your will that none should perish. Draw us to Christ in this holy season, we pray, and inspire our spirits with the hope of his coming. Help us to bear witness to this hope always, whether in plenty or in want, being confident that just as we share in Jesus's sufferings, so also we will share in his resurrection. We pray this all in his name, the name above every other, Jesus Christ, who lives and reigns with you and the Holy Spirit, one God, now and forever. Amen.

Or this prayer may be used before lighting the first Candle of Advent in Sunday worship and before the readings:

Heavenly Father, you desire all people to come to you through faith in Jesus. Today, as we worship through song, Word, and the proclamation of the gospel, send the Holy Spirit to lift our hearts with the hope of Christ's coming. And, we pray, help us to bear witness to this hope throughout the whole year, that just as we share in his sufferings, so also we will share in his resurrection. Amen.

Second Sunday of Advent and the week following:

Almighty God, renew us daily by your presence and grace that we might become agents of peace for a world that groans in bondage to conflict. Help us always to exalt Christ by both word and deed, that when he comes again, he may find in us a mansion prepared for himself and filled with the peace that passes all understanding. We ask this in his name, Jesus Christ our Lord, who lives and reigns with you in the unity of the Holy Spirit, one God, now and evermore. Amen.

Or this prayer that emphasizes peace:

Eternal God, in whose perfect kingdom no sword is drawn but the sword of righteousness and no strength known but the strength of love, spread your Spirit with great power over the whole earth, that all peoples might be gathered under the banner of your Son, the Prince of Peace, who lives and reigns with you, in the unity of the Holy Spirit, one God, now and forever. Amen.

Or this prayer may be used before lighting the second candle of Advent in Sunday worship and before the readings:

Eternal God, in your perfect kingdom no sword is drawn but the sword of righteousness and no strength is known but the strength of love. Today, as we worship through song, Word, and the proclamation of the gospel, send the Holy Spirit to fill our hearts with Christ's peace. Help us to share the faith freely with all people, that they may be gathered into the kingdom of your Son, the Prince of Peace. Amen.

Third Sunday of Advent and the week following:

Stir up your power, O Lord, and be present with us in great strength because we are greatly hindered by our sins. Let your abundant grace and mercy come quickly to help and deliver us, and let this salvation become the seedbed for a life of joy and gratitude. All this we ask through Jesus Christ our Lord, to whom, with you and the Holy Spirit, be all honor and glory, now and forevermore. Amen.

Or this prayer that emphasizes joy:

Heavenly Father, you see all things, even us, your people, as we faithfully gather this day and await the celebration of the Lord's birth. Enable us by your grace to persevere in the faith, to take joy in our salvation, and to celebrate it always with solemn worship and great rejoicing. We pray this in the name of our Lord Jesus Christ, your Son, who lives and reigns with you in the unity of the Holy Spirit, one God, forever and ever. Amen.

Or this prayer may be used before lighting the third candle of Advent in Sunday worship and before the readings:

Heavenly Father, you see all things, even your people this day, as we faithfully gather and await the celebration of Jesus' birth.

As we worship through song, Word, and the proclamation of the gospel, send the Holy Spirit so that we may take great joy in the salvation Christ alone has wrought and celebrate that salvation with full hearts. Amen.

Fourth Sunday of Advent and the week following:

Merciful God, out of your lovingkindness and patience you sent the prophets as messengers to preach repentance and prepare the way for our salvation. Give us grace to hear and to heed their warnings so that we may turn away from all sin and joyfully greet the coming of Jesus Christ our Redeemer, the one in whose name we pray, who lives and reigns with you and the Holy Spirit, one God, now and forever. Amen.

Or this prayer that emphasizes love:

Eternal Father, out of the overflowing abundance of your love and in the fullness of time, you gave the incarnate Son to be the sign and the ransom for our salvation. Plant in every heart, we pray, the love of him who is the Savior of the world, our Lord Jesus Christ, the one in whose name we pray, who lives and reigns with you and the Holy Spirit, one God, in glory everlasting. Amen.

Or this prayer may be used before lighting the fourth candle of Advent in Sunday worship and before the readings:

Eternal Father, out of the overflowing abundance of your love, and in the fullness of time, you gave your Son to be born of the virgin as the true sign and ransom of our salvation. Today, as we worship through song, Word, and the proclamation of the gospel, send the Holy Spirit to nourish and grow our love for him who is the Savior of the world. Amen.

Christmastide

<u>Christmas Eve after Sunset, Christmas Day, and all the days thereafter until the next Sunday</u>

Heavenly Father, we thank you for giving us a deep sense of joy, peace, and hope every year as we remember the birth of your only begotten Son. Just as we joyfully receive Jesus as the promised Redeemer on this holy day, grant that on the last day we may behold his coming in great confidence knowing that he will receive us into the kingdom of heaven. This we pray through your Son, our Lord Jesus Christ, who lives and reigns with you, in the unity of the Holy Spirit, one God, now and forever. Amen.

Or this:

O God, who has caused this holy night to shine with the illumination of the True Light, grant that just as we have known the mystery of that Light upon earth, so may we also perfectly know him and enjoy him forever in heaven, where with you and the Holy Spirit he lives and reigns, one God, in glory everlasting. Amen.

Or this:

Almighty God, you have given us the only-begotten Son to be born of a virgin and to take our nature upon Himself that we might be born again from above. Let us, your children by adoption and grace, be renewed daily by the Holy Spirit, through our Lord Jesus Christ, who lives and reigns with you and the same Spirit forever, one God, world without end. Amen.

Or this prayer may be used before lighting the Christ Candle in Sunday worship and before the readings:

Almighty God, you have given us the only-begotten Son to be born of a virgin and to take our nature upon himself that we might be born again from above. Today, as we worship through song, Word, and the proclamation of the gospel, send the Holy Spirit to renew us, your children by adoption and by grace, this day and throughout the whole year. Amen.

First Sunday after Christmas Day & thereafter until Jan. 1

Almighty God, you have poured out on us the new light of your incarnate Word. Grant that this same light, kindled ever anew in our hearts, may shine forth in our whole lives through Jesus Christ our Lord, who lives and reigns with you in the unity of the Holy Spirit, one God, now and forever. Amen.

From January 1 to January 5

O God, who wonderfully created and yet more wonderfully restored the dignity of human nature, grant that we may share the divine life of him who humbled himself to share in our humanity, your Son, Jesus Christ, who lives and reigns with you in the unity of the Holy Spirit, one God, forever and ever. Amen.

Epiphanytide

The Epiphany, January 6, and days thereafter until the next Sunday (The Sunday after January 6 is Baptism of the Lord)

O God, long ago you led the Gentile Magi to your only begotten Son by the light of the Advent star and so revealed his glory to the peoples of the earth. In the same way, lead us, who know you by faith, into Christ's presence in this life so we may behold his glory face to face in eternity. This we ask in the name of your Son, Jesus Christ, the name above every other, who lives and reigns with you and the Holy Spirit, one God, now and forever. Amen.

First Sunday after the Epiphany (The Baptism of the Lord) and the week following:

Father in heaven, at the baptism of Jesus in the Jordan River you proclaimed him your well-beloved Son and anointed him with the Holy Spirit. Grant that all who are baptized into his name may keep the covenant they have made with you and with your people and that they may boldly confess him as Lord and Savior unto their last breath. We ask it in Jesus' name, who with you and the Holy Spirit lives and reigns, one God, in glory everlasting. Amen.

Second Sunday after the Epiphany and the week following:

Almighty God, you have given your Son to be the light of the world. Grant that your people, illumined by his Word and strengthened by his ordinances, may shine with the radiance of Christ's glory so that he is loved, worshiped, and obeyed to the ends of the earth, through Jesus Christ our Lord, who with you and the Holy Spirit lives and reigns, one God, now and forever. Amen.

Third Sunday after the Epiphany and the week following:

Give us grace, O Lord, to gladly answer the call of our Savior, Jesus Christ, and proclaim to all people the good news of his salvation, that we and the whole world may perceive the glory of his marvelous works, who lives and reigns with you and the Holy Spirit, one God, forever and ever. Amen.

Fourth Sunday after the Epiphany and the week following:

Almighty and everlasting God, you govern all things in heaven and on earth, you give both blessing and disaster, both life and death. Hear the supplications of your people and, from your great power, have mercy on us. Grant us your peace in this season, through Jesus Christ our Lord, who lives and reigns with you and the Holy Spirit, one God, forever and ever. Amen.

Fifth Sunday after the Epiphany and the week following:

Set us free, O God, from the bondage to sin, and give us the liberty of abundant life which you have shown to us in the love and obedience of your Son, our Lord and Savior Jesus Christ, who lives and reigns with you in the unity of the Holy Spirit, one God, now and forever. Amen.

Sixth Sunday after the Epiphany and the week following:

O God, you are the strength of all who put their trust in you. In your great mercy, hear our prayers. Through the weakness of our sinful nature, we can do no good thing without you; give us the special grace of a grateful heart, that we may keep your Great Commandment and so please you by both word and deed, through Jesus Christ our Lord, who lives and reigns with you and the Holy Spirit, one God, forever and ever. Amen.

Seventh Sunday after the Epiphany and the week following:

O Lord, you have taught us that without love all our deeds are worthless. Send your Holy Spirit and pour the love of Jesus into our hearts, for this is the gift that excels all others and is the bond of peace and all virtue. Cause this love to well up in us as the overflow of a heart that has been made alive in Christ, for we pray it in his name, the name of Jesus, who lives and reigns with you and the Holy Spirit, one God, now and forever. Amen.

Eighth Sunday after the Epiphany and the week following:

Most loving Father, you are the fount of every blessing and holy desire; we give you thanks for all things. Keep us from the dread of losing anything but you. Give us grace, we pray, to cast all our cares on you because you care for us and preserve us from faithless fears and worldly anxieties. Sweep away every dark cloud of this mortal life that hides the light of the undying love you have shown us in your Son, Jesus Christ our Lord, who lives and reigns with you in the unity of the Holy Spirit, one God, now and forever. Amen.

Last Sunday before Ash Wednesday:

O God, before the suffering of your only-begotten Son, you revealed his glory upon the holy mount. Grant, we pray, that by faith we may behold the light of his face, that we may be strengthened to bear our own crosses, and that we may be changed into his likeness from glory to glory, through Jesus Christ our Lord, who lives and reigns with you and the Holy Spirit, one God, forever and ever. Amen.

Lent

Ash Wednesday and the days following until the 1st Sunday of Lent:

Almighty and everlasting God who forgives the sins of all those who are truly repentant: create in us new and contrite hearts so that we might be filled with godly sorrow for every sin and might acknowledge our wretched weakness. Grant, most merciful Father, that we will persevere in the faith and so obtain from you the crown of righteousness — a perfect remission of all our sins and the forgiveness that comes only through Christ's broken body and shed blood. This we ask in the name of Jesus Christ our Lord, who lives and reigns with you and the Holy Spirit, one God, forever and ever. Amen.

First Sunday in Lent, and the week following:

Almighty God, whose blessed Son was led by the Spirit to be tempted of Satan, make speed to help your servants because we are surrounded and worn down by many temptations. Oh God, you already know our many infirmities and so let each one of us find you mighty to save, through Jesus Christ your Son, our Lord, who lives and reigns with you and the Holy Spirit, one God, now and forever. Amen.

<u>Second Sunday in Lent, and the week following:</u>

O God, whose glory it is to always have mercy, be gracious to all who have gone astray from your ways. Grant them repentant hearts and the renewal of a steadfast faith so that they cling to the unchangeable truth of your holy Word, through Jesus Christ our Lord, who with you and the Holy Spirit lives and reigns, one God, forever and ever. Amen.

<u>Third Sunday in Lent, and the week following:</u>

Almighty God, you see that we have no power to help ourselves. Protect us outwardly in our bodies and inwardly in our souls, that we may be defended from every bodily adversity or illness and from all evil thoughts which assault and enslave the soul, through Jesus Christ our Lord, who lives and reigns with you and the Holy Spirit, one God, now and forever. Amen.

<u>Fourth Sunday in Lent, and the week following:</u>

Gracious Father, whose blessed Son, Jesus Christ, came down from heaven to be the True Bread which gives life to the world, evermore give us this Bread, that he may live in us, and we in him, who lives and reigns with you and the Holy Spirit, one God, now and forever. Amen.

<u>Fifth Sunday in Lent, and the week following:</u>

Almighty God, you alone can order the unruly wills and affections of sinful souls. Grant your people the grace to love what you have commanded and to long for that which you have promised. Grant also, we pray, that among the many disturbing changes of the world, our hearts may be fixed where true joy is found — in Jesus Christ, our Lord, who lives and reigns with you and the Holy Spirit, one God, now and forever. Amen.

Holy Week

Palm Sunday:

Almighty and ever-living God, because of your tender love for the Church, you sent your Son, our Savior Jesus Christ, to take upon himself human flesh and to suffer death upon the cross. Grant that all in his fold would follow his example with great humility. Mercifully grant that we may walk in the footsteps of his suffering, and so may also be made partakers of his resurrection, through Jesus Christ our Lord, who lives and reigns with you and the Holy Spirit, one God, forever and ever. Amen.

Holy Monday:

Almighty God, your beloved Son deferred both joy and glory by first suffering the sorrow of rejection and the pain of crucifixion. In your mercy, give us the grace to also walk first in the way of the cross. Help us to find in it the way of life and peace that leads to the glory of everlasting joy, through your Son, Jesus Christ our Lord, who lives and reigns with you and the Holy Spirit, one God, forever and ever. Amen.

Holy Tuesday:

O God, by the suffering of your blessed Son you made an instrument of shameful death into the means of eternal life. Help us to glory in the cross of Christ, that we may gladly suffer shame and loss for the sake of your Son, our Savior Jesus Christ, and so with him, and in him, obtain the resurrection of the dead;

we pray this in his name, who lives and reigns with you and the Holy Spirit, one God, forever and ever. Amen.

Spy Wednesday:

O Lord God, whose blessed Son gave his back to those who wielded the whip and did not hide his face from shame, give us grace to courageously face and endure the sufferings of this present age. Though sorrow may catch us unawares preserve our joy. Give us, in the midst of difficulty, a full and steady assurance of the glory that will one day be revealed to us, through your Son Jesus Christ, our Lord and Savior, who lives and reigns with you and the Holy Spirit, one God, forever and ever. Amen.

Maundy Thursday:

Almighty Father, your dear Son, on the night before he suffered, instituted the holy commemoration of his broken body and shed blood. Mercifully grant that our hearts may be opened to the great mystery of our faith. Help us receive the bread and wine as true signs and promises of him who gives us the gift of life eternal, your Son, Jesus Christ our Lord, who now lives and reigns with you and the Holy Spirit, one God, world without end. Amen.

Good Friday:

Almighty God, you graciously sustain all things by your outstretched hand; continue to graciously uphold the Church in her hours of darkest distress. Rescue us, your family, for whom our Lord Jesus Christ was betrayed, given into the hands of sinners, and suffered death upon the cross. This we ask in the name of Jesus, who now lives and reigns with you and the Holy Spirit, one God, forever and ever. Amen.

O God, Creator of heaven and earth, just as Jesus' crucified body was laid in the tomb and rested on this Sabbath, give us strength and patience to rest as we await with him the coming of the third day. And, heavenly Father, raise us with him to newness of life, who now lives and reigns with you and the Holy Spirit, one God, forever and ever. Amen.

Eastertide

Easter (beginning at sundown before Easter Sunday):

O God, for our redemption you gave your only-begotten Son to die on the cross; by his glorious resurrection, you have delivered us from the power of our enemy and trampled death underfoot by death. Help us, Lord, to die daily to sin so that we may live with him in the joy of eternal glory, through Jesus Christ, your Son, our Lord, who lives and reigns with you and the Holy Spirit, one God, now and forever. Amen.

Or this:

O God, long ago you made this most holy night to shine with the glory of the Lord's resurrection. Stir up in your Church the spirit of our adoption, symbolized in the waters of baptism, that we, being renewed both in body and mind, may worship you in spirit and truth, through the same Jesus Christ our Lord who lives and reigns with you in the unity of the Holy Spirit, one God, now and forever. Amen.

Or this:

Almighty God, through your only-begotten Son, Jesus Christ, you overcame death and opened the gate to everlasting life for all who turn to you in faith. Grant us a holy and enduring faith, that we who joyfully celebrate the day of the Lord's resurrection may be raised ourselves from the death of sin by your life-giving Spirit, through the same Jesus Christ our Lord who lives and reigns with you and the same Spirit, one God, now and forever. Amen.

The Monday After Easter Sunday:

Almighty God, grant that all who now joyfully anticipate the marriage supper of the Lamb may be preserved in saving faith until the day they celebrate it with Jesus face to face; through Him, who lives and reigns with you and the Holy Spirit, one God, now and forever. Amen.

The Tuesday After Easter Sunday:

O God, by the glorious resurrection of your Son, Jesus Christ, you destroyed death and brought life and immortality to your people. Grant that we, who have been raised with him, might continually abide in his presence and unceasingly rejoice in the hope of eternal glory, through the same Jesus Christ our Lord to whom, with you and the Holy Spirit, be dominion and praise forever and ever. Amen.

The Wednesday After Easter Sunday:

O God, just as your resurrected Son manifested himself to his disciples in the breaking of bread, open, we pray, the eyes of our faith, that we might behold him in all his redeeming work, through Jesus Christ our Lord, who lives and reigns with you in the unity of the Holy Spirit, one God, now and forever. Amen.

The Thursday After Easter Sunday:

Almighty and everlasting God, who, in the mystery of Christ's suffering, established the new covenant of reconciliation, grant that all who have been reborn into the fellowship of Christ's body might show forth in their lives what they profess by their faith, through the same Jesus Christ our Lord who lives and reigns with You and the Holy Spirit, one God, world without end. Amen.

The Friday After Easter Sunday:

Almighty Father, in generosity and lovingkindness you gave your only-begotten Son to die for our sins and to rise again for our justification. Give us grace to put away the leaven of malice and wickedness, that we may always serve you in pure living and the love of truth, through your Son, Jesus Christ our Lord, who lives and reigns with You and the Holy Spirit, one God, now and forever. Amen.

The Saturday After Easter Sunday:

We thank you, heavenly Father, that you have delivered us from the dominion of sin and death and have brought us into the kingdom of your Son. Grant that just as he has restored us to life by his death, so also we might die to self and rise to eternal joy. This we pray in the mighty name of your Son, Jesus, who lives and reigns with you in the unity of the Holy Spirit, one God, world without end. Amen.

The Sunday after Easter, and the week following:

Almighty and everlasting God, who, in the mystery of Christ's suffering, established the new covenant of reconciliation, grant that all who have been reborn into the fellowship of Christ's body might show forth in their lives what they profess by their faith, through the same Jesus Christ our Lord who lives and reigns with you and the Holy Spirit, one God, world without end. Amen.

The Second Sunday after Easter, and the week following:

O God, just as your resurrected Son manifested himself to his disciples in the breaking of bread, open, we pray, the eyes of our faith, that we might behold him in all his redeeming work, through Jesus Christ our Lord, who lives and reigns with you in the unity of the Holy Spirit, one God, now and forever. Amen.

The Third Sunday after Easter, and the week following:

O God, whose Son, Jesus, is the good shepherd of your people, grant that when we hear his voice, we may know him who calls us each by name and may follow wherever he leads. This we pray through your Son, our Lord, Jesus Christ, who, with You and the Holy Spirit, lives and reigns, one God, world without end. Amen.

The Fourth Sunday after Easter, and the week following:

Almighty and everlasting God, to truly know you is everlasting life; grant us grace to truly know your Son, Jesus Christ, as the way, the truth, and the life. Give us grace to follow in his steps, without wavering, on the path that leads to eternal life. This we pray through your Son, our Lord, Jesus Christ, who lives and reigns with you in the unity of the Holy Spirit, one God, in glory everlasting. Amen.

The Fifth Sunday after Easter, and the week following:

O God, in love you have prepared such good things for your people that they exceed our understanding; pour so great a love for you into our hearts. Help us to cherish you in all things and above all things, that we may obtain your promises, which exceed all that we can desire, through Jesus Christ our Lord, who lives and reigns with you and the Holy Spirit, one God, forever and ever. Amen.

<u>Ascension Day, and the days following until the Next Sunday:</u>

Almighty God, your blessed Son, our Savior Jesus Christ, ascended far above all heavens that he might glorified above every earthly power. Have mercy on us and grant us the faith to perceive that he still abides with his Church on earth, even as he has promised, unto the end of the ages, through Jesus Christ our Lord, who lives and reigns with you and the Holy Spirit, one God, in glory everlasting. Amen.

Or this:

Almighty God, we humbly ask that just as your only-begotten Son, our Lord Jesus Christ, has ascended into heaven, so may we also ascend in heart and mind and continually dwell with him who lives and reigns with you and the Holy Spirit, one God, world without end. Amen.

<u>Ascension Sunday (The Sunday before Pentecost), and the week following:</u>

O God, you are the king of glory, and, with great triumph, you have exalted your only Son, Jesus Christ, to your right hand in heaven. Do not leave us without consolation in the sorrows and struggles of this life, but send your Holy Spirit to comfort us. In due time, exalt us also, according to your will, to the place Christ has prepared for us. We pray all this in his holy name, who lives and reigns with you and the same Holy Spirit, one God, in glory everlasting. Amen.

Ordinary Time

Pentecost Sunday, and the week following:

Almighty God, on this day you opened the way of eternal life to every race and nation by the promised gift of your Holy Spirit; let this gift be spread throughout the world by the faithful preaching of the whole counsel of your word, that your chosen people might be gathered from the ends of the earth, through Jesus Christ our Lord, who lives and reigns with you, in the unity of the same Spirit, one God, forever and ever. Amen.

Or this:

O God, on this day you taught the hearts of your faithful people by sending to them the light of your Holy Spirit. Give us, by that same Spirit, godly judgment in all things and the everlasting joy and comfort he alone can bring. Grant this, we pray, according to your grace in Christ Jesus, our Lord and Savior, who lives and reigns with you in the unity of the Holy Spirit, one God, world without end. Amen.

Trinity Sunday (First Sunday after Pentecost), and the week following:

Almighty and everlasting God, you have called us and made us new by grace and have planted in our hearts the confession of a true faith, the glory of the eternal Trinity, and the power to worship the Divine Unity. We pray that you would preserve us in this faith and worship and make our hearts steadfast in every season of life. Heavenly Father bring us at last to see you in your eternal glory, where with the Son and the Holy Spirit you live and reign, one God, world without end. Amen.

Ordinary Time or Proper 1 (Week of the Sunday closest to May 11):

Remember, O Lord, not what we deserve but what you have called forth and sealed in us by your grace. And, just as you have called us to your service, make us worthy of that calling, through Jesus Christ our Lord, who lives and reigns with you and the Holy Spirit, one God, in glory everlasting. Amen.

Ordinary Time or Proper 2 (Week of the Sunday closest to May 18):

Almighty and most merciful God, in your goodness and mercy, keep us from everything that can hurt us or hurt others. Make us ready in body and soul, with free hearts, to accomplish everything you will to be done on earth, even as it is in heaven, through Jesus Christ our Lord, who lives and reigns with you and the Holy Spirit, one God, now and forever. Amen.

Ordinary Time or Proper 3 (The Sunday closest to May 25):

Almighty and most merciful God, we pray that the course of this world may be peacefully governed by your will and that your Church may joyfully serve you in confidence and dignity, through Jesus Christ our Lord, who lives and reigns with you and the Holy Spirit, one God, forever and ever. Amen.

Ordinary Time or Proper 4 (The Sunday closest to June 1):

O God, whose never-failing providence orders all things both in heaven and earth, we pray that you would drive all hurtful things far from us, and give us those things which are good for us, through Jesus Christ our Lord, who lives and reigns with you and the Holy Spirit, one God, forever and ever. Amen.

Ordinary Time or Proper 5 (The Sunday closest to June 8):

Gracious Father, all good things come from you. Grant, by your inspiration, that we will think those things that are right and pure and, by your mercy, guide us to walk in those same things, through Jesus Christ our Lord, who lives and reigns with you and the Holy Spirit, one God, in glory everlasting. Amen.

Ordinary Time or Proper 6 (The Sunday closest to June 15):

Keep, O Lord, your household, the Church, steadfast and faithful, that by the help of your grace, we may proclaim the whole truth of the gospel with boldness and minister your justice with love and compassion for the sake of our Savior, Jesus Christ, who lives and reigns with you and the Holy Spirit, one God, now and forever. Amen.

Ordinary Time or Proper 7 (The Sunday closest to June 22):

O Lord, you never fail to help and govern those whom you have set upon the sure foundation of faith, and so, we humbly ask, give us a perpetual reverence of your holy name and let our hearts be governed by the love of Christ. We pray it in his name, who lives and reigns with you and the Holy Spirit, one God, world without end. Amen.

Ordinary Time or Proper 8 (The Sunday closest to June 29):

Almighty God, you have built the Church upon the foundation of the apostles and prophets and made Jesus Christ himself the chief cornerstone; grant that the Church might be joined together in a unity of spirit by true doctrine, so perfectly revealed in Holy Scripture, that we may be made a holy temple acceptable unto you, through Jesus Christ our Lord, who lives and reigns with you and the Holy Spirit, one God, forever and ever. Amen.

Ordinary Time or Proper 9 (The Sunday closest to July 6):

O God, through your Son you taught us to love you above all else and to love our neighbor as ourselves. Grant us the grace of your Holy Spirit that we may be devoted to you with our whole heart and life, and be united to one another with a pure and holy love, through Jesus Christ our Lord, who lives and reigns with you and the Holy Spirit, one God, in glory everlasting. Amen.

Ordinary Time or Proper 10 (The Sunday closest to July 13):

O Lord, you are always ready to hear and answer the prayers of your people. Grant that we may both perceive and know the things we ought to do, and also that we may have grace and power to faithfully do them, through Jesus Christ our Lord, who lives and reigns with you and the Holy Spirit, one God, now and forever. Amen.

Ordinary Time or Proper 11 (The Sunday closest to July 20):

Almighty God, you are the fountain of all wisdom; you know our necessities before we ask and our ignorance in asking. Grant us, O Lord, those things for which, on account of our unworthiness, we dare not ask, and because of our blindness, we cannot ask. Mercifully give us these things because of the worthiness of your Son, Jesus Christ our Lord, who lives and reigns with you and the Holy Spirit, one God, in eternal glory. Amen.

Ordinary Time or Proper 12 (The Sunday closest to July 27):

O God, you are the protector of all that trust in you; without you, no one is strong and nothing is holy. Increase and multiply your mercies upon us every day that our faith might be strengthened and we might be made holy in word and deed. Send your Holy Spirit to safeguard our faith as we pass through earthly and temporary things so that we do not lose that which is eternal, through Jesus Christ our Lord, who lives and reigns with you and the Holy Spirit, one God, forever and ever. Amen.

Ordinary Time or Proper 13 (The Sunday closest to August 3):

O Lord, in your continual mercy, purify and defend your bride, the Church, because she cannot continue in safety without your aid and protection. Preserve her, we pray, from every flaming arrow of the enemy. Let your help and goodness be a shield to defend her, and let her prevail against the enemy's strongholds, just as you have promised, until the end of the age, through Jesus Christ our Lord, who lives and reigns with you and the Holy Spirit, one God, world without end. Amen.

Ordinary Time or Proper 14 (The Sunday closest to August 10):

Holy and perfect God, in every moment you uphold and sustain the whole universe by your outstretched arm. Send us your Holy Spirit to help us to always think and do what is right so that we might have the power to live according to your will, through Jesus Christ our Lord, who lives and reigns with you and the Holy Spirit, one God, in glory everlasting. Amen.

Ordinary Time or Proper 15 (The Sunday closest to August 17):

Almighty God, you gave your only Son to be both a sacrifice for sin and the example of godly living. Just so, give us grace that we may always receive him with grateful hearts as the gift surpassing all others. Help us to strive every day to follow in the blessed steps of his holy life, through the same Jesus Christ, your Son and our Lord, who lives and reigns with you and the Holy Spirit, one God, now and forever. Amen.

Ordinary Time or Proper 16 (The Sunday closest to August 24):

Eternal Father, you hold all things in the palm of your hands; grant that your Church, being gathered together in unity by the

Holy Spirit, may manifest your power among all peoples as agents of your grace, to the glory of your holy name, through Jesus Christ our Lord, who lives and reigns with you and the Holy Spirit, one God, world without end. Amen.

Ordinary Time or Proper 17 (The Sunday closest to August 31):

Lord of all power and might, you are the author and giver of all good things; graft in our hearts the love of your name; increase in us true religion; nourish us with all goodness, and bring forth in us the fruit of good works, through Jesus Christ our Lord, who lives and reigns with you and the Holy Spirit, one God, forever and ever. Amen.

Ordinary Time or Proper 18 (The Sunday closest to September 7):

Grant us, O Lord, to trust in you with all our heart. Help us to see that just as you always resist the proud who confide in their own strength, so also you never forsake those who boast only in your mercy, through Jesus Christ our Lord, who lives and reigns with you and the Holy Spirit, one God, now and forever. Amen.

Ordinary Time or Proper 19 (The Sunday closest to September 14):

Heavenly Father, your faithfulness endures forever! Without faith, we are not able to please you, and faith itself comes from you as a gift. So, mercifully grant us this faith, and cause your Holy Spirit in all things to direct and rule our hearts, through Jesus Christ our Lord, who, with you and the same Spirit, lives and reigns, one God, now and forever. Amen.

Ordinary Time or Proper 20 (The Sunday closest to September 21):

Eternal God, you are the same yesterday, today and forever. Grant us, O Lord, not to desire worldly things but to love whatever is of eternal value. Even now, while we are passing away and while we live in a world that is passing away, cause us to cling to those things that will abide forever, through Jesus Christ our Lord, who lives and reigns with you and the Holy Spirit, one God, forever and ever. Amen.

Ordinary Time or Proper 21 (The Sunday closest to September 28):

O God, you declare your almighty power chiefly by showing mercy. Mercifully grant unto us such a measure of your grace, that we, running to obtain your promises, may be made partakers of your heavenly reward, through Jesus Christ our Lord, who lives and reigns with You and the Holy Spirit, one God, forever and ever. Amen.

Ordinary Time or Proper 22 (The Sunday closest to October 5):

Almighty and everlasting God, you are always more ready to hear than we are to pray. You are always inclined to give more than we desire or deserve. Pour down on us the abundance of your mercy! Forgive us those sins which cause us fear, and give us those good things for which we are not worthy to ask, except through the merits and mediation of your Son, Jesus Christ, who lives and reigns with You and the Holy Spirit, one God, in glory everlasting. Amen.

Ordinary Time or Proper 23 (The Sunday closest to October 12):

Lord, you are the Alpha and Omega, the Beginning of life and the End for which we long. We pray that your grace may always precede and follow us and make us continually devoted to all good works, through Jesus Christ our Lord, who lives and reigns with you and the Holy Spirit, one God, now and forever. Amen.

Ordinary Time or Proper 24 (The Sunday closest to October 19):

Most merciful Father, in Christ you have revealed your glory among the nations. Preserve the works of your mercy and grant that your Church throughout the world may persevere in the true faith and in the confession of your name above every other name; through Jesus Christ our Lord, who lives and reigns with you and the Holy Spirit, one God, forever and ever. Amen.

Ordinary Time or Proper 25 (The Sunday closest to October 26):

Most gracious and loving Lord, it is by your grace alone that our faith, hope, and love increase; grant that we may obtain that which you have promised and give us hearts to love that which you have commanded, through Jesus Christ our Lord, who lives and reigns with you and the Holy Spirit, one God, in glory everlasting. Amen.

Ordinary Time or Proper 26 (The Sunday closest to November 2):

Almighty God, you generously call all people, of all walks of life, to a holy vocation in your kingdom. Grant that, in all our vocations, we may give you true and praiseworthy service and may run without stumbling to obtain a heavenly reward, through Jesus Christ our Lord, who lives and reigns with you and the Holy Spirit, one God, now and forever. Amen.

Reformation Sunday (The Last Sunday in October):

Most merciful God, you are the creator and sustainer of all life, the one who made the first man and gave him the breath of life. Through the finished work of your Son, you alone bring us back to life, you alone create repentance and justify sinners, and you alone sustain them in faith unto eternity. Even so, Lord, send your Holy Spirit to do this work in our midst and to the ends of the earth, for the glory of Christ alone. We pray this in his name, who lives and reigns with you in the unity of the Holy Spirit, one God in glory everlasting. Amen.

Ordinary Time or Proper 27 (The Sunday closest to November 9):

O God, in love you sent your Son to destroy the works of the devil and to make us children of God and heirs of eternal life. Grant that, having this hope, we may be purified even as he is pure, that, when he appears again with power and great glory, we will dwell with him in his eternal and glorious kingdom where with you, O Father, and you, O Holy Spirit, he lives and reigns forever, one God, world without end. Amen.

Ordinary Time or Proper 28 (The Sunday closest to November 16):

Blessed Lord, you have given Holy Scripture to be written for our learning and sanctification. Grant that we may hear the Bible as your own voice, that we may read and pay careful attention to all it teaches, and that our spirits might be shaped and comforted by its promises. Help us, through your Word, to embrace and cling to the hope of everlasting life, which you have given us in our Savior, Jesus Christ, who lives and reigns with you and the Holy Spirit, one God, forever and ever. Amen.

Christ the King Sunday, or Ordinary Time, or Proper 29 (The Sunday closest to November 23):

Almighty and everlasting God, whose will it is to restore all things in your well-beloved Son, the King of kings and Lord of lords, mercifully grant that the peoples of the earth, divided and enslaved by sin, may be freed and brought together under his most gracious rule, who lives and reigns with you and the Holy Spirit, one God, now and forever. Amen.

THE PSALTER

Notes about the Psalter

It is necessary to have a uniform single translation of the Psalms to facilitate their use in common prayer. When reading the Psalms responsively for worship, it is not enough to simply *hope* that everyone is using the same translation; there must be *certainty* in order to speak the psalms in unison. Even long-standing translations (i.e. KJV, NKJV, NIV 1984, NIV 2011, etc.) go through edition or revision changes that don't allow for a "word perfect" experience for group reading.

The New Living Translation is easy to read and sounds great when read aloud. We are grateful to Tyndale House Publishers for granting permission to use the NLT so that everyone can stay on the same page!

Many of the psalms include explanatory titles that place the Psalm in context — such as author (Psalm 3: "A Song of David"), how it is to be sung (Psalm 4: "to be accompanied by stringed instruments"), or even the circumstances of the writing of the song (Psalm 3: "regarding the time David fled from his son Absalom"). Several of the psalms include all three of these instructions. (Psalm 51: "For the choir director: A psalm of David, regarding the time Nathan the prophet came to him after David had committed adultery with Bathsheba.").

In addition, often the book of Psalms is interspersed with the word *interlude*, which is a rendering of the Hebrew word *selah*. The meaning of this word is uncertain, though it is probably a musical or literary term. Some believe that *selah* offered a direction to the worship leader as thirty-one of the thirty-nine psalms that include "To the Choir Director" also include *selah* somewhere in that psalm. It might be conveyed as "stop and think about," "pause," or "consider what was just sung or spoken." However, the words *selah* and *interlude* are not helpful in responsive reading. In fact, they could possibly be a distraction when doing prayer together with your children in family worship!

Thus, throughout the Psalter, these explanatory titles and musical/literary terms have been italicized to set them off from the body of the Psalm. Neither the explanatory titles or musical terms are said aloud when the Psalm is used in worship as a responsive reading. Just as in the rest of the responsive readings throughout the prayer book, the leader says the light font, and all others respond with the bolded font.

After each reading, the *Gloria Patri* is read and is included for the reference of those that are still memorizing it. The *Gloria Patri* is an ancient Christian prayer traditionally read after the reading of a Psalm; it is not a part of the book of Psalms.

Book One

(Psalms 1–41)

Psalm 1

¹Oh, the joys of those who do not
follow the advice of the wicked,
or stand around with sinners,
or join in with mockers.
²But they delight in the law of the Lord,
meditating on it day and night.
³**They are like trees planted along the riverbank,**
bearing fruit each season.
Their leaves never wither,
and they prosper in all they do.
⁴**But not the wicked!**
They are like worthless chaff, scattered by the wind.
⁵They will be condemned at the time of judgment.
Sinners will have no place among the godly.
⁶For the Lord watches over the path of the godly,
but the path of the wicked leads to destruction.

Psalm 2

¹Why are the nations so angry?
Why do they waste their time with futile plans?
²The kings of the earth prepare for battle;
the rulers plot together
against the Lord
and against his anointed one.
³"Let us break their chains," they cry,

"and free ourselves from slavery to God."

⁴But the one who rules in heaven laughs.

The Lord scoffs at them.

⁵Then in anger he rebukes them,

terrifying them with his fierce fury.

⁶**For the Lord declares, "I have placed my chosen king on the throne in Jerusalem, on my holy mountain."**

⁷The king proclaims the Lord's decree:

"The Lord said to me, 'You are my son.

Today I have become your Father.

⁸Only ask, and I will give you the nations as your inheritance,

the whole earth as your possession.

⁹**You will break them with an iron rod**

and smash them like clay pots.'"

¹⁰Now then, you kings, act wisely!

Be warned, you rulers of the earth!

¹¹Serve the Lord with reverent fear,

and rejoice with trembling.

¹²**Submit to God's royal son, or he will become angry,**

and you will be destroyed in the midst of all your activities —

for his anger flares up in an instant.

But what joy for all who take refuge in him!

Then all the people say the following praise:

Glory to the Father, and to the Son, and to the Holy Spirit, as it was in the beginning, is now, and will be forever. Amen.

Psalm 3

A psalm of David, regarding the time David fled from his son Absalom.

1 O Lord, I have so many enemies;

so many are against me.

2 **So many are saying,**

"God will never rescue him!" *Interlude*

3 But you, O Lord, are a shield around me;

you are my glory, the one who holds my head high.

4 I cried out to the Lord,

and he answered me from his holy mountain. *Interlude*

5 I lay down and slept,
  yet I woke up in safety,
  for the Lord was watching over me.
6 I am not afraid of ten thousand enemies
  who surround me on every side.
7 Arise, O Lord!
  Rescue me, my God!
Slap all my enemies in the face!
  Shatter the teeth of the wicked!
8 Victory comes from you, O Lord.
  May you bless your people. *Interlude*

Psalm 4

For the choir director: A psalm of David, to be accompanied by stringed instruments.

1 Answer me when I call to you,
  O God who declares me innocent.
Free me from my troubles.
  Have mercy on me and hear my prayer.
2 How long will you people ruin my reputation?
  How long will you make groundless accusations?
How long will you continue your lies? *Interlude*
3 **You can be sure of this:**
  The Lord set apart the godly for himself.
The Lord will answer when I call to him.
4 **Don't sin by letting anger control you.**
  Think about it overnight and remain silent. *Interlude*
5 **Offer sacrifices in the right spirit,**
  and trust the Lord.
6 **Many people say, "Who will show us better times?"**
  Let your face smile on us, Lord.
7 **You have given me greater joy**
  than those who have abundant harvests of grain and new wine.
8 **In peace I will lie down and sleep,**
  for you alone, O Lord, will keep me safe.

Then all the people say the following praise:

Glory to the Father, and to the Son, and to the Holy Spirit, as it was in the beginning, is now, and will be forever. Amen.

Psalm 5

For the choir director: A psalm of David, to be accompanied by the flute.

1 O Lord, hear me as I pray;
  pay attention to my groaning.
2 Listen to my cry for help, my King and my God,
  for I pray to no one but you.
3 Listen to my voice in the morning, Lord.
  Each morning I bring my requests to you and wait expectantly.
4 O God, you take no pleasure in wickedness;
  you cannot tolerate the sins of the wicked.
5 Therefore, the proud may not stand in your presence,
  for you hate all who do evil.
6 You will destroy those who tell lies.
  The Lord detests murderers and deceivers.
7 Because of your unfailing love, I can enter your house;
  I will worship at your Temple with deepest awe.
8 Lead me in the right path, O Lord,
  or my enemies will conquer me.
Make your way plain for me to follow.
9 **My enemies cannot speak a truthful word.**
  Their deepest desire is to destroy others.
Their talk is foul, like the stench from an open grave.
  Their tongues are filled with flattery.
10 **O God, declare them guilty.**
  Let them be caught in their own traps.
Drive them away because of their many sins,
  for they have rebelled against you.
11 **But let all who take refuge in you rejoice;**
  let them sing joyful praises forever.
Spread your protection over them,
  that all who love your name may be filled with joy.
12 **For you bless the godly, O Lord;**
  you surround them with your shield of love.

Then all the people say the following praise:

Glory to the Father, and to the Son, and to the Holy Spirit, as it was in the beginning, is now, and will be forever. Amen.

Psalm 6

For the choir director: A psalm of David, to be accompanied by an eight-stringed instrument.

1 O Lord, don't rebuke me in your anger
or discipline me in your rage.
2 Have compassion on me, Lord, for I am weak.
Heal me, Lord, for my bones are in agony.
3 I am sick at heart.
How long, O Lord, until you restore me?
4 Return, O Lord, and rescue me.
Save me because of your unfailing love.
5 For the dead do not remember you.
Who can praise you from the grave?
6 I am worn out from sobbing.
All night I flood my bed with weeping,
drenching it with my tears.
7 **My vision is blurred by grief;**
my eyes are worn out because of all my enemies.
8 **Go away, all you who do evil,**
for the Lord has heard my weeping.
9 **The Lord has heard my plea;**
the Lord will answer my prayer.
10 **May all my enemies be disgraced and terrified.**
May they suddenly turn back in shame.

Then all the people say the following praise:

Glory to the Father, and to the Son, and to the Holy Spirit, as it was in the beginning, is now, and will be forever. Amen.

Psalm 7

A psalm of David, which he sang to the Lord concerning Cush of the tribe of Benjamin.

1 I come to you for protection, O Lord my God.
Save me from my persecutors — rescue me!
2 If you don't, they will maul me like a lion,
tearing me to pieces with no one to rescue me.
3 O Lord my God, if I have done wrong
or am guilty of injustice,
4 if I have betrayed a friend
or plundered my enemy without cause,
5 then let my enemies capture me.
Let them trample me into the ground
and drag my honor in the dust. *Interlude*
6 **Arise, O Lord, in anger!**
Stand up against the fury of my enemies!
Wake up, my God, and bring justice!
7 Gather the nations before you.
Rule over them from on high.
8 The Lord judges the nations.
Declare me righteous, O Lord,
for I am innocent, O Most High!
9 **End the evil of those who are wicked,**
and defend the righteous.
For you look deep within the mind and heart,
O righteous God.
10 God is my shield,
saving those whose hearts are true and right.
11 God is an honest judge.
He is angry with the wicked every day.
12 If a person does not repent,
God will sharpen his sword;
he will bend and string his bow.
13 He will prepare his deadly weapons
and shoot his flaming arrows.
14 The wicked conceive evil;
they are pregnant with trouble
and give birth to lies.

15 They dig a deep pit to trap others,
  then fall into it themselves.
16 The trouble they make for others backfires on them.
  The violence they plan falls on their own heads.
17 I will thank the Lord because he is just;
  I will sing praise to the name of the Lord Most High.

Then all the people say the following praise:

Glory to the Father, and to the Son, and to the Holy Spirit, as it was in the beginning, is now, and will be forever. Amen.

Psalm 8

For the choir director: A psalm of David, to be accompanied by a stringed instrument.

1 O Lord, our Lord, your majestic name fills the earth!
  Your glory is higher than the heavens.
2 You have taught children and infants
  to tell of your strength,
silencing your enemies
  and all who oppose you.
3 When I look at the night sky and see the work of your fingers —
  the moon and the stars you set in place —
4 what are mere mortals that you should think about them,
  human beings that you should care for them?
5 Yet you made them only a little lower than God
  and crowned them with glory and honor.
6 You gave them charge of everything you made,
  putting all things under their authority —
7 the flocks and the herds
  and all the wild animals,
8 the birds in the sky, the fish in the sea,
  and everything that swims the ocean currents.
9 O Lord, our Lord, your majestic name fills the earth!

Then all the people say the following praise:

Glory to the Father, and to the Son, and to the Holy Spirit, as it was in the beginning, is now, and will be forever. Amen.

Psalm 9:1–10

For the choir director: A psalm of David, to be sung to the tune "Death of the Son."
1 I will praise you, Lord, with all my heart;
 I will tell of all the marvelous things you have done.
2 I will be filled with joy because of you.
 I will sing praises to your name, O Most High.
3 My enemies retreated;
 they staggered and died when you appeared.
4 For you have judged in my favor;
 from your throne you have judged with fairness.
5 You have rebuked the nations and destroyed the wicked;
 you have erased their names forever.
6 The enemy is finished, in endless ruins;
 the cities you uprooted are now forgotten.
7 But the Lord reigns forever,
 executing judgment from his throne.
8 He will judge the world with justice
 and rule the nations with fairness.
9 The Lord is a shelter for the oppressed,
 a refuge in times of trouble.
10 Those who know your name trust in you,
 for you, O Lord, do not abandon those who search for you.

Then all the people say the following praise:

**Glory to the Father, and to the Son, and to the Holy Spirit, as it was
in the beginning, is now, and will be forever. Amen.**

Psalm 9:11–20

11 Sing praises to the Lord who reigns in Jerusalem.
 Tell the world about his unforgettable deeds.
12 For he who avenges murder cares for the helpless.
 He does not ignore the cries of those who suffer.
13 Lord, have mercy on me.
 See how my enemies torment me.
 Snatch me back from the jaws of death.
14 **Save me so I can praise you publicly at Jerusalem's gates,**
 so I can rejoice that you have rescued me.

15 **The nations have fallen into the pit they dug for others.**

Their own feet have been caught in the trap they set.

16 **The Lord is known for his justice.**

The wicked are trapped by their own deeds. *Quiet Interlude*

17 **The wicked will go down to the grave.**

This is the fate of all the nations who ignore God.

18 **But the needy will not be ignored forever;**

the hopes of the poor will not always be crushed.

19 **Arise, O Lord!**

Do not let mere mortals defy you!

Judge the nations!

20 Make them tremble in fear, O Lord.

Let the nations know they are merely human. *Interlude*

Then all the people say the following praise:

Glory to the Father, and to the Son, and to the Holy Spirit, as it was in the beginning, is now, and will be forever. Amen.

Psalm 10

1 O Lord, why do you stand so far away?

Why do you hide when I am in trouble?

2 The wicked arrogantly hunt down the poor.

Let them be caught in the evil they plan for others.

3 For they brag about their evil desires;

they praise the greedy and curse the Lord.

4 The wicked are too proud to seek God.

They seem to think that God is dead.

5 Yet they succeed in everything they do.

They do not see your punishment awaiting them.

They sneer at all their enemies.

6 **They think, "Nothing bad will ever happen to us!**

We will be free of trouble forever!"

7 **Their mouths are full of cursing, lies, and threats.**

Trouble and evil are on the tips of their tongues.

8 **They lurk in ambush in the villages,**

waiting to murder innocent people.

They are always searching for helpless victims.

9 Like lions crouched in hiding,

they wait to pounce on the helpless.
Like hunters they capture the helpless
  and drag them away in nets.
10 Their helpless victims are crushed;
  they fall beneath the strength of the wicked.
11 The wicked think, "God isn't watching us!
  He has closed his eyes and won't even see what we do!"
12 Arise, O Lord!
  Punish the wicked, O God!
  Do not ignore the helpless!
13 Why do the wicked get away with despising God?
  They think, "God will never call us to account."
14 But you see the trouble and grief they cause.
  You take note of it and punish them.
The helpless put their trust in you.
  You defend the orphans.
15 Break the arms of these wicked, evil people!
  Go after them until the last one is destroyed.
16 The Lord is king forever and ever!
  The godless nations will vanish from the land.
17 Lord, you know the hopes of the helpless.
  Surely you will hear their cries and comfort them.
18 You will bring justice to the orphans and the oppressed,
  so mere people can no longer terrify them.

Then all the people say the following praise:

Glory to the Father, and to the Son, and to the Holy Spirit, as it was
in the beginning, is now, and will be forever. Amen.

Psalm 11

For the choir director: A psalm of David.

1 I trust in the Lord for protection.
So why do you say to me,
  "Fly like a bird to the mountains for safety!
2 The wicked are stringing their bows
  and fitting their arrows on the bowstrings.
They shoot from the shadows

at those whose hearts are right.
3 The foundations of law and order have collapsed.
What can the righteous do?"
4 But the Lord is in his holy Temple;
the Lord still rules from heaven.
He watches everyone closely,
examining every person on earth.
5 The Lord examines both the righteous and the wicked.
He hates those who love violence.
6 He will rain down blazing coals and burning sulfur on the wicked,
punishing them with scorching winds.
7 For the righteous Lord loves justice.
The virtuous will see his face.

Psalm 12

For the choir director: A psalm of David, to be accompanied by an eight-stringed instrument.

1 Help, O Lord, for the godly are fast disappearing!
The faithful have vanished from the earth!
2 Neighbors lie to each other,
speaking with flattering lips and deceitful hearts.
3 May the Lord cut off their flattering lips
and silence their boastful tongues.
4 They say, "We will lie to our hearts' content.
Our lips are our own — who can stop us?"
5 The Lord replies, "I have seen violence done to the helpless,
and I have heard the groans of the poor.
Now I will rise up to rescue them,
as they have longed for me to do."
6 The Lord's promises are pure,
like silver refined in a furnace,
purified seven times over.
7 **Therefore, Lord, we know you will protect the oppressed,**
preserving them forever from this lying generation,
8 **even though the wicked strut about,**
and evil is praised throughout the land.

Then all the people say the following praise:

Glory to the Father, and to the Son, and to the Holy Spirit, as it was in the beginning, is now, and will be forever. Amen.

Psalm 13

For the choir director: A psalm of David.

1 O Lord, how long will you forget me? Forever?
  How long will you look the other way?
2 How long must I struggle with anguish in my soul,
  with sorrow in my heart every day?
  How long will my enemy have the upper hand?
3 **Turn and answer me, O Lord my God!**
  Restore the sparkle to my eyes, or I will die.
4 **Don't let my enemies gloat, saying, "We have defeated him!"**
  Don't let them rejoice at my downfall.
5 **But I trust in your unfailing love.**
  I will rejoice because you have rescued me.
6 **I will sing to the Lord**
  because he is good to me.

Psalm 14

For the choir director: A psalm of David.

1 Only fools say in their hearts,
  "There is no God."
  They are corrupt, and their actions are evil;
  not one of them does good!
2 **The Lord looks down from heaven**
  on the entire human race;
  he looks to see if anyone is truly wise,
  if anyone seeks God.
3 **But no, all have turned away;**
  all have become corrupt.
  No one does good,
  not a single one!
4 **Will those who do evil never learn?**
  They eat up my people like bread
  and wouldn't think of praying to the Lord.

5 Terror will grip them,
  for God is with those who obey him.
6 The wicked frustrate the plans of the oppressed,
  but the Lord will protect his people.
7 Who will come from Mount Zion to rescue Israel?
  When the Lord restores his people,
  Jacob will shout with joy, and Israel will rejoice.

Then all the people say the following praise:

Glory to the Father, and to the Son, and to the Holy Spirit, as it was in the beginning, is now, and will be forever. Amen.

Psalm 15

A psalm of David.

1 Who may worship in your sanctuary, Lord?
  Who may enter your presence on your holy hill?
2 Those who lead blameless lives and do what is right,
  speaking the truth from sincere hearts.
3 Those who refuse to gossip
  or harm their neighbors
  or speak evil of their friends.
4 **Those who despise flagrant sinners,**
  and honor the faithful followers of the Lord,
  and keep their promises even when it hurts.
5 Those who lend money without charging interest,
  and who cannot be bribed to lie about the innocent.
  Such people will stand firm forever.

Psalm 16

A psalm of David.

1 Keep me safe, O God,
  for I have come to you for refuge.
2 I said to the Lord, "You are my Master!
  Every good thing I have comes from you."
3 The godly people in the land
  are my true heroes!

I take pleasure in them!
4 Troubles multiply for those who chase after other gods.
I will not take part in their sacrifices of blood
or even speak the names of their gods.
5 **Lord, you alone are my inheritance, my cup of blessing.**
You guard all that is mine.
6 **The land you have given me is a pleasant land.**
What a wonderful inheritance!
7 **I will bless the Lord who guides me;**
even at night my heart instructs me.
8 **I know the Lord is always with me.**
I will not be shaken, for he is right beside me.
9 **No wonder my heart is glad, and I rejoice.**
My body rests in safety.
10 **For you will not leave my soul among the dead**
or allow your holy one to rot in the grave.
11 **You will show me the way of life,**
granting me the joy of your presence
and the pleasures of living with you forever.

Then all the people say the following praise:

Glory to the Father, and to the Son, and to the Holy Spirit, as it was in the beginning, is now, and will be forever. Amen.

Psalm 17

A prayer of David.

1 O Lord, hear my plea for justice.
Listen to my cry for help.
Pay attention to my prayer,
for it comes from honest lips.
2 Declare me innocent,
for you see those who do right.
3 You have tested my thoughts and examined my heart in the night.
You have scrutinized me and found nothing wrong.
I am determined not to sin in what I say.
4 **I have followed your commands,**

which keep me from following cruel and evil people.

5 **My steps have stayed on your path;**
  I have not wavered from following you.

6 **I am praying to you because I know you will answer, O God.**
  Bend down and listen as I pray.

7 **Show me your unfailing love in wonderful ways.**
  By your mighty power you rescue
  those who seek refuge from their enemies.

8 **Guard me as you would guard your own eyes.**
  Hide me in the shadow of your wings.

9 **Protect me from wicked people who attack me,**
  from murderous enemies who surround me.

10 **They are without pity.**
  Listen to their boasting!

11 **They track me down and surround me,**
  watching for the chance to throw me to the ground.

12 **They are like hungry lions, eager to tear me apart —**
  like young lions hiding in ambush.

13 **Arise, O Lord!**
  Stand against them, and bring them to their knees!
  Rescue me from the wicked with your sword!

14 By the power of your hand, O Lord,
  destroy those who look to this world for their reward.
  But satisfy the hunger of your treasured ones.
  May their children have plenty,
  leaving an inheritance for their descendants.

15 Because I am righteous, I will see you.
  When I awake, I will see you face to face and be satisfied.

Then all the people say the following praise:

Glory to the Father, and to the Son, and to the Holy Spirit, as it was in the beginning, is now, and will be forever. Amen.

Psalm 18:1–15

*For the choir director: A psalm of David, the servant of the Lord. He sang this song
to the Lord on the day the Lord rescued him from all his enemies and from Saul. He
sang:*

1 I love you, Lord;
   you are my strength.
2 The Lord is my rock, my fortress, and my savior;
   my God is my rock, in whom I find protection.
He is my shield, the power that saves me,
   and my place of safety.
3 I called on the Lord, who is worthy of praise,
   and he saved me from my enemies.
4 The ropes of death entangled me;
   floods of destruction swept over me.
5 The grave wrapped its ropes around me;
   death laid a trap in my path.
6 But in my distress I cried out to the Lord;
   yes, I prayed to my God for help.
He heard me from his sanctuary;
   my cry to him reached his ears.
7 Then the earth quaked and trembled.
   The foundations of the mountains shook;
   they quaked because of his anger.
8 **Smoke poured from his nostrils;**
   fierce flames leaped from his mouth.
   Glowing coals blazed forth from him.
9 He opened the heavens and came down;
   dark storm clouds were beneath his feet.
10 Mounted on a mighty angelic being, he flew,
   soaring on the wings of the wind.
11 He shrouded himself in darkness,
   veiling his approach with dark rain clouds.
12 Thick clouds shielded the brightness around him
   and rained down hail and burning coals.
13 The Lord thundered from heaven;
   the voice of the Most High resounded
   amid the hail and burning coals.
14 **He shot his arrows and scattered his enemies;**

great bolts of lightning flashed, and they were confused.
15 **Then at your command, O Lord,**
  at the blast of your breath,
the bottom of the sea could be seen,
  and the foundations of the earth were laid bare.

Then all the people say the following praise:

Glory to the Father, and to the Son, and to the Holy Spirit, as it was in the beginning, is now, and will be forever. Amen.

Psalm 18:16–29

16 He reached down from heaven and rescued me;
  he drew me out of deep waters.
17 He rescued me from my powerful enemies,
  from those who hated me and were too strong for me.
18 They attacked me at a moment when I was in distress,
  but the Lord supported me.
19 He led me to a place of safety;
  he rescued me because he delights in me.
20 The Lord rewarded me for doing right;
  he restored me because of my innocence.
21 For I have kept the ways of the Lord;
  I have not turned from my God to follow evil.
22 I have followed all his regulations;
  I have never abandoned his decrees.
23 I am blameless before God;
  I have kept myself from sin.
24 The Lord rewarded me for doing right.
  He has seen my innocence.
25 To the faithful you show yourself faithful;
  to those with integrity you show integrity.
26 To the pure you show yourself pure,
  but to the crooked you show yourself shrewd.
27 You rescue the humble,
  but you humiliate the proud.
28 You light a lamp for me.
  The Lord, my God, lights up my darkness.
29 In your strength I can crush an army;
  with my God I can scale any wall.

Then all the people say the following praise:

Glory to the Father, and to the Son, and to the Holy Spirit, as it was in the beginning, is now, and will be forever. Amen.

Psalm 18:30–45

30 God's way is perfect.
All the Lord's promises prove true.
He is a shield for all who look to him for protection.
31 **For who is God except the Lord?**
Who but our God is a solid rock?
32 **God arms me with strength,**
and he makes my way perfect.
33 **He makes me as surefooted as a deer,**
enabling me to stand on mountain heights.
34 **He trains my hands for battle;**
he strengthens my arm to draw a bronze bow.
35 **You have given me your shield of victory.**
Your right hand supports me;
your help has made me great.
36 You have made a wide path for my feet
to keep them from slipping.
37 I chased my enemies and caught them;
I did not stop until they were conquered.
38 I struck them down so they could not get up;
they fell beneath my feet.
39 You have armed me with strength for the battle;
you have subdued my enemies under my feet.
40 You placed my foot on their necks.
I have destroyed all who hated me.
41 They called for help, but no one came to their rescue.
They even cried to the Lord, but he refused to answer.
42 I ground them as fine as dust in the wind.
I swept them into the gutter like dirt.
43 You gave me victory over my accusers.
You appointed me ruler over nations;
people I don't even know now serve me.
44 **As soon as they hear of me, they submit;**
foreign nations cringe before me.

45 **They all lose their courage**
and come trembling from their strongholds.

Glory to the Father, and to the Son, and to the Holy Spirit, as it was in the beginning, is now, and will be forever. Amen.

Psalm 18:46–50

46 The Lord lives! Praise to my Rock!
  May the God of my salvation be exalted!
47 He is the God who pays back those who harm me;
  he subdues the nations under me
48 and rescues me from my enemies.
You hold me safe beyond the reach of my enemies;
  you save me from violent opponents.
49 **For this, O Lord, I will praise you among the nations;**
  I will sing praises to your name.
50 **You give great victories to your king;**
  you show unfailing love to your anointed,
  to David and all his descendants forever.

Glory to the Father, and to the Son, and to the Holy Spirit, as it was in the beginning, is now, and will be forever. Amen.

Psalm 19

For the choir director: A psalm of David.

1 The heavens proclaim the glory of God.
  The skies display his craftsmanship.
2 Day after day they continue to speak;
  night after night they make him known.
3 They speak without a sound or word;
  their voice is never heard.
4 Yet their message has gone throughout the earth,
  and their words to all the world.

God has made a home in the heavens for the sun.

5 **It bursts forth like a radiant bridegroom after his wedding.**
It rejoices like a great athlete eager to run the race.

6 **The sun rises at one end of the heavens**
and follows its course to the other end.

Nothing can hide from its heat.

7 The instructions of the Lord are perfect,
reviving the soul.

The decrees of the Lord are trustworthy,
making wise the simple.

8 **The commandments of the Lord are right,**
bringing joy to the heart.

The commands of the Lord are clear,
giving insight for living.

9 **Reverence for the Lord is pure,**
lasting forever.

The laws of the Lord are true;
each one is fair.

10 **They are more desirable than gold,**
even the finest gold.

They are sweeter than honey,
even honey dripping from the comb.

11 **They are a warning to your servant,**
a great reward for those who obey them.

12 **How can I know all the sins lurking in my heart?**
Cleanse me from these hidden faults.

13 **Keep your servant from deliberate sins!**
Don't let them control me.

Then I will be free of guilt
and innocent of great sin.

14 **May the words of my mouth**
and the meditation of my heart
be pleasing to you,
O Lord, my rock and my redeemer.

Then all the people say the following praise:

Glory to the Father, and to the Son, and to the Holy Spirit, as it was in the beginning, is now, and will be forever. Amen.

Psalm 20

For the choir director: A psalm of David.

1 In times of trouble, may the Lord answer your cry.
  May the name of the God of Jacob keep you safe from all harm.
2 May he send you help from his sanctuary
  and strengthen you from Jerusalem.
3 May he remember all your gifts
  and look favorably on your burnt offerings. *Interlude*
4 May he grant your heart's desires
  and make all your plans succeed.
5 May we shout for joy when we hear of your victory
  and raise a victory banner in the name of our God.
May the Lord answer all your prayers.
6 **Now I know that the Lord rescues his anointed king.**
  He will answer him from his holy heaven
  and rescue him by his great power.
7 Some nations boast of their chariots and horses,
  but we boast in the name of the Lord our God.
8 Those nations will fall down and collapse,
  but we will rise up and stand firm.
9 Give victory to our king, O Lord!
  Answer our cry for help.

Then all the people say the following praise:

Glory to the Father, and to the Son, and to the Holy Spirit, as it was in the beginning, is now, and will be forever. Amen.

Psalm 21

For the choir director: A psalm of David.

1 How the king rejoices in your strength, O Lord!
  He shouts with joy because you give him victory.
2 For you have given him his heart's desire;
  you have withheld nothing he requested. *Interlude*
3 You welcomed him back with success and prosperity.
  You placed a crown of finest gold on his head.
4 He asked you to preserve his life,

and you granted his request.
The days of his life stretch on forever.

5 **Your victory brings him great honor,**
and you have clothed him with splendor and majesty.

6 **You have endowed him with eternal blessings**
and given him the joy of your presence.

7 **For the king trusts in the Lord.**
The unfailing love of the Most High will keep him from stumbling.

8 **You will capture all your enemies.**
Your strong right hand will seize all who hate you.

9 **You will throw them in a flaming furnace**
when you appear.
The Lord will consume them in his anger;
fire will devour them.

10 You will wipe their children from the face of the earth;
they will never have descendants.

11 Although they plot against you,
their evil schemes will never succeed.

12 For they will turn and run
when they see your arrows aimed at them.

13 Rise up, O Lord, in all your power.
With music and singing we celebrate your mighty acts.

Then all the people say the following praise:

Glory to the Father, and to the Son, and to the Holy Spirit, as it was
in the beginning, is now, and will be forever. Amen.

Psalm 22:1–24

For the choir director: A psalm of David, to be sung to the tune "Doe of the Dawn."

1 My God, my God, why have you abandoned me?
Why are you so far away when I groan for help?

2 Every day I call to you, my God, but you do not answer.
Every night I lift my voice, but I find no relief.

3 Yet you are holy,
enthroned on the praises of Israel.

4 Our ancestors trusted in you,
and you rescued them.

5 They cried out to you and were saved.

They trusted in you and were never disgraced.

6 But I am a worm and not a man.

I am scorned and despised by all!

7 Everyone who sees me mocks me.

They sneer and shake their heads, saying,

8 "Is this the one who relies on the Lord?

Then let the Lord save him!

If the Lord loves him so much,

let the Lord rescue him!"

9 Yet you brought me safely from my mother's womb

and led me to trust you at my mother's breast.

10 I was thrust into your arms at my birth.

You have been my God from the moment I was born.

11 Do not stay so far from me,

for trouble is near,

and no one else can help me.

12 **My enemies surround me like a herd of bulls;**

fierce bulls of Bashan have hemmed me in!

13 **Like lions they open their jaws against me,**

roaring and tearing into their prey.

14 **My life is poured out like water,**

and all my bones are out of joint.

My heart is like wax,

melting within me.

15 **My strength has dried up like sunbaked clay.**

My tongue sticks to the roof of my mouth.

You have laid me in the dust and left me for dead.

16 My enemies surround me like a pack of dogs;

an evil gang closes in on me.

They have pierced my hands and feet.

17 **I can count all my bones.**

My enemies stare at me and gloat.

18 **They divide my garments among themselves**

and throw dice for my clothing.

19 **O Lord, do not stay far away!**

You are my strength; come quickly to my aid!

20 **Save me from the sword;**

spare my precious life from these dogs.

21 **Snatch me from the lion's jaws**

and from the horns of these wild oxen.

22 **I will proclaim your name to my brothers and sisters.**

I will praise you among your assembled people.

23 **Praise the Lord, all you who fear him!**

Honor him, all you descendants of Jacob!

Show him reverence, all you descendants of Israel!

24 For he has not ignored or belittled the suffering of the needy.

He has not turned his back on them,

but has listened to their cries for help.

Then all the people say the following praise:

Glory to the Father, and to the Son, and to the Holy Spirit, as it was in the beginning, is now, and will be forever. Amen.

Psalm 22:25–31

25 I will praise you in the great assembly.

I will fulfill my vows in the presence of those who worship you.

26 The poor will eat and be satisfied.

All who seek the Lord will praise him.

Their hearts will rejoice with everlasting joy.

27 **The whole earth will acknowledge the Lord and return to him.**

All the families of the nations will bow down before him.

28 **For royal power belongs to the Lord.**

He rules all the nations.

29 **Let the rich of the earth feast and worship.**

Bow before him, all who are mortal,

all whose lives will end as dust.

30 Our children will also serve him.

Future generations will hear about the wonders of the Lord.

31 His righteous acts will be told to those not yet born.

They will hear about everything he has done.

Then all the people say the following praise:

Glory to the Father, and to the Son, and to the Holy Spirit, as it was in the beginning, is now, and will be forever. Amen.

Psalm 23

A psalm of David.

1 The Lord is my shepherd;
  I have all that I need.
2 He lets me rest in green meadows;
  he leads me beside peaceful streams.
3 He renews my strength.
He guides me along right paths,
  bringing honor to his name.
4 **Even when I walk**
  through the darkest valley,
I will not be afraid,
  for you are close beside me.

Your rod and your staff
  protect and comfort me.
5 You prepare a feast for me
  in the presence of my enemies.
You honor me by anointing my head with oil.
  My cup overflows with blessings.
6 Surely your goodness and unfailing love will pursue me
  all the days of my life,
and I will live in the house of the Lord
  forever.

Psalm 24

A psalm of David.

1 The earth is the Lord's, and everything in it.
  The world and all its people belong to him.
2 For he laid the earth's foundation on the seas
  and built it on the ocean depths.
3 Who may climb the mountain of the Lord?
  Who may stand in his holy place?
4 Only those whose hands and hearts are pure,
  who do not worship idols
  and never tell lies.

5 **They will receive the Lord's blessing**
and have a right relationship with God their savior.
6 **Such people may seek you**
and worship in your presence, O God of Jacob. *Interlude*
7 **Open up, ancient gates!**
Open up, ancient doors,
and let the King of glory enter.
8 Who is the King of glory?
The Lord, strong and mighty;
the Lord, invincible in battle.
9 **Open up, ancient gates!**
Open up, ancient doors,
and let the King of glory enter.
10 Who is the King of glory?
The Lord of Heaven's Armies —
he is the King of glory. *Interlude*

Then all the people say the following praise:

Glory to the Father, and to the Son, and to the Holy Spirit, as it was in the beginning, is now, and will be forever. Amen.

Psalm 25

A psalm of David.

1 O Lord, I give my life to you.
2 **I trust in you, my God!**
Do not let me be disgraced,
or let my enemies rejoice in my defeat.
3 No one who trusts in you will ever be disgraced,
but disgrace comes to those who try to deceive others.
4 Show me the right path, O Lord;
point out the road for me to follow.
5 Lead me by your truth and teach me,
for you are the God who saves me.
All day long I put my hope in you.
6 **Remember, O Lord, your compassion and unfailing love,**
which you have shown from long ages past.
7 **Do not remember the rebellious sins of my youth.**

Remember me in the light of your unfailing love,
for you are merciful, O Lord.
8 The Lord is good and does what is right;
he shows the proper path to those who go astray.
9 He leads the humble in doing right,
teaching them his way.
10 The Lord leads with unfailing love and faithfulness
all who keep his covenant and obey his demands.
11 For the honor of your name, O Lord,
forgive my many, many sins.
12 Who are those who fear the Lord?
He will show them the path they should choose.
13 They will live in prosperity,
and their children will inherit the land.
14 The Lord is a friend to those who fear him.
He teaches them his covenant.
15 My eyes are always on the Lord,
for he rescues me from the traps of my enemies.
16 Turn to me and have mercy,
for I am alone and in deep distress.
17 **My problems go from bad to worse.**
Oh, save me from them all!
18 **Feel my pain and see my trouble.**
Forgive all my sins.
19 **See how many enemies I have**
and how viciously they hate me!
20 **Protect me! Rescue my life from them!**
Do not let me be disgraced, for in you I take refuge.
21 **May integrity and honesty protect me,**
for I put my hope in you.
22 **O God, ransom Israel**
from all its troubles.

Then all the people say the following praise:

Glory to the Father, and to the Son, and to the Holy Spirit, as it was in the beginning, is now, and will be forever. Amen.

Psalm 26

A psalm of David.

1 Declare me innocent, O Lord,
  for I have acted with integrity;
  I have trusted in the Lord without wavering.
2 **Put me on trial, Lord, and cross-examine me.**
  Test my motives and my heart.
3 **For I am always aware of your unfailing love,**
  and I have lived according to your truth.
4 **I do not spend time with liars**
  or go along with hypocrites.
5 **I hate the gatherings of those who do evil,**
  and I refuse to join in with the wicked.
6 **I wash my hands to declare my innocence.**
  I come to your altar, O Lord,
7 **singing a song of thanksgiving**
  and telling of all your wonders.
8 **I love your sanctuary, Lord,**
  the place where your glorious presence dwells.
9 **Don't let me suffer the fate of sinners.**
  Don't condemn me along with murderers.
10 **Their hands are dirty with evil schemes,**
  and they constantly take bribes.
11 **But I am not like that; I live with integrity.**
  So redeem me and show me mercy.
12 **Now I stand on solid ground,**
  and I will publicly praise the Lord.

Then all the people say the following praise:

Glory to the Father, and to the Son, and to the Holy Spirit, as it was in the beginning, is now, and will be forever. Amen.

Psalm 27

A psalm of David.

1 The Lord is my light and my salvation —
  so why should I be afraid?
The Lord is my fortress, protecting me from danger,
  so why should I tremble?
2 When evil people come to devour me,
  when my enemies and foes attack me,
  they will stumble and fall.
3 Though a mighty army surrounds me,
  my heart will not be afraid.
Even if I am attacked,
  I will remain confident.
4 The one thing I ask of the Lord —
  the thing I seek most —
is to live in the house of the Lord all the days of my life,
  delighting in the Lord's perfections
  and meditating in his Temple.
5 **For he will conceal me there when troubles come;**
  he will hide me in his sanctuary.
  He will place me out of reach on a high rock.
6 Then I will hold my head high
  above my enemies who surround me.
At his sanctuary I will offer sacrifices with shouts of joy,
  singing and praising the Lord with music.
7 **Hear me as I pray, O Lord.**
  Be merciful and answer me!
8 **My heart has heard you say, "Come and talk with me."**
  And my heart responds, "Lord, I am coming."
9 **Do not turn your back on me.**
  Do not reject your servant in anger.
  You have always been my helper.
Don't leave me now; don't abandon me,
  O God of my salvation!
10 Even if my father and mother abandon me,
  the Lord will hold me close.
11 Teach me how to live, O Lord.
  Lead me along the right path,

for my enemies are waiting for me.
12 **Do not let me fall into their hands.**
For they accuse me of things I've never done;
   with every breath they threaten me with violence.
13 Yet I am confident I will see the Lord's goodness
   while I am here in the land of the living.
14 **Wait patiently for the Lord.**
Be brave and courageous.
   Yes, wait patiently for the Lord.

Then all the people say the following praise:

Glory to the Father, and to the Son, and to the Holy Spirit, as it was in the beginning, is now, and will be forever. Amen.

Psalm 28

A psalm of David.

1 I pray to you, O Lord, my rock.
   Do not turn a deaf ear to me.
For if you are silent,
   I might as well give up and die.
2 **Listen to my prayer for mercy**
   as I cry out to you for help,
   as I lift my hands toward your holy sanctuary.
3 **Do not drag me away with the wicked —**
   with those who do evil —
those who speak friendly words to their neighbors
   while planning evil in their hearts.
4 Give them the punishment they so richly deserve!
   Measure it out in proportion to their wickedness.
Pay them back for all their evil deeds!
   Give them a taste of what they have done to others.
5 They care nothing for what the Lord has done
   or for what his hands have made.
So he will tear them down,
   and they will never be rebuilt!
6 **Praise the Lord!**
   For he has heard my cry for mercy.

7 **The Lord is my strength and shield.**
I trust him with all my heart.
He helps me, and my heart is filled with joy.
I burst out in songs of thanksgiving.
8 **The Lord gives his people strength.**
He is a safe fortress for his anointed king.
9 **Save your people!**
Bless Israel, your special possession.
Lead them like a shepherd,
and carry them in your arms forever.

Then all the people say the following praise:

Glory to the Father, and to the Son, and to the Holy Spirit, as it was in the beginning, is now, and will be forever. Amen.

Psalm 29

A psalm of David.

1 Honor the Lord, you heavenly beings;
honor the Lord for his glory and strength.
2 Honor the Lord for the glory of his name.
Worship the Lord in the splendor of his holiness.
3 The voice of the Lord echoes above the sea.
The God of glory thunders.
The Lord thunders over the mighty sea.
4 **The voice of the Lord is powerful;**
the voice of the Lord is majestic.
5 **The voice of the Lord splits the mighty cedars;**
the Lord shatters the cedars of Lebanon.
6 **He makes Lebanon's mountains skip like a calf;**
he makes Mount Hermon leap like a young wild ox.
7 **The voice of the Lord strikes**
with bolts of lightning.
8 The voice of the Lord makes the barren wilderness quake;
the Lord shakes the wilderness of Kadesh.
9 The voice of the Lord twists mighty oaks
and strips the forests bare.
In his Temple everyone shouts, "Glory!"

10 **The Lord rules over the floodwaters.**
The Lord reigns as king forever.
11 **The Lord gives his people strength.**
The Lord blesses them with peace.

Then all the people say the following praise:

Glory to the Father, and to the Son, and to the Holy Spirit, as it was in the beginning, is now, and will be forever. Amen.

Psalm 30

A psalm of David. A song for the dedication of the Temple.

1 I will exalt you, Lord, for you rescued me.
You refused to let my enemies triumph over me.
2 O Lord my God, I cried to you for help,
and you restored my health.
3 You brought me up from the grave, O Lord.
You kept me from falling into the pit of death.
4 Sing to the Lord, all you godly ones!
Praise his holy name.
5 For his anger lasts only a moment,
but his favor lasts a lifetime!
Weeping may last through the night,
but joy comes with the morning.
6 When I was prosperous, I said,
"Nothing can stop me now!"
7 Your favor, O Lord, made me as secure as a mountain.
Then you turned away from me, and I was shattered.
8 I cried out to you, O Lord.
I begged the Lord for mercy, saying,
9 "What will you gain if I die,
if I sink into the grave?
Can my dust praise you?
Can it tell of your faithfulness?
10 Hear me, Lord, and have mercy on me.
Help me, O Lord."
11 You have turned my mourning into joyful dancing.
You have taken away my clothes of mourning

and clothed me with joy,
12 that I might sing praises to you and not be silent.
  O Lord my God, I will give you thanks forever!

Glory to the Father, and to the Son, and to the Holy Spirit, as it was in the beginning, is now, and will be forever. Amen.

Psalm 31:1–8

For the choir director: A psalm of David.

1 O Lord, I have come to you for protection;
  don't let me be disgraced.
  Save me, for you do what is right.
2 Turn your ear to listen to me;
  rescue me quickly.
Be my rock of protection,
  a fortress where I will be safe.
3 You are my rock and my fortress.
  For the honor of your name, lead me out of this danger.
4 Pull me from the trap my enemies set for me,
  for I find protection in you alone.
5 I entrust my spirit into your hand.
  Rescue me, Lord, for you are a faithful God.
6 I hate those who worship worthless idols.
  I trust in the Lord.
7 I will be glad and rejoice in your unfailing love,
  for you have seen my troubles,
  and you care about the anguish of my soul.
8 **You have not handed me over to my enemies**
  but have set me in a safe place.

Then all the people say the following praise:

Glory to the Father, and to the Son, and to the Holy Spirit, as it was in the beginning, is now, and will be forever. Amen.

Psalm 31:9–24

9 Have mercy on me, Lord, for I am in distress.
Tears blur my eyes.
My body and soul are withering away.
10 **I am dying from grief;**
my years are shortened by sadness.
Sin has drained my strength;
I am wasting away from within.
11 **I am scorned by all my enemies**
and despised by my neighbors —
even my friends are afraid to come near me.
When they see me on the street,
they run the other way.
12 **I am ignored as if I were dead,**
as if I were a broken pot.
13 **I have heard the many rumors about me,**
and I am surrounded by terror.
My enemies conspire against me,
plotting to take my life.
14 **But I am trusting you, O Lord,**
saying, "You are my God!"
15 **My future is in your hands.**
Rescue me from those who hunt me down relentlessly.
16 **Let your favor shine on your servant.**
In your unfailing love, rescue me.
17 **Don't let me be disgraced, O Lord,**
for I call out to you for help.
Let the wicked be disgraced;
let them lie silent in the grave.
18 **Silence their lying lips —**
those proud and arrogant lips that accuse the godly.
19 **How great is the goodness**
you have stored up for those who fear you.
You lavish it on those who come to you for protection,
blessing them before the watching world.
20 **You hide them in the shelter of your presence,**
safe from those who conspire against them.
You shelter them in your presence,

far from accusing tongues.
21 **Praise the Lord,**
 for he has shown me the wonders of his unfailing love.
 He kept me safe when my city was under attack.
22 In panic I cried out,
 "I am cut off from the Lord!"
But you heard my cry for mercy
 and answered my call for help.
23 **Love the Lord, all you godly ones!**
 For the Lord protects those who are loyal to him,
 but he harshly punishes the arrogant.
24 So be strong and courageous,
 all you who put your hope in the Lord!

Then all the people say the following praise:

Glory to the Father, and to the Son, and to the Holy Spirit, as it was in the beginning, is now, and will be forever. Amen.

Psalm 32

A psalm of David.

1 Oh, what joy for those
 whose disobedience is forgiven,
 whose sin is put out of sight!
2 Yes, what joy for those
 whose record the Lord has cleared of guilt,
 whose lives are lived in complete honesty!
3 When I refused to confess my sin,
 my body wasted away,
 and I groaned all day long.
4 **Day and night your hand of discipline was heavy on me.**
 My strength evaporated like water in the summer heat. *Interlude*
5 Finally, I confessed all my sins to you
 and stopped trying to hide my guilt.
I said to myself, "I will confess my rebellion to the Lord."
 And you forgave me! All my guilt is gone. *Interlude*
6 Therefore, let all the godly pray to you while there is still time,
 that they may not drown in the floodwaters of judgment.

7 For you are my hiding place;
you protect me from trouble.
You surround me with songs of victory. *Interlude*
8 **The Lord says, "I will guide you along the best pathway for your life.**
I will advise you and watch over you.
9 **Do not be like a senseless horse or mule**
that needs a bit and bridle to keep it under control."
10 Many sorrows come to the wicked,
but unfailing love surrounds those who trust the Lord.
11 So rejoice in the Lord and be glad, all you who obey him!
Shout for joy, all you whose hearts are pure!

Then all the people say the following praise:

Glory to the Father, and to the Son, and to the Holy Spirit, as it was in the beginning, is now, and will be forever. Amen.

Psalm 33

1 Let the godly sing for joy to the Lord;
it is fitting for the pure to praise him.
2 **Praise the Lord with melodies on the lyre;**
make music for him on the ten-stringed harp.
3 **Sing a new song of praise to him;**
play skillfully on the harp, and sing with joy.
4 **For the word of the Lord holds true,**
and we can trust everything he does.
5 **He loves whatever is just and good;**
the unfailing love of the Lord fills the earth.
6 **The Lord merely spoke,**
and the heavens were created.
He breathed the word,
and all the stars were born.
7 He assigned the sea its boundaries
and locked the oceans in vast reservoirs.
8 Let the whole world fear the Lord,
and let everyone stand in awe of him.
9 For when he spoke, the world began!
It appeared at his command.

10 The Lord frustrates the plans of the nations
  and thwarts all their schemes.
11 But the Lord's plans stand firm forever;
  his intentions can never be shaken.
12 What joy for the nation whose God is the Lord,
  whose people he has chosen as his inheritance.
13 The Lord looks down from heaven
  and sees the whole human race.
14 From his throne he observes
  all who live on the earth.
15 **He made their hearts,**
  so he understands everything they do.
16 The best-equipped army cannot save a king,
  nor is great strength enough to save a warrior.
17 Don't count on your warhorse to give you victory —
  for all its strength, it cannot save you.
18 But the Lord watches over those who fear him,
  those who rely on his unfailing love.
19 He rescues them from death
  and keeps them alive in times of famine.
20 We put our hope in the Lord.
  He is our help and our shield.
21 In him our hearts rejoice,
  for we trust in his holy name.
22 Let your unfailing love surround us, Lord,
  for our hope is in you alone.

Then all the people say the following praise:

Glory to the Father, and to the Son, and to the Holy Spirit, as it was in the beginning, is now, and will be forever. Amen.

Psalm 34

A psalm of David, regarding the time he pretended to be insane in front of Abimelech, who sent him away.

1 I will praise the Lord at all times.
  I will constantly speak his praises.
2 I will boast only in the Lord;
  let all who are helpless take heart.

3 Come, let us tell of the Lord's greatness;
  let us exalt his name together.
4 I prayed to the Lord, and he answered me.
  He freed me from all my fears.
5 Those who look to him for help will be radiant with joy;
  no shadow of shame will darken their faces.
6 In my desperation I prayed, and the Lord listened;
  he saved me from all my troubles.
7 For the angel of the Lord is a guard;
  he surrounds and defends all who fear him.
8 Taste and see that the Lord is good.
  Oh, the joys of those who take refuge in him!
9 Fear the Lord, you his godly people,
  for those who fear him will have all they need.
10 **Even strong young lions sometimes go hungry,**
  but those who trust in the Lord will lack no good thing.
11 **Come, my children, and listen to me,**
  and I will teach you to fear the Lord.
12 **Does anyone want to live a life**
  that is long and prosperous?
13 Then keep your tongue from speaking evil
  and your lips from telling lies!
14 **Turn away from evil and do good.**
  Search for peace, and work to maintain it.
15 **The eyes of the Lord watch over those who do right;**
  his ears are open to their cries for help.
16 **But the Lord turns his face against those who do evil;**
  he will erase their memory from the earth.
17 **The Lord hears his people when they call to him for help.**
  He rescues them from all their troubles.
18 **The Lord is close to the brokenhearted;**
  he rescues those whose spirits are crushed.
19 **The righteous person faces many troubles,**
  but the Lord comes to the rescue each time.
20 **For the Lord protects the bones of the righteous;**
  not one of them is broken!
21 **Calamity will surely destroy the wicked,**
  and those who hate the righteous will be punished.
22 **But the Lord will redeem those who serve him.**
  No one who takes refuge in him will be condemned.

Then all the people say the following praise:

Glory to the Father, and to the Son, and to the Holy Spirit, as it was in the beginning, is now, and will be forever. Amen.

Psalm 35:1–10

A psalm of David.

1 O Lord, oppose those who oppose me.
 Fight those who fight against me.
2 Put on your armor, and take up your shield.
 Prepare for battle, and come to my aid.
3 Lift up your spear and javelin
 against those who pursue me.
Let me hear you say,
 "I will give you victory!"
4 Bring shame and disgrace on those trying to kill me;
 turn them back and humiliate those who want to harm me.
5 Blow them away like chaff in the wind —
 a wind sent by the angel of the Lord.
6 Make their path dark and slippery,
 with the angel of the Lord pursuing them.
7 I did them no wrong, but they laid a trap for me.
 I did them no wrong, but they dug a pit to catch me.
8 So let sudden ruin come upon them!
 Let them be caught in the trap they set for me!
 Let them be destroyed in the pit they dug for me.
9 **Then I will rejoice in the Lord.**
 I will be glad because he rescues me.
10 **With every bone in my body I will praise him:**
 "Lord, who can compare with you?
Who else rescues the helpless from the strong?
 Who else protects the helpless and poor from those who rob them?"

Then all the people say the following praise:

Glory to the Father, and to the Son, and to the Holy Spirit, as it was in the beginning, is now, and will be forever. Amen.

11 Malicious witnesses testify against me.

They accuse me of crimes I know nothing about.

12 They repay me evil for good.

I am sick with despair.

13 Yet when they were ill, I grieved for them.

I denied myself by fasting for them,

but my prayers returned unanswered.

14 **I was sad, as though they were my friends or family,**

as if I were grieving for my own mother.

15 **But they are glad now that I am in trouble;**

they gleefully join together against me.

I am attacked by people I don't even know;

they slander me constantly.

16 **They mock me and call me names;**

they snarl at me.

17 **How long, O Lord, will you look on and do nothing?**

Rescue me from their fierce attacks.

Protect my life from these lions!

18 Then I will thank you in front of the great assembly.

I will praise you before all the people.

19 Don't let my treacherous enemies rejoice over my defeat.

Don't let those who hate me without cause gloat over my sorrow.

20 They don't talk of peace;

they plot against innocent people who mind their own business.

21 They shout, "Aha! Aha!

With our own eyes we saw him do it!"

22 O Lord, you know all about this.

Do not stay silent.

Do not abandon me now, O Lord.

23 **Wake up! Rise to my defense!**

Take up my case, my God and my Lord.

24 **Declare me not guilty, O Lord my God, for you give justice.**

Don't let my enemies laugh about me in my troubles.

25 **Don't let them say, "Look, we got what we wanted!**

Now we will eat him alive!"

26 **May those who rejoice at my troubles**

be humiliated and disgraced.

May those who triumph over me

be covered with shame and dishonor.

27 **But give great joy to those who came to my defense.**
Let them continually say, "Great is the Lord,
who delights in blessing his servant with peace!"

28 Then I will proclaim your justice,
and I will praise you all day long.

Then all the people say the following praise:

Glory to the Father, and to the Son, and to the Holy Spirit, as it was in the beginning, is now, and will be forever. Amen.

Psalm 36

For the choir director: A psalm of David, the servant of the Lord.

1 Sin whispers to the wicked, deep within their hearts.
They have no fear of God at all.

2 In their blind conceit,
they cannot see how wicked they really are.

3 Everything they say is crooked and deceitful.
They refuse to act wisely or do good.

4 They lie awake at night, hatching sinful plots.
Their actions are never good.
They make no attempt to turn from evil.

5 **Your unfailing love, O Lord, is as vast as the heavens;**
your faithfulness reaches beyond the clouds.

6 **Your righteousness is like the mighty mountains,**
your justice like the ocean depths.

You care for people and animals alike, O Lord.

7 How precious is your unfailing love, O God!

All humanity finds shelter
in the shadow of your wings.

8 You feed them from the abundance of your own house,
letting them drink from your river of delights.

9 For you are the fountain of life,
the light by which we see.

10 Pour out your unfailing love on those who love you;
give justice to those with honest hearts.

11 Don't let the proud trample me
or the wicked push me around.

12 Look! Those who do evil have fallen!

They are thrown down, never to rise again.

Then all the people say the following praise:

Glory to the Father, and to the Son, and to the Holy Spirit, as it was in the beginning, is now, and will be forever. Amen.

Psalm 37:1–7

A psalm of David.

1 Don't worry about the wicked
   or envy those who do wrong.
2 **For like grass, they soon fade away.**
   Like spring flowers, they soon wither.
3 **Trust in the Lord and do good.**
   Then you will live safely in the land and prosper.
4 **Take delight in the Lord,**
   and he will give you your heart's desires.
5 **Commit everything you do to the Lord.**
   Trust him, and he will help you.
6 **He will make your innocence radiate like the dawn,**
   and the justice of your cause will shine like the noonday sun.
7 **Be still in the presence of the Lord,**
   and wait patiently for him to act.
Don't worry about evil people who prosper
   or fret about their wicked schemes.

Then all the people say the following praise:

Glory to the Father, and to the Son, and to the Holy Spirit, as it was in the beginning, is now, and will be forever. Amen.

Psalm 37:8–19

8 Stop being angry!
   Turn from your rage!
Do not lose your temper —
   it only leads to harm.
9 For the wicked will be destroyed,
   but those who trust in the Lord will possess the land.

10 Soon the wicked will disappear.
Though you look for them, they will be gone.
11 The lowly will possess the land
and will live in peace and prosperity.
12 The wicked plot against the godly;
they snarl at them in defiance.
13 But the Lord just laughs,
for he sees their day of judgment coming.
14 The wicked draw their swords
and string their bows
to kill the poor and the oppressed,
to slaughter those who do right.
15 **But their swords will stab their own hearts,**
and their bows will be broken.
16 **It is better to be godly and have little**
than to be evil and rich.
17 For the strength of the wicked will be shattered,
but the Lord takes care of the godly.
18 Day by day the Lord takes care of the innocent,
and they will receive an inheritance that lasts forever.
19 They will not be disgraced in hard times;
even in famine they will have more than enough.

Then all the people say the following praise:

Glory to the Father, and to the Son, and to the Holy Spirit, as it was
in the beginning, is now, and will be forever. Amen.

Psalm 37:20–33

20 But the wicked will die.
The Lord's enemies are like flowers in a field —
they will disappear like smoke.
21 **The wicked borrow and never repay,**
but the godly are generous givers.
22 **Those the Lord blesses will possess the land,**
but those he curses will die.
23 **The Lord directs the steps of the godly.**
He delights in every detail of their lives.
24 **Though they stumble, they will never fall,**

for the Lord holds them by the hand.
25 **Once I was young, and now I am old.**
Yet I have never seen the godly abandoned
or their children begging for bread.
26 The godly always give generous loans to others,
and their children are a blessing.
27 **Turn from evil and do good,**
and you will live in the land forever.
28 **For the Lord loves justice,**
and he will never abandon the godly.
He will keep them safe forever,
but the children of the wicked will die.
29 **The godly will possess the land**
and will live there forever.
30 The godly offer good counsel;
they teach right from wrong.
31 **They have made God's law their own,**
so they will never slip from his path.
32 **The wicked wait in ambush for the godly,**
looking for an excuse to kill them.
33 **But the Lord will not let the wicked succeed**
or let the godly be condemned when they are put on trial.

Then all the people say the following praise:

**Glory to the Father, and to the Son, and to the Holy Spirit, as it was
in the beginning, is now, and will be forever. Amen.**

Psalm 37:34–40

34 Put your hope in the Lord.
Travel steadily along his path.
He will honor you by giving you the land.
You will see the wicked destroyed.
35 I have seen wicked and ruthless people
flourishing like a tree in its native soil.
36 But when I looked again, they were gone!
Though I searched for them, I could not find them!
37 Look at those who are honest and good,
for a wonderful future awaits those who love peace.

38 But the rebellious will be destroyed;
  they have no future.
39 The Lord rescues the godly;
  he is their fortress in times of trouble.
40 The Lord helps them,
  rescuing them from the wicked.
He saves them,
  and they find shelter in him.

Then all the people say the following praise:

Glory to the Father, and to the Son, and to the Holy Spirit, as it was in the beginning, is now, and will be forever. Amen.

Psalm 38

A psalm of David, asking God to remember him.

1 O Lord, don't rebuke me in your anger
  or discipline me in your rage!
2 **Your arrows have struck deep,**
  and your blows are crushing me.
3 **Because of your anger, my whole body is sick;**
  my health is broken because of my sins.
4 **My guilt overwhelms me —**
  it is a burden too heavy to bear.
5 **My wounds fester and stink**
  because of my foolish sins.
6 **I am bent over and racked with pain.**
  All day long I walk around filled with grief.
7 **A raging fever burns within me,**
  and my health is broken.
8 **I am exhausted and completely crushed.**
  My groans come from an anguished heart.
9 **You know what I long for, Lord;**
  you hear my every sigh.
10 **My heart beats wildly, my strength fails,**
  and I am going blind.
11 **My loved ones and friends stay away, fearing my disease.**
  Even my own family stands at a distance.

12 **Meanwhile, my enemies lay traps to kill me.**
Those who wish me harm make plans to ruin me.
All day long they plan their treachery.
13 But I am deaf to all their threats.
I am silent before them as one who cannot speak.
14 I choose to hear nothing,
and I make no reply.
15 For I am waiting for you, O Lord.
You must answer for me, O Lord my God.
16 I prayed, "Don't let my enemies gloat over me
or rejoice at my downfall."
17 **I am on the verge of collapse,**
facing constant pain.
18 **But I confess my sins;**
I am deeply sorry for what I have done.
19 **I have many aggressive enemies;**
they hate me without reason.
20 **They repay me evil for good**
and oppose me for pursuing good.
21 **Do not abandon me, O Lord.**
Do not stand at a distance, my God.
22 **Come quickly to help me,**
O Lord my savior.

Then all the people say the following praise:

Glory to the Father, and to the Son, and to the Holy Spirit, as it was in the beginning, is now, and will be forever. Amen.

Psalm 39

For Jeduthun, the choir director: A psalm of David.

1 I said to myself, "I will watch what I do
and not sin in what I say.
I will hold my tongue
when the ungodly are around me."
2 But as I stood there in silence —
not even speaking of good things —
the turmoil within me grew worse.

3 **The more I thought about it,**
the hotter I got,
igniting a fire of words:
4 "Lord, remind me how brief my time on earth will be.
Remind me that my days are numbered —
how fleeting my life is.
5 **You have made my life no longer than the width of my hand.**
My entire lifetime is just a moment to you;
at best, each of us is but a breath." *Interlude*
6 We are merely moving shadows,
and all our busy rushing ends in nothing.
We heap up wealth,
not knowing who will spend it.
7 And so, Lord, where do I put my hope?
My only hope is in you.
8 Rescue me from my rebellion.
Do not let fools mock me.
9 I am silent before you; I won't say a word,
for my punishment is from you.
10 But please stop striking me!
I am exhausted by the blows from your hand.
11 When you discipline us for our sins,
you consume like a moth what is precious to us.
Each of us is but a breath. *Interlude*
12 **Hear my prayer, O Lord!**
Listen to my cries for help!
Don't ignore my tears.
For I am your guest —
a traveler passing through,
as my ancestors were before me.
13 **Leave me alone so I can smile again**
before I am gone and exist no more.

Then all the people say the following praise:

Glory to the Father, and to the Son, and to the Holy Spirit, as it was in the beginning, is now, and will be forever. Amen.

Psalm 40

For the choir director: A psalm of David.

1 I waited patiently for the Lord to help me,
  and he turned to me and heard my cry.
2 He lifted me out of the pit of despair,
  out of the mud and the mire.
He set my feet on solid ground
  and steadied me as I walked along.
3 He has given me a new song to sing,
  a hymn of praise to our God.
Many will see what he has done and be amazed.
  They will put their trust in the Lord.
4 Oh, the joys of those who trust the Lord,
  who have no confidence in the proud
  or in those who worship idols.
5 **O Lord my God, you have performed many wonders for us.**
  Your plans for us are too numerous to list.
  You have no equal.
If I tried to recite all your wonderful deeds,
  I would never come to the end of them.
6 You take no delight in sacrifices or offerings.
  Now that you have made me listen, I finally understand —
  you don't require burnt offerings or sin offerings.
7 **Then I said, "Look, I have come.**
  As is written about me in the Scriptures:
8 **I take joy in doing your will, my God,**
  for your instructions are written on my heart."
9 **I have told all your people about your justice.**
  I have not been afraid to speak out,
  as you, O Lord, well know.
10 I have not kept the good news of your justice hidden in my heart;
  I have talked about your faithfulness and saving power.
I have told everyone in the great assembly
  of your unfailing love and faithfulness.
11 Lord, don't hold back your tender mercies from me.
  Let your unfailing love and faithfulness always protect me.
12 For troubles surround me —
  too many to count!

My sins pile up so high
  I can't see my way out.
They outnumber the hairs on my head.
  I have lost all courage.
13 **Please, Lord, rescue me!**
  Come quickly, Lord, and help me.
14 **May those who try to destroy me**
  be humiliated and put to shame.
May those who take delight in my trouble
  be turned back in disgrace.
15 **Let them be horrified by their shame,**
  for they said, "Aha! We've got him now!"
16 **But may all who search for you**
  be filled with joy and gladness in you.
May those who love your salvation
  repeatedly shout, "The Lord is great!"
17 As for me, since I am poor and needy,
  let the Lord keep me in his thoughts.
You are my helper and my savior.
  O my God, do not delay.

Then all the people say the following praise:

Glory to the Father, and to the Son, and to the Holy Spirit, as it was in the beginning, is now, and will be forever. Amen.

Psalm 41

For the choir director: A psalm of David.

1 Oh, the joys of those who are kind to the poor!
  The Lord rescues them when they are in trouble.
2 The Lord protects them
  and keeps them alive.
He gives them prosperity in the land
  and rescues them from their enemies.
3 The Lord nurses them when they are sick
  and restores them to health.
4 **"O Lord," I prayed, "have mercy on me.**
  Heal me, for I have sinned against you."

5 **But my enemies say nothing but evil about me.**
  "How soon will he die and be forgotten?" they ask.
6 **They visit me as if they were my friends,**
  but all the while they gather gossip,
  and when they leave, they spread it everywhere.
7 All who hate me whisper about me,
  imagining the worst.
8 "He has some fatal disease," they say.
  "He will never get out of that bed!"
9 Even my best friend, the one I trusted completely,
  the one who shared my food, has turned against me.
10 Lord, have mercy on me.
  Make me well again, so I can pay them back!
11 I know you are pleased with me,
  for you have not let my enemies triumph over me.
12 You have preserved my life because I am innocent;
  you have brought me into your presence forever.
13 Praise the Lord, the God of Israel,
  who lives from everlasting to everlasting.
Amen and amen!

Then all the people say the following praise:

Glory to the Father, and to the Son, and to the Holy Spirit, as it was in the beginning, is now, and will be forever. Amen.

Book Two

(Psalms 42–72)

Psalm 42

For the choir director: A psalm of the descendants of Korah.

1 As the deer longs for streams of water,
  so I long for you, O God.
2 I thirst for God, the living God.
  When can I go and stand before him?
3 Day and night I have only tears for food,
  while my enemies continually taunt me, saying,
  "Where is this God of yours?"
4 My heart is breaking
  as I remember how it used to be:
I walked among the crowds of worshipers,
  leading a great procession to the house of God,
singing for joy and giving thanks
  amid the sound of a great celebration!
5 Why am I discouraged?
  Why is my heart so sad?
I will put my hope in God!
  I will praise him again —
  my Savior and
6 **my God!**
Now I am deeply discouraged,
  but I will remember you —
even from distant Mount Hermon, the source of the Jordan,
  from the land of Mount Mizar.
7 I hear the tumult of the raging seas

as your waves and surging tides sweep over me.
8 But each day the Lord pours his unfailing love upon me,
and through each night I sing his songs,
praying to God who gives me life.
9 "O God my rock," I cry,
"Why have you forgotten me?
Why must I wander around in grief,
oppressed by my enemies?"
10 Their taunts break my bones.
They scoff, "Where is this God of yours?"
11 Why am I discouraged?
Why is my heart so sad?
I will put my hope in God!
I will praise him again —
my Savior and my God!

Then all the people say the following praise:

Glory to the Father, and to the Son, and to the Holy Spirit, as it was
in the beginning, is now, and will be forever. Amen.

Psalm 43

1 Declare me innocent, O God!
Defend me against these ungodly people.
Rescue me from these unjust liars.
2 For you are God, my only safe haven.
Why have you tossed me aside?
Why must I wander around in grief,
oppressed by my enemies?
3 Send out your light and your truth;
let them guide me.
Let them lead me to your holy mountain,
to the place where you live.
4 There I will go to the altar of God,
to God — the source of all my joy.
I will praise you with my harp,
O God, my God!
5 Why am I discouraged?
Why is my heart so sad?

I will put my hope in God!
I will praise him again —
my Savior and my God!

Then all the people say the following praise:

Glory to the Father, and to the Son, and to the Holy Spirit, as it was
in the beginning, is now, and will be forever. Amen.

Psalm 44

For the choir director: A psalm of the descendants of Korah.

1 O God, we have heard it with our own ears —
our ancestors have told us
of all you did in their day,
in days long ago:
2 **You drove out the pagan nations by your power**
and gave all the land to our ancestors.
You crushed their enemies
and set our ancestors free.
3 **They did not conquer the land with their swords;**
it was not their own strong arm that gave them victory.
It was your right hand and strong arm
and the blinding light from your face that helped them,
for you loved them.
4 You are my King and my God.
You command victories for Israel.
5 Only by your power can we push back our enemies;
only in your name can we trample our foes.
6 I do not trust in my bow;
I do not count on my sword to save me.
7 You are the one who gives us victory over our enemies;
you disgrace those who hate us.
8 O God, we give glory to you all day long
and constantly praise your name. *Interlude*
9 **But now you have tossed us aside in dishonor.**
You no longer lead our armies to battle.
10 **You make us retreat from our enemies**
and allow those who hate us to plunder our land.

11 **You have butchered us like sheep**
and scattered us among the nations.
12 **You sold your precious people for a pittance,**
making nothing on the sale.
13 **You let our neighbors mock us.**
We are an object of scorn and derision to those around us.
14 **You have made us the butt of their jokes;**
they shake their heads at us in scorn.
15 **We can't escape the constant humiliation;**
shame is written across our faces.
16 **All we hear are the taunts of our mockers.**
All we see are our vengeful enemies.
17 **All this has happened though we have not forgotten you.**
We have not violated your covenant.
18 **Our hearts have not deserted you.**
We have not strayed from your path.
19 **Yet you have crushed us in the jackal's desert home.**
You have covered us with darkness and death.
20 **If we had forgotten the name of our God**
or spread our hands in prayer to foreign gods,
21 **God would surely have known it,**
for he knows the secrets of every heart.
22 **But for your sake we are killed every day;**
we are being slaughtered like sheep.
23 **Wake up, O Lord! Why do you sleep?**
Get up! Do not reject us forever.
24 **Why do you look the other way?**
Why do you ignore our suffering and oppression?
25 **We collapse in the dust,**
lying face down in the dirt.
26 **Rise up! Help us!**
Ransom us because of your unfailing love.

Then all the people say the following praise:

Glory to the Father, and to the Son, and to the Holy Spirit, as it was in the beginning, is now, and will be forever. Amen.

Psalm 45

For the choir director: A love song to be sung to the tune "Lilies." A psalm of the descendants of Korah.

1 Beautiful words stir my heart.
  I will recite a lovely poem about the king,
  for my tongue is like the pen of a skillful poet.
2 **You are the most handsome of all.**
  Gracious words stream from your lips.
  God himself has blessed you forever.
3 Put on your sword, O mighty warrior!
  You are so glorious, so majestic!
4 In your majesty, ride out to victory,
  defending truth, humility, and justice.
  Go forth to perform awe-inspiring deeds!
5 **Your arrows are sharp, piercing your enemies' hearts.**
  The nations fall beneath your feet.
6 **Your throne, O God, endures forever and ever.**
  You rule with a scepter of justice.
7 **You love justice and hate evil.**
  Therefore God, your God, has anointed you,
  pouring out the oil of joy on you more than on anyone else.
8 Myrrh, aloes, and cassia perfume your robes.
  In ivory palaces the music of strings entertains you.
9 Kings' daughters are among your noble women.
  At your right side stands the queen,
  wearing jewelry of finest gold from Ophir!
10 **Listen to me, O royal daughter; take to heart what I say.**
  Forget your people and your family far away.
11 **For your royal husband delights in your beauty;**
  honor him, for he is your lord.
12 **The princess of Tyre will shower you with gifts.**
  The wealthy will beg your favor.
13 **The bride, a princess, looks glorious**
  in her golden gown.
14 In her beautiful robes, she is led to the king,
  accompanied by her bridesmaids.
15 What a joyful and enthusiastic procession
  as they enter the king's palace!

16 **Your sons will become kings like their father.**
You will make them rulers over many lands.
17 **I will bring honor to your name in every generation.**
Therefore, the nations will praise you forever and ever.

Then all the people say the following praise:

Glory to the Father, and to the Son, and to the Holy Spirit, as it was in the beginning, is now, and will be forever. Amen.

Psalm 46

For the choir director: A song of the descendants of Korah, to be sung by soprano voices.

1 God is our refuge and strength,
always ready to help in times of trouble.
2 So we will not fear when earthquakes come
and the mountains crumble into the sea.
3 Let the oceans roar and foam.
Let the mountains tremble as the waters surge! *Interlude*
4 A river brings joy to the city of our God,
the sacred home of the Most High.
5 God dwells in that city; it cannot be destroyed.
From the very break of day, God will protect it.
6 The nations are in chaos,
and their kingdoms crumble!
God's voice thunders,
and the earth melts!
7 The Lord of Heaven's Armies is here among us;
the God of Israel is our fortress. *Interlude*
8 Come, see the glorious works of the Lord:
See how he brings destruction upon the world.
9 He causes wars to end throughout the earth.
He breaks the bow and snaps the spear;
he burns the shields with fire.
10 **"Be still, and know that I am God!**
I will be honored by every nation.
I will be honored throughout the world."

11 The Lord of Heaven's Armies is here among us;
   the God of Israel is our fortress. *Interlude*

Then all the people say the following praise:

Glory to the Father, and to the Son, and to the Holy Spirit, as it was in the beginning, is now, and will be forever. Amen.

Psalm 47

For the choir director: A psalm of the descendants of Korah.

1 Come, everyone! Clap your hands!
   Shout to God with joyful praise!
2 For the Lord Most High is awesome.
   He is the great King of all the earth.
3 He subdues the nations before us,
   putting our enemies beneath our feet.
4 He chose the Promised Land as our inheritance,
   the proud possession of Jacob's descendants, whom he loves.
Interlude
5 God has ascended with a mighty shout.
   The Lord has ascended with trumpets blaring.
6 Sing praises to God, sing praises;
   sing praises to our King, sing praises!
7 For God is the King over all the earth.
   Praise him with a psalm.
8 God reigns above the nations,
   sitting on his holy throne.
9 The rulers of the world have gathered together
   with the people of the God of Abraham.
For all the kings of the earth belong to God.
   He is highly honored everywhere.

Then all the people say the following praise:

Glory to the Father, and to the Son, and to the Holy Spirit, as it was in the beginning, is now, and will be forever. Amen.

Psalm 48

A song. A psalm of the descendants of Korah.

1 How great is the Lord,
  how deserving of praise,
in the city of our God,
  which sits on his holy mountain!
2 It is high and magnificent;
  the whole earth rejoices to see it!
Mount Zion, the holy mountain,
  is the city of the great King!
3 God himself is in Jerusalem's towers,
  revealing himself as its defender.
4 The kings of the earth joined forces
  and advanced against the city.
5 But when they saw it, they were stunned;
  they were terrified and ran away.
6 They were gripped with terror
  and writhed in pain like a woman in labor.
7 You destroyed them like the mighty ships of Tarshish
  shattered by a powerful east wind.
8 **We had heard of the city's glory,**
  but now we have seen it ourselves —
  the city of the Lord of Heaven's Armies.
It is the city of our God;
  he will make it safe forever. *Interlude*
9 O God, we meditate on your unfailing love
  as we worship in your Temple.
10 As your name deserves, O God,
  you will be praised to the ends of the earth.
  Your strong right hand is filled with victory.
11 **Let the people on Mount Zion rejoice.**
  Let all the towns of Judah be glad
  because of your justice.
12 **Go, inspect the city of Jerusalem.**
  Walk around and count the many towers.
13 **Take note of the fortified walls,**
  and tour all the citadels,

that you may describe them
　　to future generations.
14 For that is what God is like.
　　He is our God forever and ever,
　　and he will guide us until we die.

Then all the people say the following praise:

Glory to the Father, and to the Son, and to the Holy Spirit, as it was in the beginning, is now, and will be forever. Amen.

Psalm 49

For the choir director: A psalm of the descendants of Korah.

1 Listen to this, all you people!
　　Pay attention, everyone in the world!
2 High and low,
　　rich and poor — listen!
3 For my words are wise,
　　and my thoughts are filled with insight.
4 I listen carefully to many proverbs
　　and solve riddles with inspiration from a harp.
5 Why should I fear when trouble comes,
　　when enemies surround me?
6 They trust in their wealth
　　and boast of great riches.
7 Yet they cannot redeem themselves from death
　　by paying a ransom to God.
8 Redemption does not come so easily,
　　for no one can ever pay enough
9 to live forever
　　and never see the grave.
10 **Those who are wise must finally die,**
　　just like the foolish and senseless,
　　leaving all their wealth behind.
11 The grave is their eternal home,
　　where they will stay forever.
They may name their estates after themselves,
12 **but their fame will not last.**

They will die, just like animals.

13 **This is the fate of fools,**
though they are remembered as being wise. *Interlude*

14 **Like sheep, they are led to the grave,**
where death will be their shepherd.
In the morning the godly will rule over them.
Their bodies will rot in the grave,
far from their grand estates.

15 But as for me, God will redeem my life.
He will snatch me from the power of the grave. *Interlude*

16 So don't be dismayed when the wicked grow rich
and their homes become ever more splendid.

17 For when they die, they take nothing with them.
Their wealth will not follow them into the grave.

18 In this life they consider themselves fortunate
and are applauded for their success.

19 But they will die like all before them
and never again see the light of day.

20 People who boast of their wealth don't understand;
they will die, just like animals.

Then all the people say the following praise:

**Glory to the Father, and to the Son, and to the Holy Spirit, as it was
in the beginning, is now, and will be forever. Amen.**

Psalm 50:1–6

A psalm of Asaph.

1 The Lord, the Mighty One, is God,
and he has spoken;
he has summoned all humanity
from where the sun rises to where it sets.

2 From Mount Zion, the perfection of beauty,
God shines in glorious radiance.

3 Our God approaches,
and he is not silent.
Fire devours everything in his way,
and a great storm rages around him.

4 He calls on the heavens above and earth below
  to witness the judgment of his people.
5 "Bring my faithful people to me —
  those who made a covenant with me by giving sacrifices."
6 Then let the heavens proclaim his justice,
  for God himself will be the judge. *Interlude*

Then all the people say the following praise:

Glory to the Father, and to the Son, and to the Holy Spirit, as it was in the beginning, is now, and will be forever. Amen.

Psalm 50:7–23

7 "O my people, listen as I speak.
  Here are my charges against you, O Israel:
  I am God, your God!
8 I have no complaint about your sacrifices
  or the burnt offerings you constantly offer.
9 But I do not need the bulls from your barns
  or the goats from your pens.
10 For all the animals of the forest are mine,
  and I own the cattle on a thousand hills.
11 I know every bird on the mountains,
  and all the animals of the field are mine.
12 If I were hungry, I would not tell you,
  for all the world is mine and everything in it.
13 **Do I eat the meat of bulls?**
  Do I drink the blood of goats?
14 **Make thankfulness your sacrifice to God,**
  and keep the vows you made to the Most High.
15 **Then call on me when you are in trouble,**
  and I will rescue you,
  and you will give me glory."
16 But God says to the wicked:
"Why bother reciting my decrees
  and pretending to obey my covenant?
17 For you refuse my discipline
  and treat my words like trash.
18 **When you see thieves, you approve of them,**

and you spend your time with adulterers.

19 **Your mouth is filled with wickedness,**
and your tongue is full of lies.

20 **You sit around and slander your brother —**
your own mother's son.

21 **While you did all this, I remained silent,**
and you thought I didn't care.

But now I will rebuke you,
listing all my charges against you.

22 **Repent, all of you who forget me,**
or I will tear you apart,
and no one will help you.

23 But giving thanks is a sacrifice that truly honors me.
If you keep to my path,
I will reveal to you the salvation of God."

Then all the people say the following praise:

**Glory to the Father, and to the Son, and to the Holy Spirit, as it was
in the beginning, is now, and will be forever. Amen.**

Psalm 51

*For the choir director: A psalm of David, regarding the time Nathan the prophet came
to him after David had committed adultery with Bathsheba.*

1 Have mercy on me, O God,
because of your unfailing love.
Because of your great compassion,
blot out the stain of my sins.

2 Wash me clean from my guilt.
Purify me from my sin.

3 For I recognize my rebellion;
it haunts me day and night.

4 Against you, and you alone, have I sinned;
I have done what is evil in your sight.
You will be proved right in what you say,
and your judgment against me is just.

5 For I was born a sinner —
yes, from the moment my mother conceived me.

6 But you desire honesty from the womb,
   teaching me wisdom even there.
7 Purify me from my sins, and I will be clean;
   wash me, and I will be whiter than snow.
8 Oh, give me back my joy again;
   you have broken me —
   now let me rejoice.
9 **Don't keep looking at my sins.**
   Remove the stain of my guilt.
10 **Create in me a clean heart, O God.**
   Renew a loyal spirit within me.
11 **Do not banish me from your presence,**
   and don't take your Holy Spirit from me.
12 **Restore to me the joy of your salvation,**
   and make me willing to obey you.
13 **Then I will teach your ways to rebels,**
   and they will return to you.
14 **Forgive me for shedding blood, O God who saves;**
   then I will joyfully sing of your forgiveness.
15 **Unseal my lips, O Lord,**
   that my mouth may praise you.
16 **You do not desire a sacrifice, or I would offer one.**
   You do not want a burnt offering.
17 **The sacrifice you desire is a broken spirit.**
   You will not reject a broken and repentant heart, O God.
18 **Look with favor on Zion and help her;**
   rebuild the walls of Jerusalem.
19 **Then you will be pleased with sacrifices offered in the right
spirit**
   with burnt offerings and whole burnt offerings.
   Then bulls will again be sacrificed on your altar.

Then all the people say the following praise:

**Glory to the Father, and to the Son, and to the Holy Spirit, as it was
in the beginning, is now, and will be forever. Amen.**

Psalm 52

For the choir director: A psalm of David, regarding the time Doeg the Edomite said to Saul, "David has gone to see Ahimelech."

1 Why do you boast about your crimes, great warrior?
  Don't you realize God's justice continues forever?
2 All day long you plot destruction.
  Your tongue cuts like a sharp razor;
  you're an expert at telling lies.
3 **You love evil more than good**
  and lies more than truth. *Interlude*
4 You love to destroy others with your words,
  you liar!
5 **But God will strike you down once and for all.**
  He will pull you from your home
  and uproot you from the land of the living. *Interlude*
6 The righteous will see it and be amazed.
  They will laugh and say,
7 "Look what happens to mighty warriors
  who do not trust in God.
They trust their wealth instead
  and grow more and more bold in their wickedness."
8 But I am like an olive tree, thriving in the house of God.
  I will always trust in God's unfailing love.
9 I will praise you forever, O God,
  for what you have done.
I will trust in your good name
  in the presence of your faithful people.

Then all the people say the following praise:

Glory to the Father, and to the Son, and to the Holy Spirit, as it was in the beginning, is now, and will be forever. Amen.

Psalm 53
For the choir director: A meditation; a psalm of David.

1 Only fools say in their hearts,
  "There is no God."

186

They are corrupt, and their actions are evil;
  not one of them does good!
2 God looks down from heaven
  on the entire human race;
he looks to see if anyone is truly wise,
  if anyone seeks God.
3 But no, all have turned away;
  all have become corrupt.
No one does good,
  not a single one!
4 Will those who do evil never learn?
  They eat up my people like bread
  and wouldn't think of praying to God.
5 **Terror will grip them,**
  terror like they have never known before.
God will scatter the bones of your enemies.
  You will put them to shame, for God has rejected them.
6 **Who will come from Mount Zion to rescue Israel?**
  When God restores his people,
  Jacob will shout with joy, and Israel will rejoice.

Psalm 54

For the choir director: A psalm of David, regarding the time the Ziphites came and said to Saul, "We know where David is hiding." To be accompanied by stringed instruments.

1 Come with great power, O God, and rescue me!
  Defend me with your might.
2 Listen to my prayer, O God.
  Pay attention to my plea.
3 For strangers are attacking me;
  violent people are trying to kill me.
  They care nothing for God. *Interlude*
4 But God is my helper.
  The Lord keeps me alive!
5 May the evil plans of my enemies be turned against them.
  Do as you promised and put an end to them.
6 I will sacrifice a voluntary offering to you;
  I will praise your name, O Lord,
  for it is good.

7 For you have rescued me from my troubles
and helped me to triumph over my enemies.

Then all the people say the following praise:

Glory to the Father, and to the Son, and to the Holy Spirit, as it was in the beginning, is now, and will be forever. Amen.

Psalm 55

For the choir director: A psalm of David, to be accompanied by stringed instruments.

1 Listen to my prayer, O God.
Do not ignore my cry for help!
2 Please listen and answer me,
for I am overwhelmed by my troubles.
3 My enemies shout at me,
making loud and wicked threats.
They bring trouble on me
and angrily hunt me down.
4 **My heart pounds in my chest.**
The terror of death assaults me.
5 **Fear and trembling overwhelm me,**
and I can't stop shaking.
6 **Oh, that I had wings like a dove;**
then I would fly away and rest!
7 **I would fly far away**
to the quiet of the wilderness. *Interlude*
8 How quickly I would escape —
far from this wild storm of hatred.
9 Confuse them, Lord, and frustrate their plans,
for I see violence and conflict in the city.
10 Its walls are patrolled day and night against invaders,
but the real danger is wickedness within the city.
11 Everything is falling apart;
threats and cheating are rampant in the streets.
12 It is not an enemy who taunts me —
I could bear that.
It is not my foes who so arrogantly insult me —
I could have hidden from them.

13 Instead, it is you — my equal,
  my companion and close friend.
14 What good fellowship we once enjoyed
  as we walked together to the house of God.
15 Let death stalk my enemies;
  let the grave swallow them alive,
  for evil makes its home within them.
16 **But I will call on God,**
  and the Lord will rescue me.
17 **Morning, noon, and night**
  I cry out in my distress,
  and the Lord hears my voice.
18 **He ransoms me and keeps me safe**
  from the battle waged against me,
  though many still oppose me.
19 **God, who has ruled forever,**
  will hear me and humble them. *Interlude*
For my enemies refuse to change their ways;
  they do not fear God.
20 **As for my companion, he betrayed his friends;**
  he broke his promises.
21 **His words are as smooth as butter,**
  but in his heart is war.
His words are as soothing as lotion,
  but underneath are daggers!
22 **Give your burdens to the Lord,**
  and he will take care of you.
  He will not permit the godly to slip and fall.
23 But you, O God, will send the wicked
  down to the pit of destruction.
Murderers and liars will die young,
  but I am trusting you to save me.

Then all the people say the following praise:
Glory to the Father, and to the Son, and to the Holy Spirit, as it was in the beginning, is now, and will be forever. Amen.

Psalm 56

For the choir director: A psalm of David, regarding the time the Philistines seized him in Gath. To be sung to the tune "Dove on Distant Oaks."

1 O God, have mercy on me,
   for people are hounding me.
   My foes attack me all day long.
2 **I am constantly hounded by those who slander me,**
   and many are boldly attacking me.
3 **But when I am afraid,**
   I will put my trust in you.
4 **I praise God for what he has promised.**
   I trust in God, so why should I be afraid?
   What can mere mortals do to me?
5 They are always twisting what I say;
   they spend their days plotting to harm me.
6 They come together to spy on me —
   watching my every step, eager to kill me.
7 Don't let them get away with their wickedness;
   in your anger, O God, bring them down.
8 You keep track of all my sorrows.
   You have collected all my tears in your bottle.
   You have recorded each one in your book.
9 **My enemies will retreat when I call to you for help.**
   This I know: God is on my side!
10 **I praise God for what he has promised;**
   yes, I praise the Lord for what he has promised.
11 **I trust in God, so why should I be afraid?**
   What can mere mortals do to me?
12 **I will fulfill my vows to you, O God,**
   and will offer a sacrifice of thanks for your help.
13 **For you have rescued me from death;**
   you have kept my feet from slipping.
So now I can walk in your presence, O God,
   in your life-giving light.

Then all the people say the following praise:

190

Glory to the Father, and to the Son, and to the Holy Spirit, as it was in the beginning, is now, and will be forever. Amen.

Psalm 57

For the choir director: A psalm of David, regarding the time he fled from Saul and went into the cave. To be sung to the tune "Do Not Destroy!"

1 Have mercy on me, O God, have mercy!
  I look to you for protection.
I will hide beneath the shadow of your wings
  until the danger passes by.
2 **I cry out to God Most High,**
  to God who will fulfill his purpose for me.
3 **He will send help from heaven to rescue me,**
  disgracing those who hound me. *Interlude*
My God will send forth his unfailing love and faithfulness.
4 I am surrounded by fierce lions
  who greedily devour human prey —
whose teeth pierce like spears and arrows,
  and whose tongues cut like swords.
5 **Be exalted, O God, above the highest heavens!**
  May your glory shine over all the earth.
6 **My enemies have set a trap for me.**
  I am weary from distress.
They have dug a deep pit in my path,
  but they themselves have fallen into it. *Interlude*
7 **My heart is confident in you, O God;**
  my heart is confident.
  No wonder I can sing your praises!
8 Wake up, my heart!
  Wake up, O lyre and harp!
  I will wake the dawn with my song.
9 **I will thank you, Lord, among all the people.**
  I will sing your praises among the nations.
10 **For your unfailing love is as high as the heavens.**
  Your faithfulness reaches to the clouds.
11 **Be exalted, O God, above the highest heavens.**
  May your glory shine over all the earth.

Glory to the Father, and to the Son, and to the Holy Spirit, as it was in the beginning, is now, and will be forever. Amen.

Psalm 58

For the choir director: A psalm of David, to be sung to the tune "Do Not Destroy!"

1 Justice — do you rulers know the meaning of the word?
Do you judge the people fairly?
2 No! You plot injustice in your hearts.
You spread violence throughout the land.
3 These wicked people are born sinners;
even from birth they have lied and gone their own way.
4 They spit venom like deadly snakes;
they are like cobras that refuse to listen,
5 ignoring the tunes of the snake charmers,
no matter how skillfully they play.
6 Break off their fangs, O God!
Smash the jaws of these lions, O Lord!
7 May they disappear like water into thirsty ground.
Make their weapons useless in their hands.
8 May they be like snails that dissolve into slime,
like a stillborn child who will never see the sun.
9 God will sweep them away, both young and old,
faster than a pot heats over burning thorns.
10 The godly will rejoice when they see injustice avenged.
They will wash their feet in the blood of the wicked.
11 Then at last everyone will say,
"There truly is a reward for those who live for God;
surely there is a God who judges justly here on earth."

Then all the people say the following praise:

Glory to the Father, and to the Son, and to the Holy Spirit, as it was in the beginning, is now, and will be forever. Amen.

Psalm 59

For the choir director: A psalm of David, regarding the time Saul sent soldiers to watch David's house in order to kill him. To be sung to the tune "Do Not Destroy!"

1 Rescue me from my enemies, O God.
  Protect me from those who have come to destroy me.
2 Rescue me from these criminals;
  save me from these murderers.
3 They have set an ambush for me.
  Fierce enemies are out there waiting, Lord,
  though I have not sinned or offended them.
4 **I have done nothing wrong,**
  yet they prepare to attack me.
  Wake up! See what is happening and help me!
5 O Lord God of Heaven's Armies, the God of Israel,
  wake up and punish those hostile nations.
  Show no mercy to wicked traitors. *Interlude*
6 **They come out at night,**
  snarling like vicious dogs
  as they prowl the streets.
7 Listen to the filth that comes from their mouths;
  their words cut like swords.
  "After all, who can hear us?" they sneer.
8 **But Lord, you laugh at them.**
  You scoff at all the hostile nations.
9 **You are my strength; I wait for you to rescue me,**
  for you, O God, are my fortress.
10 **In his unfailing love, my God will stand with me.**
  He will let me look down in triumph on all my enemies.
11 **Don't kill them, for my people soon forget such lessons;**
  stagger them with your power, and bring them to their knees,
  O Lord our shield.
12 Because of the sinful things they say,
  because of the evil that is on their lips,
let them be captured by their pride,
  their curses, and their lies.
13 Destroy them in your anger!
  Wipe them out completely!

Then the whole world will know
that God reigns in Israel. *Interlude*
14 **My enemies come out at night,**
snarling like vicious dogs
as they prowl the streets.
15 **They scavenge for food**
but go to sleep unsatisfied.
16 But as for me, I will sing about your power.
Each morning I will sing with joy about your unfailing love.
For you have been my refuge,
a place of safety when I am in distress.
17 O my Strength, to you I sing praises,
for you, O God, are my refuge,
the God who shows me unfailing love.

Then all the people say the following praise:

Glory to the Father, and to the Son, and to the Holy Spirit, as it was
in the beginning, is now, and will be forever. Amen.

Psalm 60

For the choir director: A psalm of David useful for teaching, regarding the time David
fought Aram-naharaim and Aram-zobah, and Joab returned and killed 12,000
Edomites in the Valley of Salt. To be sung to the tune "Lily of the Testimony."

1 You have rejected us, O God, and broken our defenses.
You have been angry with us; now restore us to your favor.
2 You have shaken our land and split it open.
Seal the cracks, for the land trembles.
3 You have been very hard on us,
making us drink wine that sent us reeling.
4 But you have raised a banner for those who fear you —
a rallying point in the face of attack. *Interlude*
5 Now rescue your beloved people.
Answer and save us by your power.
6 God has promised this by his holiness:
"I will divide up Shechem with joy.
I will measure out the valley of Succoth.
7 **Gilead is mine,**

194

and Manasseh, too.

Ephraim, my helmet, will produce my warriors,
and Judah, my scepter, will produce my kings.

8 **But Moab, my washbasin, will become my servant,**
and I will wipe my feet on Edom
and shout in triumph over Philistia."

9 Who will bring me into the fortified city?
Who will bring me victory over Edom?

10 Have you rejected us, O God?
Will you no longer march with our armies?

11 Oh, please help us against our enemies,
for all human help is useless.

12 With God's help we will do mighty things,
for he will trample down our foes.

Then all the people say the following praise:

Glory to the Father, and to the Son, and to the Holy Spirit, as it was in the beginning, is now, and will be forever. Amen.

Psalm 61

For the choir director: A psalm of David, to be accompanied by stringed instruments.

1 O God, listen to my cry!
Hear my prayer!

2 From the ends of the earth,
I cry to you for help
when my heart is overwhelmed.
Lead me to the towering rock of safety,

3 **for you are my safe refuge,**
a fortress where my enemies cannot reach me.

4 **Let me live forever in your sanctuary,**
safe beneath the shelter of your wings! *Interlude*

5 **For you have heard my vows, O God.**
You have given me an inheritance reserved for those who fear your name.

6 **Add many years to the life of the king!**
May his years span the generations!

7 **May he reign under God's protection forever.**

May your unfailing love and faithfulness watch over him.
8 Then I will sing praises to your name forever
as I fulfill my vows each day.

Then all the people say the following praise:

Glory to the Father, and to the Son, and to the Holy Spirit, as it was in the beginning, is now, and will be forever. Amen.

Psalm 62

For Jeduthun, the choir director: A psalm of David.

1 I wait quietly before God,
for my victory comes from him.
2 He alone is my rock and my salvation,
my fortress where I will never be shaken.
3 So many enemies against one man —
all of them trying to kill me.
To them I'm just a broken-down wall
or a tottering fence.
4 **They plan to topple me from my high position.**
They delight in telling lies about me.
They praise me to my face
but curse me in their hearts. *Interlude*
5 Let all that I am wait quietly before God,
for my hope is in him.
6 **He alone is my rock and my salvation,**
my fortress where I will not be shaken.
7 **My victory and honor come from God alone.**
He is my refuge, a rock where no enemy can reach me.
8 **O my people, trust in him at all times.**
Pour out your heart to him,
for God is our refuge. *Interlude*
9 Common people are as worthless as a puff of wind,
and the powerful are not what they appear to be.
If you weigh them on the scales,
together they are lighter than a breath of air.
10 Don't make your living by extortion
or put your hope in stealing.

And if your wealth increases,
    don't make it the center of your life.
11 God has spoken plainly,
    and I have heard it many times:
Power, O God, belongs to you;
12 unfailing love, O Lord, is yours.
Surely you repay all people
    according to what they have done.

Then all the people say the following praise:

Glory to the Father, and to the Son, and to the Holy Spirit, as it was in the beginning, is now, and will be forever. Amen.

Psalm 63

A psalm of David, regarding a time when David was in the wilderness of Judah.

1 O God, you are my God;
    I earnestly search for you.
My soul thirsts for you;
    my whole body longs for you
in this parched and weary land
    where there is no water.
2 I have seen you in your sanctuary
    and gazed upon your power and glory.
3 Your unfailing love is better than life itself;
    how I praise you!
4 I will praise you as long as I live,
    lifting up my hands to you in prayer.
5 You satisfy me more than the richest feast.
    I will praise you with songs of joy.
6 I lie awake thinking of you,
    meditating on you through the night.
7 Because you are my helper,
    I sing for joy in the shadow of your wings.
8 I cling to you;
    your strong right hand holds me securely.
9 But those plotting to destroy me will come to ruin.
    They will go down into the depths of the earth.

10 They will die by the sword
  and become the food of jackals.
11 But the king will rejoice in God.
  All who swear to tell the truth will praise him,
  while liars will be silenced.

Then all the people say the following praise:

Glory to the Father, and to the Son, and to the Holy Spirit, as it was in the beginning, is now, and will be forever. Amen.

Psalm 64

For the choir director: A psalm of David.

1 O God, listen to my complaint.
  Protect my life from my enemies' threats.
2 Hide me from the plots of this evil mob,
  from this gang of wrongdoers.
3 They sharpen their tongues like swords
  and aim their bitter words like arrows.
4 They shoot from ambush at the innocent,
  attacking suddenly and fearlessly.
5 They encourage each other to do evil
  and plan how to set their traps in secret.
  "Who will ever notice?" they ask.
6 **As they plot their crimes, they say,**
  "We have devised the perfect plan!"
  Yes, the human heart and mind are cunning.
7 But God himself will shoot them with his arrows,
  suddenly striking them down.
8 Their own tongues will ruin them,
  and all who see them will shake their heads in scorn.
9 Then everyone will be afraid;
  they will proclaim the mighty acts of God
  and realize all the amazing things he does.
10 **The godly will rejoice in the Lord**
  and find shelter in him.
And those who do what is right
  will praise him.

Then all the people say the following praise:

Glory to the Father, and to the Son, and to the Holy Spirit, as it was in the beginning, is now, and will be forever. Amen.

Psalm 65

For the choir director: A song. A psalm of David.

1 What mighty praise, O God,
   belongs to you in Zion.
We will fulfill our vows to you,
2 **for you answer our prayers.**
   All of us must come to you.
3 **Though we are overwhelmed by our sins,**
   you forgive them all.
4 **What joy for those you choose to bring near,**
   those who live in your holy courts.
What festivities await us
   inside your holy Temple.
5 You faithfully answer our prayers with awesome deeds,
   O God our savior.
You are the hope of everyone on earth,
   even those who sail on distant seas.
6 You formed the mountains by your power
   and armed yourself with mighty strength.
7 You quieted the raging oceans
   with their pounding waves
   and silenced the shouting of the nations.
8 Those who live at the ends of the earth
   stand in awe of your wonders.
From where the sun rises to where it sets,
   you inspire shouts of joy.
9 You take care of the earth and water it,
   making it rich and fertile.
The river of God has plenty of water;
   it provides a bountiful harvest of grain,
   for you have ordered it so.
10 **You drench the plowed ground with rain,**
   melting the clods and leveling the ridges.

You soften the earth with showers
and bless its abundant crops.
11 You crown the year with a bountiful harvest;
even the hard pathways overflow with abundance.
12 The grasslands of the wilderness become a lush pasture,
and the hillsides blossom with joy.
13 The meadows are clothed with flocks of sheep,
and the valleys are carpeted with grain.
They all shout and sing for joy!

Then all the people say the following praise:

Glory to the Father, and to the Son, and to the Holy Spirit, as it was
in the beginning, is now, and will be forever. Amen.

Psalm 66

For the choir director: A song. A psalm.

1 Shout joyful praises to God, all the earth!
2 Sing about the glory of his name!
Tell the world how glorious he is.
3 Say to God, "How awesome are your deeds!
Your enemies cringe before your mighty power.
4 Everything on earth will worship you;
they will sing your praises,
shouting your name in glorious songs." *Interlude*
5 Come and see what our God has done,
what awesome miracles he performs for people!
6 He made a dry path through the Red Sea,
and his people went across on foot.
There we rejoiced in him.
7 For by his great power he rules forever.
He watches every movement of the nations;
let no rebel rise in defiance. *Interlude*
8 Let the whole world bless our God
and loudly sing his praises.
9 Our lives are in his hands,
and he keeps our feet from stumbling.
10 You have tested us, O God;

you have purified us like silver.

11 **You captured us in your net
and laid the burden of slavery on our backs.**

12 Then you put a leader over us.
We went through fire and flood,
but you brought us to a place of great abundance.

13 **Now I come to your Temple with burnt offerings
to fulfill the vows I made to you —**

14 yes, the sacred vows that I made
when I was in deep trouble.

15 **That is why I am sacrificing burnt offerings to you —**
the best of my rams as a pleasing aroma,
and a sacrifice of bulls and male goats. *Interlude*

16 Come and listen, all you who fear God,
and I will tell you what he did for me.

17 For I cried out to him for help,
praising him as I spoke.

18 If I had not confessed the sin in my heart,
the Lord would not have listened.

19 But God did listen!
He paid attention to my prayer.

20 Praise God, who did not ignore my prayer
or withdraw his unfailing love from me.

Then all the people say the following praise:

**Glory to the Father, and to the Son, and to the Holy Spirit, as it was
in the beginning, is now, and will be forever. Amen.**

Psalm 67

For the choir director: A song. A psalm, to be accompanied by stringed instruments.

1 May God be merciful and bless us.
May his face smile with favor on us. *Interlude*

2 May your ways be known throughout the earth,
your saving power among people everywhere.

3 May the nations praise you, O God.
Yes, may all the nations praise you.

4 Let the whole world sing for joy,

because you govern the nations with justice
and guide the people of the whole world. *Interlude*
5 May the nations praise you, O God.
Yes, may all the nations praise you.
6 Then the earth will yield its harvests,
and God, our God, will richly bless us.
7 Yes, God will bless us,
and people all over the world will fear him.

Then all the people say the following praise:

Glory to the Father, and to the Son, and to the Holy Spirit, as it was in the beginning, is now, and will be forever. Amen.

Psalm 68:1–19

For the choir director: A song. A psalm of David.

1 Rise up, O God, and scatter your enemies.
Let those who hate God run for their lives.
2 Blow them away like smoke.
Melt them like wax in a fire.
Let the wicked perish in the presence of God.
3 **But let the godly rejoice.**
Let them be glad in God's presence.
Let them be filled with joy.
4 Sing praises to God and to his name!
Sing loud praises to him who rides the clouds.
His name is the Lord —
rejoice in his presence!
5 Father to the fatherless, defender of widows —
this is God, whose dwelling is holy.
6 God places the lonely in families;
he sets the prisoners free and gives them joy.
But he makes the rebellious live in a sun-scorched land.
7 **O God, when you led your people out from Egypt,**
when you marched through the dry wasteland, *Interlude*
8 **the earth trembled, and the heavens poured down rain**
before you, the God of Sinai,
before God, the God of Israel.

9 You sent abundant rain, O God,
  to refresh the weary land.
10 There your people finally settled,
  and with a bountiful harvest, O God,
  you provided for your needy people.
11 **The Lord gives the word,**
  and a great army brings the good news.
12 **Enemy kings and their armies flee,**
  while the women of Israel divide the plunder.
13 **Even those who lived among the sheepfolds found treasures —**
  doves with wings of silver
  and feathers of gold.
14 **The Almighty scattered the enemy kings**
  like a blowing snowstorm on Mount Zalmon.
15 **The mountains of Bashan are majestic,**
  with many peaks stretching high into the sky.
16 **Why do you look with envy, O rugged mountains,**
  at Mount Zion, where God has chosen to live,
  where the Lord himself will live forever?
17 Surrounded by unnumbered thousands of chariots,
  the Lord came from Mount Sinai into his sanctuary.
18 When you ascended to the heights,
  you led a crowd of captives.
You received gifts from the people,
  even from those who rebelled against you.
  Now the Lord God will live among us there.
19 **Praise the Lord; praise God our savior!**
  For each day he carries us in his arms. *Interlude*

Then all the people say the following praise:

**Glory to the Father, and to the Son, and to the Holy Spirit, as it was
in the beginning, is now, and will be forever. Amen.**

Psalm 68:20–35

20 Our God is a God who saves!
  The Sovereign Lord rescues us from death.
21 But God will smash the heads of his enemies,
  crushing the skulls of those who love their guilty ways.

22 The Lord says, "I will bring my enemies down from Bashan;
I will bring them up from the depths of the sea.
23 You, my people, will wash your feet in their blood,
and even your dogs will get their share!"
24 Your procession has come into view, O God —
**the procession of my God and King as he goes into the
sanctuary.**
25 Singers are in front, musicians behind;
between them are young women playing tambourines.
26 Praise God, all you people of Israel;
praise the Lord, the source of Israel's life.
27 Look, the little tribe of Benjamin leads the way.
Then comes a great throng of rulers from Judah
and all the rulers of Zebulun and Naphtali.
28 Summon your might, O God.
Display your power, O God, as you have in the past.
29 The kings of the earth are bringing tribute
to your Temple in Jerusalem.
30 Rebuke these enemy nations —
these wild animals lurking in the reeds,
this herd of bulls among the weaker calves.
Make them bring bars of silver in humble tribute.
Scatter the nations that delight in war.
31 **Let Egypt come with gifts of precious metals;**
let Ethiopia bring tribute to God.
32 **Sing to God, you kingdoms of the earth.**
Sing praises to the Lord. *Interlude*
33 **Sing to the one who rides across the ancient heavens,**
his mighty voice thundering from the sky.
34 **Tell everyone about God's power.**
His majesty shines down on Israel;
his strength is mighty in the heavens.
35 God is awesome in his sanctuary.
**The God of Israel gives power and strength to his people.
Praise be to God!**

Then all the people say the following praise:

**Glory to the Father, and to the Son, and to the Holy Spirit, as it was
in the beginning, is now, and will be forever. Amen.**

Psalm 69:1–18

For the choir director: A psalm of David, to be sung to the tune "Lilies."

1 Save me, O God,
  for the floodwaters are up to my neck.
2 Deeper and deeper I sink into the mire;
  I can't find a foothold.
I am in deep water,
  and the floods overwhelm me.
3 I am exhausted from crying for help;
  my throat is parched.
My eyes are swollen with weeping,
  waiting for my God to help me.
4 Those who hate me without cause
  outnumber the hairs on my head.
Many enemies try to destroy me with lies,
  demanding that I give back what I didn't steal.
5 **O God, you know how foolish I am;**
  my sins cannot be hidden from you.
6 **Don't let those who trust in you be ashamed because of me,**
  O Sovereign Lord of Heaven's Armies.
Don't let me cause them to be humiliated,
  O God of Israel.
7 **For I endure insults for your sake;**
  humiliation is written all over my face.
8 **Even my own brothers pretend they don't know me;**
  they treat me like a stranger.
9 **Passion for your house has consumed me,**
  and the insults of those who insult you have fallen on me.
10 **When I weep and fast,**
  they scoff at me.
11 **When I dress in burlap to show sorrow,**
  they make fun of me.
12 **I am the favorite topic of town gossip,**
  and all the drunks sing about me.
13 **But I keep praying to you, Lord,**
  hoping this time you will show me favor.
In your unfailing love, O God,
  answer my prayer with your sure salvation.

14 **Rescue me from the mud;**
don't let me sink any deeper!
Save me from those who hate me,
and pull me from these deep waters.
15 **Don't let the floods overwhelm me,**
or the deep waters swallow me,
or the pit of death devour me.
16 Answer my prayers, O Lord,
for your unfailing love is wonderful.
Take care of me,
for your mercy is so plentiful.
17 Don't hide from your servant;
answer me quickly, for I am in deep trouble!
18 Come and redeem me;
free me from my enemies.

Then all the people say the following praise:

Glory to the Father, and to the Son, and to the Holy Spirit, as it was in the beginning, is now, and will be forever. Amen.

Psalm 69:19–36

19 You know of my shame, scorn, and disgrace.
You see all that my enemies are doing.
20 Their insults have broken my heart,
and I am in despair.
If only one person would show some pity;
if only one would turn and comfort me.
21 But instead, they give me poison for food;
they offer me sour wine for my thirst.
22 Let the bountiful table set before them become a snare
and their prosperity become a trap.
23 Let their eyes go blind so they cannot see,
and make their bodies shake continually.
24 Pour out your fury on them;
consume them with your burning anger.
25 Let their homes become desolate
and their tents be deserted.
26 To the one you have punished, they add insult to injury;

206

they add to the pain of those you have hurt.
27 Pile their sins up high,
  and don't let them go free.
28 Erase their names from the Book of Life;
  don't let them be counted among the righteous.
29 I am suffering and in pain.
  Rescue me, O God, by your saving power.
30 Then I will praise God's name with singing,
  and I will honor him with thanksgiving.
31 For this will please the Lord more than sacrificing cattle,
  more than presenting a bull with its horns and hooves.
32 The humble will see their God at work and be glad.
  Let all who seek God's help be encouraged.
33 For the Lord hears the cries of the needy;
  he does not despise his imprisoned people.
34 Praise him, O heaven and earth,
  the seas and all that move in them.
35 For God will save Jerusalem
  and rebuild the towns of Judah.
His people will live there
  and settle in their own land.
36 The descendants of those who obey him will inherit the land,
  and those who love him will live there in safety.

Then all the people say the following praise:

Glory to the Father, and to the Son, and to the Holy Spirit, as it was in the beginning, is now, and will be forever. Amen.

Psalm 70

For the choir director: A psalm of David, asking God to remember him.

1 Please, God, rescue me!
  Come quickly, Lord, and help me.
2 May those who try to kill me
  be humiliated and put to shame.
May those who take delight in my trouble
  be turned back in disgrace.
3 Let them be horrified by their shame,

for they said, "Aha! We've got him now!"
4 But may all who search for you
be filled with joy and gladness in you.
May those who love your salvation
repeatedly shout, "God is great!"
5 But as for me, I am poor and needy;
please hurry to my aid, O God.
You are my helper and my savior;
O Lord, do not delay.

Then all the people say the following praise:

Glory to the Father, and to the Son, and to the Holy Spirit, as it was in the beginning, is now, and will be forever. Amen.

Psalm 71:1–16

1 O Lord, I have come to you for protection;
don't let me be disgraced.
2 Save me and rescue me,
for you do what is right.
Turn your ear to listen to me,
and set me free.
3 Be my rock of safety
where I can always hide.
Give the order to save me,
for you are my rock and my fortress.
4 **My God, rescue me from the power of the wicked,**
from the clutches of cruel oppressors.
5 **O Lord, you alone are my hope.**
I've trusted you, O Lord, from childhood.
6 **Yes, you have been with me from birth;**
from my mother's womb you have cared for me.
No wonder I am always praising you!
7 My life is an example to many,
because you have been my strength and protection.
8 That is why I can never stop praising you;
I declare your glory all day long.
9 And now, in my old age, don't set me aside.
Don't abandon me when my strength is failing.

10 For my enemies are whispering against me.

They are plotting together to kill me.

11 They say, "God has abandoned him.

Let's go and get him,

for no one will help him now."

12 O God, don't stay away.

My God, please hurry to help me.

13 Bring disgrace and destruction on my accusers.

Humiliate and shame those who want to harm me.

14 But I will keep on hoping for your help;

I will praise you more and more.

15 I will tell everyone about your righteousness.

All day long I will proclaim your saving power,

though I am not skilled with words.

16 **I will praise your mighty deeds, O Sovereign Lord.**

I will tell everyone that you alone are just.

Then all the people say the following praise:

Glory to the Father, and to the Son, and to the Holy Spirit, as it was in the beginning, is now, and will be forever. Amen.

Psalm 71:17–24

17 O God, you have taught me from my earliest childhood,

and I constantly tell others about the wonderful things you do.

18 Now that I am old and gray,

do not abandon me, O God.

Let me proclaim your power to this new generation,

your mighty miracles to all who come after me.

19 Your righteousness, O God, reaches to the highest heavens.

You have done such wonderful things.

Who can compare with you, O God?

20 **You have allowed me to suffer much hardship,**

but you will restore me to life again

and lift me up from the depths of the earth.

21 **You will restore me to even greater honor**

and comfort me once again.

22 Then I will praise you with music on the harp,

because you are faithful to your promises, O my God.

I will sing praises to you with a lyre,
  O Holy One of Israel.
23 I will shout for joy and sing your praises,
  for you have ransomed me.
24 I will tell about your righteous deeds
  all day long,
**for everyone who tried to hurt me
  has been shamed and humiliated.**

Then all the people say the following praise:

**Glory to the Father, and to the Son, and to the Holy Spirit, as it was
in the beginning, is now, and will be forever. Amen.**

Psalm 72:1–11

A psalm of Solomon.

1 Give your love of justice to the king, O God,
  and righteousness to the king's son.
2 Help him judge your people in the right way;
  let the poor always be treated fairly.
3 May the mountains yield prosperity for all,
  and may the hills be fruitful.
4 Help him to defend the poor,
  to rescue the children of the needy,
  and to crush their oppressors.
5 **May they fear you as long as the sun shines,**
  as long as the moon remains in the sky.
  Yes, forever!
6 May the king's rule be refreshing like spring rain on freshly cut grass,
  like the showers that water the earth.
7 May all the godly flourish during his reign.
  May there be abundant prosperity until the moon is no more.
8 May he reign from sea to sea,
  and from the Euphrates River to the ends of the earth.
9 Desert nomads will bow before him;
  his enemies will fall before him in the dust.
10 The western kings of Tarshish and other distant lands
  will bring him tribute.

The eastern kings of Sheba and Seba
  will bring him gifts.
11 All kings will bow before him,
  and all nations will serve him.

Glory to the Father, and to the Son, and to the Holy Spirit, as it was in the beginning, is now, and will be forever. Amen.

Psalm 72:12–20

12 He will rescue the poor when they cry to him;
  he will help the oppressed, who have no one to defend them.
13 He feels pity for the weak and the needy,
  and he will rescue them.
14 **He will redeem them from oppression and violence,**
  for their lives are precious to him.
15 Long live the king!
  May the gold of Sheba be given to him.
May the people always pray for him
  and bless him all day long.
16 **May there be abundant grain throughout the land,**
  flourishing even on the hilltops.
May the fruit trees flourish like the trees of Lebanon,
  and may the people thrive like grass in a field.
17 **May the king's name endure forever;**
  may it continue as long as the sun shines.
May all nations be blessed through him
  and bring him praise.
18 Praise the Lord God, the God of Israel,
  who alone does such wonderful things.
19 Praise his glorious name forever!
  Let the whole earth be filled with his glory.
Amen and amen!
20 *(This ends the prayers of David son of Jesse.)*

Glory to the Father, and to the Son, and to the Holy Spirit, as it was in the beginning, is now, and will be forever. Amen.

Book Three

Psalm 73:1–16

A psalm of Asaph.

1 Truly God is good to Israel,
to those whose hearts are pure.
2 But as for me, I almost lost my footing.
My feet were slipping, and I was almost gone.
3 For I envied the proud
when I saw them prosper despite their wickedness.
4 **They seem to live such painless lives;**
their bodies are so healthy and strong.
5 **They don't have troubles like other people;**
they're not plagued with problems like everyone else.
6 **They wear pride like a jeweled necklace**
and clothe themselves with cruelty.
7 These fat cats have everything
their hearts could ever wish for!
8 **They scoff and speak only evil;**
in their pride they seek to crush others.
9 **They boast against the very heavens,**
and their words strut throughout the earth.
10 **And so the people are dismayed and confused,**
drinking in all their words.
11 "What does God know?" they ask.
"Does the Most High even know what's happening?"
12 Look at these wicked people —
enjoying a life of ease while their riches multiply.

13 **Did I keep my heart pure for nothing?**
Did I keep myself innocent for no reason?
14 **I get nothing but trouble all day long;**
every morning brings me pain.
15 If I had really spoken this way to others,
I would have been a traitor to your people.
16 **So I tried to understand why the wicked prosper.**
But what a difficult task it is!

Then all the people say the following praise:

Glory to the Father, and to the Son, and to the Holy Spirit, as it was in the beginning, is now, and will be forever. Amen.

Psalm 73:17–28

17 **Then I went into your sanctuary, O God,**
and I finally understood the destiny of the wicked.
18 Truly, you put them on a slippery path
and send them sliding over the cliff to destruction.
19 In an instant they are destroyed,
completely swept away by terrors.
20 When you arise, O Lord,
you will laugh at their silly ideas
as a person laughs at dreams in the morning.
21 Then I realized that my heart was bitter,
and I was all torn up inside.
22 I was so foolish and ignorant —
I must have seemed like a senseless animal to you.
23 Yet I still belong to you;
you hold my right hand.
24 You guide me with your counsel,
leading me to a glorious destiny.
25 Whom have I in heaven but you?
I desire you more than anything on earth.
26 My health may fail, and my spirit may grow weak,
but God remains the strength of my heart;
he is mine forever.
27 **Those who desert him will perish,**
for you destroy those who abandon you.

214

28 **But as for me, how good it is to be near God!**
I have made the Sovereign Lord my shelter,
and I will tell everyone about the wonderful things you do.

Then all the people say the following praise:

Glory to the Father, and to the Son, and to the Holy Spirit, as it was in the beginning, is now, and will be forever. Amen.

Psalm 74:1–8

A psalm of Asaph.

1 O God, why have you rejected us so long?
Why is your anger so intense against the sheep of your own pasture?
2 Remember that we are the people you chose long ago,
the tribe you redeemed as your own special possession!
And remember Jerusalem, your home here on earth.
3 **Walk through the awful ruins of the city;**
see how the enemy has destroyed your sanctuary.
4 **There your enemies shouted their victorious battle cries;**
there they set up their battle standards.
5 **They swung their axes**
like woodcutters in a forest.
6 With axes and picks,
they smashed the carved paneling.
7 **They burned your sanctuary to the ground.**
They defiled the place that bears your name.
8 **Then they thought, "Let's destroy everything!"**
So they burned down all the places where God was worshiped.

Then all the people say the following praise:

Glory to the Father, and to the Son, and to the Holy Spirit, as it was in the beginning, is now, and will be forever. Amen.

9 We no longer see your miraculous signs.
  All the prophets are gone,
  and no one can tell us when it will end.
10 **How long, O God, will you allow our enemies to insult you?**
  Will you let them dishonor your name forever?
11 **Why do you hold back your strong right hand?**
  Unleash your powerful fist and destroy them.
12 **You, O God, are my king from ages past,**
  bringing salvation to the earth.
13 **You split the sea by your strength**
  and smashed the heads of the sea monsters.
14 You crushed the heads of Leviathan
  and let the desert animals eat him.
15 **You caused the springs and streams to gush forth,**
  and you dried up rivers that never run dry.
16 **Both day and night belong to you;**
  you made the starlight and the sun.
17 **You set the boundaries of the earth,**
  and you made both summer and winter.
18 **See how these enemies insult you, Lord.**
  A foolish nation has dishonored your name.
19 **Don't let these wild beasts destroy your turtledoves.**
  Don't forget your suffering people forever.
20 **Remember your covenant promises,**
  for the land is full of darkness and violence!
21 **Don't let the downtrodden be humiliated again.**
  Instead, let the poor and needy praise your name.
22 **Arise, O God, and defend your cause.**
  Remember how these fools insult you all day long.
23 **Don't overlook what your enemies have said**
  or their growing uproar.

Then all the people say the following praise:

Glory to the Father, and to the Son, and to the Holy Spirit, as it was in the beginning, is now, and will be forever. Amen.

Psalm 75

For the choir director: A psalm of Asaph. A song to be sung to the tune "Do Not Destroy!"

1 We thank you, O God!
  We give thanks because you are near.
  People everywhere tell of your wonderful deeds.
2 **God says, "At the time I have planned,**
  I will bring justice against the wicked.
3 **When the earth quakes and its people live in turmoil,**
  I am the one who keeps its foundations firm. *Interlude*
4 **"I warned the proud, 'Stop your boasting!'**
  I told the wicked, 'Don't raise your fists!
5 **Don't raise your fists in defiance at the heavens**
  or speak with such arrogance.'"
6 For no one on earth — from east or west,
  or even from the wilderness —
  should raise a defiant fist.
7 **It is God alone who judges;**
  he decides who will rise and who will fall.
8 **For the Lord holds a cup in his hand**
  that is full of foaming wine mixed with spices.
He pours out the wine in judgment,
  and all the wicked must drink it,
  draining it to the dregs.
9 **But as for me, I will always proclaim what God has done;**
  I will sing praises to the God of Jacob.
10 **For God says, "I will break the strength of the wicked,**
  but I will increase the power of the godly."

Then all the people say the following praise:

Glory to the Father, and to the Son, and to the Holy Spirit, as it was in the beginning, is now, and will be forever. Amen.

Psalm 76

For the choir director: A psalm of Asaph. A song to be accompanied by stringed instruments.

1 God is honored in Judah;
his name is great in Israel.
2 Jerusalem is where he lives;
Mount Zion is his home.
3 There he has broken the fiery arrows of the enemy,
the shields and swords and weapons of war. *Interlude*
4 You are glorious and more majestic
than the everlasting mountains.
5 **Our boldest enemies have been plundered.**
They lie before us in the sleep of death.
No warrior could lift a hand against us.
6 At the blast of your breath, O God of Jacob,
their horses and chariots lay still.
7 No wonder you are greatly feared!
Who can stand before you when your anger explodes?
8 From heaven you sentenced your enemies;
the earth trembled and stood silent before you.
9 You stand up to judge those who do evil, O God,
and to rescue the oppressed of the earth. *Interlude*
10 Human defiance only enhances your glory,
for you use it as a weapon.
11 Make vows to the Lord your God, and keep them.
Let everyone bring tribute to the Awesome One.
12 For he breaks the pride of princes,
and the kings of the earth fear him.

Then all the people say the following praise:

Glory to the Father, and to the Son, and to the Holy Spirit, as it was in the beginning, is now, and will be forever. Amen.

Psalm 77

For Jeduthun, the choir director: A psalm of Asaph.

1 I cry out to God; yes, I shout.
 Oh, that God would listen to me!
2 When I was in deep trouble,
 I searched for the Lord.
All night long I prayed, with hands lifted toward heaven,
 but my soul was not comforted.
3 I think of God, and I moan,
 overwhelmed with longing for his help. *Interlude*
4 You don't let me sleep.
 I am too distressed even to pray!
5 I think of the good old days,
 long since ended,
6 when my nights were filled with joyful songs.
 I search my soul and ponder the difference now.
7 Has the Lord rejected me forever?
 Will he never again be kind to me?
8 Is his unfailing love gone forever?
 Have his promises permanently failed?
9 Has God forgotten to be gracious?
 Has he slammed the door on his compassion? *Interlude*
10 And I said, "This is my fate;
 the Most High has turned his hand against me."
11 But then I recall all you have done, O Lord;
 I remember your wonderful deeds of long ago.
12 They are constantly in my thoughts.
 I cannot stop thinking about your mighty works.
13 O God, your ways are holy.
 Is there any god as mighty as you?
14 You are the God of great wonders!
 You demonstrate your awesome power among the nations.
15 By your strong arm, you redeemed your people,
 the descendants of Jacob and Joseph. *Interlude*
16 When the Red Sea saw you, O God,
 its waters looked and trembled!
The sea quaked to its very depths.
17 **The clouds poured down rain;**

the thunder rumbled in the sky.
Your arrows of lightning flashed.
18 Your thunder roared from the whirlwind;
the lightning lit up the world!
The earth trembled and shook.
19 **Your road led through the sea,**
your pathway through the mighty waters —
a pathway no one knew was there!
20 You led your people along that road like a flock of sheep,
with Moses and Aaron as their shepherds.

Then all the people say the following praise:

Glory to the Father, and to the Son, and to the Holy Spirit, as it was in the beginning, is now, and will be forever. Amen.

Psalm 78:1–16

A psalm of Asaph.

1 O my people, listen to my instructions.
Open your ears to what I am saying,
2 for I will speak to you in a parable.
I will teach you hidden lessons from our past —
3 stories we have heard and known,
stories our ancestors handed down to us.
4 We will not hide these truths from our children;
we will tell the next generation
about the glorious deeds of the Lord,
about his power and his mighty wonders.
5 **For he issued his laws to Jacob;**
he gave his instructions to Israel.
He commanded our ancestors
to teach them to their children,
6 so the next generation might know them —
even the children not yet born —
and they in turn will teach their own children.
7 **So each generation should set its hope anew on God,**
not forgetting his glorious miracles
and obeying his commands.

8 **Then they will not be like their ancestors —**
stubborn, rebellious, and unfaithful,
refusing to give their hearts to God.
9 The warriors of Ephraim, though armed with bows,
turned their backs and fled on the day of battle.
10 They did not keep God's covenant
and refused to live by his instructions.
11 **They forgot what he had done —**
the great wonders he had shown them,
12 **the miracles he did for their ancestors**
on the plain of Zoan in the land of Egypt.
13 For he divided the sea and led them through,
making the water stand up like walls!
14 In the daytime he led them by a cloud,
and all night by a pillar of fire.
15 He split open the rocks in the wilderness
to give them water, as from a gushing spring.
16 He made streams pour from the rock,
making the waters flow down like a river!

Then all the people say the following praise:

Glory to the Father, and to the Son, and to the Holy Spirit, as it was in the beginning, is now, and will be forever. Amen.

Psalm 78:17–31

17 Yet they kept on sinning against him,
rebelling against the Most High in the desert.
18 They stubbornly tested God in their hearts,
demanding the foods they craved.
19 They even spoke against God himself, saying,
"God can't give us food in the wilderness.
20 Yes, he can strike a rock so water gushes out,
but he can't give his people bread and meat."
21 When the Lord heard them, he was furious.
The fire of his wrath burned against Jacob.
Yes, his anger rose against Israel,
22 **for they did not believe God**
or trust him to care for them.

23 But he commanded the skies to open;

he opened the doors of heaven.

24 He rained down manna for them to eat;

he gave them bread from heaven.

25 They ate the food of angels!

God gave them all they could hold.

26 He released the east wind in the heavens

and guided the south wind by his mighty power.

27 He rained down meat as thick as dust —

birds as plentiful as the sand on the seashore!

28 He caused the birds to fall within their camp

and all around their tents.

29 **The people ate their fill.**

He gave them what they craved.

30 **But before they satisfied their craving,**

while the meat was yet in their mouths,

31 **the anger of God rose against them,**

and he killed their strongest men.

He struck down the finest of Israel's young men.

Then all the people say the following praise:

Glory to the Father, and to the Son, and to the Holy Spirit, as it was in the beginning, is now, and will be forever. Amen.

Psalm 78:32–39

32 But in spite of this, the people kept sinning.

Despite his wonders, they refused to trust him.

33 So he ended their lives in failure,

their years in terror.

34 When God began killing them,

they finally sought him.

They repented and took God seriously.

35 **Then they remembered that God was their rock,**

that God Most High was their redeemer.

36 **But all they gave him was lip service;**

they lied to him with their tongues.

37 **Their hearts were not loyal to him.**

They did not keep his covenant.

38 **Yet he was merciful and forgave their sins**
  and did not destroy them all.
Many times he held back his anger
  and did not unleash his fury!
39 **For he remembered that they were merely mortal,**
  gone like a breath of wind that never returns.

Then all the people say the following praise:

Glory to the Father, and to the Son, and to the Holy Spirit, as it was in the beginning, is now, and will be forever. Amen.

Psalm 78:40–55

40 Oh, how often they rebelled against him in the wilderness
  and grieved his heart in that dry wasteland.
41 Again and again they tested God's patience
  and provoked the Holy One of Israel.
42 They did not remember his power
  and how he rescued them from their enemies.
43 They did not remember his miraculous signs in Egypt,
  his wonders on the plain of Zoan.
44 For he turned their rivers into blood,
  so no one could drink from the streams.
45 He sent vast swarms of flies to consume them
  and hordes of frogs to ruin them.
46 He gave their crops to caterpillars;
  their harvest was consumed by locusts.
47 He destroyed their grapevines with hail
  and shattered their sycamore-figs with sleet.
48 He abandoned their cattle to the hail,
  their livestock to bolts of lightning.
49 He loosed on them his fierce anger —
  all his fury, rage, and hostility.
He dispatched against them
  a band of destroying angels.
50 He turned his anger against them;
  he did not spare the Egyptians' lives
  but ravaged them with the plague.
51 He killed the oldest son in each Egyptian family,

the flower of youth throughout the land of Egypt.
52 But he led his own people like a flock of sheep,
guiding them safely through the wilderness.
53 He kept them safe so they were not afraid;
but the sea covered their enemies.
54 He brought them to the border of his holy land,
to this land of hills he had won for them.
55 He drove out the nations before them;
he gave them their inheritance by lot.
He settled the tribes of Israel into their homes.

Then all the people say the following praise:

Glory to the Father, and to the Son, and to the Holy Spirit, as it was in the beginning, is now, and will be forever. Amen.

Psalm 78:56–64

56 But they kept testing and rebelling against God Most High.
They did not obey his laws.
57 They turned back and were as faithless as their parents.
They were as undependable as a crooked bow.
58 They angered God by building shrines to other gods;
they made him jealous with their idols.
59 When God heard them, he was very angry,
and he completely rejected Israel.
60 Then he abandoned his dwelling at Shiloh,
the Tabernacle where he had lived among the people.
61 He allowed the Ark of his might to be captured;
he surrendered his glory into enemy hands.
62 He gave his people over to be butchered by the sword,
because he was so angry with his own people — his special possession.
63 Their young men were killed by fire;
their young women died before singing their wedding songs.
64 Their priests were slaughtered,
and their widows could not mourn their deaths.

Then all the people say the following praise:

Glory to the Father, and to the Son, and to the Holy Spirit, as it was in the beginning, is now, and will be forever. Amen.

Psalm 78:65–72

65 Then the Lord rose up as though waking from sleep,
  like a warrior aroused from a drunken stupor.
66 He routed his enemies
  and sent them to eternal shame.
67 But he rejected Joseph's descendants;
  he did not choose the tribe of Ephraim.
68 He chose instead the tribe of Judah,
  and Mount Zion, which he loved.
69 There he built his sanctuary as high as the heavens,
  as solid and enduring as the earth.
70 He chose his servant David,
  calling him from the sheep pens.
71 He took David from tending the ewes and lambs
  and made him the shepherd of Jacob's descendants —
  God's own people, Israel.
72 He cared for them with a true heart
  and led them with skillful hands.

Then all the people say the following praise:

Glory to the Father, and to the Son, and to the Holy Spirit, as it was in the beginning, is now, and will be forever. Amen.

Psalm 79

A psalm of Asaph.

1 O God, pagan nations have conquered your land,
  your special possession.
They have defiled your holy Temple
  and made Jerusalem a heap of ruins.
2 They have left the bodies of your servants
  as food for the birds of heaven.
The flesh of your godly ones
  has become food for the wild animals.

3 Blood has flowed like water all around Jerusalem;
no one is left to bury the dead.
**4 We are mocked by our neighbors,
an object of scorn and derision to those around us.**
5 O Lord, how long will you be angry with us? Forever?
How long will your jealousy burn like fire?
6 Pour out your wrath on the nations that refuse to acknowledge you
on kingdoms that do not call upon your name.
**7 For they have devoured your people Israel,
making the land a desolate wilderness.**
8 Do not hold us guilty for the sins of our ancestors!
**Let your compassion quickly meet our needs,
for we are on the brink of despair.**
9 Help us, O God of our salvation!
Help us for the glory of your name.
**Save us and forgive our sins
for the honor of your name.**
10 Why should pagan nations be allowed to scoff,
asking, "Where is their God?"
**Show us your vengeance against the nations,
for they have spilled the blood of your servants.**
11 Listen to the moaning of the prisoners.
**Demonstrate your great power
by saving those condemned to die.**
12 O Lord, pay back our neighbors seven times
for the scorn they have hurled at you.
**13 Then we your people, the sheep of your pasture,
will thank you forever and ever,
praising your greatness from generation to generation.**

Then all the people say the following praise:

**Glory to the Father, and to the Son, and to the Holy Spirit, as it was
in the beginning, is now, and will be forever. Amen.**

Psalm 80

*For the choir director: A psalm of Asaph, to be sung to the tune "Lilies of the
Covenant."*

1 Please listen, O Shepherd of Israel,
you who lead Joseph's descendants like a flock.

O God, enthroned above the cherubim,

display your radiant glory

2 to Ephraim, Benjamin, and Manasseh.

Show us your mighty power.

Come to rescue us!

3 **Turn us again to yourself, O God.**

Make your face shine down upon us.

Only then will we be saved.

4 O Lord God of Heaven's Armies,

how long will you be angry with our prayers?

5 You have fed us with sorrow

and made us drink tears by the bucketful.

6 **You have made us the scorn of neighboring nations.**

Our enemies treat us as a joke.

7 **Turn us again to yourself, O God of Heaven's Armies.**

Make your face shine down upon us.

Only then will we be saved.

8 You brought us from Egypt like a grapevine;

you drove away the pagan nations and transplanted us into your land.

9 You cleared the ground for us,

and we took root and filled the land.

10 Our shade covered the mountains;

our branches covered the mighty cedars.

11 We spread our branches west to the Mediterranean Sea;

our shoots spread east to the Euphrates River.

12 But now, why have you broken down our walls

so that all who pass by may steal our fruit?

13 The wild boar from the forest devours it,

and the wild animals feed on it.

14 Come back, we beg you, O God of Heaven's Armies.

Look down from heaven and see our plight.

Take care of this grapevine

15   that you yourself have planted,

this son you have raised for yourself.

16 For we are chopped up and burned by our enemies.

May they perish at the sight of your frown.

17 Strengthen the man you love,

the son of your choice.

18 Then we will never abandon you again.

Revive us so we can call on your name once more.
19 Turn us again to yourself, O Lord God of Heaven's Armies.
Make your face shine down upon us.
Only then will we be saved.

Then all the people say the following praise:

Glory to the Father, and to the Son, and to the Holy Spirit, as it was in the beginning, is now, and will be forever. Amen.

Psalm 81

For the choir director: A psalm of Asaph, to be accompanied by a stringed instrument.

1 Sing praises to God, our strength.
Sing to the God of Jacob.
2 Sing! Beat the tambourine.
Play the sweet lyre and the harp.
3 Blow the ram's horn at new moon,
and again at full moon to call a festival!
4 For this is required by the decrees of Israel;
it is a regulation of the God of Jacob.
5 He made it a law for Israel
when he attacked Egypt to set us free.
I heard an unknown voice say,
6 "Now I will take the load from your shoulders;
I will free your hands from their heavy tasks.
7 You cried to me in trouble, and I saved you;
I answered out of the thundercloud
and tested your faith when there was no water
at Meribah. *Interlude*
8 "Listen to me, O my people, while I give you stern warnings.
O Israel, if you would only listen to me!
9 You must never have a foreign god;
you must not bow down before a false god.
10 For it was I, the Lord your God,
who rescued you from the land of Egypt.
Open your mouth wide, and I will fill it with good things.
11 **"But no, my people wouldn't listen.**
Israel did not want me around.

12 **So I let them follow their own stubborn desires,**
living according to their own ideas.
13 **Oh, that my people would listen to me!**
Oh, that Israel would follow me, walking in my paths!
14 **How quickly I would then subdue their enemies!**
How soon my hands would be upon their foes!
15 **Those who hate the Lord would cringe before him;**
they would be doomed forever.
16 **But I would feed you with the finest wheat.**
I would satisfy you with wild honey from the rock."

Then all the people say the following praise:

Glory to the Father, and to the Son, and to the Holy Spirit, as it was in the beginning, is now, and will be forever. Amen.

Psalm 82

A psalm of Asaph.

1 God presides over heaven's court;
he pronounces judgment on the heavenly beings:
2 "How long will you hand down unjust decisions
by favoring the wicked? *Interlude*
3 "Give justice to the poor and the orphan;
uphold the rights of the oppressed and the destitute.
4 Rescue the poor and helpless;
deliver them from the grasp of evil people.
5 But these oppressors know nothing;
they are so ignorant!
They wander about in darkness,
while the whole world is shaken to the core.
6 I say, 'You are gods;
you are all children of the Most High.
7 But you will die like mere mortals
and fall like every other ruler.'"
8 Rise up, O God, and judge the earth,
for all the nations belong to you.

Then all the people say the following praise:

Glory to the Father, and to the Son, and to the Holy Spirit, as it was in the beginning, is now, and will be forever. Amen.

Psalm 83

A song. A psalm of Asaph.

1 O God, do not be silent!
Do not be deaf.
Do not be quiet, O God.
2 **Don't you hear the uproar of your enemies?**
Don't you see that your arrogant enemies are rising up?
3 **They devise crafty schemes against your people;**
they conspire against your precious ones.
4 **"Come," they say, "let us wipe out Israel as a nation.**
We will destroy the very memory of its existence."
5 **Yes, this was their unanimous decision.**
They signed a treaty as allies against you —
6 **these Edomites and Ishmaelites;**
Moabites and Hagrites;
7 **Gebalites, Ammonites, and Amalekites;**
and people from Philistia and Tyre.
8 **Assyria has joined them, too,**
and is allied with the descendants of Lot. *Interlude*
9 **Do to them as you did to the Midianites**
and as you did to Sisera and Jabin at the Kishon River.
10 They were destroyed at Endor,
and their decaying corpses fertilized the soil.
11 Let their mighty nobles die as Oreb and Zeeb did.
Let all their princes die like Zebah and Zalmunna,
12 for they said, "Let us seize for our own use
these pasturelands of God!"
13 **O my God, scatter them like tumbleweed,**
like chaff before the wind!
14 **As a fire burns a forest**
and as a flame sets mountains ablaze,
15 chase them with your fierce storm;
terrify them with your tempest.
16 Utterly disgrace them
until they submit to your name, O Lord.

17 **Let them be ashamed and terrified forever.**
Let them die in disgrace.
18 **Then they will learn that you alone are called the Lord,**
that you alone are the Most High,
supreme over all the earth.

Then all the people say the following praise:

Glory to the Father, and to the Son, and to the Holy Spirit, as it was in the beginning, is now, and will be forever. Amen.

Psalm 84

For the choir director: A psalm of the descendants of Korah, to be accompanied by a stringed instrument.

1 How lovely is your dwelling place,
O Lord of Heaven's Armies.
2 I long, yes, I faint with longing
to enter the courts of the Lord.
With my whole being, body and soul,
I will shout joyfully to the living God.
3 Even the sparrow finds a home,
and the swallow builds her nest and raises her young
at a place near your altar,
O Lord of Heaven's Armies, my King and my God!
4 **What joy for those who can live in your house,**
always singing your praises. *Interlude*
5 **What joy for those whose strength comes from the Lord,**
who have set their minds on a pilgrimage to Jerusalem.
6 **When they walk through the Valley of Weeping,**
it will become a place of refreshing springs.
The autumn rains will clothe it with blessings.
7 They will continue to grow stronger,
and each of them will appear before God in Jerusalem.
8 O Lord God of Heaven's Armies, hear my prayer.
Listen, O God of Jacob. *Interlude*
9 O God, look with favor upon the king, our shield!
Show favor to the one you have anointed.

10 A single day in your courts
  is better than a thousand anywhere else!
I would rather be a gatekeeper in the house of my God
  than live the good life in the homes of the wicked.
11 For the Lord God is our sun and our shield.
  He gives us grace and glory.
The Lord will withhold no good thing
  from those who do what is right.
12 **O Lord of Heaven's Armies,**
  what joy for those who trust in you.

Then all the people say the following praise:

**Glory to the Father, and to the Son, and to the Holy Spirit, as it was
in the beginning, is now, and will be forever. Amen.**

Psalm 85

For the choir director: A psalm of the descendants of Korah.

1 Lord, you poured out blessings on your land!
  You restored the fortunes of Israel.
2 You forgave the guilt of your people —
  yes, you covered all their sins. *Interlude*
3 You held back your fury.
  You kept back your blazing anger.
4 Now restore us again, O God of our salvation.
  Put aside your anger against us once more.
5 Will you be angry with us always?
  Will you prolong your wrath to all generations?
6 Won't you revive us again,
  so your people can rejoice in you?
7 Show us your unfailing love, O Lord,
  and grant us your salvation.
8 I listen carefully to what God the Lord is saying,
  for he speaks peace to his faithful people.
But let them not return to their foolish ways.
9 **Surely his salvation is near to those who fear him,**
  so our land will be filled with his glory.
10 **Unfailing love and truth have met together.**

Righteousness and peace have kissed!
11 **Truth springs up from the earth,**
and righteousness smiles down from heaven.
12 **Yes, the Lord pours down his blessings.**
Our land will yield its bountiful harvest.
13 **Righteousness goes as a herald before him,**
preparing the way for his steps.

Then all the people say the following praise:

Glory to the Father, and to the Son, and to the Holy Spirit, as it was
in the beginning, is now, and will be forever. Amen.

Psalm 86

A prayer of David.

1 Bend down, O Lord, and hear my prayer;
answer me, for I need your help.
2 Protect me, for I am devoted to you.
Save me, for I serve you and trust you.
You are my God.
3 **Be merciful to me, O Lord,**
for I am calling on you constantly.
4 **Give me happiness, O Lord,**
for I give myself to you.
5 **O Lord, you are so good, so ready to forgive,**
so full of unfailing love for all who ask for your help.
6 **Listen closely to my prayer, O Lord;**
hear my urgent cry.
7 **I will call to you whenever I'm in trouble,**
and you will answer me.
8 **No pagan god is like you, O Lord.**
None can do what you do!
9 **All the nations you made**
will come and bow before you, Lord;
they will praise your holy name.
10 **For you are great and perform wonderful deeds.**
You alone are God.
11 **Teach me your ways, O Lord,**

that I may live according to your truth!
Grant me purity of heart,
so that I may honor you.
12 **With all my heart I will praise you, O Lord my God.**
I will give glory to your name forever,
13 **for your love for me is very great.**
You have rescued me from the depths of death.
14 **O God, insolent people rise up against me;**
a violent gang is trying to kill me.
You mean nothing to them.
15 But you, O Lord,
are a God of compassion and mercy,
slow to get angry
and filled with unfailing love and faithfulness.
16 Look down and have mercy on me.
Give your strength to your servant;
save me, the son of your servant.
17 **Send me a sign of your favor.**
Then those who hate me will be put to shame,
for you, O Lord, help and comfort me.

Then all the people say the following praise:

Glory to the Father, and to the Son, and to the Holy Spirit, as it was in the beginning, is now, and will be forever. Amen.

Psalm 87

A song. A psalm of the descendants of Korah.

1 On the holy mountain
stands the city founded by the Lord.
2 **He loves the city of Jerusalem**
more than any other city in Israel.
3 O city of God,
what glorious things are said of you! *Interlude*
4 I will count Egypt and Babylon among those who know me —
also Philistia and Tyre, and even distant Ethiopia.
They have all become citizens of Jerusalem!
5 **Regarding Jerusalem it will be said,**

"Everyone enjoys the rights of citizenship there."
And the Most High will personally bless this city.
6 When the Lord registers the nations, he will say,
"They have all become citizens of Jerusalem." *Interlude*
7 The people will play flutes and sing,
"The source of my life springs from Jerusalem!"

Then all the people say the following praise:

Glory to the Father, and to the Son, and to the Holy Spirit, as it was in the beginning, is now, and will be forever. Amen.

Psalm 88

For the choir director: A psalm of the descendants of Korah. A song to be sung to the tune "The Suffering of Affliction." A psalm of Heman the Ezrahite.

1 O Lord, God of my salvation,
I cry out to you by day.
I come to you at night.
2 **Now hear my prayer;**
listen to my cry.
3 **For my life is full of troubles,**
and death draws near.
4 **I am as good as dead,**
like a strong man with no strength left.
5 **They have left me among the dead,**
and I lie like a corpse in a grave.
I am forgotten,
cut off from your care.
6 **You have thrown me into the lowest pit,**
into the darkest depths.
7 **Your anger weighs me down;**
with wave after wave you have engulfed me. *Interlude*
8 You have driven my friends away
by making me repulsive to them.
I am in a trap with no way of escape.
9 **My eyes are blinded by my tears.**
Each day I beg for your help, O Lord;
I lift my hands to you for mercy.

10 Are your wonderful deeds of any use to the dead?

Do the dead rise up and praise you? *Interlude*

11 Can those in the grave declare your unfailing love?

Can they proclaim your faithfulness in the place of destruction?

12 Can the darkness speak of your wonderful deeds?

Can anyone in the land of forgetfulness talk about your righteousness?

13 O Lord, I cry out to you.

I will keep on pleading day by day.

14 O Lord, why do you reject me?

Why do you turn your face from me?

15 I have been sick and close to death since my youth.

I stand helpless and desperate before your terrors.

16 Your fierce anger has overwhelmed me.

Your terrors have paralyzed me.

17 They swirl around me like floodwaters all day long.

They have engulfed me completely.

18 You have taken away my companions and loved ones.

Darkness is my closest friend.

Then all the people say the following praise:

Glory to the Father, and to the Son, and to the Holy Spirit, as it was in the beginning, is now, and will be forever. Amen.

Psalm 89:1–14

A psalm of Ethan the Ezrahite.

1 I will sing of the Lord's unfailing love forever!

Young and old will hear of your faithfulness.

2 Your unfailing love will last forever.

Your faithfulness is as enduring as the heavens.

3 The Lord said, "I have made a covenant with David, my chosen servant.

I have sworn this oath to him:

4 'I will establish your descendants as kings forever;

they will sit on your throne from now until eternity.'" *Interlude*

5 All heaven will praise your great wonders, Lord;

myriads of angels will praise you for your faithfulness.

6 For who in all of heaven can compare with the Lord?
 What mightiest angel is anything like the Lord?
7 The highest angelic powers stand in awe of God.
 He is far more awesome than all who surround his throne.
8 O Lord God of Heaven's Armies!
 Where is there anyone as mighty as you, O Lord?
 You are entirely faithful.
9 **You rule the oceans.**
 You subdue their storm-tossed waves.
10 **You crushed the great sea monster.**
 You scattered your enemies with your mighty arm.
11 **The heavens are yours, and the earth is yours;**
 everything in the world is yours — you created it all.
12 **You created north and south.**
 Mount Tabor and Mount Hermon praise your name.
13 **Powerful is your arm!**
 Strong is your hand!
 Your right hand is lifted high in glorious strength.
14 Righteousness and justice are the foundation of your throne.
 Unfailing love and truth walk before you as attendants.

Then all the people say the following praise:

Glory to the Father, and to the Son, and to the Holy Spirit, as it was in the beginning, is now, and will be forever. Amen.

Psalm 89:15–37

15 Happy are those who hear the joyful call to worship,
 for they will walk in the light of your presence, Lord.
16 They rejoice all day long in your wonderful reputation.
 They exult in your righteousness.
17 You are their glorious strength.
 It pleases you to make us strong.
18 Yes, our protection comes from the Lord,
 and he, the Holy One of Israel, has given us our king.
19 Long ago you spoke in a vision to your faithful people.
You said, "I have raised up a warrior.
 I have selected him from the common people to be king.
20 **I have found my servant David.**

I have anointed him with my holy oil.
21 **I will steady him with my hand;**
with my powerful arm I will make him strong.
22 **His enemies will not defeat him,**
nor will the wicked overpower him.
23 **I will beat down his adversaries before him**
and destroy those who hate him.
24 My faithfulness and unfailing love will be with him,
and by my authority he will grow in power.
25 I will extend his rule over the sea,
his dominion over the rivers.
26 And he will call out to me, 'You are my Father,
my God, and the Rock of my salvation.'
27 I will make him my firstborn son,
the mightiest king on earth.
28 I will love him and be kind to him forever;
my covenant with him will never end.
29 I will preserve an heir for him;
his throne will be as endless as the days of heaven.
30 But if his descendants forsake my instructions
and fail to obey my regulations,
31 if they do not obey my decrees
and fail to keep my commands,
32 **then I will punish their sin with the rod,**
and their disobedience with beating.
33 **But I will never stop loving him**
nor fail to keep my promise to him.
34 No, I will not break my covenant;
I will not take back a single word I said.
35 I have sworn an oath to David,
and in my holiness I cannot lie:
36 His dynasty will go on forever;
his kingdom will endure as the sun.
37 It will be as eternal as the moon,
my faithful witness in the sky!" *Interlude*

Then all the people say the following praise:

Glory to the Father, and to the Son, and to the Holy Spirit, as it was in the beginning, is now, and will be forever. Amen.

38 But now you have rejected him and cast him off.
You are angry with your anointed king.
39 You have renounced your covenant with him;
you have thrown his crown in the dust.
40 You have broken down the walls protecting him
and ruined every fort defending him.
41 **Everyone who comes along has robbed him,**
and he has become a joke to his neighbors.
42 **You have strengthened his enemies**
and made them all rejoice.
43 You have made his sword useless
and refused to help him in battle.
44 **You have ended his splendor**
and overturned his throne.
45 You have made him old before his time
and publicly disgraced him. *Interlude*
46 **O Lord, how long will this go on?**
Will you hide yourself forever?
How long will your anger burn like fire?
47 Remember how short my life is,
how empty and futile this human existence!
48 No one can live forever; all will die.
No one can escape the power of the grave. *Interlude*
49 Lord, where is your unfailing love?
You promised it to David with a faithful pledge.
50 Consider, Lord, how your servants are disgraced!
I carry in my heart the insults of so many people.
51 Your enemies have mocked me, O Lord;
they mock your anointed king wherever he goes.
52 Praise the Lord forever!
Amen and amen!

Then all the people say the following praise:

Glory to the Father, and to the Son, and to the Holy Spirit, as it was in the beginning, is now, and will be forever. Amen.

Book Four

(Psalms 90–106)

Psalm 90

A prayer of Moses, the man of God.

1 Lord, through all the generations
   you have been our home!
2 **Before the mountains were born,**
   before you gave birth to the earth and the world,
   from beginning to end, you are God.
3 You turn people back to dust, saying,
   "Return to dust, you mortals!"
4 For you, a thousand years are as a passing day,
   as brief as a few night hours.
5 You sweep people away like dreams that disappear.
   They are like grass that springs up in the morning.
6 In the morning it blooms and flourishes,
   but by evening it is dry and withered.
7 We wither beneath your anger;
   we are overwhelmed by your fury.
8 You spread out our sins before you —
   our secret sins — and you see them all.
9 We live our lives beneath your wrath,
   ending our years with a groan.
10 Seventy years are given to us!
   Some even live to eighty.
But even the best years are filled with pain and trouble;
   soon they disappear, and we fly away.
11 Who can comprehend the power of your anger?

Your wrath is as awesome as the fear you deserve.
12 Teach us to realize the brevity of life,
  so that we may grow in wisdom.
13 O Lord, come back to us!
  How long will you delay?
  Take pity on your servants!
14 **Satisfy us each morning with your unfailing love,**
  so we may sing for joy to the end of our lives.
15 **Give us gladness in proportion to our former misery!**
  Replace the evil years with good.
16 **Let us, your servants, see you work again;**
  let our children see your glory.
17 **And may the Lord our God show us his approval**
  and make our efforts successful.
  Yes, make our efforts successful!

Then all the people say the following praise:

Glory to the Father, and to the Son, and to the Holy Spirit, as it was in the beginning, is now, and will be forever. Amen.

Psalm 91

1 Those who live in the shelter of the Most High
  will find rest in the shadow of the Almighty.
2 **This I declare about the Lord:**
  He alone is my refuge, my place of safety;
  he is my God, and I trust him.
3 For he will rescue you from every trap
  and protect you from deadly disease.
4 **He will cover you with his feathers.**
  He will shelter you with his wings.
  His faithful promises are your armor and protection.
5 Do not be afraid of the terrors of the night,
  nor the arrow that flies in the day.
6 Do not dread the disease that stalks in darkness,
  nor the disaster that strikes at midday.
7 Though a thousand fall at your side,
  though ten thousand are dying around you,
  these evils will not touch you.

242

8 **Just open your eyes,**
and see how the wicked are punished.
9 **If you make the Lord your refuge,**
if you make the Most High your shelter,
10 **no evil will conquer you;**
no plague will come near your home.
11 **For he will order his angels**
to protect you wherever you go.
12 They will hold you up with their hands
so you won't even hurt your foot on a stone.
13 **You will trample upon lions and cobras;**
you will crush fierce lions and serpents under your feet!
14 **The Lord says, "I will rescue those who love me.**
I will protect those who trust in my name.
15 **When they call on me, I will answer;**
I will be with them in trouble.
I will rescue and honor them.
16 I will reward them with a long life
and give them my salvation."

Then all the people say the following praise:

Glory to the Father, and to the Son, and to the Holy Spirit, as it was
in the beginning, is now, and will be forever. Amen.

Psalm 92

A psalm. A song to be sung on the Sabbath Day.

1 It is good to give thanks to the Lord,
to sing praises to the Most High.
2 It is good to proclaim your unfailing love in the morning,
your faithfulness in the evening,
3 accompanied by a ten-stringed instrument, a harp,
and the melody of a lyre.
4 You thrill me, Lord, with all you have done for me!
I sing for joy because of what you have done.
5 O Lord, what great works you do!
And how deep are your thoughts.
6 Only a simpleton would not know,

and only a fool would not understand this:
7 Though the wicked sprout like weeds
and evildoers flourish,
they will be destroyed forever.
8 But you, O Lord, will be exalted forever.
9 **Your enemies, Lord, will surely perish;**
all evildoers will be scattered.
10 **But you have made me as strong as a wild ox.**
You have anointed me with the finest oil.
11 **My eyes have seen the downfall of my enemies;**
my ears have heard the defeat of my wicked opponents.
12 **But the godly will flourish like palm trees**
and grow strong like the cedars of Lebanon.
13 For they are transplanted to the Lord's own house.
They flourish in the courts of our God.
14 Even in old age they will still produce fruit;
they will remain vital and green.
15 They will declare, "The Lord is just!
He is my rock!
There is no evil in him!"

Then all the people say the following praise:

Glory to the Father, and to the Son, and to the Holy Spirit, as it was in the beginning, is now, and will be forever. Amen.

Psalm 93

1 The Lord is king! He is robed in majesty.
Indeed, the Lord is robed in majesty and armed with strength.
The world stands firm
and cannot be shaken.
2 **Your throne, O Lord, has stood from time immemorial.**
You yourself are from the everlasting past.
3 **The floods have risen up, O Lord.**
The floods have roared like thunder;
the floods have lifted their pounding waves.
4 But mightier than the violent raging of the seas,
mightier than the breakers on the shore —
the Lord above is mightier than these!

5 **Your royal laws cannot be changed.**
  Your reign, O Lord, is holy forever and ever.

Then all the people say the following praise:

Glory to the Father, and to the Son, and to the Holy Spirit, as it was in the beginning, is now, and will be forever. Amen.

Psalm 94

1 O Lord, the God of vengeance,
  O God of vengeance, let your glorious justice shine forth!
2 Arise, O Judge of the earth.
  Give the proud what they deserve.
3 How long, O Lord?
  How long will the wicked be allowed to gloat?
4 How long will they speak with arrogance?
  How long will these evil people boast?
5 They crush your people, Lord,
  hurting those you claim as your own.
6 They kill widows and foreigners
  and murder orphans.
7 **"The Lord isn't looking," they say,**
  "and besides, the God of Israel doesn't care."
8 **Think again, you fools!**
  When will you finally catch on?
9 **Is he deaf — the one who made your ears?**
  Is he blind — the one who formed your eyes?
10 **He punishes the nations — won't he also punish you?**
  He knows everything — doesn't he also know what you are doing?
11 **The Lord knows people's thoughts;**
  he knows they are worthless!
12 **Joyful are those you discipline, Lord,**
  those you teach with your instructions.
13 **You give them relief from troubled times**
  until a pit is dug to capture the wicked.
14 The Lord will not reject his people;
  he will not abandon his special possession.
15 Judgment will again be founded on justice,
  and those with virtuous hearts will pursue it.

16 Who will protect me from the wicked?
Who will stand up for me against evildoers?
17 Unless the Lord had helped me,
I would soon have settled in the silence of the grave.
18 I cried out, "I am slipping!"
but your unfailing love, O Lord, supported me.
19 When doubts filled my mind,
your comfort gave me renewed hope and cheer.
20 Can unjust leaders claim that God is on their side —
leaders whose decrees permit injustice?
21 They gang up against the righteous
and condemn the innocent to death.
22 **But the Lord is my fortress;**
my God is the mighty rock where I hide.
23 **God will turn the sins of evil people back on them.**
He will destroy them for their sins.
The Lord our God will destroy them.

Then all the people say the following praise:

Glory to the Father, and to the Son, and to the Holy Spirit, as it was in the beginning, is now, and will be forever. Amen.

Psalm 95

1 Come, let us sing to the Lord!
Let us shout joyfully to the Rock of our salvation.
2 Let us come to him with thanksgiving.
Let us sing psalms of praise to him.
3 For the Lord is a great God,
a great King above all gods.
4 He holds in his hands the depths of the earth
and the mightiest mountains.
5 **The sea belongs to him, for he made it.**
His hands formed the dry land, too.
6 **Come, let us worship and bow down.**
Let us kneel before the Lord our maker,
7 **for he is our God.**
We are the people he watches over,
the flock under his care.

If only you would listen to his voice today!
8 **The Lord says, "Don't harden your hearts as Israel did at Meribah,**
as they did at Massah in the wilderness.
9 **For there your ancestors tested and tried my patience,**
even though they saw everything I did.
10 **For forty years I was angry with them, and I said,**
'They are a people whose hearts turn away from me.
They refuse to do what I tell them.'
11 So in my anger I took an oath:
'They will never enter my place of rest.'"

Then all the people say the following praise:

Glory to the Father, and to the Son, and to the Holy Spirit, as it was in the beginning, is now, and will be forever. Amen.

Psalm 96

1 Sing a new song to the Lord!
Let the whole earth sing to the Lord!
2 Sing to the Lord; praise his name.
Each day proclaim the good news that he saves.
3 Publish his glorious deeds among the nations.
Tell everyone about the amazing things he does.
4 Great is the Lord! He is most worthy of praise!
He is to be feared above all gods.
5 The gods of other nations are mere idols,
but the Lord made the heavens!
6 Honor and majesty surround him;
strength and beauty fill his sanctuary.
7 O nations of the world, recognize the Lord;
recognize that the Lord is glorious and strong.
8 Give to the Lord the glory he deserves!
Bring your offering and come into his courts.
9 Worship the Lord in all his holy splendor.
Let all the earth tremble before him.
10 Tell all the nations, "The Lord reigns!"
The world stands firm and cannot be shaken.
He will judge all peoples fairly.

11 **Let the heavens be glad, and the earth rejoice!**
Let the sea and everything in it shout his praise!
12 **Let the fields and their crops burst out with joy!**
Let the trees of the forest sing for joy
13 before the Lord, for he is coming!
He is coming to judge the earth.
He will judge the world with justice,
and the nations with his truth.

Then all the people say the following praise:

Glory to the Father, and to the Son, and to the Holy Spirit, as it was in the beginning, is now, and will be forever. Amen.

Psalm 97

1 The Lord is king!
Let the earth rejoice!
Let the farthest coastlands be glad.
2 **Dark clouds surround him.**
Righteousness and justice are the foundation of his throne.
3 **Fire spreads ahead of him**
and burns up all his foes.
4 His lightning flashes out across the world.
The earth sees and trembles.
5 The mountains melt like wax before the Lord,
before the Lord of all the earth.
6 The heavens proclaim his righteousness;
every nation sees his glory.
7 Those who worship idols are disgraced —
all who brag about their worthless gods —
for every god must bow to him.
8 **Jerusalem has heard and rejoiced,**
and all the towns of Judah are glad
because of your justice, O Lord!
9 **For you, O Lord, are supreme over all the earth;**
you are exalted far above all gods.
10 **You who love the Lord, hate evil!**
He protects the lives of his godly people
and rescues them from the power of the wicked.

11 **Light shines on the godly,**
and joy on those whose hearts are right.
12 **May all who are godly rejoice in the Lord**
and praise his holy name!

Then all the people say the following praise:

Glory to the Father, and to the Son, and to the Holy Spirit, as it was
in the beginning, is now, and will be forever. Amen.

Psalm 98

A psalm.

1 Sing a new song to the Lord,
  for he has done wonderful deeds.
His right hand has won a mighty victory;
  his holy arm has shown his saving power!
2 The Lord has announced his victory
  and has revealed his righteousness to every nation!
3 **He has remembered his promise to love and be faithful to**
Israel.
  The ends of the earth have seen the victory of our God.
4 **Shout to the Lord, all the earth;**
  break out in praise and sing for joy!
5 **Sing your praise to the Lord with the harp,**
  with the harp and melodious song,
6 **with trumpets and the sound of the ram's horn.**
  Make a joyful symphony before the Lord, the King!
7 **Let the sea and everything in it shout his praise!**
  Let the earth and all living things join in.
8 **Let the rivers clap their hands in glee!**
  Let the hills sing out their songs of joy
9 before the Lord,
  for he is coming to judge the earth.
He will judge the world with justice,
  and the nations with fairness.

Then all the people say the following praise:

Glory to the Father, and to the Son, and to the Holy Spirit, as it was in the beginning, is now, and will be forever. Amen.

Psalm 99

1 The Lord is king!
Let the nations tremble!
He sits on his throne between the cherubim.
Let the whole earth quake!
2 The Lord sits in majesty in Jerusalem,
exalted above all the nations.
3 Let them praise your great and awesome name.
Your name is holy!
4 Mighty King, lover of justice,
you have established fairness.
You have acted with justice
and righteousness throughout Israel.
5 **Exalt the Lord our God!**
Bow low before his feet, for he is holy!
6 **Moses and Aaron were among his priests;**
Samuel also called on his name.
They cried to the Lord for help,
and he answered them.
7 **He spoke to Israel from the pillar of cloud,**
and they followed the laws and decrees he gave them.
8 **O Lord our God, you answered them.**
You were a forgiving God to them,
but you punished them when they went wrong.
9 Exalt the Lord our God,
and worship at his holy mountain in Jerusalem,
for the Lord our God is holy!

Then all the people say the following praise:

Glory to the Father, and to the Son, and to the Holy Spirit, as it was in the beginning, is now, and will be forever. Amen.

Psalm 100

A psalm of thanksgiving.

1 Shout with joy to the Lord, all the earth!
2 **Worship the Lord with gladness.**
  Come before him, singing with joy.
3 **Acknowledge that the Lord is God!**
  He made us, and we are his.
  We are his people, the sheep of his pasture.
4 Enter his gates with thanksgiving;
  go into his courts with praise.
  Give thanks to him and praise his name.
5 **For the Lord is good.**
  His unfailing love continues forever,
  and his faithfulness continues to each generation.

Psalm 101

A psalm of David.

1 I will sing of your love and justice, Lord.
  I will praise you with songs.
2 I will be careful to live a blameless life —
  when will you come to help me?
  I will lead a life of integrity
  in my own home.
3 **I will refuse to look at**
  anything vile and vulgar.
  I hate all who deal crookedly;
  I will have nothing to do with them.
4 I will reject perverse ideas
  and stay away from every evil.
5 **I will not tolerate people who slander their neighbors.**
  I will not endure conceit and pride.
6 **I will search for faithful people**
  to be my companions.
  Only those who are above reproach
  will be allowed to serve me.
7 **I will not allow deceivers to serve in my house,**

and liars will not stay in my presence.
8 **My daily task will be to ferret out the wicked
and free the city of the Lord from their grip.**

Then all the people say the following praise:

**Glory to the Father, and to the Son, and to the Holy Spirit, as it was
in the beginning, is now, and will be forever. Amen.**

Psalm 102:1–17

A prayer of one overwhelmed with trouble, pouring out problems before the Lord.

1 Lord, hear my prayer!
  Listen to my plea!
2 Don't turn away from me
  in my time of distress.
Bend down to listen,
  and answer me quickly when I call to you.
3 **For my days disappear like smoke,**
  and my bones burn like red-hot coals.
4 **My heart is sick, withered like grass,**
  and I have lost my appetite.
5 **Because of my groaning,**
  I am reduced to skin and bones.
6 **I am like an owl in the desert,**
  like a little owl in a far-off wilderness.
7 **I lie awake,**
  lonely as a solitary bird on the roof.
8 **My enemies taunt me day after day.**
  They mock and curse me.
9 **I eat ashes for food.**
  My tears run down into my drink
10 because of your anger and wrath.
  For you have picked me up and thrown me out.
11 My life passes as swiftly as the evening shadows.
  I am withering away like grass.
12 But you, O Lord, will sit on your throne forever.
  Your fame will endure to every generation.
13 You will arise and have mercy on Jerusalem —

and now is the time to pity her,
now is the time you promised to help.
14 **For your people love every stone in her walls**
and cherish even the dust in her streets.
15 Then the nations will tremble before the Lord.
The kings of the earth will tremble before his glory.
16 For the Lord will rebuild Jerusalem.
He will appear in his glory.
17 He will listen to the prayers of the destitute.
He will not reject their pleas.

Then all the people say the following praise:

Glory to the Father, and to the Son, and to the Holy Spirit, as it was
in the beginning, is now, and will be forever. Amen.

Psalm 102:18–28

18 Let this be recorded for future generations,
so that a people not yet born will praise the Lord.
19 Tell them the Lord looked down
from his heavenly sanctuary.
He looked down to earth from heaven
20 **to hear the groans of the prisoners,**
to release those condemned to die.
21 **And so the Lord's fame will be celebrated in Zion,**
his praises in Jerusalem,
22 **when multitudes gather together**
and kingdoms come to worship the Lord.
23 He broke my strength in midlife,
cutting short my days.
24 But I cried to him, "O my God, who lives forever,
don't take my life while I am so young!
25 Long ago you laid the foundation of the earth
and made the heavens with your hands.
26 **They will perish, but you remain forever;**
they will wear out like old clothing.
You will change them like a garment
and discard them.

27 But you are always the same;
  you will live forever.
28 The children of your people
  will live in security.
**Their children's children
  will thrive in your presence."**

Then all the people say the following praise:

**Glory to the Father, and to the Son, and to the Holy Spirit, as it was
in the beginning, is now, and will be forever. Amen.**

Psalm 103

A psalm of David.

1 Let all that I am praise the Lord;
  with my whole heart, I will praise his holy name.
2 Let all that I am praise the Lord;
  may I never forget the good things he does for me.
3 He forgives all my sins
  and heals all my diseases.
4 **He redeems me from death
  and crowns me with love and tender mercies.**
5 He fills my life with good things.
  My youth is renewed like the eagle's!
6 The Lord gives righteousness
  and justice to all who are treated unfairly.
7 **He revealed his character to Moses
  and his deeds to the people of Israel.**
8 The Lord is compassionate and merciful,
  slow to get angry and filled with unfailing love.
9 He will not constantly accuse us,
  nor remain angry forever.
10 He does not punish us for all our sins;
  he does not deal harshly with us, as we deserve.
11 For his unfailing love toward those who fear him
  is as great as the height of the heavens above the earth.
12 **He has removed our sins as far from us
  as the east is from the west.**

13 The Lord is like a father to his children,
  tender and compassionate to those who fear him.
14 For he knows how weak we are;
  he remembers we are only dust.
15 Our days on earth are like grass;
  like wildflowers, we bloom and die.
16 The wind blows, and we are gone —
  as though we had never been here.
17 But the love of the Lord remains forever
  with those who fear him.
His salvation extends to the children's children
18   **of those who are faithful to his covenant,**
  of those who obey his commandments!
19 **The Lord has made the heavens his throne;**
  from there he rules over everything.
20 **Praise the Lord, you angels,**
  you mighty ones who carry out his plans,
  listening for each of his commands.
21 Yes, praise the Lord, you armies of angels
  who serve him and do his will!
22 **Praise the Lord, everything he has created,**
  everything in all his kingdom.
Let all that I am praise the Lord.

Then all the people say the following praise:

Glory to the Father, and to the Son, and to the Holy Spirit, as it was in the beginning, is now, and will be forever. Amen.

Psalm 104:1–18

1 Let all that I am praise the Lord.
O Lord my God, how great you are!
  You are robed with honor and majesty.
2   **You are dressed in a robe of light.**
You stretch out the starry curtain of the heavens;
3   **you lay out the rafters of your home in the rain clouds.**
You make the clouds your chariot;
  you ride upon the wings of the wind.

4 The winds are your messengers;
  flames of fire are your servants.
5 You placed the world on its foundation
  so it would never be moved.
6 You clothed the earth with floods of water,
  water that covered even the mountains.
7 At your command, the water fled;
  at the sound of your thunder, it hurried away.
8 Mountains rose and valleys sank
  to the levels you decreed.
9 **Then you set a firm boundary for the seas,**
  so they would never again cover the earth.
10 **You make springs pour water into the ravines,**
  so streams gush down from the mountains.
11 **They provide water for all the animals,**
  and the wild donkeys quench their thirst.
12 **The birds nest beside the streams**
  and sing among the branches of the trees.
13 You send rain on the mountains from your heavenly home,
  and you fill the earth with the fruit of your labor.
14 You cause grass to grow for the livestock
  and plants for people to use.
You allow them to produce food from the earth —
15 wine to make them glad,
olive oil to soothe their skin,
  and bread to give them strength.
16 **The trees of the Lord are well cared for —**
  the cedars of Lebanon that he planted.
17 **There the birds make their nests,**
  and the storks make their homes in the cypresses.
18 **High in the mountains live the wild goats,**
  and the rocks form a refuge for the hyraxes.

Then all the people say the following praise:

Glory to the Father, and to the Son, and to the Holy Spirit, as it was in the beginning, is now, and will be forever. Amen.

Psalm 104:19–35

19 You made the moon to mark the seasons,
and the sun knows when to set.
20 You send the darkness, and it becomes night,
when all the forest animals prowl about.
21 Then the young lions roar for their prey,
stalking the food provided by God.
22 At dawn they slink back
into their dens to rest.
23 **Then people go off to their work,**
where they labor until evening.
24 **O Lord, what a variety of things you have made!**
In wisdom you have made them all.
The earth is full of your creatures.
25 Here is the ocean, vast and wide,
teeming with life of every kind,
both large and small.
26 **See the ships sailing along,**
and Leviathan, which you made to play in the sea.
27 **They all depend on you**
to give them food as they need it.
28 When you supply it, they gather it.
You open your hand to feed them,
and they are richly satisfied.
29 **But if you turn away from them, they panic.**
When you take away their breath,
they die and turn again to dust.
30 When you give them your breath, life is created,
and you renew the face of the earth.
31 May the glory of the Lord continue forever!
The Lord takes pleasure in all he has made!
32 The earth trembles at his glance;
the mountains smoke at his touch.
33 I will sing to the Lord as long as I live.
I will praise my God to my last breath!
34 May all my thoughts be pleasing to him,
for I rejoice in the Lord.
35 Let all sinners vanish from the face of the earth;
let the wicked disappear forever.

Let all that I am praise the Lord.
Praise the Lord!

Then all the people say the following praise:

Glory to the Father, and to the Son, and to the Holy Spirit, as it was in the beginning, is now, and will be forever. Amen.

Psalm 105:1–15

1 Give thanks to the Lord and proclaim his greatness.
Let the whole world know what he has done.
2 Sing to him; yes, sing his praises.
Tell everyone about his wonderful deeds.
3 Exult in his holy name;
rejoice, you who worship the Lord.
4 Search for the Lord and for his strength;
continually seek him.
5 Remember the wonders he has performed,
his miracles, and the rulings he has given,
6 you children of his servant Abraham,
you descendants of Jacob, his chosen ones.
7 He is the Lord our God.
His justice is seen throughout the land.
8 He always stands by his covenant —
the commitment he made to a thousand generations.
9 This is the covenant he made with Abraham
and the oath he swore to Isaac.
10 **He confirmed it to Jacob as a decree,**
and to the people of Israel as a never-ending covenant:
11 **"I will give you the land of Canaan**
as your special possession."
12 He said this when they were few in number,
a tiny group of strangers in Canaan.
13 They wandered from nation to nation,
from one kingdom to another.
14 Yet he did not let anyone oppress them.
He warned kings on their behalf:
15 "Do not touch my chosen people,
and do not hurt my prophets."

Then all the people say the following praise:

Glory to the Father, and to the Son, and to the Holy Spirit, as it was in the beginning, is now, and will be forever. Amen.

Psalm 105:16–25

16 He called for a famine on the land of Canaan,
  cutting off its food supply.
17 Then he sent someone to Egypt ahead of them —
  Joseph, who was sold as a slave.
18 They bruised his feet with fetters
  and placed his neck in an iron collar.
19 **Until the time came to fulfill his dreams,**
  the Lord tested Joseph's character.
20 **Then Pharaoh sent for him and set him free;**
  the ruler of the nation opened his prison door.
21 **Joseph was put in charge of all the king's household;**
  he became ruler over all the king's possessions.
22 **He could instruct the king's aides as he pleased**
  and teach the king's advisers.
23 Then Israel arrived in Egypt;
  Jacob lived as a foreigner in the land of Ham.
24 And the Lord multiplied the people of Israel
  until they became too mighty for their enemies.
25 **Then he turned the Egyptians against the Israelites,**
  and they plotted against the Lord's servants.

Then all the people say the following praise:

Glory to the Father, and to the Son, and to the Holy Spirit, as it was in the beginning, is now, and will be forever. Amen.

Psalm 105:26–45

26 But the Lord sent his servant Moses,
  along with Aaron, whom he had chosen.
27 They performed miraculous signs among the Egyptians,
  and wonders in the land of Ham.

28 The Lord blanketed Egypt in darkness,
  for they had defied his commands to let his people go.
29 He turned their water into blood,
  poisoning all the fish.
30 Then frogs overran the land
  and even invaded the king's bedrooms.
31 When the Lord spoke, flies descended on the Egyptians,
  and gnats swarmed across Egypt.
32 He sent them hail instead of rain,
  and lightning flashed over the land.
33 He ruined their grapevines and fig trees
  and shattered all the trees.
34 He spoke, and hordes of locusts came —
  young locusts beyond number.
35 They ate up everything green in the land,
  destroying all the crops in their fields.
36 Then he killed the oldest son in each Egyptian home,
  the pride and joy of each family.
37 The Lord brought his people out of Egypt, loaded with silver and gold;
  and not one among the tribes of Israel even stumbled.
38 Egypt was glad when they were gone,
  for they feared them greatly.
39 The Lord spread a cloud above them as a covering
  and gave them a great fire to light the darkness.
40 They asked for meat, and he sent them quail;
  he satisfied their hunger with manna — bread from heaven.
41 He split open a rock, and water gushed out
  to form a river through the dry wasteland.
42 For he remembered his sacred promise
  to his servant Abraham.
43 So he brought his people out of Egypt with joy,
  his chosen ones with rejoicing.
44 He gave his people the lands of pagan nations,
  and they harvested crops that others had planted.
45 All this happened so they would follow his decrees
  and obey his instructions.
Praise the Lord!

Then all the people say the following praise:

Glory to the Father, and to the Son, and to the Holy Spirit, as it was in the beginning, is now, and will be forever. Amen.

Psalm 106:1–11

1 Praise the Lord!
Give thanks to the Lord, for he is good!
  His faithful love endures forever.
2 **Who can list the glorious miracles of the Lord?**
  Who can ever praise him enough?
3 **There is joy for those who deal justly with others**
  and always do what is right.
4 Remember me, Lord, when you show favor to your people;
  come near and rescue me.
5 **Let me share in the prosperity of your chosen ones.**
  Let me rejoice in the joy of your people;
  let me praise you with those who are your heritage.
6 Like our ancestors, we have sinned.
  We have done wrong! We have acted wickedly!
7 Our ancestors in Egypt
  were not impressed by the Lord's miraculous deeds.
They soon forgot his many acts of kindness to them.
  Instead, they rebelled against him at the Red Sea.
8 **Even so, he saved them —**
  to defend the honor of his name
  and to demonstrate his mighty power.
9 **He commanded the Red Sea to dry up.**
  He led Israel across the sea as if it were a desert.
10 **So he rescued them from their enemies**
  and redeemed them from their foes.
11 Then the water returned and covered their enemies;
  not one of them survived.

Then all the people say the following praise:

Glory to the Father, and to the Son, and to the Holy Spirit, as it was in the beginning, is now, and will be forever. Amen.

12 Then his people believed his promises.
Then they sang his praise.
13 Yet how quickly they forgot what he had done!
They wouldn't wait for his counsel!
14 In the wilderness their desires ran wild,
testing God's patience in that dry wasteland.
**15 So he gave them what they asked for,
but he sent a plague along with it.**
16 The people in the camp were jealous of Moses
and envious of Aaron, the Lord's holy priest.
17 Because of this, the earth opened up;
**it swallowed Dathan
and buried Abiram and the other rebels.**
18 Fire fell upon their followers;
a flame consumed the wicked.
19 The people made a calf at Mount Sinai;
they bowed before an image made of gold.
20 They traded their glorious God
for a statue of a grass-eating bull.
**21 They forgot God, their savior,
who had done such great things in Egypt —**
22 such wonderful things in the land of Ham,
such awesome deeds at the Red Sea.
23 So he declared he would destroy them.
But Moses, his chosen one, stepped between the Lord and the people.
He begged him to turn from his anger and not destroy them.
24 The people refused to enter the pleasant land,
for they wouldn't believe his promise to care for them.
**25 Instead, they grumbled in their tents
and refused to obey the Lord.**
26 Therefore, he solemnly swore
that he would kill them in the wilderness,
**27 that he would scatter their descendants among the nations,
exiling them to distant lands.**

Then all the people say the following praise:

Glory to the Father, and to the Son, and to the Holy Spirit, as it was in the beginning, is now, and will be forever. Amen.

Psalm 106:28–39

28 Then our ancestors joined in the worship of Baal at Peor;
they even ate sacrifices offered to the dead!
29 They angered the Lord with all these things,
so a plague broke out among them.
30 But Phinehas had the courage to intervene,
and the plague was stopped.
31 So he has been regarded as a righteous man
ever since that time.
32 **At Meribah, too, they angered the Lord,**
causing Moses serious trouble.
33 **They made Moses angry,**
and he spoke foolishly.
34 **Israel failed to destroy the nations in the land,**
as the Lord had commanded them.
35 **Instead, they mingled among the pagans**
and adopted their evil customs.
36 They worshiped their idols,
which led to their downfall.
37 They even sacrificed their sons
and their daughters to the demons.
38 **They shed innocent blood,**
the blood of their sons and daughters.
By sacrificing them to the idols of Canaan,
they polluted the land with murder.
39 **They defiled themselves by their evil deeds,**
and their love of idols was adultery in the Lord's sight.

Then all the people say the following praise:

Glory to the Father, and to the Son, and to the Holy Spirit, as it was in the beginning, is now, and will be forever. Amen.

40 That is why the Lord's anger burned against his people,
and he abhorred his own special possession.
41 He handed them over to pagan nations,
and they were ruled by those who hated them.
42 Their enemies crushed them
and brought them under their cruel power.
43 **Again and again he rescued them,**
but they chose to rebel against him,
and they were finally destroyed by their sin.
44 Even so, he pitied them in their distress
and listened to their cries.
45 **He remembered his covenant with them**
and relented because of his unfailing love.
46 He even caused their captors
to treat them with kindness.
47 **Save us, O Lord our God!**
Gather us back from among the nations,
so we can thank your holy name
and rejoice and praise you.
48 Praise the Lord, the God of Israel,
who lives from everlasting to everlasting!
Let all the people say, "Amen!"
Praise the Lord!

Then all the people say the following praise:

Glory to the Father, and to the Son, and to the Holy Spirit, as it was in the beginning, is now, and will be forever. Amen

Book Five

(Psalms 107–150)

Psalm 107:1–16

1 Give thanks to the Lord, for he is good!
   His faithful love endures forever.
2 Has the Lord redeemed you? Then speak out!
   Tell others he has redeemed you from your enemies.
3 For he has gathered the exiles from many lands,
   from east and west,
   from north and south.
4 **Some wandered in the wilderness,**
   lost and homeless.
5 **Hungry and thirsty,**
   they nearly died.
6 **"Lord, help!" they cried in their trouble,**
   and he rescued them from their distress.
7 **He led them straight to safety,**
   to a city where they could live.
8 **Let them praise the Lord for his great love**
   and for the wonderful things he has done for them.
9 For he satisfies the thirsty
   and fills the hungry with good things.
10 **Some sat in darkness and deepest gloom,**
   imprisoned in iron chains of misery.
11 **They rebelled against the words of God,**
   scorning the counsel of the Most High.
12 **That is why he broke them with hard labor;**
   they fell, and no one was there to help them.
13 **"Lord, help!" they cried in their trouble,**

and he saved them from their distress.

14 **He led them from the darkness and deepest gloom;**
he snapped their chains.

15 **Let them praise the Lord for his great love**
and for the wonderful things he has done for them.

16 For he broke down their prison gates of bronze;
he cut apart their bars of iron.

Then all the people say the following praise:

Glory to the Father, and to the Son, and to the Holy Spirit, as it was
in the beginning, is now, and will be forever. Amen.

Psalm 107:17–32

17 Some were fools; they rebelled
and suffered for their sins.

18 **They couldn't stand the thought of food,**
and they were knocking on death's door.

19 **"Lord, help!" they cried in their trouble,**
and he saved them from their distress.

20 **He sent out his word and healed them,**
snatching them from the door of death.

21 **Let them praise the Lord for his great love**
and for the wonderful things he has done for them.

22 Let them offer sacrifices of thanksgiving
and sing joyfully about his glorious acts.

23 **Some went off to sea in ships,**
plying the trade routes of the world.

24 **They, too, observed the Lord's power in action,**
his impressive works on the deepest seas.

25 **He spoke, and the winds rose,**
stirring up the waves.

26 **Their ships were tossed to the heavens**
and plunged again to the depths;
the sailors cringed in terror.

27 **They reeled and staggered like drunkards**
and were at their wits' end.

28 "Lord, help!" they cried in their trouble,
and he saved them from their distress.

29 He calmed the storm to a whisper
   and stilled the waves.
30 **What a blessing was that stillness
   as he brought them safely into harbor!**
31 Let them praise the Lord for his great love
   and for the wonderful things he has done for them.
32 **Let them exalt him publicly before the congregation
   and before the leaders of the nation.**

Then all the people say the following praise:

**Glory to the Father, and to the Son, and to the Holy Spirit, as it was
in the beginning, is now, and will be forever. Amen.**

Psalm 107:33–43

33 He changes rivers into deserts,
   and springs of water into dry, thirsty land.
34 He turns the fruitful land into salty wastelands,
   because of the wickedness of those who live there.
35 But he also turns deserts into pools of water,
   the dry land into springs of water.
36 He brings the hungry to settle there
   and to build their cities.
37 **They sow their fields, plant their vineyards,**
   and harvest their bumper crops.
38 **How he blesses them!**
   They raise large families there,
   and their herds of livestock increase.
39 When they decrease in number and become impoverished
   through oppression, trouble, and sorrow,
40 **the Lord pours contempt on their princes,**
   causing them to wander in trackless wastelands.
41 **But he rescues the poor from trouble
   and increases their families like flocks of sheep.**
42 The godly will see these things and be glad,
   while the wicked are struck silent.
43 Those who are wise will take all this to heart;
   they will see in our history the faithful love of the Lord.

Then all the people say the following praise:

Glory to the Father, and to the Son, and to the Holy Spirit, as it was in the beginning, is now, and will be forever. Amen.

Psalm 108

A song. A psalm of David.

1 My heart is confident in you, O God;
   no wonder I can sing your praises with all my heart!
2 Wake up, lyre and harp!
   I will wake the dawn with my song.
3 I will thank you, Lord, among all the people.
   I will sing your praises among the nations.
4 For your unfailing love is higher than the heavens.
   Your faithfulness reaches to the clouds.
5 Be exalted, O God, above the highest heavens.
   May your glory shine over all the earth.
6 Now rescue your beloved people.
   Answer and save us by your power.
7 God has promised this by his holiness:
   "I will divide up Shechem with joy.
   I will measure out the valley of Succoth.
8 **Gilead is mine,**
   and Manasseh, too.
   Ephraim, my helmet, will produce my warriors,
   and Judah, my scepter, will produce my kings.
9 **But Moab, my washbasin, will become my servant,**
   and I will wipe my feet on Edom
   and shout in triumph over Philistia."
10 **Who will bring me into the fortified city?**
   Who will bring me victory over Edom?
11 **Have you rejected us, O God?**
   Will you no longer march with our armies?
12 **Oh, please help us against our enemies,**
   for all human help is useless.
13 **With God's help we will do mighty things,**
   for he will trample down our foes.

Then all the people say the following praise:

Glory to the Father, and to the Son, and to the Holy Spirit, as it was in the beginning, is now, and will be forever. Amen.

Psalm 109:1–19

For the choir director: A psalm of David.

1 O God, whom I praise,
   don't stand silent and aloof
2 **while the wicked slander me**
   and tell lies about me.
3 They surround me with hateful words
   and fight against me for no reason.
4 **I love them, but they try to destroy me with accusations**
   even as I am praying for them!
5 They repay evil for good,
   and hatred for my love.
6 They say, "Get an evil person to turn against him.
   Send an accuser to bring him to trial.
7 When his case comes up for judgment,
   let him be pronounced guilty.
   Count his prayers as sins.
8 **Let his years be few;**
   let someone else take his position.
9 **May his children become fatherless,**
   and his wife a widow.
10 **May his children wander as beggars**
   and be driven from their ruined homes.
11 May creditors seize his entire estate,
   and strangers take all he has earned.
12 Let no one be kind to him;
   let no one pity his fatherless children.
13 May all his offspring die.
   May his family name be blotted out in the next generation.
14 May the Lord never forget the sins of his fathers;
   may his mother's sins never be erased from the record.
15 May the Lord always remember these sins,
   and may his name disappear from human memory.

16 For he refused all kindness to others;
  he persecuted the poor and needy,
  and he hounded the brokenhearted to death.
17 **He loved to curse others;**
  now you curse him.
He never blessed others;
  now don't you bless him.
18 **Cursing is as natural to him as his clothing,**
  or the water he drinks,
  or the rich food he eats.
19 Now may his curses return and cling to him like clothing;
  may they be tied around him like a belt."

Then all the people say the following praise:

Glory to the Father, and to the Son, and to the Holy Spirit, as it was in the beginning, is now, and will be forever. Amen.

Psalm 109:20–31

20 May those curses become the Lord's punishment
  for my accusers who speak evil of me.
21 **But deal well with me, O Sovereign Lord,**
  for the sake of your own reputation!
Rescue me
  because you are so faithful and good.
22 For I am poor and needy,
  and my heart is full of pain.
23 I am fading like a shadow at dusk;
  I am brushed off like a locust.
24 My knees are weak from fasting,
  and I am skin and bones.
25 I am a joke to people everywhere;
  when they see me, they shake their heads in scorn.
26 Help me, O Lord my God!
  Save me because of your unfailing love.
27 Let them see that this is your doing,
  that you yourself have done it, Lord.
28 Then let them curse me if they like,
  but you will bless me!

When they attack me, they will be disgraced!
But I, your servant, will go right on rejoicing!
29 May my accusers be clothed with disgrace;
may their humiliation cover them like a cloak.
30 But I will give repeated thanks to the Lord,
praising him to everyone.
31 For he stands beside the needy,
ready to save them from those who condemn them.

Then all the people say the following praise:

Glory to the Father, and to the Son, and to the Holy Spirit, as it was in the beginning, is now, and will be forever. Amen.

Psalm 110

A psalm of David.

1 The Lord said to my Lord,
"Sit in the place of honor at my right hand
until I humble your enemies,
making them a footstool under your feet."
2 **The Lord will extend your powerful kingdom from Jerusalem;**
you will rule over your enemies.
3 **When you go to war,**
your people will serve you willingly.
You are arrayed in holy garments,
and your strength will be renewed each day like the morning dew.
4 **The Lord has taken an oath and will not break his vow:**
"You are a priest forever in the order of Melchizedek."
5 **The Lord stands at your right hand to protect you.**
He will strike down many kings when his anger erupts.
6 **He will punish the nations**
and fill their lands with corpses;
he will shatter heads over the whole earth.
7 **But he himself will be refreshed from brooks along the way.**
He will be victorious.

Then all the people say the following praise:

Glory to the Father, and to the Son, and to the Holy Spirit, as it was in the beginning, is now, and will be forever. Amen.

Psalm 111

1 Praise the Lord!
I will thank the Lord with all my heart
as I meet with his godly people.
2 How amazing are the deeds of the Lord!
All who delight in him should ponder them.
3 Everything he does reveals his glory and majesty.
His righteousness never fails.
4 He causes us to remember his wonderful works.
How gracious and merciful is our Lord!
5 He gives food to those who fear him;
he always remembers his covenant.
6 He has shown his great power to his people
by giving them the lands of other nations.
7 **All he does is just and good,**
and all his commandments are trustworthy.
8 **They are forever true,**
to be obeyed faithfully and with integrity.
9 **He has paid a full ransom for his people.**
He has guaranteed his covenant with them forever.
What a holy, awe-inspiring name he has!
10 Fear of the Lord is the foundation of true wisdom.
All who obey his commandments will grow in wisdom.
Praise him forever!

Then all the people say the following praise:

Glory to the Father, and to the Son, and to the Holy Spirit, as it was in the beginning, is now, and will be forever. Amen.

Psalm 112

1 Praise the Lord!
How joyful are those who fear the Lord
and delight in obeying his commands.

2 Their children will be successful everywhere;
  an entire generation of godly people will be blessed.
3 They themselves will be wealthy,
  and their good deeds will last forever.
4 Light shines in the darkness for the godly.
  They are generous, compassionate, and righteous.
5 Good comes to those who lend money generously
  and conduct their business fairly.
6 **Such people will not be overcome by evil.**
  Those who are righteous will be long remembered.
7 **They do not fear bad news;**
  they confidently trust the Lord to care for them.
8 **They are confident and fearless**
  and can face their foes triumphantly.
9 They share freely and give generously to those in need.
  Their good deeds will be remembered forever.
  They will have influence and honor.
10 **The wicked will see this and be infuriated.**
  They will grind their teeth in anger;
  they will slink away, their hopes thwarted.

Then all the people say the following praise:

Glory to the Father, and to the Son, and to the Holy Spirit, as it was in the beginning, is now, and will be forever. Amen.

Psalm 113

1 Praise the Lord!
Yes, give praise, O servants of the Lord.
  Praise the name of the Lord!
2 **Blessed be the name of the Lord**
  now and forever.
3 Everywhere — from east to west —
  praise the name of the Lord.
4 For the Lord is high above the nations;
  his glory is higher than the heavens.
5 Who can be compared with the Lord our God,
  who is enthroned on high?

6 He stoops to look down
  on heaven and on earth.
7 **He lifts the poor from the dust**
  and the needy from the garbage dump.
8 He sets them among princes,
  even the princes of his own people!
9 He gives the childless woman a family,
  making her a happy mother.
  Praise the Lord!

Psalm 114

1 When the Israelites escaped from Egypt —
  when the family of Jacob left that foreign land —
2 the land of Judah became God's sanctuary,
  and Israel became his kingdom.
3 The Red Sea saw them coming and hurried out of their way!
  The water of the Jordan River turned away.
4 The mountains skipped like rams,
  the hills like lambs!
5 What's wrong, Red Sea, that made you hurry out of their way?
  What happened, Jordan River, that you turned away?
6 Why, mountains, did you skip like rams?
  Why, hills, like lambs?
7 Tremble, O earth, at the presence of the Lord,
  at the presence of the God of Jacob.
8 He turned the rock into a pool of water;
  yes, a spring of water flowed from solid rock.

Then all the people say the following praise:

Glory to the Father, and to the Son, and to the Holy Spirit, as it was
in the beginning, is now, and will be forever. Amen.

Psalm 115

1 Not to us, O Lord, not to us,
  but to your name goes all the glory
  for your unfailing love and faithfulness.

2 Why let the nations say,
   "Where is their God?"
3 Our God is in the heavens,
   and he does as he wishes.
4 Their idols are merely things of silver and gold,
   shaped by human hands.
5 They have mouths but cannot speak,
   and eyes but cannot see.
6 They have ears but cannot hear,
   and noses but cannot smell.
7 They have hands but cannot feel,
   and feet but cannot walk,
   and throats but cannot make a sound.
8 **And those who make idols are just like them,**
   as are all who trust in them.
9 **O Israel, trust the Lord!**
   He is your helper and your shield.
10 **O priests, descendants of Aaron, trust the Lord!**
   He is your helper and your shield.
11 **All you who fear the Lord, trust the Lord!**
   He is your helper and your shield.
12 **The Lord remembers us and will bless us.**
   He will bless the people of Israel
   and bless the priests, the descendants of Aaron.
13 **He will bless those who fear the Lord,**
   both great and lowly.
14 **May the Lord richly bless**
   both you and your children.
15 May you be blessed by the Lord,
   who made heaven and earth.
16 The heavens belong to the Lord,
   but he has given the earth to all humanity.
17 The dead cannot sing praises to the Lord,
   for they have gone into the silence of the grave.
18 But we can praise the Lord
   both now and forever!
Praise the Lord!

Then all the people say the following praise:

Glory to the Father, and to the Son, and to the Holy Spirit, as it was in the beginning, is now, and will be forever. Amen.

Psalm 116

1 I love the Lord because he hears my voice
and my prayer for mercy.
2 **Because he bends down to listen,**
I will pray as long as I have breath!
3 **Death wrapped its ropes around me;**
the terrors of the grave overtook me.
I saw only trouble and sorrow.
4 Then I called on the name of the Lord:
"Please, Lord, save me!"
5 How kind the Lord is! How good he is!
So merciful, this God of ours!
6 The Lord protects those of childlike faith;
I was facing death, and he saved me.
7 Let my soul be at rest again,
for the Lord has been good to me.
8 He has saved me from death,
my eyes from tears,
my feet from stumbling.
9 **And so I walk in the Lord's presence**
as I live here on earth!
10 I believed in you, so I said,
"I am deeply troubled, Lord."
11 In my anxiety I cried out to you,
"These people are all liars!"
12 What can I offer the Lord
for all he has done for me?
13 **I will lift up the cup of salvation**
and praise the Lord's name for saving me.
14 I will keep my promises to the Lord
in the presence of all his people.
15 **The Lord cares deeply**
when his loved ones die.
16 O Lord, I am your servant;
yes, I am your servant, born into your household;

you have freed me from my chains.
**17 I will offer you a sacrifice of thanksgiving
and call on the name of the Lord.**
18 I will fulfill my vows to the Lord
in the presence of all his people —
**19 in the house of the Lord
in the heart of Jerusalem.
Praise the Lord!**

Psalm 117

1 Praise the Lord, all you nations.
Praise him, all you people of the earth.
2 For his unfailing love for us is powerful;
**the Lord's faithfulness endures forever.
Praise the Lord!**

Then all the people say the following praise:

**Glory to the Father, and to the Son, and to the Holy Spirit, as it was
in the beginning, is now, and will be forever. Amen.**

Psalm 118:1–18

1 Give thanks to the Lord, for he is good!
His faithful love endures forever.
2 Let all Israel repeat:
"His faithful love endures forever."
3 Let Aaron's descendants, the priests, repeat:
"His faithful love endures forever."
4 Let all who fear the Lord repeat:
"His faithful love endures forever."
5 In my distress I prayed to the Lord,
and the Lord answered me and set me free.
6 The Lord is for me, so I will have no fear.
What can mere people do to me?
7 Yes, the Lord is for me; he will help me.
I will look in triumph at those who hate me.

8 It is better to take refuge in the Lord
   than to trust in people.
9 **It is better to take refuge in the Lord**
   than to trust in princes.
10 Though hostile nations surrounded me,
   I destroyed them all with the authority of the Lord.
11 Yes, they surrounded and attacked me,
   but I destroyed them all with the authority of the Lord.
12 They swarmed around me like bees;
   they blazed against me like a crackling fire.
   But I destroyed them all with the authority of the Lord.
13 **My enemies did their best to kill me,**
   but the Lord rescued me.
14 **The Lord is my strength and my song;**
   he has given me victory.
15 **Songs of joy and victory are sung in the camp of the godly.**
   The strong right arm of the Lord has done glorious things!
16 **The strong right arm of the Lord is raised in triumph.**
   The strong right arm of the Lord has done glorious things!
17 **I will not die; instead, I will live**
   to tell what the Lord has done.
18 The Lord has punished me severely,
   but he did not let me die.

Then all the people say the following praise:

Glory to the Father, and to the Son, and to the Holy Spirit, as it was in the beginning, is now, and will be forever. Amen.

Psalm 118:19–29

19 Open for me the gates where the righteous enter,
   and I will go in and thank the Lord.
20 These gates lead to the presence of the Lord,
   and the godly enter there.
21 I thank you for answering my prayer
   and giving me victory!
22 **The stone that the builders rejected**
   has now become the cornerstone.

23 This is the Lord's doing,
  and it is wonderful to see.
24 This is the day the Lord has made.
  We will rejoice and be glad in it.
25 Please, Lord, please save us.
  Please, Lord, please give us success.
26 Bless the one who comes in the name of the Lord.
  We bless you from the house of the Lord.
27 The Lord is God, shining upon us.
  Take the sacrifice and bind it with cords on the altar.
28 You are my God, and I will praise you!
  You are my God, and I will exalt you!
29 Give thanks to the Lord, for he is good!
  His faithful love endures forever.

Then all the people say the following praise:

Glory to the Father, and to the Son, and to the Holy Spirit, as it was in the beginning, is now, and will be forever. Amen.

Psalm 119:1–16

Aleph

1 Joyful are people of integrity,
  who follow the instructions of the Lord.
2 Joyful are those who obey his laws
  and search for him with all their hearts.
3 **They do not compromise with evil,**
  and they walk only in his paths.
4 **You have charged us**
  to keep your commandments carefully.
5 Oh, that my actions would consistently
  reflect your decrees!
6 **Then I will not be ashamed**
  when I compare my life with your commands.
7 As I learn your righteous regulations,
  I will thank you by living as I should!
8 I will obey your decrees.
  Please don't give up on me!

9 How can a young person stay pure?
By obeying your word.
10 I have tried hard to find you —
don't let me wander from your commands.
11 I have hidden your word in my heart,
that I might not sin against you.
12 I praise you, O Lord;
teach me your decrees.
13 I have recited aloud
all the regulations you have given us.
14 **I have rejoiced in your laws**
as much as in riches.
15 I will study your commandments
and reflect on your ways.
16 **I will delight in your decrees**
and not forget your word.

Then all the people say the following praise:

Glory to the Father, and to the Son, and to the Holy Spirit, as it was in the beginning, is now, and will be forever. Amen.

Psalm 119:17–32

Gimel

17 Be good to your servant,
that I may live and obey your word.
18 Open my eyes to see
the wonderful truths in your instructions.
19 **I am only a foreigner in the land.**
Don't hide your commands from me!
20 **I am always overwhelmed**
with a desire for your regulations.
21 You rebuke the arrogant;
those who wander from your commands are cursed.
22 Don't let them scorn and insult me,
for I have obeyed your laws.

23 Even princes sit and speak against me,
but I will meditate on your decrees.
24 Your laws please me;
they give me wise advice.

Daleth

25 I lie in the dust;
revive me by your word.
26 I told you my plans, and you answered.
Now teach me your decrees.
27 Help me understand the meaning of your commandments,
and I will meditate on your wonderful deeds.
28 I weep with sorrow;
encourage me by your word.
29 Keep me from lying to myself;
give me the privilege of knowing your instructions.
30 I have chosen to be faithful;
I have determined to live by your regulations.
31 I cling to your laws.
Lord, don't let me be put to shame!
32 I will pursue your commands,
for you expand my understanding.

Then all the people say the following praise:

Glory to the Father, and to the Son, and to the Holy Spirit, as it was in the beginning, is now, and will be forever. Amen.

Psalm 119:33–40

He

33 Teach me your decrees, O Lord;
I will keep them to the end.
34 Give me understanding and I will obey your instructions;
I will put them into practice with all my heart.
35 Make me walk along the path of your commands,
for that is where my happiness is found.
36 Give me an eagerness for your laws

rather than a love for money!

37 **Turn my eyes from worthless things,**
  and give me life through your word.

38 **Reassure me of your promise,**
  made to those who fear you.

39 **Help me abandon my shameful ways;**
  for your regulations are good.

40 **I long to obey your commandments!**
  Renew my life with your goodness.

Then all the people say the following praise:

Glory to the Father, and to the Son, and to the Holy Spirit, as it was in the beginning, is now, and will be forever. Amen.

Psalm 119:41–48

Waw

41 Lord, give me your unfailing love,
  the salvation that you promised me.

42 Then I can answer those who taunt me,
  for I trust in your word.

43 Do not snatch your word of truth from me,
  for your regulations are my only hope.

44 I will keep on obeying your instructions
  forever and ever.

45 I will walk in freedom,
  for I have devoted myself to your commandments.

46 I will speak to kings about your laws,
  and I will not be ashamed.

47 How I delight in your commands!
  How I love them!

48 I honor and love your commands.
  I meditate on your decrees.

Then all the people say the following praise:

Glory to the Father, and to the Son, and to the Holy Spirit, as it was in the beginning, is now, and will be forever. Amen.

Psalm 119:49–56

Zayin

49 Remember your promise to me;
  it is my only hope.
50 Your promise revives me;
  it comforts me in all my troubles.
51 The proud hold me in utter contempt,
  but I do not turn away from your instructions.
52 I meditate on your age-old regulations;
  O Lord, they comfort me.
53 I become furious with the wicked,
  because they reject your instructions.
54 Your decrees have been the theme of my songs
  wherever I have lived.
55 I reflect at night on who you are, O Lord;
  therefore, I obey your instructions.
56 This is how I spend my life:
  obeying your commandments.

Then all the people say the following praise:

Glory to the Father, and to the Son, and to the Holy Spirit, as it was in the beginning, is now, and will be forever. Amen.

Psalm 119:57–80

Heth

57 Lord, you are mine!
  I promise to obey your words!
58 With all my heart I want your blessings.
  Be merciful as you promised.
59 I pondered the direction of my life,
  and I turned to follow your laws.
60 I will hurry, without delay,
  to obey your commands.
61 Evil people try to drag me into sin,
  but I am firmly anchored to your instructions.

62 I rise at midnight to thank you
for your just regulations.
63 **I am a friend to anyone who fears you —**
anyone who obeys your commandments.
64 **O Lord, your unfailing love fills the earth;**
teach me your decrees.

Teth

65 You have done many good things for me, Lord,
just as you promised.
66 I believe in your commands;
now teach me good judgment and knowledge.
67 I used to wander off until you disciplined me;
but now I closely follow your word.
68 You are good and do only good;
teach me your decrees.
69 Arrogant people smear me with lies,
but in truth I obey your commandments with all my heart.
70 Their hearts are dull and stupid,
but I delight in your instructions.
71 My suffering was good for me,
for it taught me to pay attention to your decrees.
72 Your instructions are more valuable to me
than millions in gold and silver.

Yodh

73 You made me; you created me.
Now give me the sense to follow your commands.
74 May all who fear you find in me a cause for joy,
for I have put my hope in your word.
75 I know, O Lord, that your regulations are fair;
you disciplined me because I needed it.
76 Now let your unfailing love comfort me,
just as you promised me, your servant.
77 Surround me with your tender mercies so I may live,
for your instructions are my delight.
78 Bring disgrace upon the arrogant people who lied about me;
meanwhile, I will concentrate on your commandments.

79 Let me be united with all who fear you,
   with those who know your laws.
80 May I be blameless in keeping your decrees;
   then I will never be ashamed.

Then all the people say the following praise:

Glory to the Father, and to the Son, and to the Holy Spirit, as it was in the beginning, is now, and will be forever. Amen.

Psalm 119:81–96

Kaph

81 I am worn out waiting for your rescue,
   but I have put my hope in your word.
82 My eyes are straining to see your promises come true.
   When will you comfort me?
83 I am shriveled like a wineskin in the smoke,
   but I have not forgotten to obey your decrees.
84 How long must I wait?
   When will you punish those who persecute me?
85 These arrogant people who hate your instructions
   have dug deep pits to trap me.
86 **All your commands are trustworthy.**
   Protect me from those who hunt me down without cause.
87 **They almost finished me off,**
   but I refused to abandon your commandments.
88 **In your unfailing love, spare my life;**
   then I can continue to obey your laws.

Lamedh

89 Your eternal word, O Lord,
   stands firm in heaven.
90 Your faithfulness extends to every generation,
   as enduring as the earth you created.
91 Your regulations remain true to this day,
   for everything serves your plans.

92 If your instructions hadn't sustained me with joy,
I would have died in my misery.
93 I will never forget your commandments,
for by them you give me life.
94 I am yours; rescue me!
For I have worked hard at obeying your commandments.
95 Though the wicked hide along the way to kill me,
I will quietly keep my mind on your laws.
96 Even perfection has its limits,
but your commands have no limit.

Then all the people say the following praise:

Glory to the Father, and to the Son, and to the Holy Spirit, as it was in the beginning, is now, and will be forever. Amen.

Psalm 119:97–104

Mem

97 Oh, how I love your instructions!
I think about them all day long.
98 Your commands make me wiser than my enemies,
for they are my constant guide.
99 Yes, I have more insight than my teachers,
for I am always thinking of your laws.
100 I am even wiser than my elders,
for I have kept your commandments.
101 I have refused to walk on any evil path,
so that I may remain obedient to your word.
102 I haven't turned away from your regulations,
for you have taught me well.
103 How sweet your words taste to me;
they are sweeter than honey.
104 Your commandments give me understanding;
no wonder I hate every false way of life.

Then all the people say the following praise:

Glory to the Father, and to the Son, and to the Holy Spirit, as it was in the beginning, is now, and will be forever. Amen.

Psalm 119:105–112

Nun

105 Your word is a lamp to guide my feet
   and a light for my path.
106 **I've promised it once, and I'll promise it again:**
   I will obey your righteous regulations.
107 **I have suffered much, O Lord;**
   restore my life again as you promised.
108 **Lord, accept my offering of praise,**
   and teach me your regulations.
109 **My life constantly hangs in the balance,**
   but I will not stop obeying your instructions.
110 **The wicked have set their traps for me,**
   but I will not turn from your commandments.
111 **Your laws are my treasure;**
   they are my heart's delight.
112 **I am determined to keep your decrees**
   to the very end.

Then all the people say the following praise:

Glory to the Father, and to the Son, and to the Holy Spirit, as it was in the beginning, is now, and will be forever. Amen.

Psalm 119:113–128

Samekh

113 I hate those with divided loyalties,
   but I love your instructions.
114 You are my refuge and my shield;
   your word is my source of hope.
115 Get out of my life, you evil-minded people,
   for I intend to obey the commands of my God.

116 Lord, sustain me as you promised, that I may live!
Do not let my hope be crushed.
117 Sustain me, and I will be rescued;
then I will meditate continually on your decrees.
118 But you have rejected all who stray from your decrees.
They are only fooling themselves.
119 You skim off the wicked of the earth like scum;
no wonder I love to obey your laws!
120 I tremble in fear of you;
I stand in awe of your regulations.

Ayin

121 Don't leave me to the mercy of my enemies,
for I have done what is just and right.
122 Please guarantee a blessing for me.
Don't let the arrogant oppress me!
123 My eyes strain to see your rescue,
to see the truth of your promise fulfilled.
124 I am your servant; deal with me in unfailing love,
and teach me your decrees.
125 Give discernment to me, your servant;
then I will understand your laws.
126 Lord, it is time for you to act,
for these evil people have violated your instructions.
127 Truly, I love your commands
more than gold, even the finest gold.
128 Each of your commandments is right.
That is why I hate every false way.

Then all the people say the following praise:

Glory to the Father, and to the Son, and to the Holy Spirit, as it was in the beginning, is now, and will be forever. Amen.

Psalm 119:129–144

Pe

129 Your laws are wonderful.
No wonder I obey them!

130 The teaching of your word gives light,
  so even the simple can understand.
131 I pant with expectation,
  longing for your commands.
132 Come and show me your mercy,
  as you do for all who love your name.
133 Guide my steps by your word,
  so I will not be overcome by evil.
134 Ransom me from the oppression of evil people;
  then I can obey your commandments.
135 Look upon me with love;
  teach me your decrees.
136 Rivers of tears gush from my eyes
  because people disobey your instructions.

Tsadhe

137 O Lord, you are righteous,
  and your regulations are fair.
138 Your laws are perfect
  and completely trustworthy.
139 I am overwhelmed with indignation,
  for my enemies have disregarded your words.
140 Your promises have been thoroughly tested;
  that is why I love them so much.
141 I am insignificant and despised,
  but I don't forget your commandments.
142 Your justice is eternal,
  and your instructions are perfectly true.
143 As pressure and stress bear down on me,
  I find joy in your commands.
144 Your laws are always right;
  help me to understand them so I may live.

Then all the people say the following praise:

**Glory to the Father, and to the Son, and to the Holy Spirit, as it was
in the beginning, is now, and will be forever. Amen.**

Psalm 119:145–152

Qoph

145 I pray with all my heart; answer me, Lord!
I will obey your decrees.
146 I cry out to you; rescue me,
that I may obey your laws.
147 I rise early, before the sun is up;
I cry out for help and put my hope in your words.
148 I stay awake through the night,
thinking about your promise.
149 In your faithful love, O Lord, hear my cry;
let me be revived by following your regulations.
150 Lawless people are coming to attack me;
they live far from your instructions.
151 But you are near, O Lord,
and all your commands are true.
152 I have known from my earliest days
that your laws will last forever.

Then all the people say the following praise:

Glory to the Father, and to the Son, and to the Holy Spirit, as it was in the beginning, is now, and will be forever. Amen.

Psalm 119:153–160

Resh

153 Look upon my suffering and rescue me,
for I have not forgotten your instructions.
154 Argue my case; take my side!
Protect my life as you promised.
155 The wicked are far from rescue,
for they do not bother with your decrees.
156 Lord, how great is your mercy;
let me be revived by following your regulations.
157 Many persecute and trouble me,
yet I have not swerved from your laws.

158 Seeing these traitors makes me sick at heart,
because they care nothing for your word.
159 See how I love your commandments, Lord.
Give back my life because of your unfailing love.
160 The very essence of your words is truth;
all your just regulations will stand forever.

Then all the people say the following praise:

Glory to the Father, and to the Son, and to the Holy Spirit, as it was in the beginning, is now, and will be forever. Amen.

Psalm 119:161–176

Shin

161 Powerful people harass me without cause,
but my heart trembles only at your word.
162 I rejoice in your word
like one who discovers a great treasure.
163 **I hate and abhor all falsehood,**
but I love your instructions.
164 **I will praise you seven times a day**
because all your regulations are just.
165 Those who love your instructions have great peace
and do not stumble.
166 **I long for your rescue, Lord,**
so I have obeyed your commands.
167 **I have obeyed your laws,**
for I love them very much.
168 **Yes, I obey your commandments and laws**
because you know everything I do.

Taw

169 O Lord, listen to my cry;
give me the discerning mind you promised.
170 Listen to my prayer;
rescue me as you promised.
171 Let praise flow from my lips,

for you have taught me your decrees.
172 Let my tongue sing about your word,
  for all your commands are right.
173 Give me a helping hand,
  for I have chosen to follow your commandments.
174 O Lord, I have longed for your rescue,
  and your instructions are my delight.
175 Let me live so I can praise you,
  and may your regulations help me.
176 I have wandered away like a lost sheep;
  come and find me,
  for I have not forgotten your commands.

Then all the people say the following praise:

Glory to the Father, and to the Son, and to the Holy Spirit, as it was in the beginning, is now, and will be forever. Amen.

Psalm 120

A song for pilgrims ascending to Jerusalem.

1 I took my troubles to the Lord;
  I cried out to him, and he answered my prayer.
2 Rescue me, O Lord, from liars
  and from all deceitful people.
3 **O deceptive tongue, what will God do to you?**
  How will he increase your punishment?
4 **You will be pierced with sharp arrows**
  and burned with glowing coals.
5 How I suffer in far-off Meshech.
  It pains me to live in distant Kedar.
6 I am tired of living
  among people who hate peace.
7 **I search for peace;**
  but when I speak of peace, they want war!

Psalm 121

A song for pilgrims ascending to Jerusalem.

1 I look up to the mountains —
does my help come from there?
2 My help comes from the Lord,
who made heaven and earth!
3 He will not let you stumble;
the one who watches over you will not slumber.
4 Indeed, he who watches over Israel
never slumbers or sleeps.
5 **The Lord himself watches over you!**
The Lord stands beside you as your protective shade.
6 **The sun will not harm you by day,**
nor the moon at night.
7 **The Lord keeps you from all harm**
and watches over your life.
8 The Lord keeps watch over you as you come and go,
both now and forever.

Then all the people say the following praise:

Glory to the Father, and to the Son, and to the Holy Spirit, as it was
in the beginning, is now, and will be forever. Amen.

Psalm 122

A song for pilgrims ascending to Jerusalem. A psalm of David.

1 I was glad when they said to me,
"Let us go to the house of the Lord."
2 And now here we are,
standing inside your gates, O Jerusalem.
3 Jerusalem is a well-built city;
its seamless walls cannot be breached.
4 All the tribes of Israel — the Lord's people —
make their pilgrimage here.
They come to give thanks to the name of the Lord,
as the law requires of Israel.

5 Here stand the thrones where judgment is given,
the thrones of the dynasty of David.
6 Pray for peace in Jerusalem.
May all who love this city prosper.
7 O Jerusalem, may there be peace within your walls
and prosperity in your palaces.
8 **For the sake of my family and friends, I will say,
"May you have peace."**
9 For the sake of the house of the Lord our God,
I will seek what is best for you, O Jerusalem.

Psalm 123

A song for pilgrims ascending to Jerusalem.

1 I lift my eyes to you,
O God, enthroned in heaven.
2 We keep looking to the Lord our God for his mercy,
just as servants keep their eyes on their master,
as a slave girl watches her mistress for the slightest signal.
3 **Have mercy on us, Lord, have mercy,**
for we have had our fill of contempt.
4 **We have had more than our fill of the scoffing of the proud
and the contempt of the arrogant.**

Psalm 124

A song for pilgrims ascending to Jerusalem. A psalm of David.

1 What if the Lord had not been on our side?
Let all Israel repeat:
2 What if the Lord had not been on our side
when people attacked us?
3 **They would have swallowed us alive
in their burning anger.**
4 The waters would have engulfed us;
a torrent would have overwhelmed us.
5 Yes, the raging waters of their fury
would have overwhelmed our very lives.
6 **Praise the Lord,**

who did not let their teeth tear us apart!

7 **We escaped like a bird from a hunter's trap.**

The trap is broken, and we are free!

8 **Our help is from the Lord,**

who made heaven and earth.

Then all the people say the following praise:

Glory to the Father, and to the Son, and to the Holy Spirit, as it was in the beginning, is now, and will be forever. Amen.

Psalm 125

A song for pilgrims ascending to Jerusalem.

1 Those who trust in the Lord are as secure as Mount Zion;

they will not be defeated but will endure forever.

2 Just as the mountains surround Jerusalem,

so the Lord surrounds his people, both now and forever.

3 The wicked will not rule the land of the godly,

for then the godly might be tempted to do wrong.

4 O Lord, do good to those who are good,

whose hearts are in tune with you.

5 But banish those who turn to crooked ways, O Lord.

Take them away with those who do evil.

May Israel have peace!

Psalm 126

A song for pilgrims ascending to Jerusalem.

1 When the Lord brought back his exiles to Jerusalem,

it was like a dream!

2 We were filled with laughter,

and we sang for joy.

And the other nations said,

"What amazing things the Lord has done for them."

3 Yes, the Lord has done amazing things for us!

What joy!

4 Restore our fortunes, Lord,
  as streams renew the desert.
5 Those who plant in tears
  will harvest with shouts of joy.
6 **They weep as they go to plant their seed,**
  but they sing as they return with the harvest.

Psalm 127

A song for pilgrims ascending to Jerusalem. A psalm of Solomon.

1 Unless the Lord builds a house,
  the work of the builders is wasted.
Unless the Lord protects a city,
  guarding it with sentries will do no good.
2 It is useless for you to work so hard
  from early morning until late at night,
anxiously working for food to eat;
  for God gives rest to his loved ones.
3 **Children are a gift from the Lord;**
  they are a reward from him.
4 **Children born to a young man**
  are like arrows in a warrior's hands.
5 How joyful is the man whose quiver is full of them!
**He will not be put to shame when he confronts his accusers at the
city gates.**

Then all the people say the following praise:

**Glory to the Father, and to the Son, and to the Holy Spirit, as it was
in the beginning, is now, and will be forever. Amen.**

Psalm 128

A song for pilgrims ascending to Jerusalem.

1 How joyful are those who fear the Lord —
  all who follow his ways!
2 You will enjoy the fruit of your labor.
  How joyful and prosperous you will be!

3 Your wife will be like a fruitful grapevine,
flourishing within your home.
Your children will be like vigorous young olive trees
as they sit around your table.
4 **That is the Lord's blessing**
for those who fear him.
5 May the Lord continually bless you from Zion.
May you see Jerusalem prosper as long as you live.
6 May you live to enjoy your grandchildren.
May Israel have peace!

Psalm 129

A song for pilgrims ascending to Jerusalem.

1 From my earliest youth my enemies have persecuted me.
Let all Israel repeat this:
2 From my earliest youth my enemies have persecuted me,
but they have never defeated me.
3 My back is covered with cuts,
as if a farmer had plowed long furrows.
4 But the Lord is good;
he has cut me free from the ropes of the ungodly.
5 May all who hate Jerusalem
be turned back in shameful defeat.
6 **May they be as useless as grass on a rooftop,**
turning yellow when only half grown,
7 **ignored by the harvester,**
despised by the binder.
8 **And may those who pass by**
refuse to give them this blessing:
"The Lord bless you;
we bless you in the Lord's name."

Then all the people say the following praise:

Glory to the Father, and to the Son, and to the Holy Spirit, as it was
in the beginning, is now, and will be forever. Amen.

Psalm 130

A song for pilgrims ascending to Jerusalem.

1 From the depths of despair, O Lord,
I call for your help.
2 Hear my cry, O Lord.
Pay attention to my prayer.
3 Lord, if you kept a record of our sins,
who, O Lord, could ever survive?
4 But you offer forgiveness,
that we might learn to fear you.
5 I am counting on the Lord;
yes, I am counting on him.
I have put my hope in his word.
6 **I long for the Lord**
more than sentries long for the dawn,
yes, more than sentries long for the dawn.
7 **O Israel, hope in the Lord;**
for with the Lord there is unfailing love.
His redemption overflows.
8 He himself will redeem Israel
from every kind of sin.

Psalm 131

A song for pilgrims ascending to Jerusalem. A psalm of David.

1 **Lord, my heart is not proud;**
my eyes are not haughty.
I don't concern myself with matters too great
or too awesome for me to grasp.
2 Instead, I have calmed and quieted myself,
like a weaned child who no longer cries for its mother's milk.
Yes, like a weaned child is my soul within me.
3 **O Israel, put your hope in the Lord —**
now and always.

Then all the people say the following praise:

Glory to the Father, and to the Son, and to the Holy Spirit, as it was in the beginning, is now, and will be forever. Amen.

Psalm 132

A song for pilgrims ascending to Jerusalem.

1 Lord, remember David
and all that he suffered.
2 **He made a solemn promise to the Lord.**
He vowed to the Mighty One of Israel,
3 **"I will not go home;**
I will not let myself rest.
4 **I will not let my eyes sleep**
nor close my eyelids in slumber
5 until I find a place to build a house for the Lord,
a sanctuary for the Mighty One of Israel."
6 We heard that the Ark was in Ephrathah;
then we found it in the distant countryside of Jaar.
7 Let us go to the sanctuary of the Lord;
let us worship at the footstool of his throne.
8 Arise, O Lord, and enter your resting place,
along with the Ark, the symbol of your power.
9 May your priests be clothed in godliness;
may your loyal servants sing for joy.
10 For the sake of your servant David,
do not reject the king you have anointed.
11 The Lord swore an oath to David
with a promise he will never take back:
"I will place one of your descendants
on your throne.
12 **If your descendants obey the terms of my covenant**
and the laws that I teach them,
then your royal line
will continue forever and ever."
13 **For the Lord has chosen Jerusalem;**
he has desired it for his home.
14 **"This is my resting place forever," he said.**
"I will live here, for this is the home I desired.
15 **I will bless this city and make it prosperous;**

I will satisfy its poor with food.
16 **I will clothe its priests with godliness;**
 its faithful servants will sing for joy.
17 **Here I will increase the power of David;**
 my anointed one will be a light for my people.
18 **I will clothe his enemies with shame,**
 but he will be a glorious king."

Then all the people say the following praise:

Glory to the Father, and to the Son, and to the Holy Spirit, as it was in the beginning, is now, and will be forever. Amen.

Psalm 133

A song for pilgrims ascending to Jerusalem. A psalm of David.

1 How wonderful and pleasant it is
 when brothers live together in harmony!
2 **For harmony is as precious as the anointing oil**
 that was poured over Aaron's head,
 that ran down his beard
 and onto the border of his robe.
3 **Harmony is as refreshing as the dew from Mount Hermon**
 that falls on the mountains of Zion.
And there the Lord has pronounced his blessing,
 even life everlasting.

Psalm 134

A song for pilgrims ascending to Jerusalem.

1 Oh, praise the Lord, all you servants of the Lord,
 you who serve at night in the house of the Lord.
2 Lift your hands toward the sanctuary,
 and praise the Lord.
3 May the Lord, who made heaven and earth,
 bless you from Jerusalem.

Then all the people say the following praise:

Glory to the Father, and to the Son, and to the Holy Spirit, as it was in the beginning, is now, and will be forever. Amen.

Psalm 135

1 Praise the Lord!
Praise the name of the Lord!
 Praise him, you who serve the Lord,
2 **you who serve in the house of the Lord,**
 in the courts of the house of our God.
3 **Praise the Lord, for the Lord is good;**
 celebrate his lovely name with music.
4 **For the Lord has chosen Jacob for himself,**
 Israel for his own special treasure.
5 **I know the greatness of the Lord —**
 that our Lord is greater than any other god.
6 **The Lord does whatever pleases him**
 throughout all heaven and earth,
 and on the seas and in their depths.
7 **He causes the clouds to rise over the whole earth.**
 He sends the lightning with the rain
 and releases the wind from his storehouses.
8 **He destroyed the firstborn in each Egyptian home,**
 both people and animals.
9 **He performed miraculous signs and wonders in Egypt**
 against Pharaoh and all his people.
10 He struck down great nations
 and slaughtered mighty kings —
11 **Sihon king of the Amorites,**
 Og king of Bashan,
 and all the kings of Canaan.
12 He gave their land as an inheritance,
 a special possession to his people Israel.
13 Your name, O Lord, endures forever;
 your fame, O Lord, is known to every generation.
14 For the Lord will give justice to his people
 and have compassion on his servants.
15 **The idols of the nations are merely things of silver and gold,**
 shaped by human hands.
16 **They have mouths but cannot speak,**

and eyes but cannot see.
17 **They have ears but cannot hear,**
and mouths but cannot breathe.
18 **And those who make idols are just like them,**
as are all who trust in them.
19 **O Israel, praise the Lord!**
O priests — descendants of Aaron — praise the Lord!
20 **O Levites, praise the Lord!**
All you who fear the Lord, praise the Lord!
21 **The Lord be praised from Zion,**
for he lives here in Jerusalem.
Praise the Lord!

Then all the people say the following praise:

Glory to the Father, and to the Son, and to the Holy Spirit, as it was in the beginning, is now, and will be forever. Amen.

Psalm 136:1–16

1 Give thanks to the Lord, for he is good!
His faithful love endures forever.
2 Give thanks to the God of gods.
His faithful love endures forever.
3 Give thanks to the Lord of lords.
His faithful love endures forever.
4 Give thanks to him who alone does mighty miracles.
His faithful love endures forever.
5 Give thanks to him who made the heavens so skillfully.
His faithful love endures forever.
6 Give thanks to him who placed the earth among the waters.
His faithful love endures forever.
7 Give thanks to him who made the heavenly lights —
His faithful love endures forever.
8 the sun to rule the day,
His faithful love endures forever.
9 and the moon and stars to rule the night.
His faithful love endures forever.
10 Give thanks to him who killed the firstborn of Egypt.
His faithful love endures forever.

11 He brought Israel out of Egypt.

His faithful love endures forever.

12 He acted with a strong hand and powerful arm.

His faithful love endures forever.

13 Give thanks to him who parted the Red Sea.

His faithful love endures forever.

14 He led Israel safely through,

His faithful love endures forever.

15 but he hurled Pharaoh and his army into the Red Sea.

His faithful love endures forever.

16 Give thanks to him who led his people through the wilderness.

His faithful love endures forever.

Then all the people say the following praise:

Glory to the Father, and to the Son, and to the Holy Spirit, as it was in the beginning, is now, and will be forever. Amen.

Psalm 136:17–26

17 Give thanks to him who struck down mighty kings.

His faithful love endures forever.

18 He killed powerful kings —

His faithful love endures forever.

19 Sihon king of the Amorites,

His faithful love endures forever.

20 and Og king of Bashan.

His faithful love endures forever.

21 God gave the land of these kings as an inheritance —

His faithful love endures forever.

22 a special possession to his servant Israel.

His faithful love endures forever.

23 He remembered us in our weakness.

His faithful love endures forever.

24 He saved us from our enemies.

His faithful love endures forever.

25 He gives food to every living thing.

His faithful love endures forever.

26 Give thanks to the God of heaven.

His faithful love endures forever.

Then all the people say the following praise:

Glory to the Father, and to the Son, and to the Holy Spirit, as it was in the beginning, is now, and will be forever. Amen.

Psalm 137

1 Beside the rivers of Babylon, we sat and wept
as we thought of Jerusalem.
2 **We put away our harps,**
hanging them on the branches of poplar trees.
3 **For our captors demanded a song from us.**
Our tormentors insisted on a joyful hymn:
"Sing us one of those songs of Jerusalem!"
4 But how can we sing the songs of the Lord
while in a pagan land?
5 **If I forget you, O Jerusalem,**
let my right hand forget how to play the harp.
6 **May my tongue stick to the roof of my mouth**
if I fail to remember you,
if I don't make Jerusalem my greatest joy.
7 **O Lord, remember what the Edomites did**
on the day the armies of Babylon captured Jerusalem.
"Destroy it!" they yelled.
"Level it to the ground!"
8 O Babylon, you will be destroyed.
Happy is the one who pays you back
for what you have done to us.
9 Happy is the one who takes your babies
and smashes them against the rocks!

Then all the people say the following praise:

Glory to the Father, and to the Son, and to the Holy Spirit, as it was in the beginning, is now, and will be forever. Amen.

Psalm 138

A psalm of David.

1 I give you thanks, O Lord, with all my heart;
I will sing your praises before the gods.

2 I bow before your holy Temple as I worship.
  I praise your name for your unfailing love and faithfulness;
for your promises are backed
  by all the honor of your name.
3 **As soon as I pray, you answer me;**
  you encourage me by giving me strength.
4 **Every king in all the earth will thank you, Lord,**
  for all of them will hear your words.
5 **Yes, they will sing about the Lord's ways,**
  for the glory of the Lord is very great.
6 **Though the Lord is great, he cares for the humble,**
  but he keeps his distance from the proud.
7 **Though I am surrounded by troubles,**
  you will protect me from the anger of my enemies.
You reach out your hand,
  and the power of your right hand saves me.
8 **The Lord will work out his plans for my life —**
  for your faithful love, O Lord, endures forever.
Don't abandon me, for you made me.

Then all the people say the following praise:

Glory to the Father, and to the Son, and to the Holy Spirit, as it was in the beginning, is now, and will be forever. Amen.

Psalm 139:1–12

For the choir director: A psalm of David.

1 O Lord, you have examined my heart
  and know everything about me.
2 **You know when I sit down or stand up.**
  You know my thoughts even when I'm far away.
3 **You see me when I travel**
  and when I rest at home.
  You know everything I do.
4 **You know what I am going to say**
  even before I say it, Lord.
5 You go before me and follow me.
  You place your hand of blessing on my head.
6 Such knowledge is too wonderful for me,

too great for me to understand!
7 I can never escape from your Spirit!
 I can never get away from your presence!
8 If I go up to heaven, you are there;
 if I go down to the grave, you are there.
9 If I ride the wings of the morning,
 if I dwell by the farthest oceans,
10 even there your hand will guide me,
 and your strength will support me.
11 I could ask the darkness to hide me
 and the light around me to become night —
12 **but even in darkness I cannot hide from you.**
To you the night shines as bright as day.
 Darkness and light are the same to you.

Then all the people say the following praise:

**Glory to the Father, and to the Son, and to the Holy Spirit, as it was
in the beginning, is now, and will be forever. Amen.**

Psalm 139:13–24

13 You made all the delicate, inner parts of my body
 and knit me together in my mother's womb.
14 **Thank you for making me so wonderfully complex!**
 Your workmanship is marvelous — how well I know it.
15 **You watched me as I was being formed in utter seclusion,**
 as I was woven together in the dark of the womb.
16 **You saw me before I was born.**
 Every day of my life was recorded in your book.
Every moment was laid out
 before a single day had passed.
17 How precious are your thoughts about me, O God.
 They cannot be numbered!
18 I can't even count them;
 they outnumber the grains of sand!
And when I wake up,
 you are still with me!
19 O God, if only you would destroy the wicked!
 Get out of my life, you murderers!

20 They blaspheme you;

your enemies misuse your name.

21 O Lord, shouldn't I hate those who hate you?

Shouldn't I despise those who oppose you?

22 Yes, I hate them with total hatred,

for your enemies are my enemies.

23 Search me, O God, and know my heart;

test me and know my anxious thoughts.

24 Point out anything in me that offends you,

and lead me along the path of everlasting life.

Then all the people say the following praise:

Glory to the Father, and to the Son, and to the Holy Spirit, as it was in the beginning, is now, and will be forever. Amen.

Psalm 140

For the choir director: A psalm of David.

1 O Lord, rescue me from evil people.

Protect me from those who are violent,

2 those who plot evil in their hearts

and stir up trouble all day long.

3 **Their tongues sting like a snake;**

the venom of a viper drips from their lips. *Interlude*

4 **O Lord, keep me out of the hands of the wicked.**

Protect me from those who are violent,

for they are plotting against me.

5 The proud have set a trap to catch me;

they have stretched out a net;

they have placed traps all along the way. *Interlude*

6 **I said to the Lord, "You are my God!"**

Listen, O Lord, to my cries for mercy!

7 **O Sovereign Lord, the strong one who rescued me,**

you protected me on the day of battle.

8 **Lord, do not let evil people have their way.**

Do not let their evil schemes succeed,

or they will become proud. *Interlude*

9 Let my enemies be destroyed

by the very evil they have planned for me.
10 **Let burning coals fall down on their heads.**
Let them be thrown into the fire
or into watery pits from which they can't escape.
11 **Don't let liars prosper here in our land.**
Cause great disasters to fall on the violent.
12 **But I know the Lord will help those they persecute;**
he will give justice to the poor.
13 **Surely righteous people are praising your name;**
the godly will live in your presence.

Then all the people say the following praise:

Glory to the Father, and to the Son, and to the Holy Spirit, as it was in the beginning, is now, and will be forever. Amen.

Psalm 141

A psalm of David.

1 O Lord, I am calling to you. Please hurry!
Listen when I cry to you for help!
2 Accept my prayer as incense offered to you,
and my upraised hands as an evening offering.
3 Take control of what I say, O Lord,
and guard my lips.
4 Don't let me drift toward evil
or take part in acts of wickedness.
Don't let me share in the delicacies
of those who do wrong.
5 Let the godly strike me!
It will be a kindness!
If they correct me, it is soothing medicine.
Don't let me refuse it.
But I pray constantly
against the wicked and their deeds.
6 **When their leaders are thrown down from a cliff,**
the wicked will listen to my words and find them true.
7 **Like rocks brought up by a plow,**
the bones of the wicked will lie scattered without burial.

8 **I look to you for help, O Sovereign Lord.**
 You are my refuge; don't let them kill me.
9 **Keep me from the traps they have set for me,**
 from the snares of those who do wrong.
10 **Let the wicked fall into their own nets,**
 but let me escape.

Then all the people say the following praise:

Glory to the Father, and to the Son, and to the Holy Spirit, as it was in the beginning, is now, and will be forever. Amen.

Psalm 142

A psalm of David, regarding his experience in the cave. A prayer.

1 I cry out to the Lord;
 I plead for the Lord's mercy.
2 I pour out my complaints before him
 and tell him all my troubles.
3 **When I am overwhelmed,**
 you alone know the way I should turn.
Wherever I go,
 my enemies have set traps for me.
4 **I look for someone to come and help me,**
 but no one gives me a passing thought!
No one will help me;
 no one cares a bit what happens to me.
5 **Then I pray to you, O Lord.**
 I say, "You are my place of refuge.
 You are all I really want in life.
6 Hear my cry,
 for I am very low.
Rescue me from my persecutors,
 for they are too strong for me.
7 Bring me out of prison
 so I can thank you.
The godly will crowd around me,
 for you are good to me."

Then all the people say the following praise:

Glory to the Father, and to the Son, and to the Holy Spirit, as it was in the beginning, is now, and will be forever. Amen.

Psalm 143

A psalm of David.

1 Hear my prayer, O Lord;
   listen to my plea!
   Answer me because you are faithful and righteous.
2 **Don't put your servant on trial,**
   for no one is innocent before you.
3 **My enemy has chased me.**
   He has knocked me to the ground
   and forces me to live in darkness like those in the grave.
4 **I am losing all hope;**
   I am paralyzed with fear.
5 **I remember the days of old.**
   I ponder all your great works
   and think about what you have done.
6 **I lift my hands to you in prayer.**
   I thirst for you as parched land thirsts for rain. *Interlude*
7 **Come quickly, Lord, and answer me,**
   for my depression deepens.
Don't turn away from me,
   or I will die.
8 **Let me hear of your unfailing love each morning,**
   for I am trusting you.
Show me where to walk,
   for I give myself to you.
9 **Rescue me from my enemies, Lord;**
   I run to you to hide me.
10 **Teach me to do your will,**
   for you are my God.
May your gracious Spirit lead me forward
   on a firm footing.
11 For the glory of your name, O Lord, preserve my life.
   Because of your faithfulness, bring me out of this distress.

12 In your unfailing love, silence all my enemies
and destroy all my foes,
for I am your servant.

Then all the people say the following praise:

**Glory to the Father, and to the Son, and to the Holy Spirit, as it was
in the beginning, is now, and will be forever. Amen.**

Psalm 144

A psalm of David.

1 Praise the Lord, who is my rock.
**He trains my hands for war
and gives my fingers skill for battle.**
2 He is my loving ally and my fortress,
my tower of safety, my rescuer.
He is my shield, and I take refuge in him.
He makes the nations submit to me.
3 O Lord, what are human beings that you should notice them,
mere mortals that you should think about them?
4 For they are like a breath of air;
their days are like a passing shadow.
5 Open the heavens, Lord, and come down.
Touch the mountains so they billow smoke.
6 Hurl your lightning bolts and scatter your enemies!
Shoot your arrows and confuse them!
7 Reach down from heaven and rescue me;
rescue me from deep waters,
from the power of my enemies.
8 **Their mouths are full of lies;**
they swear to tell the truth, but they lie instead.
9 **I will sing a new song to you, O God!**
I will sing your praises with a ten-stringed harp.
10 **For you grant victory to kings!**
You rescued your servant David from the fatal sword.
11 **Save me!**
Rescue me from the power of my enemies.
Their mouths are full of lies;

they swear to tell the truth, but they lie instead.

12 **May our sons flourish in their youth**
like well-nurtured plants.
May our daughters be like graceful pillars,
  carved to beautify a palace.
13 May our barns be filled
  with crops of every kind.
May the flocks in our fields multiply by the thousands,
  even tens of thousands,
14   **and may our oxen be loaded down with produce.**
May there be no enemy breaking through our walls,
  no going into captivity,
  no cries of alarm in our town squares.
15 **Yes, joyful are those who live like this!**
Joyful indeed are those whose God is the Lord.

Then all the people say the following praise:

Glory to the Father, and to the Son, and to the Holy Spirit, as it was
in the beginning, is now, and will be forever. Amen.

Psalm 145:1–13

A psalm of praise of David.

1 I will exalt you, my God and King,
  and praise your name forever and ever.
2 I will praise you every day;
  yes, I will praise you forever.
3 Great is the Lord! He is most worthy of praise!
  No one can measure his greatness.
4 Let each generation tell its children of your mighty acts;
  let them proclaim your power.

5 I will meditate on your majestic, glorious splendor
  and your wonderful miracles.
6 **Your awe-inspiring deeds will be on every tongue;**
  I will proclaim your greatness.
7 **Everyone will share the story of your wonderful goodness;**
  they will sing with joy about your righteousness.

312

8 **The Lord is merciful and compassionate,**
slow to get angry and filled with unfailing love.
9 **The Lord is good to everyone.**
He showers compassion on all his creation.
10 **All of your works will thank you, Lord,**
and your faithful followers will praise you.
11 **They will speak of the glory of your kingdom;**
they will give examples of your power.
12 **They will tell about your mighty deeds**
and about the majesty and glory of your reign.
13 For your kingdom is an everlasting kingdom.
You rule throughout all generations.
The Lord always keeps his promises;
he is gracious in all he does.

Then all the people say the following praise:

Glory to the Father, and to the Son, and to the Holy Spirit, as it was in the beginning, is now, and will be forever. Amen.

Psalm 145:14–21

14 The Lord helps the fallen
and lifts those bent beneath their loads.
15 **The eyes of all look to you in hope;**
you give them their food as they need it.
16 When you open your hand,
you satisfy the hunger and thirst of every living thing.
17 **The Lord is righteous in everything he does;**
he is filled with kindness.
18 The Lord is close to all who call on him,
yes, to all who call on him in truth.
19 **He grants the desires of those who fear him;**
he hears their cries for help and rescues them.
20 The Lord protects all those who love him,
but he destroys the wicked.
21 **I will praise the Lord,**
and may everyone on earth bless his holy name
forever and ever.

Then all the people say the following praise:

Glory to the Father, and to the Son, and to the Holy Spirit, as it was in the beginning, is now, and will be forever. Amen.

Psalm 146

1 Praise the Lord!
Let all that I am praise the Lord.
2   I will praise the Lord as long as I live.
I will sing praises to my God with my dying breath.
3 Don't put your confidence in powerful people;
there is no help for you there.
4 When they breathe their last, they return to the earth,
and all their plans die with them.
5 But joyful are those who have the God of Israel as their helper,
whose hope is in the Lord their God.
6 He made heaven and earth,
the sea, and everything in them.
He keeps every promise forever.
7 **He gives justice to the oppressed**
and food to the hungry.
The Lord frees the prisoners.
8   **The Lord opens the eyes of the blind.**
The Lord lifts up those who are weighed down.
The Lord loves the godly.
9 The Lord protects the foreigners among us.
He cares for the orphans and widows,
but he frustrates the plans of the wicked.
10 **The Lord will reign forever.**
He will be your God, O Jerusalem, throughout the generations.
Praise the Lord!

Then all the people say the following praise:
Glory to the Father, and to the Son, and to the Holy Spirit, as it was in the beginning, is now, and will be forever. Amen.

Psalm 147

1 Praise the Lord!
How good to sing praises to our God!

314

How delightful and how fitting!

2 **The Lord is rebuilding Jerusalem**
and bringing the exiles back to Israel.

3 He heals the brokenhearted
and bandages their wounds.

4 **He counts the stars**
and calls them all by name.

5 How great is our Lord! His power is absolute!
His understanding is beyond comprehension!

6 The Lord supports the humble,
but he brings the wicked down into the dust.

7 Sing out your thanks to the Lord;
sing praises to our God with a harp.

8 He covers the heavens with clouds,
provides rain for the earth,
and makes the grass grow in mountain pastures.

9 **He gives food to the wild animals**
and feeds the young ravens when they cry.

10 He takes no pleasure in the strength of a horse
or in human might.

11 **No, the Lord's delight is in those who fear him,**
those who put their hope in his unfailing love.

12 **Glorify the Lord, O Jerusalem!**
Praise your God, O Zion!

13 **For he has strengthened the bars of your gates**
and blessed your children within your walls.

14 He sends peace across your nation
and satisfies your hunger with the finest wheat.

15 **He sends his orders to the world —**
how swiftly his word flies!

16 **He sends the snow like white wool;**
he scatters frost upon the ground like ashes.

17 **He hurls the hail like stones.**
Who can stand against his freezing cold?

18 **Then, at his command, it all melts.**
He sends his winds, and the ice thaws.

19 **He has revealed his words to Jacob,**
his decrees and regulations to Israel.

20 **He has not done this for any other nation;**

they do not know his regulations.
Praise the Lord!

Then all the people say the following praise:

Glory to the Father, and to the Son, and to the Holy Spirit, as it was in the beginning, is now, and will be forever. Amen.

Psalm 148

1 Praise the Lord!
Praise the Lord from the heavens!
  Praise him from the skies!
2 **Praise him, all his angels!**
  Praise him, all the armies of heaven!
3 **Praise him, sun and moon!**
  Praise him, all you twinkling stars!
4 **Praise him, skies above!**
  Praise him, vapors high above the clouds!
5 **Let every created thing give praise to the Lord,**
  for he issued his command, and they came into being.
6 **He set them in place forever and ever.**
  His decree will never be revoked.
7 **Praise the Lord from the earth,**
  you creatures of the ocean depths,
8 **fire and hail, snow and clouds,**
  wind and weather that obey him,
9 **mountains and all hills,**
  fruit trees and all cedars,
10 **wild animals and all livestock,**
  small scurrying animals and birds,
11 **kings of the earth and all people,**
  rulers and judges of the earth,
12 **young men and young women,**
  old men and children.
13 **Let them all praise the name of the Lord.**
  For his name is very great;
  his glory towers over the earth and heaven!
14 He has made his people strong,
  Honoring his faithful ones —

the people of Israel who are close to him.
Praise the Lord!

Then all the people say the following praise:

Glory to the Father, and to the Son, and to the Holy Spirit, as it was in the beginning, is now, and will be forever. Amen.

Psalm 149

1 Praise the Lord!
Sing to the Lord a new song.
Sing his praises in the assembly of the faithful.
2 **O Israel, rejoice in your Maker.**
O people of Jerusalem, exult in your King.
3 **Praise his name with dancing,**
accompanied by tambourine and harp.
4 **For the Lord delights in his people;**
he crowns the humble with victory.
5 **Let the faithful rejoice that he honors them.**
Let them sing for joy as they lie on their beds.
6 **Let the praises of God be in their mouths,**
and a sharp sword in their hands —
7 **to execute vengeance on the nations**
and punishment on the peoples,
8 to bind their kings with shackles
and their leaders with iron chains,
9 **to execute the judgment written against them.**
This is the glorious privilege of his faithful ones.
Praise the Lord!

Psalm 150

1 Praise the Lord!
Praise God in his sanctuary;
praise him in his mighty heaven!
2 **Praise him for his mighty works;**
praise his unequaled greatness!
3 **Praise him with a blast of the ram's horn;**

praise him with the lyre and harp!
4 **Praise him with the tambourine and dancing;**
  praise him with strings and flutes!
5 **Praise him with a clash of cymbals;**
  praise him with loud clanging cymbals.
6 **Let everything that breathes sing praises to the Lord!
Praise the Lord!**

Then all the people say the following praise:

Glory to the Father, and to the Son, and to the Holy Spirit, as it was in the beginning, is now, and will be forever. Amen.

THE JOURNEY OF DISCIPLESHIP

Dedication of a Child

About the Service of Child Dedication

The Service of Child Dedication allows parents, friends, and church family to enter into a holy covenant to partner in a child's journey of discipleship.

Spiritual sponsors are individuals chosen by the parents to have a special relationship and care for the welfare of both the family and child as they move through the journey of discipleship together. It is best for there to be no fewer than two sponsors, and no more than six. The spiritual sponsors are committing to help through regular prayer, as well as other forms of spiritual and material support; even watching the kids so parents can have a night out can be an important form of ministry.

Ideally, within the Sunday morning worship setting, the Service of Child Dedication should occur after the readings and before the sermon.

Presentation for Dedication

The pastor should call parents and children to the front of the church where they will group together with their sponsors, preferably near to or in front of the altar. Children should stand or be held in front of the parents; spiritual sponsors should stand behind the parents.

The pastor or minister begins the dedication by saying:

Today is an opportunity for the whole church to covenant together by dedicating a child/children to the service of Christ's kingdom and the glory of God. Parents, who is/are the child/children you wish to dedicate?

Parents: We wish to dedicate _____ (*full name, including middle of any*), to the service of Christ's kingdom and the glory of God.

The Parent's Covenant

Pastor: Parents, will you raise your child in the fear and admonition of the Lord, teaching him/her/them by word and deed to hold fast to the essentials of the Christian faith, to keep God's commandments, and to serve him in righteousness and holiness, all his/her/their days?

Parents: **We will, with God's help.**

Pastor: And will you keep your family in the fellowship of the church, live a life of continual repentance, and continually devote yourselves to the breaking of bread and to prayer?

Parents: **We will, with God's help.**

The Sponsor's Covenant

Pastor: Sponsors, do you promise to help these parents as they raise their child in the fear and admonition of the Lord, to support them with prayer, encouragement, counsel, and through the gifts of your time and resources, as may be necessary?

Spiritual Sponsors: **We will, with God's help.**

The Church's Covenant

The Church's covenant is made after all parents and sponsors have given their covenants.

Pastor: Church family, do you promise to support the instruction of this child/these children by continually holding their parents and sponsors up in prayer, by giving faithfully and generously to support their instruction in the Lord through the ministry of this church, and by providing them with a safe, peaceable, and holy environment as they grow in the journey of discipleship?

Church Family: **We will, with God's help.**

Prayer of Dedication

Pastor: Amen and Amen. Let us pray.

Then the pastor will either say a prayer extemporaneously or say the following dedication prayer (or something similar).

Heavenly Father, you are a good and gracious Father, tender and compassionate to all your children, abounding in good and perfect gifts. We praise you for the gift of new life that we see expressed today through the heartbeat(s) of this child/these children; we bring them before you and dedicate them to your hands. We realize that everything we have comes from you and we are simply offering this child/these children back to you as an act of honor and praise.

Lord Jesus Christ, we are grateful for the example you gave during your earthly ministry to bless and minister to little children, and to treat them with dignity. You wouldn't allow the children to be sent away but asked that the little ones come to you. Therefore, in obedience to your command, we bring this child/these children to you and pray that he/she/they may learn to follow your example and grow to become more and more like you each and every day of his/her/their lives.

Holy Spirit, we ask that you come and fill our lives with your wisdom and knowledge as we disciple this child/these children who have been placed in our care. Preserve us in faith and help us to always walk in you, as we live out Christ's example in our homes and this church family.

Holy God, we dedicate this child/these children to you, confident not in ourselves, but in your wonderful faithfulness. We pray this in the name of our Lord Jesus Christ, your Son, who lives and reigns with you in the unity of the Holy Spirit, one God, forever and ever. Amen.

Presentation of Bible and Sealed Letter

At this time the pastor presents the child's parents with a Bible and presents the sponsors with a sealed letter from the church leadership. The letter describes the day, reiterates the dedication of the parents, sponsors, and the church to help the child grow in their journey of discipleship, and provides encouragement to the child and family. The letter is to be given by the sponsors to the family on the day of the child's baptism.

The following may be said to the parents and sponsors separately or all at once while a helper hands out the Bible(s) and letter(s).

Pastor: Parents, please accept this/these Bible/Bibles from your church family as a token of our covenant with you. The Word of God is living and active, so read it and memorize it and God will be faithful to lead you always.

Pastor: Sponsors, please accept this/these letter/letters as the bond of your pledge to help this/these families in their journey of discipleship. In the upper room, Jesus consecrated friendship and made it holy, so walk faithfully as friends of this family, and give this letter as an encouragement and reminder of God's faithfulness on the day this/these child/children is/are baptized.

The Benediction

Then the pastor will close with this Benediction:

Parents, Sponsors and Church: "Let the message about Christ, in all its richness, fill your lives. Teach and counsel each other with all the wisdom he gives. Sing psalms and hymns and spiritual songs to God with thankful hearts. And whatever you do or say, do it as a representative of the Lord Jesus, giving thanks through him to God the Father." Amen.

Colossians 3:16–17 (NLT)

After the Benediction, the families will return to their seats.

A New Baptist Catechism

This New Baptist Catechism (2020) can be used to shape instruction for the unconverted in the home and in the church. It is also suitable to shape instruction for believing persons whom the church is preparing for baptism.

This catechism is based primarily on the 1963 and 2000 versions of the Baptist Faith and Message, but it contains additional material that seeks to add clarity and to reflect upon the current situation and diversity of Southern Baptist witness while remaining faithful to historic Baptist commitments. Language borrowed directly from the Baptist Faith and Message is used with the written acknowledgement of the Executive Committee of The Southern Baptist Convention. Each group of questions provides scriptural proofs at the end of the section.

It is not necessary for a local church to agree with every point of the catechism to use it in their context, so long as they are in agreement on the essential elements of doctrine. In fact, points of disagreement on secondary matters can provide natural conversational contexts to point out local or personal distinctives.

Nevertheless, in order to avoid needless controversy, any person authorized to teach in the church should read the whole catechism carefully, reflect on it, and obtain permission from appropriate church authorities before using it in formal instruction in the church.

Holy Scripture

1: What is the Bible?

The Bible is the perfect record of God's revelation of himself to humanity.

2: How did the Bible come to exist?

Long ago, God inspired certain men to write the sixty-six works that comprise the Bible. The Holy Spirit inspired the people of God throughout history to gather these works together into one canon of Holy Scripture.

3: Is the Bible trustworthy?

The Bible is trustworthy because it is inspired by God. He has ensured that it contains every truth necessary for our salvation and that it is without error.

4: Will the Bible ever become irrelevant?

No. The Bible reveals the character and nature of God and his unchanging standards for righteousness. It will therefore remain relevant to the end of the world.

5: What is the role of the Bible in the life of the Church?

The Holy Bible is a totally unique and precious repository of every truth necessary for our salvation and is the only formal authority for Christian faith and practice. Holy Scripture is the wellspring of all orthodox Christian preaching, teaching, and spiritual formation, and should therefore be personally studied and publicly read in worship.

6: What is the principle aim of the Bible?

All of Scripture bears testimony to Christ, who is himself the incarnate and personal self-revelation of God.

7: Is it proper to reverence Holy Scripture in the same way that we reverence Jesus Christ?

No. Jesus Christ is the direct, personal, and incarnate self-revelation of God's own being. Reverencing Holy Scripture in the same way that we reverence Jesus Christ is idolatry. God is not a book, nor can the fullness of his being ever be contained in any sensible sign besides Jesus Christ.

8: Can the revelation of God in Scripture and the self-revelation of God in Christ contradict each other?

No. Even though we do not reverence them identically, they are in perfect accord. It is an improper use of the Bible to claim the behaviors or nature of Christ as a justification for ignoring or subverting the authority of the full canon of Scripture, or for subverting any clear moral teaching of Holy Scripture.

Scriptural References for Questions 1–8:

Exodus 20:3-6; Exodus 24:4; Deuteronomy 4:1–2; Deut. 17:19; Joshua 8:34; Psalms 19:7–10; Ps. 119:11,89,105,140; Isaiah 34:16; Isa. 40:8; Jeremiah 15:16; Jer. 36:1–32; Matthew 5:17–18; Matt. 22:29; Luke 21:33; Lk. 24:44–46; John 1:1-18; John 5:39; Jn. 16:13–15; Jn. 17:17; Acts 2:16ff.; Acts 17:11; Romans 15:4; Rom. 16:25–26; 2 Timothy 3:15–17; Hebrews 1:1–2; Heb. 4:12; 1 Peter 1:25; 2 Peter 1:19–21;

The Godhead & God the Father

9: How many Gods are there?

There is only one true and living God.

10: How does this God exist?

God is triune; he exists and reveals himself to us as Father, Son, and Holy Spirit, with distinct personal attributes but without division of nature, essence, or being.

11: What is the nature and character of God?

God is an intelligent, spiritual, and personal being. He is the Creator, Redeemer, Preserver, and Ruler of the universe. God is infinite in holiness and in all other perfections. God is all powerful and all knowing; his perfect knowledge extends to all things past, present, and future, including the future decisions of his creatures.

12: What is our obligation to God?

We owe God the highest love, reverence, and obedience.

13: What does Scripture teach about the person of God the Father?

God the Father reigns with providential care over his universe and his creatures and governs the unfolding of all human history according to the purposes of his grace. He is all powerful, all knowing, all loving, and all wise.

14: What is the Father's relationship to the Church?

God is Father in truth to those who become children of God through faith in Jesus Christ.

15: What is the Father's relationship to those outside the Church?

Though God's covenant relationship with his people is special, he is fatherly in his attitude toward all people.

Scriptural References for Questions 9–15:

Genesis 1:1; Gen. 2:7; Exodus 3:14; Ex. 6:2–3; Ex. 15:11ff.; Ex. 20:1ff.; Leviticus 22:2; Deuteronomy 6:4; Deut. 32:6; 1 Chronicles 29:10; Psalm 19:1–3; Isaiah 43:3,15; Isa. 64:8; Jeremiah 10:10; Jer. 17:13; Matthew 6:9ff.; Matt. 7:11; Matt. 23:9; Matt 28:19; Mark 1:9–11; John 4:24; Jn. 5:26; Jn. 14:6–13; Jn. 17:1–8; Acts 1:7; Romans 8:14–15; 1 Corinthians 8:6; Galatians 4:6; Ephesians 4:6; Colossians 1:15; 1 Timothy 1:17; Hebrews 11:6; Heb. 12:9; 1 Peter 1:17; 1 John 5:7.

God the Son

16: What does Scripture teach about the nature and incarnation of God the Son?

Jesus Christ is the eternal Son of God. In his incarnation, the Son of God was conceived of the Holy Spirit and born of the virgin Mary. As a man, Christ took upon himself the fullness of human nature with its demands and necessities, identifying himself completely with mankind, yet was without sin.

17: What does Scripture teach about the life of Jesus?

As the last and greatest of all prophets, Jesus perfectly proclaimed the will of God. In all ways, he honored the divine law by his personal obedience.

18: What does Scripture teach concerning the death of Jesus?

In his substitutionary death on the cross, the Lord Jesus Christ acted as High Priest for the people of God, offering himself up to make provision for the redemption of his people from sin.

19: What does Scripture teach about the resurrection of Jesus?

On the third day, Christ was raised from the dead with a glorified body and appeared to his disciples as the person who was with them before his crucifixion. He ascended into heaven and is now exalted at the right hand of God.

20: What does Scripture teach about the ongoing life and work of the Son?

Jesus lives as a High Priest forever, living to make intercession for his people, the One Mediator between God and humanity, fully God, fully man, in whose person is effected reconciliation between God and sinners.

21: What does Scripture teach concerning the reign of Christ?

Jesus now dwells in and with all believers as their living and ever-present Lord and King. He will return in power and glory to judge the world and to consummate his redemptive mission by establishing the kingdom.

Scriptural References for Questions 16–21:

Genesis 18:1ff.; Psalms 2:7ff.; Ps. 110:1ff.; Isaiah 7:14; Isa. 53:1–12; Matthew 1:18–23; Matt. 3:17; Matt. 8:29; Matt. 11:27; Matt. 14:33; Matt. 16:16,27; Matt. 17:5; Matt. 27; Matt. 28:1–6,19; Mark 1:1; Mk. 3:11; Luke 1:35; Lk. 4:41; Lk. 22:70; Lk. 24:46; John 1:1–18,29; Jn. 10:30,38; Jn. 11:25–27; Jn. 12:44–50; Jn. 14:7–11; Jn. 16:15–16,28; Jn. 17:1–5, 21–22; Jn. 20:1–20,28; Acts 1:9; Acts 2:22–24; Acts 7:55–56; Acts 9:4–5,20; Romans 1:3–4; Rom. 3:23–

26; Rom. 5:6–21; Rom. 8:1–3,34; Rom. 10:4; 1 Corinthians 1:30; 1 Cor. 2:2; 1 Cor. 8:6; 1 Cor. 15:1–8,24–28; 2 Corinthians 5:19–21; 2 Cor. 8:9; Galatians 4:4–5; Ephesians 1:20; Eph. 3:11; Eph. 4:7–10; Philippians 2:5–11; Colossians 1:13–22; Col. 2:9; 1 Thessalonians 4:14–18; 1 Timothy 2:5–6; 1 Tim. 3:16; Titus 2:13–14; Hebrews 1:1–3; Heb. 4:14–15; Heb. 7:14–28; Heb. 9:12–15,24–28; Heb. 12:2; Heb. 13:8; 1 Peter 2:21–25; 1 Pet. 3:22; 1 John 1:7–9; 1 Jn. 3:2; 1 Jn. 4:14–15; 1 Jn. 5:9; 2 John 7–9; Revelation 1:13–16; Rev. 5:9–14; Rev. 12:10–11; Rev. 13:8; Rev. 19:16.

God the Holy Spirit

22: Who is the Holy Spirit?

The Holy Spirit is a person, the Lord and Giver of Life, and the fully divine Spirit of God.

23: What is the relationship of the Holy Spirit to the origin and transmission of the Bible?

It was the Holy Spirit who inspired holy men of old to write the scriptures. Through his ministration, the Bible has been preserved in substance, inviolate, from generation to generation.

24: What is the ongoing work of the Holy Spirit?

Through illumination, he enables mankind to understand truth. He exalts Christ. He convicts people of sin, of righteousness, and of judgment. He effectually calls his people to the Savior and effects regeneration.

25: What is the Baptism of the Holy Spirit?

The Holy Spirit baptizes every believer into the body of Christ at the moment of regeneration. This baptism of the Holy Spirit is the one and only baptism for the remission of sins, of which water baptism provides a sensible sign.

26: How does the Holy Spirit equip believers for service in the Church and in the world?

The Holy Spirit cultivates Christian character, comforts believers, and bestows the spiritual gifts by which they serve God through his Church. He enlightens and empowers the believer and the Church in worship, evangelism, and service.

27: What is the effect of the Spirit's indwelling?

The Spirit seals the believer unto the day of final redemption. His presence in the Christian is the guarantee that God will bring the believer into the fullness of the stature of Christ.

Scriptural References for Questions 21–27:

Genesis 1:2; Judges 14:6; Job 26:13; Psalms 51:11; 139:7ff.; Isaiah 61:1–3; Joel 2:28–32; Matthew 1:18; Matt. 3:16; Matt. 4:1; Matt. 12:28–32; Matt. 28:19; Mark 1:10,12; Luke 1:35; Lk. 4:1,18–19; Lk. 11:13; Lk. 12:12; Lk. 24:49; John 4:24; Jn. 14:16–17,26; Jn. 15:26; Jn. 16:7–14; Acts 1:8; Acts 2:1–4,38; Acts 4:31; Acts 5:3; Acts 6:3; Acts 7:55; Acts 8:17,39; Acts 10:44; Acts 13:2; Acts 15:28; Acts 16:6; Acts 19:1–6; Romans 8:9–11,14–16,26–27; 1 Corinthians 2:10–14; 1 Cor. 3:16; 1 Cor. 12:3–11,13; Galatians 4:6; Ephesians 1:13–14; Eph. 4:30; Eph. 5:18; 1 Thessalonians 5:19; 1 Timothy 3:16; 1 Tim. 4:1; 2 Timothy 1:14; 2 Tim. 3:16; Hebrews 9:8,14; 2 Peter 1:21; 1 John 4:13; 1 Jn. 5:6–7; Revelation 1:10; Rev. 22:17.

Humanity

28: What is humanity?

Humanity is the special creation of God, both male and female, made in God's own image.

29: How did God create humanity?

God created humanity, male and female, as the crowning work of his creation. The gift of natural biological gender is thus a part of the goodness of God's creation.

30: What was the original condition of humanity?

In the beginning, humans were innocent of sin and its consequences and were endowed by the Creator with freedom of choice.

31: How did sin enter the world?

By their free choice, Adam and Eve succumbed to temptation, sinned against God, and brought sin into the human race.

32: What is the effect of the fall on human nature?

When humanity transgressed the command of God, it fell from its original state of innocence. Consequently, all humans inherit a nature and an environment in bondage to sin. Therefore, as soon as they are capable of moral action, they become actual transgressors and ratify their guilt.

33: How are people returned to a state of peace and reconciliation with God?

Only the grace of God can return humanity to a state of peace and holy fellowship with God, and enable people to fulfill the creative purpose of God.

34: How is the sacredness, dignity, and worth of every human person established?

The sacredness of human personality is established by God, who created people in his own image. Therefore, every person of every race possesses full dignity and is worthy of respect and Christian love.

Scriptural References for Questions 28–34:

Genesis 1:26–30; Gen. 2:5,7,18–22; Gen. 3; Gen. 9:6; Psalms 1; Ps. 8:3–6; Ps. 32:1–5; Ps. 51:5; Isaiah 6:5; Jeremiah 17:5; Matthew 16:26; Acts 17:26–31; Romans 1:19–32; Rom. 3:10–18,23; Rom. 5:6,12,19; Rom. 6:6; Rom. 7:14–25; Rom. 8:14–18,29; 1 Corinthians 1:21–31; 1 Cor. 15:19,21–22; Ephesians 2:1–22; Colossians 1:21–22; Col. 3:9–11.

Salvation

35: What is the scope of personal salvation?

Personal salvation involves the redemption of the whole person — body and soul.

36: To whom is salvation offered?

Salvation is offered freely to all who accept Jesus Christ as Lord and Savior, who, by his own blood, obtained eternal redemption for the believer.

37: Are there other religions or paths that lead to salvation?

There is no salvation outside the one true Church, the bride of Christ, which consists of all those who have a personal, saving faith in Jesus Christ as risen Lord.

38: What are the scriptural phases of salvation?

In its broadest sense, salvation includes the phases of regeneration, justification, sanctification, and glorification.

39: What is regeneration?

Regeneration, or the new birth, is a work of God's grace whereby believers become new creatures in Christ Jesus. It is a change of heart wrought by the Holy Spirit through conviction of sin, to which the sinner responds in repentance toward God and faith in the Lord Jesus Christ.

40: What is the relationship between faith and repentance?

Repentance and faith are inseparable experiences and gifts of grace.

41: What is repentance?

Repentance is a genuine turning away from sin toward God.

42: What is faith?

Faith is a gift from God; it is the acceptance of Jesus Christ as the Son of God and the promised Messiah. It is the trust that we will rise to eternal life on the last day because of Christ's finished work, and the commitment of the entire personality to him as Lord and Savior.

43: What is justification?

Justification is God's gracious and full acquittal, upon principles of his love and righteousness, of all sinners who repent and believe in Christ.

44: What is the effect of justification?

Justification brings the believer into a relationship of peace and favor with God.

45: What is sanctification?

Sanctification is the process, beginning in regeneration, by which the believer is set apart for God's purposes. The believer is enabled to cooperate in their progress toward moral and spiritual maturity through the indwelling presence and power of the Holy Spirit.

46: What is the course of sanctification?

Sanctification should continue throughout the regenerate person's life.

47: What is glorification?

Glorification is the culmination of salvation and is the final blessed and abiding state of the redeemed.

Scriptural References for Questions 35–47:

Genesis 3:15; Exodus 3:14–17; Ex. 6:2–8; Matthew 1:21; Matt. 4:17; Matt. 16:21–26; Matt. 27:22–28:6; Luke 1:68–69; Lk. 2:28–32; John 1:11–14,29; Jn. 3:3–21,36; Jn. 5:24; Jn. 10:9,28–29; Jn. 15:1–16; Jn. 17:17; Acts 2:21; Acts 4:12; Acts 15:11; Acts 16:30–31; Acts 17:30–31; Acts 20:32; Romans 1:16–18; Rom. 2:4; Rom. 3:23–25; Rom. 4:3ff.; Rom. 5:8–10; Rom. 6:1–23; Rom. 8:1–18,29–39; Rom. 10:9–10,13; Rom. 13:11–14; 1 Corinthians

1:18,30; 1 Cor. 6:19–20; 1 Cor. 15:10; 2 Corinthians 5:17–20; Galatians 2:20; Gal. 3:13; Gal. 5:22–25; Gal. 6:15; Ephesians 1:7; Eph. 2:8–22; Eph. 4:11–16; Philippians 2:12–13; Colossians 1:9–22; Col. 3:1ff.; 1 Thessalonians 5:23–24; 2 Timothy 1:12; Titus 2:11–14; Hebrews 2:1–3; Heb. 5:8–9; Heb. 9:24–28; Heb. 11:1–12:8,14; James 2:14–26; 1 Peter 1:2–23; 1 John 1:6–2:11; Revelation 3:20; Rev. 21:1–22:5.

God's Sovereign Choice

48: What is election?

Election is God's sovereign choice, according to which he calls, regenerates, justifies, sanctifies, and glorifies sinners.

49: Does election contradict human responsibility?

No. It is consistent with human responsibility and includes all the means God uses to persuade, shape, and keep the human will unto the day of salvation.

50: What is the nature and purpose of election?

Election is infinitely wise, holy, and unchangeable. The purpose of election is to put God's sovereign goodness and grace on glorious display for all the world to see.

51: What is the effect of a true understanding of election?

A true understanding of election excludes boasting and promotes humility.

52: What is the relationship between election and final salvation?

Because all those whom God has accepted in Christ and sanctified by his Spirit are elect, they will never fall away from the state of grace. They shall persevere in faith and the fellowship of the church to the end of their earthly lives.

53: Does election mean believers do not commit individual sins or go through seasons of sinfulness?

No. Believers may fall into sin through neglect and temptation, grieve the Spirit, impair their graces and comforts, and bring reproach on the cause of Christ and temporal judgments on themselves. Even so, God is faithful to return these believers to repentance and to keep them by his own power unto the day of salvation.

Scriptural References for Questions 48–53:

Genesis 12:1–3; Exodus 19:5–8; 1 Samuel 8:4–7,19–22; Isaiah 5:1–7; Jeremiah 31:31ff.; Matthew 16:18–19; Matt. 21:28–45; Matt. 24:22,31; Matt. 25:34; Luke 1:68–79; Lk. 2:29–32; Lk. 19:41–44; Lk. 24:44–48; John 1:12–14; Jn. 3:16; Jn. 5:24; Jn. 6:44–45,65; Jn. 10:27–29; Jn. 15:16; Jn. 17:6,12,17–18; Acts 20:32; Romans 5:9–10; Rom. 8:28–39; Rom. 10:12–15; Rom. 11:5–7,26–36; 1 Corinthians 1:1–2; 1 Cor. 15:24–28; Ephesians 1:4–23; Eph. 2:1–10; Eph. 3:1–11; Colossians 1:12–14; 2 Thessalonians 2:13–14; 2 Timothy 1:12; 2 Tim. 2:10,19; Hebrews 11:39–12:2; James 1:12; 1 Peter 1:2–5,13; 1 Pet. 2:4–10; 1 John 1:7–9; 1 Jn. 2:19; 1 Jn. 3:2.

The Church

54: What is the New Testament Church?

A New Testament church of the Lord Jesus Christ is an autonomous local congregation of baptized believers, associated by covenant in the faith and fellowship of the gospel, where the word of God is faithfully preached and the two ordinances of Christ are rightly administered.

55: What is the vocation of the church?

The vocation of the church is to worship, love, and obey God. It fulfills this vocation by exercising the gifts, rights, and privileges invested in it by God's Word, and by seeking to extend the gospel to the ends of the earth.

56: How should the local church be governed?

Each congregation operates under the Lordship of Christ through congregational processes. In such a congregation, each member is responsible and accountable to Christ as Lord, to fellow members of the church as brothers and sisters, and to the leadership of the church inasmuch as that leadership walks in humility, holiness, and obedience to the revealed will of God.

57: What are the scriptural offices of the church?

The scriptural officers of the church are elders (πρεσβύτερος) and deacons (διάκονος). The pastor is an elder charged with overseeing a local church (ἐπίσκοπος). While both men and women are gifted for ministry, as qualified by Scripture, only men may serve as elders (πρεσβύτερος).

58: What is the one, holy, universal, and apostolic Church?

The New Testament also speaks of the Church as the body of Christ, a mystical union that includes all the redeemed through all the ages, believers from every tribe, tongue, people, and nation. This alone is the one, holy, universal, and apostolic Church.

Scriptural References for Questions 54–58:

Matthew 16:15–19; Matt. 18:15–20; Acts 2:41–42,47; Acts 5:11–14; Acts 6:3–6; Acts 13:1–3; Acts 14:23,27; Acts 15:1–30; Acts 16:5; Acts 20:28; Romans 1:7; 1 Corinthians 1:2; 1 Cor. 3:16; 1 Cor. 5:4–5; 1 Cor. 7:17; 1 Cor. 9:13–14; 1 Cor. 12; Ephesians 1:22–23; Eph. 2:19–22; Eph. 3:8–11,21; Eph. 5:22–32; Philippians 1:1; Colossians 1:18; 1 Timothy 2:9–14; 1 Tim. 3:1–15; 1 Tim. 4:14; Hebrews 11:39–40; 1 Peter 5:1–4; Revelation 2–3; Rev. 21:2–3.

Baptism and Communion

59: What are the two ordinances of Christ?

The two ordinances of Christ are baptism and the Lord's Supper.

60: What is the New Testament mode of Christian baptism?

In the New Testament, Christian baptism is the immersion of a believer in water in the name of the Father, the Son, and the Holy Spirit.

61: What is the symbolic value of baptism?

Baptism symbolizes the believer's faith in a crucified, buried, and risen Savior, the believer's death to sin, the burial of the old life, and the resurrection to walk in newness of life in Christ Jesus.

62: To what promise does the visible sign of baptism bear witness?

As a visible sign, baptism bears witness to the promise of final victory over death in the resurrection to glory of all the dead in Christ.

63: What is the relationship between baptism and the privileges of church membership and the Lord's Supper?

Baptism is a prerequisite to the privileges of church membership and to participation in the Lord's Supper.

64: What is the symbolic value of the Lord's Supper?

The Lord's Supper symbolizes the broken body and shed blood of the Lord Jesus Christ. Believers partake of the Lord's Supper as an act of obedience whereby they memorialize the death of the Redeemer for the remission of their sins.

65: To what promises does the Lord's Supper bear witness?

The Lord's Supper is a visible sign that reminds the church of the fact that Christ's body and blood were given for her and of the promise that he will gather her to joyous celebration at the final Marriage Supper of the Lamb.

66: What is the spiritual value of the Lord's Supper?

Those who receive the visible elements of this ordinance worthily, and by faith, spiritually receive and feed upon Christ crucified and all the benefits of his death and in this way are nourished and strengthened to a life of holiness.[21]

---

[21] This answer is derived from the Baptist Confession of 1689, Chapter 30, article 7.

67: Does the spiritual value of the Lord's Supper require that the substance of the elements be changed or transformed?

No. The doctrine which maintains a change of the substance of the bread and wine into the substance of Christ's body and blood, commonly called transubstantiation, is not necessary to the spiritual value of the Lord's Supper.

Scriptural References for Questions 59–67:

Matthew 3:13–17; Matt. 26:26–30; Matt. 28:19–20; Mark 1:9–11; Mk. 14:22–26; Luke 3:21–22; Lk. 22:19–20; Lk. 24:6; John 3:23; Acts 2:41–42; Acts 3:21; Acts 8:35–39; Acts 16:30–33; Acts 20:7; Acts 39; Romans 6:3–5; 1 Corinthians 10:16,21; 1 Cor. 11:23–29; Colossians 2:12.

The Lord's Day

68: What is the Lord's Day?

Sunday, the first day of the week, is the Lord's Day.

69: What is the proper use of the Lord's Day?

The Lord's Day is a Christian institution for regular observance that commemorates the resurrection of Christ from the dead. It should include exercises of worship and spiritual devotion, both public and private.

70: What activities are allowed on the Lord's Day?

Activities on the Lord's Day should be commensurate with the Christian's conscience under the Lordship of Jesus Christ.

The Kingdom of God

71: What is the extent of God's reign?

God's reign includes both his general sovereignty over the whole universe and his particular kingship over all those who willfully acknowledge him as King.

72: How do people enter into the Kingdom of God?

The Kingdom of Heaven is the realm of salvation into which people enter by trustful, childlike commitment to Jesus Christ.

73: How should Christians labor for the kingdom?

Christians ought to pray and labor so that the kingdom may come and God's will be done on earth.

74: When will the full consummation of the kingdom occur?

The full consummation of the kingdom awaits the return of Jesus Christ and the end of this age.

Acts 17:22–31; Romans 5:17; Rom. 8:19; 1 Corinthians 15:24–28; Colossians 1:13; Hebrews 11:10,16; Heb. 12:28; 1 Peter 2:4–10; 1 Pet. 4:13; Revelation 1:6,9; Rev. 5:10; Rev. 11:15; Rev. 21–22.

The Last Things

75: When and how will the end times come to pass?

God, in his own time and in his own way, will bring the world to its appropriate end.

76: What will happen at the end of human history?

According to his promise, Jesus Christ will return personally and visibly in glory to the earth, the dead will be raised, and Christ will judge all people in righteousness.

77: What will be the eternal fate of the unrighteous?

The unrighteous will be consigned to hell, the place of everlasting punishment.

78: What will be the eternal fate of the righteous?

The righteous, in their resurrected and glorified bodies, will receive their reward and will dwell forever in the new heaven and the new earth with the Lord.

Scriptural References for Questions 75–78:

Isaiah 2:4; Isa. 11:9; Matthew 16:27; Matt. 18:8–9; Matt. 19:28; Matt. 24:27,30,36,44; Matt. 25:31–46; Matt. 26:64; Mark 8:38; Mk. 9:43–48; Luke 12:40,48; Lk. 16:19–26; Lk. 17:22–37; Lk. 21:27–28; John 14:1–3; Acts 1:11; Acts 17:31; Romans 14:10; 1 Corinthians 4:5; 1 Cor. 15:24–28,35–58; 2 Corinthians 5:10; Philippians 3:20–21; Colossians 1:5; Col. 3:4; 1 Thessalonians 4:14–18; 1 Thess.

5:1ff.; 2 Thessalonians 1:7ff.; 2 Thess. 2; 1 Timothy 6:14; 2 Timothy 4:1,8; Titus 2:13; Hebrews 9:27–28; James 5:8; 2 Peter 3:7ff.; 1 John 2:28; 1 Jn. 3:2; Jude 14; Revelation 1:18; Rev. 3:11; Rev. 20:1–22:13.

Evangelism and Missions

79: What is the vocation and privilege of every believer to grow the kingdom of God?

It is the vocation and privilege of every follower of Christ and of every church of the Lord Jesus Christ to grow the kingdom by making disciples of all nations and by proclaiming the Gospel in word and deed to a world lost in sin.

80: What gives rise to the evangelistic impulse?

The new birth of man's spirit by God's Holy Spirit means the birth of love for others. Evangelism is the overflow of Christian love.

81: Why is missionary activity necessary?

Missionary effort rests upon a spiritual necessity of the regenerate life and is expressly and repeatedly commanded in the teachings of Christ. The Lord Jesus Christ has commanded the preaching of the gospel to all nations.

82: How is the duty and privilege of evangelism to be carried out?

It is the duty of every child of God to seek constantly to win the lost to Christ by verbal witness undergirded by a Christian lifestyle and by other methods in harmony with the gospel of Christ.

Scriptural References for Questions 79–82:

Genesis 12:1–3; Exodus 19:5–6; Isaiah 6:1–8; Matthew 9:37–38; Matt. 10:5–15; Matt. 13:18–30,37–43; Matt. 16:19; Matt. 22:9–10; Matt. 24:14; Matt. 28:18–20; Luke 10:1–18; Lk. 24:46–53; John 14:11–12; Jn. 15:7–8,16; Jn. 17:15; Jn. 20:21; Acts 1:8; Acts 2; Acts 8:26–40; Acts 10:42–48; Acts 13:2–3; Romans 10:13–15; Ephesians 3:1–11; 1 Thessalonians 1:8; 2 Timothy 4:5; Hebrews 2:1–3; Heb. 11:39–12:2; 1 Peter 2:4–10; Revelation 22:17.

Education

83: What is the relationship of the Christian religion to learning?

Christianity is the faith of enlightenment and intelligence. In Jesus Christ abide all the treasures of wisdom and knowledge. All sound learning is, therefore, a part of our Christian heritage.

84: What is the relationship of the Christian religion to knowledge?

The new birth opens all human faculties and creates a thirst for knowledge.

85: Why should local churches support education?

The cause of education in the kingdom of Christ is co-ordinate with the causes of missions and general benevolence and should receive, along with these, the liberal support of the churches. An adequate system of Christian education is necessary for a complete spiritual program for Christ's people.

86: What is the relationship between academic freedom and academic responsibility in Christian education?

In Christian education, there should be a proper balance between academic freedom and academic responsibility. Freedom in any orderly relationship of human life is always limited and never absolute. The freedom of a teacher in a Christian school, college, or seminary is limited by the preeminence of Jesus Christ, by the authoritative nature of the scriptures, and by the distinct purpose for which the school exists.

Scriptural References for Questions 83–86:

Deuteronomy 4:1,5,9,14; Deut. 6:1–10; Deut. 31:12–13; Nehemiah 8:1–8; Job 28:28; Psalms 19:7ff.; Ps. 119:11; Proverbs 3:13ff.; Prov. 4:1–10; Prov. 8:1–7,11; Prov. 15:14; Ecclesiastes 7:19; Matthew 5:2; Matt. 7:24ff.; Matt. 28:19–20; Luke 2:40; 1 Corinthians 1:18–31; Ephesians 4:11–16; Philippians 4:8; Colossians 2:3,8–9; 1 Timothy 1:3–7; 2 Timothy 2:15; 2 Tim. 3:14–17; Hebrews 5:12–6:3; James 1:5; Jas. 3:17.

Stewardship

87: Who is the source of all our blessings, temporal and spiritual?

God is the source of all blessings, temporal and spiritual; all that we have and are we owe to him.

88: How are Christians to understand all their blessings?

Christians should understand their material and spiritual blessings as entrusted to them to use for the glory of God and for helping others; they confer on Christians a holy obligation to the whole world and trusteeship in the gospel.

89: How are Christians obliged to exercise stewardship?

Christians are obliged to serve Christ with their time, talents, and material possessions.

90: How is the work of the church supported?

The work of the church is supported as believers give of their means — cheerfully, regularly, systematically, proportionately, and liberally — for the advancement of the Redeemer's cause on earth.

Scriptural References for Questions 87–90:

Genesis 14:20; Leviticus 27:30–32; Deuteronomy 8:18; Malachi 3:8–12; Matthew 6:1–4,19–21; Matt. 19:21; Matt. 23:23; Matt. 25:14–29; Luke 12:16–21,42; Lk. 16:1–13; Acts 2:44–47; Acts 5:1–11; Acts 17:24–25; Acts 20:35; Romans 6:6–22; Romans 12:1–2; 1 Corinthians 4:1–2; 1 Cor. 6:19–20; 1 Cor. 12; 1 Cor. 16:1–4; 2 Corinthians 8–9; 2 Cor. 12:15; Philippians 4:10–19; 1 Peter 1:18–19.

Christian Cooperation

91: What should occasion Christian cooperation?

Christ's people should, as occasion requires, organize such associations and conventions as may best secure cooperation for the great objects of the kingdom of God.

92: What are Baptist associations and conventions?

They are voluntary and advisory bodies designed to elicit, combine, and direct the energies of Baptists in the most effective manner.

93: What is the authority of associations and conventions?

Associations and conventions have no authority over one another or over the churches, except insofar as a local church, by its own autonomy and authority, may prescribe. [22]

94: How should the members of local churches cooperate with one another?

Members of New Testament churches should cooperate with one another in carrying forward missional, educational, and charitable ministries for the extension of Christ's kingdom.

95: What is Christian unity?

Christian unity in the New Testament sense is spiritual harmony and voluntary cooperation for common ends by various groups of Christ's people.

96: Should Baptists cooperate with other denominations?

Cooperation is desirable between the various orthodox Christian denominations when the end to be attained is itself justified and when such cooperation involves no violation of conscience or compromise of loyalty to Christ and his word as revealed in the New Testament.

Scriptural References for Questions 90–96:

Exodus 17:12; Ex. 18:17ff.; Judges 7:21; Ezra 1:3–4; Ez. 2:68–69; Ez. 5:14–15; Nehemiah 4; Neh. 8:1–5; Matthew 10:5–15; Matt.

---

22 This nuance was thought necessary to allow for the increasingly prevalent phenomenon of multi-site ministries and churches and church planting networks, situations in which it might be convincingly argued that several local "churches" are acting in concert, with central leadership exercising an authority delegated by those local congregations.

20:1–16; Matt. 22:1–10; Matt. 28:19–20; Mark 2:3; Luke 10:1ff.; Acts 1:13–14; Acts 2:1ff.; Acts 4:31–37; Acts 13:2–3; Acts 15:1–35; 1 Corinthians 1:10–17; 1 Cor. 3:5–15; 1 Cor. 12; 2 Corinthians 8–9; Galatians 1:6–10; Ephesians 4:1–16; Philippians 1:15–18.

The Christian and Social Order

97: How should Christians understand Christ's will in their own life of the believer and in the life society at large?

All Christians are under obligation to seek to make Christ's will the supreme organizing principle for our own lives and for human society at large.

98: What is the only true foundation of the improvement of society and the establishment of righteousness?

The only true means and methods for the permanent improvement of society and the establishment of righteousness are rooted in the regeneration of the individual by the saving grace of God in Jesus Christ.

99: What are Christians obligated to oppose in the public square?

In the spirit of Christ, Christians should oppose racism, every form of greed, selfishness, vice, and all forms of sexual immorality, including adultery, homosexuality, and pornography.

100: For whom are Christians obliged to become advocates and defenders?

We should work to provide for the orphaned, the needy, the abused, the aged, the helpless, and the sick. We should speak on behalf of the unborn and contend for the sanctity of all human life from conception to natural death.

101: What should Christians labor to make the common principles for industry, government, and society?

Every Christian should seek to bring industry, government, and society as a whole under the sway of the principles of righteousness, justice, truth, and brotherly love.

102: With whom should Christians work in the attainment of these goals?

In order to promote these ends, Christians should be ready to work with all people of good will in any good cause, always being careful to act in the spirit of love without compromising their loyalty to Christ and his truth.

Scriptural References for Questions 97–102:

Exodus 20:3–17; Leviticus 6:2–5; Deuteronomy 10:12; Deut. 27:17; Psalm 101:5; Micah 6:8; Zechariah 8:16; Matthew 5:13–16,43–48; Matt. 22:36–40; Matt. 25:35; Mark 1:29–34; Mk. 2:3ff.; Mk. 10:21; Luke 4:18–21; Lk. 10:27–37; Lk. 20:25; John 15:12; Jn. 17:15; Romans 12–14; 1 Corinthians 5:9–10; 1 Cor. 6:1–7; 1 Cor. 7:20–24; 1 Cor. 10:23–11:1; Galatians 3:26–28; Ephesians 6:5–9; Colossians 3:12–17; 1 Thessalonians 3:12; Philemon; James 1:27; Jas. 2:8.

Peace and War

103: How should Christians seek to live in relationship to their fellow human beings?

It is the duty of Christians to seek peace with all persons on principles of righteousness.

104: How should Christians believe and act with respect to war?

In accordance with the spirit and teachings of Christ, they should do all in their power to put an end to war.

105: What is the only true remedy for war?

The only true remedy for the spirit of war is the gospel of our Lord. The supreme need of the world is the acceptance of his teachings in all the affairs of humankind and of nations and the practical application of his law of love. Christian people throughout the world should pray for the reign of the Prince of Peace.

Scriptural References for Questions 103–105:

Isaiah 2:4; Matthew 5:9,38–48; Matt. 6:33; Matt. 26:52; Luke 22:36,38; Romans 12:18–19; Rom. 13:1–7; Rom. 14:19; Hebrews 12:14; James 4:1–2.

The Relationship of Church and State

106: What is the proper allegiance of the human conscience?

God alone is Lord of the conscience, and he has left it free from human doctrines and commandments which are contrary to his word or not contained in it. The state must not attempt to command a loyalty or adulation that is reserved to God alone, and Christians ought never to render such unconditional loyalty or adulation to the state.

107: What is the proper relationship between church and state?

Church and state should be separate.

108: For what purpose has God created the civil state?

The state exists to ensure justice and restrain wickedness. The laws that it creates, to that effect, only encompass life, property, and the realities of this world. Any civil law that seeks to control, dominate, or manipulate the human spirit exceeds the divine vocation of the civil government.

109: What does the state owe the church?

The state owes to every church protection and full freedom in the pursuit of its spiritual ends. In providing for such freedom, no ecclesiastical group or denomination should be favored by the state over another.

110: What is the obligation of the Christian to the state?

Civil government is ordained of God. It is the duty of Christians to render loyal obedience to the civil government so long as that obedience does not violate the command of Christ. However, Christians are under a holy obligation to peacefully disobey any decree that violates the command of Christ or seeks to elevate the state to a station reserved for God alone.

111: What means should the church employ to carry out its vocation?

The gospel of Christ contemplates spiritual means alone for the pursuit of its ends. The church should not resort to the civil power to carry on its work.

112: What are the limits of the powers of the state with respect to religious penalties and taxes?

The state has no right to impose penalties for religious opinions of any kind. The state has no right to impose taxes for the support of any form of religion.

113: What is the ideal constitution of the state with respect to the exercise of religion?

A free church in a free state is the Christian ideal, and this implies the right of free and unhindered access to God on the part of all people and the right to form and propagate opinions in the sphere of religion without interference by the civil power.

Scriptural References for Questions 106–113:

Genesis 1:27; Gen. 2:7; Matthew 6:6–7,24; Matt. 16:26; Matt. 22:21; John 8:36; Acts 4:19–20; Romans 6:1–2; Rom. 13:1–7; Galatians 5:1,13; Philippians 3:20; 1 Timothy 2:1–2; James 4:12; 1 Peter 2:12–17; 1 Pet. 3:11–17; 1 Pet. 4:12–19.

The Family

114: What is the biblical, orthodox understanding of Christian marriage?

The biblical, orthodox understanding of Christian marriage is a union of one man and one woman, as defined by the two natural biological genders, in covenant commitment for a lifetime.

115: What is the highest vocation of Christian marriage?

The highest vocation of marriage is to act as a parable of the mystical union between Christ and the Church.

116: How does marriage provide for human needs?

Marriage provides men and women the framework for intimate companionship, the channel of sexual expression according to biblical standards, and the means for procreation of the human race.

117: What is the relationship of the family to society?

God has ordained the family as the foundational institution of human society. It is composed of persons related to one another by marriage, blood, or adoption.

118: In the marriage relationship, who is of greater value?

Neither the husband nor the wife is of greater value than the other; both are of equal dignity and worth before God since both are created in God's image.

119: How should men and women relate to one another in the context of marriage?

Since the marriage relationship models the way God relates to his people, those who are married should take heed of the holy covenant that binds them together and honor the solemn and joyful obligations that arise from that covenant.

120: What is the obligation of the husband to the wife?

The husband is to sacrificially love his wife as Christ loved the Church.

121: How did Christ model a husband's love?

Christ modeled this this kind of sacrificial love when he took up the basin and the towel to serve the disciples, and ultimately when he gave his life to ransom sinners. So also, the husband must serve his family; just as Christ came not to be served but to serve and give his life as a ransom for many.

122: What is the obligation of the husband to his family?

The husband has a God-given responsibility to disciple, provide for, protect, and lead his family.

123: What is the obligation of the wife to her husband?

A wife is to submit herself graciously to the godly leadership of her husband even as the Church willingly submits to the headship of Christ.

124: How did Christ model this obligation?

By graciously submitting himself to the Father's will.

125: What is the obligation of a wife to her family?

The wife has a God-given responsibility to help in managing the household and nurturing the next generation.

126: What is the obligation of Christian parenthood?

Christian parents are to demonstrate to their children God's pattern for marriage. Parents are to teach their children to value biblical truth, spiritually form their children through worship and prayer, lead their children through the example of a consistent lifestyle and loving discipline, and to make choices for the family that are based on biblical truth. The obligation of Christian parenthood, however, is not a warrant for cruelty or callousness.

127: What is the beginning and the nature of human life?

Children are persons, from the moment of conception, and are a blessing and heritage from the Lord.

128: What is the obligation of Christian childhood?

Children are to honor and obey their parents in the Lord.

Scriptural References for Questions 114–124:

Genesis 1:26–28; Gen. 2:15–25; Gen. 3:1–20; Exodus 20:12; Deuteronomy 6:4–9; Joshua 24:15; 1 Samuel 1:26–28; Psalms 51:5; Ps. 78:1–8; Ps. 127; Ps. 128; Ps. 139:13–16; Proverbs 1:8; Prov. 5:15–20; Prov. 6:20–22; Prov. 12:4; Prov. 13:24; Prov. 14:1; Prov. 17:6; Prov. 18:22; Prov. 22:6,15; Prov. 23:13–14; Prov. 24:3; Prov. 29:15,17; Prov. 31:10–31; Ecclesiastes 4:9–12; Prov. 9:9; Malachi 2:14–16; Matthew 5:31–32; Matt. 18:2–5; Matt. 19:3–9; Mark 10:6–12; Romans 1:18–32; 1 Corinthians 7:1–16; Ephesians 5:21–33; Eph. 6:1–4; Colossians 3:18–21; 1 Timothy 5:8,14; 2 Timothy 1:3–5; Titus 2:3–5; Hebrews 13:4; 1 Peter 3:1–7.

Believer's Baptism

Presentation of the Candidate

The pastor will enter the baptistry or river or other natural waters. If the baptismal waters will not accommodate both the pastor and the baptismal candidate, the pastor will situate himself behind the baptismal waters.[23]

Then the pastor may read an appropriate passage from Scripture, such as: Matthew 3:13–17, 28:18–20, Romans 6:3–12, Galatians 3:26–27, or Mark 1:4–8.

Then the pastor may present the candidate for baptism with these words:

Friends, [Name] has come today to be baptized in obedience to Christ's command.

> *Or, after inviting the candidate into the baptismal waters, by asking the candidate this question:*

Pastor: [Full Given Name], why have you come here today?
Baptismal Candidate: **To be baptized in obedience to our Lord's command.**

Then the pastor may offer a few words of testimony to the congregation about the candidate and his or her salvation experience, or may allow another person to do so, or may simply proceed to the Examination.

---

23 Many modern baptisms are occurring in swimming pools, portable baptismals, or cattle troughs that will not accommodate two persons.

Examination of the Candidate

Then, the pastor will invite the candidate to enter the baptismal waters if he or she has not already entered, offering assistance as needed.

In river baptisms, the candidate should face downstream so that the current assists in bringing the candidate out of the water.

Upon entering the baptismal waters, the candidate should be directed to stand on the pastor's left.

Then the pastor asks the following questions of the candidate:

Pastor: Have you repented of sin and renounced Satan and all the forces of spiritual darkness that war against God?
Baptismal Candidate: **Yes, I have.**

Pastor: And have you turned to Jesus Christ in faith and accepted him as your Lord and Savior?
Baptismal Candidate: **Yes, I have.**

Pastor: And will you promise to follow and obey him the rest of your life and to remain in the fellowship of his church?
Baptismal Candidate: **Yes, I will.**

Baptism

After the examination, the candidate will grasp his or her left wrist with the right hand and will hold his or her hands together above the water as instructed.

Then the pastor will hold up his left hand and will say:

[Name], based on your public profession of faith, and in obedience to the command of our Lord and Savior Jesus Christ, I baptize you, my brother/sister, in the name of the Father, and of the Son, and of the Holy Spirit.

Then the pastor will gently guide the candidate's left hand towards the face so that the nose can be covered by the left hand prior to immersion and will firmly grasp the candidate's right wrist.

Then the pastor will brace himself, placing his left hand on the shoulder blades of the candidate. The candidate will bend his or her knees slightly as the pastor lowers them completely into the water.

While the pastor is lowering the candidate into the water, he will say:

Buried with Christ in baptism.

As the candidate emerges from the water, the pastor will say:

Raised to walk in newness of life.

Prayer for the Candidate(s)

When all candidates have been baptized, the pastor will say:

Let us pray.

Then the pastor may pray an extemporaneous prayer asking God to bless the candidate(s) and preserve him or her in a life of godliness and faith. Or the pastor may say this prayer:

Grant, O Lord, that all who receive/are receiving the holy sign of baptism, and have made a public profession of faith through that sign, may live in the power of Christ's resurrection and look eagerly for him to come again in glory. Amen.

Holy Communion

Communion By Two Distributions

This order of communion is designed for communion ware that holds each element in separate trays.

The Great Thanksgiving

After having come to stand behind or near the alter, the pastor may begin with an excerpt of the Great Thanksgiving or may simply proceed to the last declaration of the Great Thanksgiving by saying:

Blessed indeed are all those Jesus has invited to his table, the wedding supper of the Lamb!

If a fuller form of the Great Thanksgiving is used, the pastor will proceed with these words:

Brothers and sisters/Friends, it is a good and joyful thing to give thanks to our God, the Father Almighty, Creator of heaven and earth! For great is his lovingkindness and wonderful the salvation he has made for us through the body and blood of his only Son!

For this reason, we praise him, joining our voices with all the company of heaven, who forever proclaim the glory of his name:

Holy, Holy, Holy Lord,
God of power and might,
heaven and earth are full of your glory!
Hosanna in the highest!
Blessed is he who comes in the name of the Lord!

And blessed indeed are all those he has invited to his table, the wedding supper of the Lamb!

The Prayer of Consecration

Then the pastor will say: Let us pray; *and he, or another minister will say this prayer of consecration (or something very similar in his own words):*

Most Merciful Father, with thankful hearts we celebrate our redemption in this memorial of the Last Supper. As we recall Christ's death, resurrection, and ascension, we offer you every part of this remembrance as a gift of praise and thanksgiving.

Sanctify every part of this service, by your Holy Spirit, so that your people might be nourished by Christ, who is himself the true Bread of Heaven and the Water of Eternal Life.

Sanctify us also that we may truly keep the feast, not with the old bread leavened with malice and wickedness, but with the unleavened bread of sincerity and truth. And grant that we may serve you in unity, faithfulness, and peace until you bring us into the joy of your eternal kingdom.

All this we ask through your Son Jesus Christ: by him, and with him, and in him, in the unity of the Holy Spirit, all honor and glory are yours, Almighty Father, now and forevermore. Amen.

The Admonition of Scripture

Then the pastor will continue by saying:

Now hear the admonition of Holy Scripture concerning the Lord's Supper:

Then he will read the following passage from 1 Cor. 11:27-29 (ESV):

"whoever eats this bread or drinks the Lord's cup in a way unworthy of the Lord will be guilty of the body and the blood of the Lord. [28] But let a man examine himself, and so let him eat of the bread, and drink of the cup. [29] For he who eats and drinks in an unworthy way eats and drinks judgment to himself if he doesn't discern the Lord's body."

And then he will continue:

Therefore, let us all keep silence, putting away every worldly thought, for the Lord is in his holy temple.

Then, after a sufficient pause, the pastor, looking up, proclaims this truth to the congregation:

Friends, this is the Lord's table, and we are not worthy even to gather the crumbs that fall from it. But God, in his great mercy, has given these signs as gifts to his people until he returns. Take them in remembrance of him and let your hearts be nourished by faith and hope and filled with thanksgiving!

The Bread and the Cup

The Bread

After having said these words the pastor will uncover the bread and, taking up a piece, will break it and place a piece in each tray, and then he will hand a tray to each congregant or ushers/deacons. Then they will distribute the bread to the congregation.

After serving the congregation, the ushers/deacons return and hand their trays to the pastor. The first tray(s) will be set on the table. The pastor will use the last tray to serve the deacons and ushers.

The last deacon or usher to be served will take the tray from the pastor and serve him. After the last tray is set down, the pastor will motion for an usher or deacon to say a prayer over the bread.

When the prayer is finished, the pastor, standing behind the alter, will say these words from 1 Corinthians 11:23b-24 (WEB):

> "the Lord Jesus on the night in which he was betrayed took bread. When he had given thanks, he broke it and said, "Take, eat. This is my body, which is broken for you. Do this in memory of me.""

After having said these words, the pastor will eat the bread, and the congregation with him will do likewise.

The Cup

After eating the bread, the pastor will uncover the cup and hand a tray to each congregant or ushers/deacons. They will distribute to the congregation.

After serving the congregation, the ushers/deacons return and hand their trays to the pastor. The first tray(s) will be set on the table. The pastor will use the last tray to serve the deacons and ushers.

The last deacon or usher to be served will take the tray from the pastor and serve him. After the last tray is set down, the pastor will motion for an usher or deacon to say a prayer over the cup.

When the prayer is finished, the pastor, standing behind the alter continue with these words from 1 Corinthians 11:25–26 (WEB):

"In the same way, after supper he took the cup, saying, 'This cup is the new covenant in my blood; do this, whenever you drink it, in remembrance of me. For as often as you eat this bread and drink the cup, you proclaim the Lord's death until he comes.'"

After having said these words, the pastor will drink the cup, and the congregation with him will do likewise.

After everyone has taken the cup, the pastor will end by saying:

Let us pray.

The Response of Thanksgiving

Then the pastor will say this prayer (or something similar) on behalf of the congregation:

Heavenly Father, we give you praise because you are the Holy One, the Lord God of Hosts, creator of Heaven and Earth. We thank you for pouring out your mercy on us so freely and generously.

Lamb of God, we praise you and thank you for taking away the sins of the world, even our own. Strengthen us by your presence that we might grow more like you every day.

Holy Spirit, help us to grow in grace and to persevere in the faith. Cause us, we pray, to remember the life, death, and resurrection of Jesus every day, even as we have remembered it this day, just as he taught us.

Holy God, One and Triune, let us depart this day in your peace. All these things we pray in the mighty name of Jesus. Amen.

In lieu of, or in addition to the above prayer, the pastor may ask all present to stand and sing the Doxology, or another suitable anthem.

The Benediction

Then the pastor may dismiss the congregation with one of these benedictions:

"Let the message about Christ, in all its richness, fill your lives. Teach and counsel each other with all the wisdom he gives. Sing psalms and hymns and spiritual songs to God with thankful hearts. And whatever you do or say, do it as a representative of the Lord Jesus, giving thanks through him to God the Father." Amen. (Colossians 3:16–17, NLT)

"Now all glory to God, who is able, through his mighty power at work within us, to accomplish infinitely more than we might ask or think. Glory to him in the church and in Christ Jesus through all generations forever and ever! Amen." (Ephesians 3:20–21, NLT)

Communion by a Single Distribution

This order of communion is designed for communion trays that hold both elements in one tray.

After having come to stand behind the alter, the pastor will begin by saying:
Please Stand.

After the congregation stands, if the elements are not already on the altar, the deacons/ushers will bring the elements in, carrying them in from the entrance or narthex of the church and will place them on the altar.

The Great Thanksgiving

The pastor may choose to incorporate this version of the Great Thanksgiving or may simply proceed to the last declaration of the Great Thanksgiving by saying:

Blessed indeed are all those Jesus has invited to his table, the wedding supper of the Lamb! You may be seated.

If the Great Thanksgiving is used, after the elements are on the table, the pastor will proceed with these words:

Pastor: The Lord be with you.
People: **And also with you.**

Pastor: Lift up your hearts.
People: **We lift them up to the Lord.**

Pastor: Let us give thanks to the Lord our God.
People: **It is right and good for us give him our thanks and praise.**

371

Then the pastor will continue with this excerpt of the Great Thanksgiving:

Brothers and sisters, it is a good and joyful thing to give thanks to our God, the Father Almighty, Creator of heaven and earth! For great is his lovingkindness and wonderful the salvation he has made for us through the body and blood of his only Son!

Therefore, let us join our voices with all the company of heaven, who forever proclaim the glory of his name:

Then the people will join together in this reading (or the pastor may read it himself):

Holy, Holy, Holy Lord,
God of power and might,
heaven and earth are full of your glory!
Hosanna in the highest!
Blessed is he who comes in the name of the Lord!

Then the pastor will respond to the people or simply continue with these words:

And blessed indeed are all those he has invited to his table; to the wedding supper of the Lamb!

You may be seated.

The Words of Institution

Then the pastor will continue with the words of institution from 1 Corinthians 11:23b–26 (WEB). The pastor may carefully uncover the elements so that a piece of bread can be elevated and broken at the appropriate moment. He will say:

"the Lord Jesus on the night in which he was betrayed took bread. When he had given thanks, he broke it and said, "Take, eat. This is my body, which is broken for you. Do this in memory of me.""

Then the pastor may hold up and break a piece of the bread and say:

"In the same way, after supper he took the cup, saying, 'This cup is the new covenant in my blood; do this, whenever you drink it, in remembrance of me. For as often as you eat this bread and drink the cup, you proclaim the Lord's death until he comes.'

The Prayer of Consecration

Then the pastor will say:

Let us pray.

And he will say this prayer of consecration (or something very similar in his own words). Or the pastor may motion for a deacon to say this prayer (or something very similar):

Most Merciful Father, with thankful hearts we celebrate our redemption in this memorial of the Last Supper. As we recall Christ's death, resurrection, and ascension, we offer you every part of this remembrance as a gift of praise and thanksgiving.

Sanctify every part of this service, by your Holy Spirit, so that your people might be nourished by Christ, who is himself the true Bread of Heaven and the Water of Eternal Life.

Sanctify us also that we may truly keep the feast, not with the old bread, leavened with malice and wickedness, but with the unleavened bread of sincerity and truth. And grant that we may serve you in unity, faithfulness, and peace until you bring us into the joy of your eternal kingdom.

All this we ask through your Son, Jesus Christ: By him, and with him, and in him, in the unity of the Holy Spirit, all honor and glory is yours, Almighty Father, now and forevermore. Amen.

The Admonition of Scripture

Then the pastor will continue by saying:

Now hear the admonition of Holy Scripture concerning the Lord's Supper.

Then he will read the following passage from 1 Cor. 11:27-29 (ESV):

"whoever eats this bread or drinks the Lord's cup in a way unworthy of the Lord will be guilty of the body and the blood of the Lord. 28 But let a man examine himself, and so let him eat of the bread, and drink of the cup. 29 For he who eats and drinks in an unworthy way eats and drinks judgment to himself if he doesn't discern the Lord's body."

Therefore, let us all keep silence, putting away every worldly thought, for the Lord is in his holy temple.

The Prayer of Humility

Then after a brief pause the people will join together in the following prayer, or the pastor may say it on behalf of all:

Heavenly Father, we do not presume to come to your table trusting in our own righteousness but trusting only in your great mercy. We are not worthy to even gather up the crumbs under your table. But you are the same Lord who takes delight in showing mercy. Give us grace therefore to participate in this holy sign and to believe the promise you have given in it. Lord, let us be spiritually nourished by it; use it to shape and to mold us, according to your will, for your glory alone. Amen.

Then the pastor, looking up, proclaims this truth to the congregation:

This is the Lord's table and these signs are his gifts to his people. Take them in remembrance of him and let your hearts be nourished by faith and hope and filled with thanksgiving!

Distribution

Beginning, at the word "thanksgiving", *and throughout the distribution, music should play softly in the background. The pastor will uncover the elements or, if they are already uncovered, will hand a tray to each usher or deacon, and they will distribute the elements to the congregation.*

After serving the congregation, the ushers or deacons return and hand their trays to the pastor. The pastor will set the trays on the table and will use the last tray to serve the ushers or deacons.

Then the pastor will set down the last tray, and taking the bread in his right hand, he will signal for a deacon to say a prayer over the elements.

The Bread and The Cup

Then, after the prayer is complete, the pastor will hold up the bread before the congregation and will say the following words (or something similar):

The body of our Lord Jesus Christ given for you. Take and eat it in remembrance of him.

After the pastor says these words, all will take their bread and will eat it.

Then the pastor will take a cup in his right hand and, holding it up before the congregation, will say the following words (or something similar):

The blood of our Lord Jesus Christ shed for the forgiveness of sins. Drink from it all of you.

After the pastor says these words, all will take their cup and will drink the wine.

The Response of Thanksgiving

Then the pastor will say:

Let us pray.

And all will say this prayer in unison, or the pastor may read it alone or say something similar on behalf of the congregation:

Heavenly Father, we give you praise because you are the Holy One, the Lord God of Hosts, creator of Heaven and Earth. We thank you for pouring out your mercy on us so freely and generously.

Lamb of God, we praise you and thank you for taking away the sins of the world, even our own. Strengthen us by your presence that we might grow more like you every day.

Holy Spirit, help us to grow in grace and to persevere in the faith. Cause us, we pray, to remember the life, death, and resurrection of Jesus every day, even as we have remembered it this day, just as he taught us.

Holy God, One and Triune, let us depart this day in your peace. All these things we pray in the mighty name of Jesus. Amen.

Or, in lieu of or in addition to the above prayer, the pastor may ask all present to stand and sing the Doxology.

The Benediction

After the doxology, the pastor may dismiss the congregation with one of these benedictions:

"May the grace of the Lord Jesus Christ, the love of God, and the fellowship of the Holy Spirit be with you all." Amen.
2 Corinthians 13:14 (NLT)

"Let the message about Christ, in all its richness, fill your lives. Teach and counsel each other with all the wisdom he gives. Sing psalms and hymns and spiritual songs to God with thankful hearts. And whatever you do or say, do it as a representative of the Lord Jesus, giving thanks through him to God the Father." Amen.
Colossians 3:16,17 (NLT)

"May you experience the love of Christ, though it is too great to understand fully. Then you will be made complete with all the fullness of life and power that comes from God. Now all glory to God, who is able, through his mighty power at work within us, to accomplish infinitely more than we might ask or think. Glory to him in the church and in Christ Jesus through all generations forever and ever! Amen."
Ephesians 3:19–21 (NLT)

Communion by Intinction

After having come to stand behind the alter, the pastor will begin by saying:
Please Stand.

After the congregation stands, the deacons will bring in the elements from the back of the church and place them on the altar.

The Great Thanksgiving

The pastor may choose to incorporate the Great Thanksgiving or may simply proceed to the last declaration of the Great Thanksgiving by saying:

Blessed indeed are all those Jesus has invited to his table: the wedding supper of the Lamb! You may be seated.

If the Great Thanksgiving is used, after the elements are on the table, the pastor will proceed with these words:

Pastor: The Lord be with you.
People: **And also with you.**

Pastor: Lift up your hearts.
People: **We lift them up to the Lord.**

Pastor: Let us give thanks to the Lord our God.
People: **It is right and good for us give him our thanks and praise.**

Then the pastor will continue with this excerpt of the Great Thanksgiving:

Brothers and sisters, it is a good and joyful thing to give thanks to our God, the Father Almighty, Creator of heaven and earth! For great is his lovingkindness and wonderful the salvation he has made for us through the body and blood of his only Son!

Therefore let us join our voices with all the company of heaven, who forever proclaim the glory of his name:

Then the people will join together in this reading (or the pastor may read it himself on behalf of all):

Holy, Holy, Holy Lord, God of power and might,
heaven and earth are full of your glory!
Hosanna in the highest!
Blessed is he who comes in the name of the Lord!

Then the pastor will respond to the people or simply continue with these words:

And blessed indeed are we and all those he has invited to his table; to the wedding supper of the Lamb! You may be seated.

The Words of Institution

Then the pastor will carefully uncover the elements and will continue with the words of institution from 1 Corinthians 11:23b–26 (WEB). (As he is saying them, he may choose to pick up a piece of bread so that it can be broken at the appropriate moment.)

"the Lord Jesus on the night in which he was betrayed took bread. When he had given thanks, he broke it and said, "Take, eat. This is my body, which is broken for you. Do this in memory of me.""

Then the pastor may hold up and break a piece of the bread.

"In the same way, after supper he took the cup, saying, 'This cup is the new covenant in my blood; do this, whenever you drink it, in remembrance of me. For as often as you eat this bread and drink the cup, you proclaim the Lord's death until he comes."

The Prayer of Consecration

Then the pastor will say: Let us pray.

And he will say this prayer of consecration (or something very similar):

Most Merciful Father, with thankful hearts we celebrate our redemption in this memorial of the Last Supper. As we recall Christ's death, resurrection, and ascension, we offer you every part of this remembrance as a gift of praise and thanksgiving.

Sanctify every part of this service, by your Holy Spirit, so that your people might be nourished by Christ, who is himself the true Bread of Heaven and the Water of Eternal Life.

Sanctify us also that we may truly keep the feast, not with the old bread, leavened with malice and wickedness, but with the unleavened bread of sincerity and truth. And grant that we may serve you in unity, faithfulness, and peace until you bring us into the joy of your eternal kingdom.

All this we ask through your Son, Jesus Christ: By him, and with him, and in him, in the unity of the Holy Spirit, all honor and glory are yours, Almighty Father, now and forevermore. Amen.

The Admonition of Scripture

Then the pastor will continue by saying:

Now hear the admonition of Holy Scripture concerning the Lord's Supper.

Then he will read the following passage from 1 Cor. 11:27-29 (ESV):

"whoever eats this bread or drinks the Lord's cup in a way unworthy of the Lord will be guilty of the body and the blood of the Lord. [28] But let a man examine himself, and so let him eat of the bread, and drink of the cup. [29] For he who eats and drinks in an unworthy way eats and drinks judgment to himself if he doesn't discern the Lord's body."

Therefore, let us all keep silence, put away every worldly thought, and examine their own hearts, for the Lord is in his holy temple.

The Prayer of Humility

Then, after a brief pause, the people will join together in the following prayer, or the pastor may say it on behalf of all:

Heavenly Father, we do not presume to come to your table trusting in our own righteousness, for we are not even worthy to gather up the crumbs under your table. But you are the same Lord who takes delight in showing kindness and mercy. Give us grace, therefore, to participate in this holy sign with unburdened hearts and to believe the promise you have given in it. Lord, let us be spiritually nourished by this remembrance; use it to shape and to mold us, according to your will, for your glory alone. Amen."

Then the pastor, looking up, proclaims this truth to the congregation:

This is the Lord's table and these signs are his gifts to his people. Take them in remembrance of him and let your hearts be nourished by faith and hope and filled with thanksgiving!

The Communication of Officiants

At the word "Thanksgiving", and throughout communication, music should play in the background. This music can be congregational.

The pastor will begin by carefully uncovering all the elements and reverently folding up the cloths.

Then, the pastor will take a paten and will place a piece of unleavened bread into the cupped hands of each minister or deacon, saying to each in turn the following words (or something similar):

The body of our Lord Jesus Christ broken for you.

Or:

The body of the Lord.

Then, the pastor will take a chalice to each deacon and, offering the chalice to each, will say the following words (or something similar):

The blood of our Lord Jesus Christ shed for the forgiveness of sins.

As the pastor says these words to each communicant, they will dip the bread in the wine and will eat it.

Then the pastor returns to stand behind the altar and sets down the chalice. At the same time, the last minister or deacon to receive communion should come to stand directly in front of the altar and should repeat the steps above for the pastor. After serving the pastor, the deacon should set down the chalice and return to his place.

Then the pastor will give a chalice to each deacon furthest from the alter. The pastor will give a paten to the minister or deacon nearest to the altar and will take a paten for himself.

Then the pastor takes his place while the deacons turn to face the congregation.

The Communication of the Congregation

When the pastor, elders, and deacons are all facing the congregation, that will be the cue for an usher to begin dismissing rows to go forward and receive communion. The communion line should be kept full, but not too long. Unbaptized children may come forward but should not receive communion. Instead, the pastor or elder may lay hands on them and say the following prayer:

May the Lord Jesus draw you to himself in repentance, give you saving faith, and preserve you unto everlasting life. Amen.

The pastor, elder, or deacon should place the bread into the cupped hand of each baptized believer with the following words (or something similar):

The body of our Lord Jesus Christ broken for you.

Or:

The body of the Lord.

Then each baptized believer will go stand in front of the pastor, elder, or deacon holding the chalice on the side of the altar nearest to them. The pastor, elder, or deacon will offer each the chalice while saying the following words (or something similar):

The blood of our Lord Jesus Christ shed for the forgiveness of sins.

When the pastor, elder, or deacon has said these words, the baptized believer will dip his bread in the wine and will eat it.

When all have taken communion, the pastor, elders, or deacons will be seated until the current song ends.

The Response of Thanksgiving

Then the pastor will return to stand behind the altar and will say:

Let us pray.

And all will say this prayer in unison, or the pastor may read it alone or say something similar on behalf of the congregation:

Heavenly Father, we give you praise because you are the Holy One, the Lord God of Hosts, creator of Heaven and Earth. We thank you for pouring out your mercy on us so freely and generously.

Lamb of God, we praise you and thank you for taking away the sins of the world, even our own. Strengthen us by your presence that we might grow more like you every day.

Holy Spirit, help us to grow in grace and to persevere in the faith. Cause us, we pray, to remember the life, death, and resurrection of Jesus every day, even as we have remembered it this day, just as he taught us.

Holy God, One and Triune, let us depart this day in your peace. All these things we pray in the mighty name of Jesus. Amen.

Or, in lieu of or in addition to the above prayer, the pastor may ask all present to stand and sing the Doxology.

The Benediction

Then the pastor may dismiss the congregation with one of these benedictions:

"May the grace of the Lord Jesus Christ, the love of God, and the fellowship of the Holy Spirit be with you all." Amen.
2 Corinthians 13:14 (NLT)

"Let the message about Christ, in all its richness, fill your lives. Teach and counsel each other with all the wisdom he gives. Sing psalms and hymns and spiritual songs to God with thankful hearts. And whatever you do or say, do it as a representative of the Lord Jesus, giving thanks through him to God the Father." Amen.
Colossians 3:16–17 (NLT)

"May you experience the love of Christ, though it is too great to understand fully. Then you will be made complete with all the fullness of life and power that comes from God. Now all glory to God, who is able, through his mighty power at work within us, to accomplish infinitely more than we might ask or think. Glory to him in the church and in Christ Jesus through all generations forever and ever! Amen."
Ephesians 3:19–21 (NLT)

Last Communion

When a believer is near death but unable to celebrate communion outside of their home or other place of care, then it is appropriate for an elder or elders and deacons to take the elements to the believer and celebrate it where they are able.

On occasion, it may be necessary for the one performing this ministry to briefly provide some theological perspective. Baptists do not believe such a communion conveys saving grace, nor do they believe that the minister provides any sacerdotal spiritual benefit. Nevertheless, such a celebration can be a deeply holy moment of remembrance in the believer's journey toward death and can strengthen and fortify their spirit for what lies ahead. Such a request should not be refused, except if there is very serious reason to doubt whether a person has come to saving faith in Christ. In such a case, the Last Communion may unintentionally serve to comfort one who should not yet be comforted by the assurance of an eternity with Christ.

This form of communion may be celebrated immediately before the ministry to the dying believer, but it need not be. It can also be celebrated whenever the whole family is able to gather to the bedside of the dying believer.

Since this method for communion differs somewhat from communion in a church setting, the pastor should familiarize himself with the order of service in advance of providing this ministry.

The Service of the Word

The pastor or other minister should begin by ensuring there is a small table near the place he will be seated, so that the elements and a Bible can be placed there. The pastor will hold the prayer book as a guide, except when it is necessary to administer the elements.

Then the pastor should invite all present to gather and be seated, if they are not already. If possible, all should gather as near as possible to the dying believer.

If copies of this prayer book are available, then the pastor may use the Shortened Order for Morning Prayer as the Service of the Word. If copies of this prayer book are not available, or if the pastor believes a shorter Order may be more appropriate, then he should proceed as follows.

The Invocation

After all are seated, the pastor begins with this brief invocation:

O Lord, open thou our lips. And our mouth shall show forth thy praise.

Glory to the Father, and to the Son, and to the Holy Spirit, as it was in the beginning, is now, and will be forever. Amen.

The Old Testament Reading

If brevity is desired, the Old Testament reading may be omitted. If the Old Testament reading will be used the pastor will say the following:

Hear the words of Holy Scripture from the Old Testament, in the book of_____, beginning in the _____chapter.

Then the pastor, or another person appointed beforehand will read the Old Testament scripture. After the reading, the one reading should pause, and then close by saying:

The word of the Lord.

The Psalm

Then, if prayer books are available, all may say a psalm responsively, or if they are not available, the pastor may decide to read Psalm 46 (ESV) as provided or another suitable Psalm.

1 God is our refuge and strength,
  a very present help in trouble.
2 Therefore we will not fear though the earth gives way,
  though the mountains be moved into the heart of the sea,
3 though its waters roar and foam,
  though the mountains tremble at its swelling. *Selah*
4 There is a river whose streams make glad the city of God,
  the holy habitation of the Most High.
5 **God is in the midst of her; she shall not be moved;**
  God will help her when morning dawns.
6 The nations rage, the kingdoms totter;
  he utters his voice, the earth melts.
7 The Lord of hosts is with us;
  the God of Jacob is our fortress. *Selah*
8 Come, behold the works of the Lord,
  how he has brought desolations on the earth.
9 He makes wars cease to the end of the earth;
  he breaks the bow and shatters the spear;
  he burns the chariots with fire.
10 "Be still, and know that I am God.
  I will be exalted among the nations,
  I will be exalted in the earth!"
11 The Lord of hosts is with us;
  the God of Jacob is our fortress. *Selah*

The New Testament Reading

Then the pastor will say:

Now hear these words of Holy Scripture from the New Testament, the book of_____, beginning in the _____chapter.

Then the pastor, or another person appointed beforehand, will read the New Testament scripture. After the reading, the one reading should pause and then close by saying:

The word of the Lord.

The Lord's Prayer

Then, after the reading of the New Testament scripture, the pastor will say:
And now, Lord, we pray as you taught us.

Then all gathered will say the Lord's Prayer in unison (Matt. 6:9–13 KJV):

Our Father, who art in heaven,
hallowed be thy Name,
thy kingdom come,
thy will be done,
in earth as it is in heaven.
Give us this day our daily bread.
And forgive us our trespasses,
as we forgive those who trespass against us.
And lead us not into temptation,
but deliver us from evil.
For thine is the kingdom, and the power, and the glory,
forever and ever. Amen.

The Service of Holy Communion

The Great Thanksgiving

After the Lord's Prayer, the pastor may choose to proceed with this version of the Great Thanksgiving or may simply proceed to the last declaration of the Great Thanksgiving by saying:

Blessed indeed are all those Jesus has invited to his table: the wedding supper of the Lamb!

If the Great Thanksgiving is used, after the elements are on the table, the pastor will proceed with these words:

Pastor: The Lord be with you.
People: **And also with you.**

Pastor: Lift up your hearts.
People: **We lift them up to the Lord.**

Pastor: Let us give thanks to the Lord our God.
People: **It is right and good for us give him our thanks and praise.**

Then, on behalf of all, the pastor will continue with this excerpt of the Great Thanksgiving:

Friends, it is a good and joyful thing to give thanks to our God, the Father Almighty, Creator of heaven and earth! For great is his lovingkindness and wonderful the salvation he has made for us through the body and blood of his only Son!

For this reason, we do praise him, joining our voices with all the company of heaven who forever proclaim the glory of his name:

Holy, Holy, Holy Lord,
God of power and might,
Heaven and earth are full of your glory!
Hosanna in the highest!
Blessed is he who comes in the name of the Lord!

And blessed indeed are we and all those he has invited to his table, the wedding supper of the Lamb!

The Prayer of Consecration

Then the pastor will say: Let us pray.

And he will say this prayer of consecration (or something very similar in his own words):

Most Merciful Father, with thankful hearts we celebrate our redemption in this memorial of the Last Supper. As we recall Christ's death, resurrection, and ascension, we offer you every part of this remembrance as a gift of praise and thanksgiving.

Sanctify every part of this service, by your Holy Spirit, so that your people might be nourished by Christ, who is himself the true Bread of Heaven and the Water of Eternal Life.

Sanctify us also that we may truly keep the feast, not with the old bread, leavened with malice and wickedness, but with the unleavened bread of sincerity and truth. And grant that we may serve you in unity, faithfulness, and peace until you bring us into the joy of your eternal kingdom.

All this we ask through your Son, Jesus Christ: By him, and with him, and in him, in the unity of the Holy Spirit, all honor and glory is yours, Almighty Father, now and forevermore. Amen.

The Admonition of Scripture

Then the pastor will continue by saying:

Now hear the admonition of Holy Scripture concerning the Lord's Supper.

Then he will read the following passage from 1 Cor. 11:27-29,32 (ESV):

"Whoever eats the bread or drinks the cup of the Lord in an unworthy manner will be guilty of sinning against the body and blood of the Lord. Everyone ought to examine themselves before they eat of the bread and drink from the cup. For those who eat and drink without discerning the body of Christ eat and drink judgment on themselves."

Therefore, let us keep silence, putting away every worldly thought, for the Lord is in his holy Temple.

The Prayer of Humility

Then, after a brief pause, the pastor will say this prayer (or something similar) on behalf of all:

Heavenly Father, we do not presume to come to your table trusting in our own righteousness, for we are not even worthy to gather up the crumbs under your table. But you are the same Lord who takes delight in showing kindness and mercy. Give us grace therefore to participate in this holy sign with unburdened hearts and to believe the promise you have given in it. Lord, let us be spiritually nourished by this remembrance; use it to shape and to mold us, according to your will, for your glory alone. Amen.

The Bread and The Cup

<u>The Bread</u>

After the Prayer of Humility, the pastor will continue with these words from 1 Corinthians 11:23b–24 (WEB):

Scripture tells us how "the Lord Jesus on the night in which he was betrayed took bread. When he had given thanks, he broke it and said, "Take, eat. This is my body, which is broken for you. Do this in memory of me.""

Then the pastor will distribute the bread, individually to each person, if possible, or by passing the paten, if necessary.

When all have their bread, the pastor will pause briefly, hold up his bread, and say these words:

The body of our Lord Jesus Christ given for you. Take and eat it in remembrance of him.

After having said these words, the pastor will eat the bread, and those gathered with him will follow suit.

<u>The Cup</u>

Then the pastor will continue reading from 1 Cor. 11:25–26 (WEB):

"In the same way, after supper he took the cup, saying, 'This cup is the new covenant in my blood; do this, whenever you drink it, in remembrance of me. For as often as you eat this bread and drink the cup, you proclaim the Lord's death until he comes.'"

Then the pastor will distribute the cups to each, individually, if possible, or by passing the tray, if necessary.

When all have their cup, the pastor will pause briefly, hold up his cup, and say these words:

The blood of our Lord Jesus Christ shed for the forgiveness of sins. Drink from it all of you.

Or, if the cup is common, then the pastor may offer it to each person and say the same words to each as they partake.

After everyone has taken the cup, the pastor will end by saying:

Let us pray.

The Response of Thanksgiving

Then the pastor will say: Let us pray.

And all will say this prayer in unison, or the pastor may read it alone or say something similar on behalf of those gathered.

Heavenly Father, we give you praise because you are the Holy One, the Lord God of Hosts, creator of Heaven and Earth. We thank you for pouring out your mercy on us so freely and generously. Lamb of God, we praise you and thank you for taking away the sins of the world, even our own. Strengthen us by your presence that we might grow more like you every day. Holy Spirit, help us to grow in grace and to persevere in the faith. Cause us, we pray, to remember the life, death, and resurrection of Jesus every day, even as we have remembered it this day, just as he taught us. Holy God, One and Triune, let us depart this day in your peace. All these things we pray in the mighty name of Jesus. Amen.

The Benediction

Then the pastor may end the service with this benediction (or with something similar):

"May you experience the love of Christ, though it is too great to understand fully. Then you will be made complete with all the fullness of life and power that comes from God. Now all glory to God, who is able, through his mighty power at work within us, to accomplish infinitely more than we might ask or think. Glory to him in the church and in Christ Jesus through all generations forever and ever! Amen." Ephesians 3:19–21 (NLT)

Group Bible Reading

Guidance for Group Bible Reading Facilitators

What follows is a method for reading and listening to scripture and freely and openly discussing it in a group setting. The facilitator of the group bible reading is not absolved from thorough study and preparation for the group reading and should be personally prepared to answer the following types of questions:

1. Is there a command stated or implied in the passage?
2. How did people in Scripture or in the ancient world fail to keep this command?
3. How do modern people fail to keep this command?
4. How is God's grace present in the passage?
5. How is that same grace present in the church and world today?
6. What are the implications of this scripture for Christian living?
7. How should this scripture impact the way I behave toward my family?
8. How should this scripture impact the way I behave toward my church?
9. How should this scripture impact the way I behave toward unbelievers?

Opening Silence

Begin by encouraging people to eliminate distractions. Depending on the group, you may ask them to simply close their eyes.

Historically, Christians have sometimes helped to eliminate distractions by focusing on an icon (for example: a Christian painting like the Isenheim Altarpiece) or by repeating a prayer like the 'Jesus Prayer' (Lord Jesus Christ, Son of God, have mercy on me, a sinner) or the Lord's Prayer.

The main point here is to simply push away life's distractions: the waiting chores, PTA meetings, leaky faucets, upcoming business meetings, or whatever keeps us from being present and listening to scripture "with the ears of the heart."

This process of preparation should last one minute, and silence should be maintained throughout.

Listening

First Reading

The facilitator breaks the first silence by asking people to listen for something that *catches their attention* as the passage is read a first time (this could be as simple as a color, an image, or a word).

Then the facilitator reads the passage.

After the scripture is read, the facilitator allows everyone to sit in silence for one minute before breaking the silence. Then discussion of the passage and listening prompt may follow.

Or, the facilitator may move immediately to the second reading, deferring discussion until after the fourth reading.

Second Reading

The facilitator prefaces the second reading by asking people to listen for something that *they may not understand* as the passage is read a second time.

Then the facilitator or another person reads the passage.

After the scripture is read, the facilitator allows everyone to sit in silence for one minute before breaking the silence. Then discussion of the passage and listening prompt may follow.

Or, the facilitator may move immediately to the third reading, deferring discussion until after the fourth reading.

Third Reading

The facilitator prefaces the third reading by asking people to listen for something that *points to the gospel* as the passage is read a third time.

Then the facilitator or another person reads the passage.

After the scripture is read, the facilitator allows everyone to sit in silence for one minute before breaking the silence. Then discussion of the passage and listening prompt may follow.

Or, the facilitator may move immediately to the fourth reading.

Fourth Reading

The facilitator prefaces the fourth reading by asking people to listen for something that *God may be inviting them to do* as the passage is read a fourth time.

Then the facilitator or another person reads the passage.

After the scripture is read, the facilitator allows everyone to sit in silence for one minute before breaking the silence. Then the facilitator moves to Application. Or, if all discussion has been deferred, the facilitator should move to a General Discussion.

General Discussion

The facilitator will break the fifth silence by asking people to open their eyes (if they have been closed) and discuss what they may have "heard."

A word of caution is in order here. Clearly, there is a fine line between allowing people the space to share their experience and allowing them the space to share the kind of heresy that confuses people and imperils souls. As the author of 1 John says, we are not to "believe every spirit, but test the spirits to see whether they are from God, because many false prophets have gone out into the world" (1 Jn. 4:1). Serious error should be gently and lovingly but firmly corrected by recourse to Scripture.

On the other hand, it is not really reasonable to expect that there will never be theological error in these kinds of discussions, especially when people who are far from the Lord participate (which is the aim!). Moreover, since we can't really peer into anyone else's heart to know their relationship with God or their struggles, a certain degree of humility and circumspection is also in order. The facilitator should discern very carefully whether it is necessary or helpful to publicly correct a publicly shared experience or insight — "in essentials unity, in non-essentials liberty, and in all things charity."

Life Application

Finally, the facilitator begins the concluding movement by asking people, as the passage is read a fifth time, to close their eyes and listen.

Then the facilitator reads the passage a final time.

After the scripture is read, the facilitator allows everyone to sit in silence for one minute before breaking the silence.

Then the facilitator may briefly offer some of his or her own concluding thoughts or insights about the scripture drawn from his or her own study and reflection, as well as an application of the scripture to the believer's life. After the application, the facilitator should close by saying: "

In the name of Jesus, amen.

Or:

In the name of the Father, the Son, and the Holy Spirit. Amen.

Individual Bible Study

This method can be used to prepare for teaching, leading group bible reading, or even for basic sermon preparation. Before beginning it is a good idea to have a Bible, a pen or pencil, and a piece of paper or journal ready.

Before you begin, select a scripture for study using either the Schedule of Readings in this prayer book or another suitable scripture reading schedule or plan.

Silence

Before you begin, spend a few moments in silence and prayer. Ask the Lord to open your mind, spirit, and heart to learn from Holy Scripture and for God to shape your heart through it.

Reading

After a few moments of prayer, read the selected passage, highlighting key ideas or words as necessary.

Reflection

Next, take a few moments to prayerfully reflect on the passage using the following questions as a guide:

1. Is there a command stated or implied in the passage?
2. How did people in Scripture or in the ancient world fail to keep this command?

3. How do modern people fail to keep this command?
4. How is God's grace present in the passage?
5. How is that same grace present in the church and world today?

Study

Follow your time of reflection with a brief time of study. If you have not been able to answer the reflection questions above, try to answer them through study. Helpful resources include Bible commentaries and Bible dictionaries. Be careful to choose a reputable site if you reference internet resources. Take brief notes if you wish to but do not get bogged down in extensive note taking.

Life Application

Next, take a few moments to prayerfully reflect on what this scripture means for how you live. You may find it helpful to use the following questions to guide your reflection:

1. How should this scripture impact the way I behave toward my family?
2. How should this scripture impact the way I behave toward my church?
3. How should this scripture impact the way I behave toward unbelievers?

Prayer

Finally, conclude your study with a time of worship and prayer using the Order for Midday Devotion and selecting the elements in that Order appropriate to the time of day. Or, you may conclude by writing a prayer in your journal, using the following structure as a guide:

1. **Praise the Father:** In this part of the prayer, you will praise God the Father for his work as evidenced in the scripture you have read. Take time to reflect seriously on this, and write a sentence or two to summarize your thoughts.

2. **Glorify Christ**: Next, write a sentence or two about how this work of God is present in the life and obedience of Jesus.

3. **Invite the Work of the Holy Spirit**: Next, write a sentence or two about how God can do this work in your life through the ministry of the Holy Spirit.

4. **Worship the Trinity**: Finally, make reference to God's whole being, the Holy Trinity, and give the Amen.

So, for example, if you have read Psalm 8, you might write a prayer in your journal that sounds something like this:

Heavenly Father, you are mighty and strong, the only God and the one who has created the beauty of the heavens and the earth. Just as you made the world beautiful, so also Christ made his life a beautiful and pleasing offering to you and recreated the beauty of human life and of the whole world through the obedience of his broken body and shed blood. Help us Lord also, by your Holy Spirit, to live such a holy and pleasing life, so that we might show forth the beauty of your Son to the whole world. All this we pray in Jesus' name, who lives and reigns with you in heaven, together with the Holy Spirit, One God, forever and ever. Amen.

The Ministry of Confession
and Consolation

Corporate Christian worship should always include time set aside for the confession of sins, and for congregants to hear the assurance of forgiveness for all those who truly repent.

The method outlined in this chapter is for personal confession, and may be used as a general form whenever one believer wishes to make a personal, audible confession of sin to another believer.

It is recommended that the *confessor* (the one receiving the confession), in accordance with his or her own conscience, make the following disclosures to the *penitent* (the one making confession) before beginning. The disclosures can occur immediately before the confession, but are probably best given in an initial contact or at some other prior time.

First, the confessor may wish to disclose that Baptists have not historically held that a minister, in whatever capacity or ordination status, has the right to actually confer absolution or the forgiveness of sin. Nevertheless, there are biblical grounds for the practice of confession. James 5:16 admonishes believers to confess their sins, one to another, and to pray for one another. Additionally, Scripture implores believers to "bear one another's burdens, and so fulfill the law of Christ" (Gal. 6:2). So, while Baptists do not believe the pastor or minister grants absolution, it is perfectly scriptural for believers, including ministers, to give and receive confessions. And, in fact, as simple common sense makes clear, believers can experience great relief by getting things "off their chest." In making audible confessions, sin and Satan are deprived of the power they exercise through secrecy. Ultimately, we receive great comfort through the audible reminder that we have found grace and forgiveness in Jesus Christ.

Second, the confessor should disclose that there are some crimes that the law may require laypersons to report. Those who are ordained or actually employed in ministry are protected in many cases by the "seal of the confessional." (All Christian ministers are protected by the seal, not merely Roman Catholics). Thus, ordination or licensure may come to bear on secular obligations, even if, as most Baptists believe, it makes no indelible mark or substantive distinction before God, since all believers are priests. On the other hand, some jurisdictions do not acknowledge or protect the confidentiality of pastoral communications. Accordingly, before receiving confession, every person must ensure that they are well aware of the legal obligations established in their place of residence.

Third, the confessor may wish to disclose that there are some sins he or she may be personally unwilling or unable hold in confidence, regardless of what the law may or may not allow. Examples may include certain crimes against children.

Receiving a Confession

Before beginning, the confessor should allow the penitent to express why they have come. It is best for this to take the form of a natural conversation. During this time, the confessor may wish, especially if he or she is a minister of the church, to offer counsel, direction, and comfort.

After this opening conversation is complete, the confessor will invite both persons to kneel, may lay hands on the fellow believer, and will begin with these words:

May the Lord be in your heart and upon your lips so that you may honestly and humbly confess your sins, in the name of the Father, and of the Son, and of the Holy Spirit. Amen.

Then the penitent will respond audibly using this form (or something similar as the Spirit leads):

I freely confess to Almighty God that I have sinned in many ways, but especially by _____. For this sin I am truly sorry. I ask God to have mercy on me and to forgive me. I firmly intend to go and sin no more, as he gives me grace.

The confessor then announces the general grace of forgiveness in this way:

[Name of penitent], In the mercy of Almighty God, Jesus Christ was given to die for you, and for his sake, God is faithful to forgive all your sins. To those who repent and believe in Jesus Christ he gives the power to become the children of God and bestows on them the Holy Spirit.

Do you believe this?

Then the penitent will respond:

I do.

The confessor then announces the particular grace of forgiveness in this way:

Then, [penitent's name], on the basis of your confession of faith, I declare to you that the Lord has put away all your sins. May the Lord, who has begun this good work in you, bring it to completion in the day of our Lord Jesus Christ.

Go, in the power of the Holy Spirit, and sin no more.

Amen.

Holy Matrimony

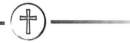

About Holy Matrimony

Christian marriage is a union of one man and one woman in covenant commitment for a lifetime. The wedding ceremony is a Christian worship service in which the couple exchanges vows to establish this covenant. The ceremony is conducted before God and in the presence of witnesses, who join with the couple in prayer that God will bless their life together until death.

The highest and holiest vocation of Christian marriage is to act as a parable of the mystical union of Christ Jesus and his Church (Eph. 5:32). Since the marriage relationship models the way God relates to his people, those who are married should take heed of the holy covenant that binds them together and honor the solemn and joyful obligations that arise from that covenant. In addition to its first vocation, Christian marriage also provides men and women the framework for intimate companionship, the channel of sexual expression according to biblical standards, and the means for procreation of the human race. Both husband and wife are made in the image of God, and are equal in dignity and in worth, as individual souls before God.

The husband is to sacrificially love his wife as Christ loved the Church. Christ modeled this this kind of sacrificial love when he took up the basin and the towel to serve the disciples. Just so, the husband must serve his family; for Christ came not to be served but to serve and give his life as a ransom for many. In this way, the husband teaches his wife to love as Christ loved, in great humility, by giving up honor, prestige, and power for the sake of his beloved. The husband has a God-given responsibility and privilege to provide for, protect, and lead his family.

The wife should submit graciously to the godly leadership of her husband, even as the Church willingly and joyfully submits to the headship of Christ. In this way, the wife teaches her husband to yield as Christ has yielded himself to the Father. In accordance with the teaching of Holy Scripture, wives have a God-given responsibility to respect their husbands and to serve as helpers in managing the household and in nurturing the next generation.

While not all Christians are called to marry, God has ordained the family as the foundational institution of human society. It is composed of persons related to one another by marriage, blood, or adoption.

This Prayer Book approaches preparation for holy matrimony and the wedding ceremony as a processing consisting of a minimum of four distinct phases: preparation through premarital counseling, publication through the reading of the Banns, further preparation through the rehearsal and, of course, the wedding ceremony. Other elements such as rehearsal dinners or event consultations may be added in accordance with the wishes of the couple and the tradition of the local church.

Premarital Counseling

Many couples focus on planning the wedding ceremony but fail to adequately think through the larger issues involved in the meaning and preparation for biblical marriage. Premarital counseling, if administered effectively, can help to remedy this deficiency in the practice of ministry and can help young couples avoid some of the pitfalls that are most common in young marriages. Some of the struggles and conflicts premarital counseling will help to unearth are not new to the couple but simply haven't been viewed in a systematic and objective way. All too often, these issues start out seeming like simple quirks and minor disagreements but quickly mushroom into full scale crisis when the "newness" has worn off the relationship.

Premarital counseling requires absolute confidentiality. Ideally, it should include no fewer than six and no more than eight hour-long sessions. If there are too few sessions, the process will lack necessary thoroughness. If there are too many sessions, a sense of weariness begins to set in on the couple (and the pastor/counselor too!). Each session should include the reading of Scripture, probing questions designed to examine preconceptions and personal histories, and the application of biblical truth to married life.

Counseling sessions should, at a minimum, focus on the following subjects in light of the witness of Scripture and the truth of the gospel:

1. The biblical definition and meaning of marriage
2. Conflict resolution and forgiveness
3. Personal sexual history and godly sexuality
4. Financial stewardship and related issues
5. Managing extended family relationships

The final session (or sessions) should focus on planning the ceremony itself (personnel, music, scripture readings, etc.).

Some pastors will choose to have the couple consult other counselors or pastors to do the lion's share of the premarital counseling. If a pastor or minister is not able to provide premarital counseling, the couple should consider inquiring with other local churches of like practice about premarital classes or small groups. These classes can be a wonderful way to dialogue with others who are walking through similar experiences. If outside counsel is used, the pastor would still need to meet a minimum of two times with the couple to get acquainted with them and to plan the actual ceremony.

The Reading of the Banns

Explanation of the Banns

Historically, the Banns of Marriage were read on a given number of Sundays before a wedding (often three) in order to publicly announce the intention of a couple to marry. On some public occasion, usually before a worship service, a priest or minister would stand before the congregation and make an announcement that would have been similar to this:

> This is the first (or second or third) announcement that John and Jane intend to be married in this place, three weeks from today, on the _____ day of January in the year of our Lord _____. If there are any who can give just cause why they should not be married, let them speak now.

This practice of public announcement has been adopted by both Protestants and Roman Catholics alike and remains a legal alternative to the civil marriage license in some jurisdictions outside the United States.

Today, in the United States, state law typically requires that a couple obtain a marriage license before their marriage ceremony and that ministers execute or witness that license before proceeding with the formal marriage ceremony. This process is intended to ensure that no legal impediment exists to the proposed marriage. Often there are civil or criminal penalties for failure to comply with this process that can include fines or even jail time.

Why Read the Banns?

There are at least a couple of reasons why reading the Banns may be beneficial in a modern Baptist context. Baptist ministers often realize that additional pastoral discernment may be necessary before performing a marriage ceremony. This is even more the case as the civil license, on its face, does not provide a sufficient theological or biblical warrant to perform the public Christian marriage ceremony. A formal church process requiring the Banns may provide a natural impediment to overly hasty or ill-considered marriages, even in situations where a couple declines premarital counseling.

Also, there is a growing concern that the minster's willingness to participate in the execution of a civil marriage license may eventually compromise his independent theological judgement and have serious long-term consequences for the separation of Church and state. It is no longer impossible to envision a time when a minister's freedom to perform wedding ceremonies is severely curtailed by public policy if he is not willing to act as an impartial agent of the state in all scenarios. Any dissenting minister who performs a marriage ceremony under this type of sanction, or in any case without a civil marriage license, must do so as an act of civil disobedience.

On the other hand, Scripture is clear that marriage does have public and communal import; thus, so-called "secret marriages" may be problematic for legal and theological reasons.

While reading the Banns certainly does not protect a minister from prosecution by the state for the performance of any so-called "illegal" marriage, it may allow the minister to satisfy the obligation of personal conscience on the one hand and the public nature of the Christian wedding ceremony on the other.

Hopefully, God willing, it will never be "necessary" to read the Banns in order to protect the freedom of conscience. If it does become necessary, in lieu of a civil license, then the minister ought to be well acquainted with the process and should consider very carefully whether he may be called to take such a potentially serious step for the sake of his witness and in obedience to our Lord.

Procedure for Reading the Banns

If a minister and the couple believe that the Banns should be read as a necessary alternative to obtaining a civil license, or if they simply wish to read the Banns for the sake of tradition, then the Banns should be read no less than three times, in public, preferably before Sunday morning church. If there are any that object, the pastor or other minister should take note and refer the matter to appropriate church or civil authorities.

The fourth or final announcement may occur during the marriage ceremony itself.

The Unity Candle

Explanation of the Unity Candle

The lighting of a unity candle is a relatively recent addition to the traditional wedding ceremony and is most popular in the United States. The unity candle ceremony uses two taper "family candles" on either side of a large central pillar candle called the "unity candle".

At the beginning of the wedding ceremony, a representative from each family (usually the mothers of the bride and groom) light the two taper family candles. Later in the ceremony, usually after the vows, the bride and groom use the two taper candles to light the large central unity candle together.

Often a unity candle is decorated with the wedding invitation, an inscription, a picture of the couple, or other ornamentation. The candles are almost always white. The lighting ceremony may be accompanied by special music. In some circles, it is customary for the couple to save the unity candle and relight it on anniversaries.

Symbolism

The lighting of the unity candle is performed to symbolize the joining together of the two families who, for the sake of their love for bride and groom, consent to join together into one new family.

The candle also symbolizes the union of two individuals, bound together as one flesh in a holy covenant. Representatives from each family light the taper candles on either side of the unity candle to symbolize the love and allegiance that each family has for either the bride or the groom. As the bride and groom use these two flames to light the unity candle, they bring the love of both families together in a united love of the new couple.

Generally, the two tapers are left burning and replaced in their holders because each family's love for their own will continue.

416

When the ceremony is performed to symbolize only the joining together of the bride and groom, the tapers may be extinguished to indicate that the two lives have been permanently merged, or they may remain lit beside the central candle, symbolizing that the now married partners have not lost their individuality.

Procedure for Lighting of the Unity Candle

The most common time for lighting the family candles is immediately after the mothers have been escorted into the sanctuary. Each mother (or other family representative) will proceed together to the unity candle on the dais. They each will light a candle on the side of the center unity candle. The taper candles on the side may remain lit throughout the entire ceremony until the bride and groom extinguish them after lighting the center unity candle.

The Wedding Rehearsal

The Wedding Overview Sheet

The pastor or other minister should meet with the couple during the final premarital session to discuss the actual wedding ceremony and create an overview sheet to be used at the wedding rehearsal and ceremony. Make sure that all details are discussed before the rehearsal and written down on the sheet. Each person at the rehearsal will receive a copy of the overview sheet so that all participants know what to do at any point during the ceremony. The wedding overview sheet should include these details at a minimum:

- Full names of each participant in the wedding ceremony along with the order of standing on the dais.

- The physical blocking indicating where each person will stand and move, the cues for movement, and the times they are expected to move.
- Full order of service with each element in the service, including scripture passages, titles of songs, key transition words, audio cues, etc.
- Details about the day of the ceremony that each member of the wedding party needs to know such as: what time to arrive for the ceremony, when and where are pictures, where are the two dressing rooms located, etc.

Walkthrough – Cue to Cue

A thorough rehearsal is important to insure a God-honoring ceremony. If at all possible, make sure each and every participant is able to attend the rehearsal. Before the rehearsal, the pastor and couple should meet with the wedding coordinator (if any), church officials, photographers, videographers, sound technicians, musicians, and any other parties that need a copy of the wedding overview sheet.

The rehearsal itself should include a minimum of one full walkthrough; more may be conducted if necessary.

The Marriage Ceremony

Wedding traditions and practices vary from place to place. What follows here is a template that incorporates elements and practices from the broader Christian tradition and from the patterns set forth in this book. Couples and ministers should feel free to modify them or simplify them as necessary for local and personal preference, so long as those modifications are consistent with the theological import and symbolism of the day.

Commencement

Gathering

At the appointed time, the family and friends of the couple will gather in the church. As they gather, hymns or appropriate instrumental music may be played.

Traditionally, ushers are chosen to help seat the bride's guests on the stage right side of sanctuary and the groom's guests on the stage left side of the sanctuary.

After the congregation is seated, the Ushers will escort Grandparents first; grandmothers are escorted with their husbands following behind.

Parents of the groom enter; the mother is escorted with her husband following behind.

Mother of the bride enters, escorted by an usher. The father will escort the bride.

After all parties are seated, the congregation may join together in a hymn such as "Joyful, Joyful we Adore Thee" or another appropriate hymn or spiritual song.

After the hymn ceases, close family, mothers or family members will light family candles on either side of the unity candle.

Procession

After the family candles are lit, the pastor and groom proceed to the front of the church and face the congregation. Groomsmen will join the groom unless they are escorting the bridesmaids.

After the pastor, groom and groomsmen have entered, junior bridesmaids, bridesmaids, maid or matron of honor, flower girl(s), and ring bearer proceed to the front, in that order.

Before the bride prepares to enter, the doors of the sanctuary are closed. Then the pastor will say:

Please Stand.

Then the bride enters, escorted by her father or another family member, and proceeds to the front of the altar. Music may play as she processes.

As the bride approaches the front of the church, the groom will move down to greet the bride and will stand beside the father of the bride (or her escort).

Then the pastor, facing the people and the persons to be married, with the woman stage right, the man stage left, and the father of the bride in the middle, addresses the congregation with the words of The Greeting.

The Greeting

Dearly beloved, we have gathered today at the invitation of [groom's name] and [bride's name] to share in the joy and celebration of their wedding.

In this outward celebration, we observe a sign of the love and devotion a man and woman hold unseen in their hearts. By faith, we perceive in this sign a living parable of the gospel of Jesus Christ. He is, in himself, the union in which our togetherness finds its beginning and end, and every Christian marriage, in sickness and health, bears the promise of our once and future union with him.

God loves us and has created us to love each other. He has set marriage aside as a holy vocation to love and to be loved. He is glorified as we enjoy and persist in that vocation, even as he has found great joy and persisted in his love for us.

Giving of the Bride

[Groom's name] and [bride's name] come today desiring to be united in marriage.

Who gives this woman to be married to this man?

The father of the bride says:

Her mother and I (or something similar).

Then the father raises the veil, kisses the bride, hands her to the groom, and the couple joins hands. Then the wedding party joins the pastor on the stage.

Then the pastor says:

Please be seated.

Declaration of Consent

Then the pastor will address the groom:

[Groom's name], do you come of your own free will, to take [bride's name] as your wedded wife, to live together in the holy covenant of marriage?

The groom responds: **Yes** *or* **I Do.**

Then the pastor will address the bride:

And, [Bride's name], do you come of your own free will, to take [groom's name] to be your wedded husband, to live together in the holy covenant of marriage?

The bride responds: **Yes** *or* **I Do.**

The Final Bann

The pastor will proceed immediately, in a loud voice, with the Final Bann:

Friends, in the presence of Almighty God and all here gathered as witnesses, [groom's name] and [bride's name] have come, of their own free will, to be joined together in the holy covenant of Christian marriage. If any of you can show just cause why they may not be lawfully married, speak now, or forever hold your peace.

Then the pastor will pause, and if none object, the pastor will continue:

Seeing that none object, let us pray.

Then the pastor will pray the Prayer of Invocation (or something similar in his own words).

It is not likely that any will object, but if there is any objection, the pastor will maintain good order and will insist that objector stand, face the congregation, state his or her name, and state the objection in a loud and clear voice. Then the bride and groom may be seated or may join the pastor as he consults with the parents and bridal parties to make a determination.

If the pastor determines the ceremony should continue, then he will invite the bride, groom, and bridal parties to return to their places and will continue with these words:
We have heard the objection of [objector's name] and found that it gives insufficient cause to prevent this marriage. Let us pray.

If, however, the pastor determines the ceremony should not continue, then the bride and groom and bridal parties will be seated, and the pastor will address the congregation with these words:

We have heard the objection of [objector's name] and found that it gives sufficient cause to delay this marriage.

Let us pray for grace and for the wisdom of God.

Then the pastor will pray and dismiss the congregation with these words:

This ceremony is adjourned until such a day and time as it may be fitting that it reconvenes. Go in God's peace.

The Prayer of Invocation

Most gracious and loving Father, in the beginning you said it was not good that we should be alone. Out of your great kindness, you joined man and woman together that their union might be a sign of your own holy love and faithfulness. Lord, look with favor upon [groom's name] and [bride's name] as they seek your blessing this day. Give them the grace to love as you have loved, with true fidelity and steadfastness, that they might honor and keep the vows they make this day, through Jesus Christ our Savior, who lives and reigns with you in the unity of the Holy Spirit, one God, in glory everlasting. Amen.

The Service of the Word

The Old Testament Reading

Then someone will read a selected Old Testament passage. Before reading the appointed passage, the reader may begin by saying:

A reading from [a citation giving book and chapter]. *Or the reader may say:* Hear the word of the Lord from [a citation giving book and chapter].

Depending on where the appointed reading begins, it may be necessary to provide some context. For example:

"This is from the reply of the Lord to Job," *or:* "This is while Jesus was teaching on the mount."

The scripture reading ends as follows:

Reader: The word of the Lord.
Or the reader may say: May God bless the reading of his word.

People: **Thanks be to God.**

Then an appointed Psalm will be read or said responsively, or a hymn or other appropriate spiritual song may be sung. Suggested psalms include 67, 127, and 128.

If a Psalm is read, it may be followed by the Gloria Patri, either spoken or sung:

Glory to the Father, and to the Son, and to the Holy Spirit, as it was in the beginning, is now, and will be forever. Amen.

The New Testament Reading

Then someone will read a selected New Testament passage. Before reading the appointed passage, the reader may begin by saying:

A reading from [a citation giving book and chapter]. *Or the reader may say:* Hear the word of the Lord from [a citation giving book and chapter].

Depending on where the appointed reading begins, it may be necessary to provide some context. For example:

"This is from the reply of the Lord to Job," *or:* "This is while Jesus was teaching on the mount."

The scripture reading ends as follows:

Reader: The word of the Lord.
Or the reader may say: May God bless the reading of his word.

People: **Thanks be to God.**

<u>Sermon</u>

*Then the pastor will offer a brief sermon drawn from one of the readings or
another suitable passage of Scripture.*

*During this time, the pastor may choose to include other scripture or readings
that the couple would like to be included to personalize the ceremony.*

*The pastor may conclude the sermon with either the invocation of the Trinity or
by saying:*

In the name of our Lord Jesus Christ, let it be so.

<u>The Lord's Prayer</u>

*Then the Lord's prayer may be sung, or may spoken by the congregation in
unison. If the Lord's Prayer is spoken, the pastor will begin by saying:*

And now, Lord, we pray as you taught us.

*Then all gathered may say the Lord's Prayer in unison (Matt. 6:9–13
KJV):*

Our Father, who art in heaven,
  hallowed be thy Name,
  thy kingdom come,
  thy will be done,
  on earth as it is in heaven.
Give us this day our daily bread.
And forgive us our trespasses,
  as we forgive those who trespass against us.
And lead us not into temptation,
  but deliver us from evil.

For thine is the kingdom, and the power, and the glory,
  forever and ever. Amen.

The Wedding

The Exchange of Vows

Then after the sermon, the Maid or Matron of Honor will take the bride's bouquet, and the groom will face the bride and take her hands into his, and the pastor will ask the husband to repeat after him:

I, [groom's name] take you [bride's name] to be my wife,
to have and to hold from this day forward,
for better, for worse,
for richer, for poorer,
in sickness and in health,
to love and to comfort,
To honor and to cherish,
forsaking all others,
until death do us part.
This is my solemn vow.

Then pastor will ask the bride to repeat after him:

I, [bride's name] take you [groom's name] to be my husband,
to have and to hold from this day forward,
for better, for worse,
for richer, for poorer,
in sickness and in health,
to love and to comfort,
To honor and to cherish,
forsaking all others,
until death do us part.
This is my solemn vow.

Then the couple will loose their hands.

The Exchange of Rings

Then the pastor says:

Having this kind of love in your hearts, you have chosen to exchange rings as the sign and seal of the vows you are making today. May I have the rings?

The pastor will hold out his hand and receive the rings from the maid or matron of honor and the best man. Holding them out in front of his body in an open hand the pastor says:

Although these rings are small in size, what they signify is of great importance; made of precious metal, they remind us that love is neither cheap nor common; indeed, godly love is costly. Fashioned in a circle, their design reminds us that godly love does not end.

As you wear these rings, whether together or apart, let them be a sign and a constant reminder of these truths and the promises you have made today in the presence of Almighty God and loved ones.

The ring should be initially placed on the ring finger just over the first knuckle during the first question (Do you give… I do.). After the response of the second question (Do you accept… I do.), then the ring is placed completely on the finger.

Then the pastor will address this question to the groom:

[Groom's name], do you give this ring to [bride's name], whom you have taken as your lawful wife, as a sign and token of your love and enduring commitment?

The groom responds: **I do.**

And the pastor addresses this question to the bride:

> [Bride's name], do you accept this ring from [groom's name], whom you have taken as your lawful husband, and promise to wear it as a sign and token of your love and esteem for him?

The bride responds: **I do.**

And the pastor addresses this question to the bride:

> And [bride's name], do you give this ring to [groom's name], whom you have taken as your lawful husband, as a sign and token of your love and enduring commitment?

The bride responds: **I do.**

And the pastor addresses this question to the groom:

> [Groom's name], do you accept this ring from [bride's name], whom you have taken as your lawful wife, and promise to wear it as a sign and token of your love and esteem for her?

The groom responds: **I do.**

Song & Unity Candle

Then, if a unity candle is part of the ceremony, the pastor will explain the lighting of the unity candle:

These candles represent your lives.

The two outside candles have been lighted by your families to represent your lives up to this moment. They are two distinct lights, each of them capable of going its own separate way. Now, for the sake of the joy set out before you, these two flames must merge into one.

As each of you take a candle and together light the Unity Candle, let it represent the union of your two lives into one flesh. As this center light cannot be divided, in the same way do not let your lives be divided, but be united in the testimony of a Christian home, as Christ gives you light.

Then the pastor steps aside so the couple can light the candle.

Music may be played or a solo performed as the unity candle is lit.

The couple stays in front of the candle until the music is completed. They may listen to the music, pray together, or spend a few private moments together.

Prayer of Consecration

Then the pastor says:

Join with me as we ask God's blessing on this new couple.

Eternal Father, Redeemer, we now turn to you, and as the first act of this couple in their newly formed union, we ask you to protect their home. May they always turn to you for guidance, for strength, for provision, and for direction. May they glorify you in the choices they make, in the ministries they involve themselves in, and in all that they do. Use them to draw others to yourself, and let them stand as a testimony to the world of your faithfulness. We ask this in Jesus' name. Amen.

Holy Communion

If the couple chooses to have communion in the ceremony, it is best to use a modified form of the Order for Communion by Intinction. If they are believers, the bride and groom, and members of the bridal party may administer the elements to the congregation, which adds a personal touch to the ceremony.

Ushers may dismiss rows to receive communion.

Remaining members of the bridal party may be communicated first, and then may sit on the front row as the remaining congregants are communicated.

After the Response of Thanksgiving, the couple will place remaining elements on the altar or will hand them to the pastor to replace on the altar, and then the couple will return to their place, facing the pastor, and the bridal party will return to their places.

Benediction

The Declaration of Marriage

Then, after all are done, the pastor will proceed with these words:

Having taken these wedding vows and pledged yourself to one another till death do you part, it is now my privilege as a minister of the gospel, sanctioned by divine authority and the laws of this state,[24] to declare you legally married, husband and wife. What God has put together let no man or woman put asunder.

The Blessing

Then the pastor proceeds immediately to pronounce a blessing upon the couple:

The Lord bless you and keep you.
The Lord make his face to shine upon you
  and be gracious to you.
The Lord lift up his countenance upon you
  and give you peace. Amen.

The Holy Kiss

[Groom's name], you may kiss your bride!

---

[24] If so sanctioned.

Presentation of the Couple

Then the bride and groom will turn to face the audience.

Ladies and Gentlemen, for the first time, I present to you: Mr. & Mrs. [groom's last name] *or* [groom's name] and [bride's name]

Recessional

Then, as the couple and wedding party depart, a Recessional Hymn is performed.

After the wedding party exits the sanctuary, the pastor will again address the congregation saying:

_____ and _____ are so grateful that you joined them on this joyous occasion. Thank you again for being a part of their wedding ceremony.

Housekeeping remarks may be spoken here, such as how the congregation will exit the sanctuary, details about a receiving line, or directions to the reception.

Music should continue to play as guests depart.

Ministry to the Sick or Suffering

The Church prioritizes visitation to the sick and suffering in obedience to the Lord's command and to show the love of God for those that suffer. Therefore, in visitation, the minister must avoid behaviors and mannerisms that might inadvertently cause the sick person to feel like a burden or "just another stop" on a long list of things to do. Body language, and non-verbal communication are critical when providing this ministry.

Anyone ministering to the sick or suffering should be considerate of their time and the physical drain that pastoral visitation may cause. Therefore, visits to the sick and suffering should be kept brief.

All scriptures in this section are quoted from the World English Bible, unless otherwise noted, or are slightly modified from the World English Bible and so left unattributed. The minister should select scriptures and prayers before entering the room.

Greeting

Upon entering the room, it has been customary in many places to greet the one who is sick by first praying a blessing for him or her, and all who are gathered or dwell in that place. If the one ministering feels it appropriate, he may say the following (or something similar):

May God's peace be with all who dwell in this house (*or* place).

Or some other suitable greeting may be used instead.

After the greeting, or immediately upon entering, the minister should make eye contact with and greet the one who is sick or suffering. Then, if the person's medical condition allows, the minister should make physical contact, either by shaking a hand or gently touching a shoulder or arm. These types of gestures reassure and give comfort (Matt. 8:3).

After the greeting, if physical or medical conditions allow it, the minister may wish to sit or stand at the bedside and make pleasant conversation for a few minutes, so as to put the one who is sick or suffering at ease.

The Reading of Scripture

After a few moments of conversation, the minster should offer to read one of the following passages of Scripture:

<u>For those who are physically sick:</u>

A reading from Psalm 46:1–11

1 God is our refuge and strength,
    a very present help in trouble.
2 Therefore we won't be afraid, though the earth changes,
    though the mountains are shaken into the heart of the seas;
3 though its waters roar and are troubled,
    though the mountains tremble with their swelling. *Selah.*
4 There is a river, the streams of which make glad
    the city of God,
    the holy place of the tents of the Most High.
5 God is within her. She shall not be moved.
    God will help her at dawn.
6 The nations raged. The kingdoms were moved.
    He lifted his voice and the earth melted.
7 The LORD of Armies is with us.
    The God of Jacob is our refuge. *Selah.*
8 Come, see The LORD's works,
    what desolations he has made in the earth.
9 He makes wars cease to the end of the earth.

He breaks the bow, and shatters the spear.
He burns the chariots in the fire.
10 "Be still, and know that I am God.
I will be exalted among the nations.
I will be exalted in the earth."
11 The LORD of Armies is with us.
The God of Jacob is our refuge. *Selah.*

A reading from Psalm 91:9–16

9 Because you have made The LORD your refuge,
and the Most High your dwelling place,
10 no evil shall happen to you,
neither shall any plague come near your dwelling.
11 For he will put his angels in charge of you,
to guard you in all your ways.
12 They will bear you up in their hands,
so that you won't dash your foot against a stone.
13 You will tread on the lion and cobra.
You will trample the young lion and the serpent underfoot.
14 "Because he has set his love on me,
therefore I will deliver him.
I will set him on high, because he has known my name.
15 He will call on me, and I will answer him.
I will be with him in trouble.
I will deliver him, and honor him.
16 I will satisfy him with long life,
and show him my salvation."

A reading from Isaiah 26:1–4

1 In that day, this song will be sung in the land of Judah:
"We have a strong city.
God appoints salvation for walls and bulwarks.
2 Open the gates, that the righteous nation may enter:
the one which keeps faith.
3 You will keep whoever's mind is steadfast in perfect peace,

because he trusts in you.
4 Trust in the LORD forever;
    for in The LORD GOD, is an everlasting Rock.

A reading from Matthew 11:25–30

25 At that time, Jesus answered, "I thank you, Father, Lord of heaven and earth, that you hid these things from the wise and understanding, and revealed them to infants. 26 Yes, Father, for so it was well-pleasing in your sight. 27 All things have been delivered to me by my Father. No one knows the Son, except the Father; neither does anyone know the Father, except the Son and he to whom the Son desires to reveal him.

28 "Come to me, all you who labor and are heavily burdened, and I will give you rest. 29 Take my yoke upon you and learn from me, for I am gentle and humble in heart; and you will find rest for your souls.30 For my yoke is easy, and my burden is light."

A reading from Luke 17:11–19

11 As he was on his way to Jerusalem, he was passing along the borders of Samaria and Galilee. 12 As he entered into a certain village, ten men who were lepers met him, who stood at a distance. 13 They lifted up their voices, saying, "Jesus, Master, have mercy on us!"

14 When he saw them, he said to them, "Go and show yourselves to the priests." As they went, they were cleansed. 15 One of them, when he saw that he was healed, turned back, glorifying God with a loud voice. 16 He fell on his face at Jesus' feet, giving him thanks; and he was a Samaritan. 17 Jesus answered, "Weren't the ten cleansed? But where are the nine? 18 Were there none found who returned to give glory to God, except this foreigner?" 19 Then he said to him, "Get up, and go your way. Your faith has healed you."

A reading from 2 Corinthians 1:3–5

3 Blessed be the God and Father of our Lord Jesus Christ, the Father of mercies and God of all comfort; 4 who comforts us in all our affliction, that we may be able to comfort those who are in any affliction, through the comfort with which we ourselves are comforted by God. 5 For as the sufferings of Christ abound to us, even so our comfort also abounds through Christ.

A reading from 2 Corinthians 4:13–18

13 But having the same spirit of faith, according to that which is written, "I believed, and therefore I spoke." We also believe, and therefore we also speak; 14 knowing that he who raised the Lord Jesus will raise us also with Jesus, and will present us with you. 15 For all things are for your sakes, that the grace, being multiplied through the many, may cause the thanksgiving to abound to the glory of God.

16 Therefore we don't faint, but though our outward person is decaying, yet our inward person is renewed day by day. 17 For our light affliction, which is for the moment, works for us more and more exceedingly an eternal weight of glory, 18 while we don't look at the things which are seen, but at the things which are not seen. For the things which are seen are temporal, but the things which are not seen are eternal.

For those who are suffering in other ways:

A reading from Psalm 23 (ESV)

1 The Lord is my shepherd; I shall not want.
2 He makes me lie down in green pastures.
    He leads me beside still waters.
3 He restores my soul.
    He leads me in paths of righteousness
    for his name's sake.

⁴ Even though I walk through the valley
    of the shadow of death,
    I will fear no evil,
for you are with me;
    your rod and your staff,
    they comfort me.
⁵ You prepare a table before me
    in the presence of my enemies;
you anoint my head with oil;
    my cup overflows.
⁶ Surely goodness and mercy shall follow me
    all the days of my life,
and I shall dwell in the house of the Lord
    forever.

A reading from Psalm 121:1–7

¹ I will lift up my eyes to the hills.
    Where does my help come from?
² My help comes from The LORD,
    who made heaven and earth.
³ He will not allow your foot to be moved.
    He who keeps you will not slumber.
⁴ Behold, he who keeps Israel
    will neither slumber nor sleep.
⁵ The LORD is your keeper.
    The LORD is your shade on your right hand.
⁶ The sun will not harm you by day,
    nor the moon by night.
⁷ The LORD will keep you from all evil.
    He will keep your soul.

A reading from Isaiah 40:28–31:

²⁸ Haven't you known?
    Haven't you heard?
    The everlasting God, The LORD,

the Creator of the ends of the earth, does not faint.
He isn't weary.
His understanding is unsearchable.
29 He gives power to the weak.
He increases the strength of him who has no might.
30 Even the youths faint and get weary,
and the young men utterly fall;
31 but those who wait for The LORD
will renew their strength.
They will mount up with wings like eagles.
They will run, and not be weary.
They will walk, and not faint.

A reading from Matthew 6:25–26 (WEB)

25 Therefore I tell you, don't be anxious for your life: what you will eat, or what you will drink; nor yet for your body, what you will wear. Isn't life more than food, and the body more than clothing? 26 See the birds of the sky, that they don't sow, neither do they reap, nor gather into barns. Your heavenly Father feeds them. Aren't you of much more value than they?

A reading from John 14:1–3, 25-27: (WEB)

"Don't let your heart be troubled. Believe in God. Believe also in me. 2 In my Father's house are many homes. If it weren't so, I would have told you. I am going to prepare a place for you. 3 If I go and prepare a place for you, I will come again, and will receive you to myself; that where I am, you may be there also.

25 I have said these things to you while still living with you. 26 But the Counselor, the Holy Spirit, whom the Father will send in my name, will teach you all things, and will remind you of all that I said to you. 27 Peace I leave with you. My peace I give to you; not as the world gives, I give to you. Don't let your heart be troubled, neither let it be fearful.

18 For I consider that the sufferings of this present time are not worthy to be compared with the glory which will be revealed toward us. 19 For the creation waits with eager expectation for the children of God to be revealed. 20 For the creation was subjected to vanity, not of its own will, but because of him who subjected it, in hope 21 that the creation itself also will be delivered from the bondage of decay into the liberty of the glory of the children of God. 22 For we know that the whole creation groans and travails in pain together until now. 23 Not only so, but ourselves also, who have the first fruits of the Spirit, even we ourselves groan within ourselves, waiting for adoption, the redemption of our body. 24 For we were saved in hope, but hope that is seen is not hope. For who hopes for that which he sees? 25 But if we hope for that which we don't see, we wait for it with patience.

26 In the same way, the Spirit also helps our weaknesses, for we don't know how to pray as we ought. But the Spirit himself makes intercession for us with groanings which can't be uttered.

A reading from Philippians 4:4–9: (WEB)

4 Rejoice in the Lord always! Again I will say, "Rejoice!" 5 Let your gentleness be known to all men. The Lord is at hand. 6 In nothing be anxious, but in everything, by prayer and petition with thanksgiving, let your requests be made known to God. 7 And the peace of God, which surpasses all understanding, will guard your hearts and your thoughts in Christ Jesus.

8 Finally, brothers, whatever things are true, whatever things are honorable, whatever things are just, whatever things are pure, whatever things are lovely, whatever things are of good report: if there is any virtue and if there is any praise, think about these

things. [9] The things which you learned, received, heard, and saw in me: do these things, and the God of peace will be with you.

A reading from 1 Peter 5:6–11: (WEB)

[6] Humble yourselves therefore under the mighty hand of God, that he may exalt you in due time, [7] casting all your worries on him, because he cares for you.

[8] Be sober and self-controlled. Be watchful. Your adversary, the devil, walks around like a roaring lion, seeking whom he may devour. [9] Withstand him steadfast in your faith, knowing that your brothers who are in the world are undergoing the same sufferings. [10] But may the God of all grace, who called you to his eternal glory by Christ Jesus, after you have suffered a little while, perfect, establish, strengthen, and settle you. [11] To him be the glory and the power forever and ever. Amen.

The Prayer

After the scripture has been read, the minister should say:

Let us pray.

He may pray extemporaneously or may say one of the following prayers:

For One Who Is Unwell in Body or in Spirit

This prayer may be suitable for one will may not recover from physical illness:

Father of mercies and God of all comfort, you are our only help in time of need. We humbly ask you to look upon the sickness of [unwell person's name], and to give him/her relief. Look upon him/her with mercy; comfort him/her with a sense of your goodness; preserve him/her from the temptations of the enemy; and give him/her patience in this season of difficulty. Above all, Lord, grant that [unwell person's name] may live with you in eternity, through Jesus Christ our Lord. Amen.

For Recovery from an Illness

Heavenly Father, you are the strength of those who are weak and the comfort of all who suffer. Hear our prayers and have mercy on [name]. Give him/her the help of your healing power, that this illness may be turned into health and our sorrow into joy, through Jesus Christ our Lord. Amen.

Or this:

Almighty God, you are the Lord of Hosts. By the might of your outstretched hand, you are able to drive away from our bodies all illness and all infirmity. We ask you to be present with your servant [name], that his/her illness may be cured, and his/her strength restored. Oh Lord, give him/her grace, that in sickness or in health he/she might bless your holy name, through Jesus Christ our Lord. Amen.

For a Sick Child

Heavenly Father, watch with us over your child [child's name]. Lord Jesus Christ, Son of God, have mercy on him/her. Holy Spirit, give grace and comfort to his/her spirit and to his/her family. Holy and Triune God, we ask that you allow him/her to be fully restored to the perfect health which it is yours alone to give, through Jesus Christ our Lord. Amen.

Or this:

Lord Jesus Christ, Good Shepherd of the sheep, you gather your lambs in your arms and protect them. We commend to your loving care this child, [child's name]. Relieve his/her pain and grant him/her, by your grace, eternal life in the light of your presence. Hear us, we pray, for the sake of your well-beloved Son, for it is in his name that we pray. Amen.

Before a Surgical Procedure

Almighty God, our heavenly Father, comfort your servant [patient's name], and bless the doctors, nurses, and others that will minister to him/her. Bless the medicines and treatments that will be used. Fill his/her heart with confidence that, though at times he/she may be afraid, he/she may put his/her trust in you, through Jesus Christ our Lord. Amen.

Or this:

Heavenly Father, strengthen your servant [patient's name], to do what he/she has to do and bear what he/she has to bear. Give him/her grace to humbly accept your healing gifts through the skill of surgeons and nurses, that he/she may be restored and may dwell in this world with a thankful heart, through Jesus Christ our Lord. Amen.

For Strength and Confidence

Heavenly Father, you are the giver of life and health. We ask you to comfort and relieve [person's name], and give your strength and power of healing to those who are caring for his/her needs. Through these acts of kindness help [person's name] to have confidence in your own lovingkindness and provision, through Jesus Christ our Lord. Amen.

For the Consecration of Illness

Consecrate, O Lord, this illness of [sick person's name], that his/her feeling of weakness might add strength to his/her faith, urgency to his/her repentance, and power to his/her testimony.

Above all Lord, grant that he/she may live with you in everlasting life, through Jesus Christ our Lord. Amen.

For Health of Body and Soul

May God the Father bless you; God the Son heal you; God the Holy Spirit give you strength. May God the holy and Triune Trinity guard your body, save your soul, and bring you safely to his heavenly country, where he lives and reigns forever and ever. Amen.

For the Doctors and Nurses

O Lord, watch over and guide all those whom you have called to study and practice medicine. Strengthen them by your life-giving Spirit, that through their ministry, diseases of every sort might be prevented and defeated. Help them, Lord, to understand their calling as a holy vocation that strengthens the Church for its labors, promotes the welfare of the community, and exercises biblical stewardship over your creation, through Jesus Christ our Lord. Amen.

Thanksgiving for a Beginning of Recovery

Heavenly Father, you are good, your compassions never fail, and your mercies are new every morning! We give you thanks and praise for giving our brother/sister, [person's name], both healing from _____ and the hope that comes with renewed health. Continue in him/her, we pray, the good work you have begun. Heavenly Father, we ask that you give [person's name] increasing strength every day, and the grace to rejoice in your goodness. Help [person's name] to order his/her life and conduct as an expression of gratitude, so that in all things, they might be found pleasing to you, through Jesus Christ our Lord. Amen.

Anointing with Oil

If the person has requested anointing, the elder will begin by reading the following passage of Scripture from James 5:13–16 (WEB)

13 Is any among you suffering? Let him pray. Is any cheerful? Let him sing praises. 14 Is any among you sick? Let him call for the elders of the assembly, and let them pray over him, anointing him with oil in the name of the Lord, 15 and the prayer of faith will heal him who is sick, and the Lord will raise him up. If he has committed sins, he will be forgiven. 16 Confess your offenses to one another, and pray for one another, that you may be healed. The insistent prayer of a righteous person is powerfully effective.

Then, the elder will say the following prayer (or something similar):

Almighty God, you are the giver of health and salvation, and so the scriptures tell us how the apostles anointed many that were sick and healed them. We ask you to send the Holy Spirit to sanctify this anointing. We pray that those who receive this oil in faith and repentance might be made whole. This we ask in the name of our Lord Jesus Christ, who lives and reigns with you in the unity of the Holy Spirit, one God, forever and ever. Amen.

Then the elder lays hands upon the sick person and says one of the following:

[Name], I lay my hands upon you in the name of the Father, and of the Son, and of the Holy Spirit, asking our Lord Jesus Christ to sustain you with his presence, to drive away all sickness of body and spirit, and to give you that victory of life and peace which will enable you to serve him both now and evermore. Amen.
  Or this:

[Name], I lay hands upon you in the name the Father who has created and called you, in the Name of the Son who has redeemed you, and in the name of the Holy Spirit that sustains you in faith.

Holy God, we ask you to uphold [name] and fill him/her with your grace, that he/she may know the healing power of his love. Amen.

Then the elder will dip his thumb in the oil and will make the sign of the cross on the sick person's forehead, saying:

[Name], I anoint you with oil in the name of the Father, and of the Son, and of the Holy Spirit. Amen.

Then the elder may administer communion, or if communion is not to follow, the Lord's Prayer is now said (Matt. 6:9–13 KJV):

Our Father, who art in heaven,
 hallowed be thy Name,
 thy kingdom come,
 thy will be done,
  on earth as it is in heaven.
Give us this day our daily bread.
And forgive us our trespasses,
 as we forgive those who trespass against us.
And lead us not into temptation,
 but deliver us from evil.
For thine is the kingdom, and the power, and the glory,
 forever and ever. Amen.

Then the elder may conclude by saying the following:

The Lord is a strong tower to all who put their trust in him, and to him, all things in heaven, on earth, and under the earth bow. May he be your only comfort in life or in death. And may you rest in the sure knowledge that health and salvation are found in our Lord Jesus Christ alone. To him be glory, now and forevermore. Amen.

Ministry to the Dying Believer

When a confessing Christian is near death, a pastor, elder, or deacon should be called to the bedside. There, he may provide the following ministry to the believer and gathered family. If no pastor, elder, or deacon is available or willing, any believer may perform this service to the dying believer.

Upon entering the room, the minister should greet the family with appropriate solemnity. Then the minister should proceed to the side of the bed and, if it is possible given the arrangement of the room, should kneel. At this time, if the minister and family prefer, the minister may decide to don a prayer stole as a sign of the yoke of Christ.

Then the minister should lay a hand or hands upon the one who is dying, pause briefly to make a silent confession of sin, and ask for the strength to minister as Christ.

Invocation

The minister then begins with the following invocation:

In the name of the Father, and of the Son, and of the Holy Spirit. Amen.

The Scripture Reading

Then, immediately after the invocation, the minister should proceed reading with these words (or something similar):

Hear the word of the Lord from Paul's letter to the Romans.

Then the scripture is read:

For I consider that the sufferings of this present time are not worth comparing with the glory that is to be revealed to us. For the creation waits with eager longing for the revealing of the sons of God. For the creation was subjected to futility, not willingly, but because of him who subjected it, in hope that the creation itself will be set free from its bondage to corruption and obtain the freedom of the glory of the children of God. For we know that the whole creation has been groaning together in the pains of childbirth until now. And not only the creation, but we ourselves, who have the first fruits of the Spirit, groan inwardly as we wait eagerly for adoption as sons, the redemption of our bodies. For in this hope we were saved. Now hope that is seen is not hope. For who hopes for what he sees? But if we hope for what we do not see, we wait for it with patience (Rom. 8:18–25, ESV).

A Prayer for Comfort

The minister should continue with the following prayer, or a brief prayer of similar content, first saying: Let us pray.

Almighty God, look on this your servant, lying in great weakness, and comfort him/her with the promise of eternal life given by the resurrection of your Son, Jesus Christ our Lord. Amen.

The Litany at the Time of Death

If prayer books are available to all gathered, and if the family so desires, all may join together in the following litany. Or, the minister may continue by saying it alone:

God the Father,
have mercy on your servant.
God the Son,
have mercy on your servant.
God the Holy Spirit,
have mercy on your servant.
Holy Trinity, one God,
have mercy on your servant.

From all evil, from all sin, from all tribulation,
Good Lord, deliver him/her.
By your holy incarnation, by your cross and passion,
by your precious death and burial,
Good Lord, deliver him/her.
By your glorious resurrection and ascension,
and by the Coming of the Holy Spirit,
Good Lord, deliver him/her.
We sinners beseech you to hear us, Lord Christ:

That it may please you to deliver the soul of your servant
from the power of evil, and from eternal death,
we beseech you to hear us, good Lord.
That it may please you mercifully to pardon all his/her sins,
we beseech you to hear us, good Lord.
That it may please you to grant him/her a place of refreshment
and everlasting blessedness,
we beseech you to hear us, good Lord.
That it may please you to give him joy and gladness
in your kingdom, with your saints in light,
we beseech you to hear us, good Lord.

Jesus, Lamb of God,
  have mercy on him/her.
Jesus, bearer of our sins,
  have mercy on him/her.
Jesus, redeemer of the world,
  give him/her your peace.

  Lord, have mercy.
  Christ, have mercy.
  Lord, have mercy.

The Lord's Prayer

If the gathered family members desire it, all may join together in saying the Lord's Prayer, or the minister may continue by saying it alone.

If the prayer is to be said in unison, the minister should begin with these words:

And now, Lord, we pray as you taught us.

All gathered will say the Lord's prayer in unison (or the minister alone) will say the Lord's Prayer (Matt. 6:9–13 KJV):

  Our Father, who art in heaven,
  hallowed be thy Name,
  thy kingdom come,
  thy will be done,
  in earth as it is in heaven.
  Give us this day our daily bread.
  And forgive us our trespasses,
  as we forgive those who trespass against us.
  And lead us not into temptation,
  but deliver us from evil.

  For thine is the kingdom, and the power, and the glory,
  forever and ever. Amen.

The Pastoral Prayers

The minister should continue immediately to the following prayers, or something very similar in theological content, interjecting the believer's name as appropriate:

Prayer for Mercy

O Sovereign Lord Christ, deliver your servant, [Name], from all evil and set him/her free from every earthly bond, that he/she may rest with all your saints in the eternal habitations where, with the Father and the Holy Spirit, you live and reign, one God, forever and ever. Amen.

Release to a Holy Death

Then the minister should read this prayer, releasing the believer to a holy death:

Depart, O Christian soul, out of this world, in the name of God the Father Almighty who created you, in the name of Jesus Christ who redeemed you, in the name of the Holy Spirit who sanctifies you. May your eternal rest be in peace, and your dwelling place in the paradise of God."

Commendation

Then the minister should read this commendation of the believer to God:
Into your hands, O merciful Savior, we commend your servant [Name]. Acknowledge, we humbly ask you, a sheep of your own fold, a lamb of your own flock, a sinner of your own redeeming. Receive him/her into the arms of your mercy, into the blessed rest of everlasting peace, and into the glorious company of the saints in light. Amen.

Benediction

Then the minister should conclude by saying:

May our brother/sister, [Name], go quickly into the presence of the Lord, where faith becomes sight, and there, through the mercy of almighty God, rest in peace forevermore. Amen.

Christian Burial

About the Funeral and Commitment Service

The basic form for Christian burial is similar to many worship services, and its purpose is three-fold: the memorialization or celebration of life, the comfort of the surviving family, and, most important of all, the exaltation of Christ. All parts of the services in this book assume that the decedent was a believer.

Before conducting the funeral service, the pastor should make time to meet with the family to comfort them in their grief, to counsel them about the nature and purpose of Christian burial, and to help guide them in the selection of scriptures and songs. It may be helpful to ask for a Bible of the decedent, as passages that have been underlined or noted can help in the selection of scriptures.

Certain traditional elements in the Service of Commitment, such as the prayers or lowering of the casket, may be unknown in some ministry settings. These elements may strike family members as strange or even unsettling. Nevertheless, their use should gently encouraged, chiefly for pastoral reasons, but also because they can help pastors avoid the errors and embarrassment that often accompany improvisation during holy moments. In particular, the lowering of the casket, though it may make some individuals uncomfortable, should be explained as a visible sign of the reality of death and a strong encouragement for all to take its coming seriously and prepare accordingly. However, pastors should feel liberty to adapt the forms as may best suit their congregation and local custom.

The Funeral Service

This service may be modified, as appropriate, in accordance with the wishes of the family.

The Greeting

The pastor begins the service with this greeting taken from John 11:25–26 (NLT):

Jesus said, "I am the resurrection and the life. He who believes in me will live, even though he dies. And everyone who lives and believes in me will never die."

Or this from 2 Corinthians 1:3–4 (ESV):

Blessed be the God and Father of our Lord Jesus Christ, the Father of mercies and God of all comfort, who comforts us in all our affliction, so that we may be able to comfort those who are in any affliction, with the comfort with which we ourselves are comforted by God.

The Opening Prayer

Then the pastor continues by saying:

Let us pray.

And he will say this prayer (or something similar):

Almighty Father, your mercies are new every morning and your kindness is great beyond our understanding. Accept our prayers this day on behalf of the family of your servant, [name of decedent], and on behalf of all those who mourn and suffer. Comfort us Lord, and remind us to be grateful for your faithfulness and mercy, that this day you have granted him/her an entrance into the land of light and joy, in the fellowship of those who have truly believed; this we ask in the name of our Lord Jesus Christ, who lives and reigns with you and the Holy Spirit, one God, now and forever. Amen.

The Opening Hymn or Hymns

Then a hymn or hymns or other songs appropriate to the occasion may be sung or performed, I accordance with wishes of the family.

Old Testament Reading:

Then the Old Testament scripture is read. The family should choose this scripture beforehand, and if possible, a willing family member should also be designated to read it. Suggested Old Testament Scriptures include the following:

Ecclesiastes 3:1–8
Isaiah 25:6–9
Isaiah 61:1–3
Lamentations 3:22–33
Job 19:21–27

The Psalm

The Psalm may be read in unison, or may be read responsively, or may be sung if a suitable version is available. Suggested psalms include the following:

Psalm 23
Psalm 39:4–7
Psalm 48:8–14
Psalm 116:12–19

New Testament Reading

Then the New Testament scripture is read. The family should choose this scripture beforehand, and if possible, a willing family member should also be designated to read it. Suggested New Testament Scriptures include the following:

John 10:27–29
John: 14:1–4
1 Corinthians 15:50–58
1 Thessalonians 4:13–18
Revelation 21:1–7

Reflections of the Family

Then a designated person or persons may offer testimonies or reflections on the life of their loved one.

The Pastoral Reflection

Then the pastor will offer a closing homily or sermonette drawn from the scripture or scriptures that have been read. Whenever possible, the sermon should include a presentation of the gospel. The pastor may choose, in this instance, to close his sermon with the invocation of the Trinity, or may say:

In the name of our Lord Jesus Christ. Amen.

Litany of The Mourners

Then the pastor will say "Let us pray."

Pastor. God our Father, you are the source of all wisdom and love. We thank you for the life of [decedent's name]. We thank you for creating him/her in your image, for calling him/her from darkness into light, for the grace of repentance and the gift of faith, and for bringing him/her into the glory of your presence.

God of all mercies, we lift up our voices to you.

> *People:* **Lord, hear our prayer.**

Pastor: Son of Righteousness, you are the Good Shepherd. We thank you for our salvation, for the promise of comfort to those who mourn, and for the gift of a yoke that is easy and a burden that is light. Give rest, we pray to those who are weary with grief.

God of all mercies, we lift up our voices to you.

> *People:* **Lord, hear our prayer.**

Pastor: Holy Spirit, you are the giver of all comfort and the bringer and sustainer of faith, hope, and love. Give comfort, we pray, to those who grieve; lift up those who are suffering, and give endurance to those who grow tired with sorrow.

God of all mercies, we lift up our voices to you.

> *People:* **Lord, hear our prayer.**

The Proclamation of Easter Hope (*Paschal Troparion*)

Then, after the Litany of Mourners, the pastor should immediately continue with these words:

Brothers and sisters, take heart! Christ is indeed risen from the dead, trampling down death by death, and giving life to those in the tomb. The Son of Righteousness is gloriously risen, giving light to those who sat in darkness and in the shadow of death. The Lord will guide our feet into the way of peace, having taken away the sin of the world. Christ will open the kingdom of

heaven to all who believe in his name, saying, "Come, O blessed
of my Father; inherit the kingdom prepared for you."

Benediction

Then the pastor dismisses the people with these words:

The Lord bless you and keep you.
The Lord make his face to shine upon you
  and be gracious to you.
The Lord lift up his countenance upon you
  and give you peace.

The Graveside

Opening Acclimation

After all the family, friends, and others are gathered around the graveside, the pastor will begin with these words:

Jesus said, "All that the Father gives me will come to me, and whoever comes to me I will never cast out. (Jn. 6:37 ESV).

He who raised Jesus Christ from the dead will also give new life to our mortal bodies through his indwelling Spirit.

He will show us the path of life; in his presence there is fullness of joy, and in his right hand are pleasures forevermore.

Opening Prayer

Then the pastor continues by saying:

Let us pray.

And he will say this prayer (or something similar):

Most merciful God, your wisdom and kindness are beyond our understanding. Give comfort this day to those who grieve. Surround them with your love and give them strength that they may not be overwhelmed by their loss. Above all, give them an unshakable confidence in your goodness, both now and forevermore. Amen.

Internment

Then a suitable hymn or song may be sung.

Then the pastor will take a handful of dirt, or a flower, and place it on the casket, followed by other family members if the family wishes.

Then the casket may be lowered into the grave, and silence is kept.

After the casket is lowered, or, if the casket is not to be lowered, the pastor continues with these words:

In sure and certain hope of the resurrection to eternal life through our Lord Jesus Christ, we commend to almighty God our brother/sister, and we commit his/her body to the ground; earth to earth, ashes to ashes, dust to dust.

Then others who wish may follow suit in casting or placing either dirt or a flower upon the casket. Or the casket may be physically buried, if it is to be buried by hand.

Then the pastor continues with these words:

May the Lord bless him/her and keep him/her.
May the Lord make his face to shine upon him/her
and be gracious to him/her.
May the Lord lift up his countenance upon
Him/her and give him/her peace.

Closing Prayer

Then the pastor continues by saying:

Let us pray.

And he will say this prayer (or something similar):

Almighty and most merciful God, we thank you for calling, justifying, and sanctifying our friend and brother/sister. In gratitude, we commend him/her to you, together with all the souls of those departed in Christ, to rest in peace.

Amen.

Benediction

Then the pastor dismisses the people with these words:

May the God of peace, who brought again from the dead our Lord Jesus Christ, the great Shepherd of the sheep, through the blood of the eternal covenant, make you perfect in every good work to do his will, working in you that which is well-pleasing in his sight, through Jesus Christ, to whom be glory forever and ever.

Amen.

Worship on Holy Days

Ash Wednesday

The Greeting

The pastor and other ministers may choose to process in at the beginning of the service.

The pastor should position himself in front of the altar or pulpit and then will begin the following responsive reading:

Pastor: The Lord be with you.
People: **And also with you.**

Pastor: Lift up your hearts.
People: **We lift them up to the Lord.**

Pastor: Let us give thanks to the Lord our God.
People: **It is right and good for us give him our thanks and praise.**

Then the pastor will say:

Let us pray.

The Written Prayer

Then the pastor will say the following prayer:

Almighty and everlasting God, who forgives the sins of all those who are truly repentant, create in us new hearts so that we might be filled with godly sorrow for every sin and a true knowledge of our wretched weakness. Grant, most merciful Father, that having a true knowledge of our guilt, we may cast all our hopes on your mercy, that all our sins may be perfectly forgiven through Christ's broken body and shed blood. This we ask in the name of our Lord and Savior Jesus Christ, who lives and reigns with you and the Holy Spirit, one God, forever and ever. Amen.

The Old Testament Reading

Then someone will read from the Old Testament, either Joel 2:1–2, 12–17, or Isaiah 58:1–12. Before reading the appointed passage, the reader may begin by saying:

A reading from [a citation giving book and chapter]. *Or the reader may say:* Hear the word of the Lord from [a citation giving book and chapter].

Depending on where the appointed reading begins, it may be necessary to provide some context. For example:

"This is from the reply of the Lord to Job," *or:* "This is while Jesus was teaching on the mount."

The scripture reading ends as follows:

Reader: The word of the Lord.
Or the reader may say: May God bless the reading of his word.

People: **Thanks be to God.**

Psalm 51 (NLT)

1 Have mercy on me, O God,
   because of your unfailing love.
Because of your great compassion,
   blot out the stain of my sins.
2 Wash me clean from my guilt.
   Purify me from my sin.
3 For I recognize my rebellion;
   it haunts me day and night.
4 Against you, and you alone, have I sinned;
   I have done what is evil in your sight.
You will be proved right in what you say,
   and your judgment against me is just.
5 For I was born a sinner —
   yes, from the moment my mother conceived me.
6 But you desire honesty from the womb,
   teaching me wisdom even there.
7 Purify me from my sins, and I will be clean;
   wash me, and I will be whiter than snow.
8 Oh, give me back my joy again;
   you have broken me —
   now let me rejoice.
9 **Don't keep looking at my sins.**
   Remove the stain of my guilt.
10 **Create in me a clean heart, O God.**
   Renew a loyal spirit within me.
11 **Do not banish me from your presence,**
   and don't take your Holy Spirit from me.
12 **Restore to me the joy of your salvation,**
   and make me willing to obey you.
13 **Then I will teach your ways to rebels,**
   and they will return to you.
14 **Forgive me for shedding blood, O God who saves;**
   then I will joyfully sing of your forgiveness.
15 **Unseal my lips, O Lord,**

that my mouth may praise you.

16 **You do not desire a sacrifice, or I would offer one.**

You do not want a burnt offering.

17 **The sacrifice you desire is a broken spirit.**

You will not reject a broken and repentant heart, O God.

18 **Look with favor on Zion and help her;**

rebuild the walls of Jerusalem.

19 **Then you will be pleased with sacrifices offered in the right spirit.**

The New Testament Reading

Then someone will read from the New Testament, either Matthew 6:1–6, 16–21 or Corinthians 5:20b–6:10. Before reading the appointed passage, the reader may begin by saying:

A reading from [a citation giving book and chapter]. *Or the reader may say:* Hear the word of the Lord from [a citation giving book and chapter].

Depending on where the appointed reading begins, it may be necessary to provide some context. For example:

"This is from the reply of the Lord to Job," *or:* "This is while Jesus was teaching on the mount."

The scripture reading ends as follows:

Reader: The word of the Lord.

Or the reader may say: May God bless the reading of his word.

People: **Thanks be to God.**

The Sermon

Then the pastor or other minister should offer a brief sermon on one of the readings.

The Imposition of Ashes

After the sermon, the pastor will invite all present to stand.

Then the pastor invites the people to the observance of the season of Lent with the following words:

Brothers and sisters, with great devotion, every year, from ancient time, Christians have solemnly remembered the holy week in which our Lord suffered, died, and was resurrected. And so it also became the custom of those ancient believers to prepare themselves for Holy Week through a season of fasting and godly sorrow for sin. In the English language, this season became known as Lent, a name derived from the ancient word in our language for springtime.

For these early Christians, the season also provided a time in which new converts were prepared for holy baptism and in which those who had committed very serious and public sins, and so come under discipline, could be restored to the fellowship of the church.

Through all these things, the season constantly reminded believers about the most central tenets of our faith, that, in Christ, God was reconciling the world to himself and no longer remembering the sins of any that would come to him through repentance and faith.

I invite you all, therefore, to this same ancient and holy observance. I invite you to take the days between now and Easter to read God's word and to examine yourself in the holy light of its eternal truth. I invite you to repent of sins, old and new, to pray and to fast, and so to deny yourself, take up your cross and follow Jesus.

And so, to make a right beginning of this season of repentance, let us now keep silence before the Lord, and with penitent and obedient hearts, confess our sins to almighty God.

Let us pray.

If ashes are to be imposed, the pastor or one leading will say the following prayer:

Almighty God, you have created us out of the dust of the earth. Grant that these ashes may be to us a sign of our mortality and contrition, that we may remember it is only by your gracious gift that we are given everlasting life, through Jesus Christ our Savior. Amen.

Then all will come forward to receive the imposition of ashes. And, as the pastor or other leader imposes them, he will say the following words:

Remember that you are dust, and to dust you shall return.

Or this:

Repent and believe the gospel.

The Common Confession

Then, after all have returned to their seats, the pastor may invite all present to kneel, he kneeling with them.

Or he may continue directly to the invitation to common confession with these words:

Here in the presence of God and of each other, let us make a common confession of our sins so that we may cast off that which so easily ensnares and run with diligence the race God has laid out for us.

Then all gathered will say the following common confession in unison:

**Most merciful God,
we confess that we have sinned against you
in thought, word, and deed
by what we have done
and by what we have left undone.
We have not loved you with our whole heart;
we have not loved our neighbors as ourselves.
We are truly sorry, and we humbly repent.
For the sake of your Son, Jesus Christ,
have mercy on us and forgive us;
give us grace to delight in your will
and to walk in your ways,
for the glory of your name.
Amen.**

Then the pastor may continue with the following litany of confession, or may use the litany of common confession alone, he reading the light print and the people responding with the bolded print.

We have been deaf to your call to serve, as Christ served us. We have not been true to the mind of Christ.
**We have grieved your Holy Spirit.
Have mercy on us, O Lord.**

All our past unfaithfulness, pride, hypocrisy, and impatience —
we confess to you, O Lord.

Our self-indulgent appetites and exploitation of other people —
we confess to you, O Lord.

Our anger at unrealized ambition and our envy of those more fortunate than ourselves —
we confess to you, O Lord.

Our love of worldly goods and comforts and our dishonesty in
daily life and work —
we confess to you, O Lord.

Our negligence in prayer and worship and our failure to boldly
proclaim the truth of the gospel —
we confess to you, O Lord.

For our blindness to human need and suffering and our
indifference to injustice and cruelty —
accept our repentance, O Lord.

For all false judgments and for all unkind and unloving thoughts
toward our neighbors —
accept our repentance, O Lord.

For all our prejudice and contempt toward those who differ from
us —
accept our repentance, O Lord.

For all the wrongs we have done —
accept our repentance, O Lord.

Restore us, good Lord, and let your anger depart from us;
Favorably hear us, for your mercy is great.

Accomplish in us the work of your salvation,
that we may show forth your glory in the world.

By the cross and passion of your Son our Lord,
bring us with all your saints to the joy of eternal life.

The Words of Consolation

*Then one who has been ordained should stand and, facing the people, say the
following:*

472

In the mercy of almighty God, Jesus Christ was given to die for you, and for his sake, God is faithful to forgive all your sins. To those who believe in Jesus Christ he gives the power to become the children of God and bestows on them the Holy Spirit. May the Lord, who has begun this good work in us, bring it to completion in the day of our Lord Jesus Christ.

Therefore, believing his promise, we ask the Lord to grant us true repentance and the grace of the Holy Spirit, that everything we do this day might please him and that all the rest of our lives may be pure and holy, for the glory of his name, through Jesus Christ our Lord. Amen.

Then people should freely and warmly greet each and shake hands, with the following greeting: The peace of Christ be with you.

The Benediction

Then the leader will say: Let us bless the Lord.
The people will respond: **Thanks be to God.**

Then the pastor will dismiss everyone with these words:

The Lord bless you and keep you.
The Lord make his face to shine upon you
  and be gracious to you.
The Lord lift up his countenance upon you
  and give you peace.

Maundy Thursday

About Maundy Thursday

Maundy Thursday begins a period in traditional Church observance called the Triduum (the sacred three days). The name "Maundy Thursday" is derived from the Latin noun *mandatum* which means "commandment." The Gospel of John tells how, on the night of the Last Supper, in the upper room, Jesus said, "A new commandment I give to you, that you love one another: just as I have loved you, you also love one another" (Jn. 13:34, WEB).

This service commemorates Jesus' institution of the Lord's Supper, his anguish in the Garden of Gethsemane, and the betrayal of Judas that lead to his crucifixion and death. Accordingly, it is a solemn occasion. Singing is kept to a minimum, the sermon is brief, and congregants depart from the service in silence.

An Order for Worship on Maundy Thursday

The Opening Acclimation

The pastor will begin by standing in front of the altar, or stage, or at the front of the place of worship and will say the following words:

Pastor: Blessed be the God of our salvation.
Congregation: **Who bears our burdens and forgives our sins.**

The Call to Worship

Following the opening acclamation, the pastor, or an elder or deacon, will begin with these words:

Brothers and sisters (or Friends), this is the night that Christ, the Son of Man, gathered with his disciples in the upper room.

This is the night that Christ, our Lord and Master, took a towel and washed the disciples' feet, calling us to love one another as he has loved us.

This is the night that Christ our God gave us this holy feast, that we who eat this bread and drink this cup may here proclaim his perfect sacrifice until he returns.

This is the night that Christ the Lamb of God gave himself into the hands of those who would slay him.

The Opening Prayer

Then, either an elder or deacon will come forward to pray. The subject of the prayer should revolve around thankfulness for the work of Christ, and for the ordinance of the Lord's Supper. Or, the elder or deacon may read the following prayer:

Almighty Father, on the night before he suffered your dear Son instituted the Lord's Supper as a memorial of his broken body and shed blood. Holy Spirit, grant that we may gratefully receive and soberly participate in this in remembrance, being humbled by your great love. We ask this in the name of Jesus, our Lord and Savior, who through this holy mystery gives us both the sign and the promise of eternal life. Amen.

The Opening Praise

The congregation will then sing a hymn or hymns appropriate to the occasion (for example "O Sacred Head Now Wounded").

476

The Responsive Reading: *Ubi Caritas*

The pastor will lead the congregation in the following responsive reading:

Where charity and love are, God is there.
Christ's love has gathered us into one.
Let us rejoice and be pleased in him.

Let us fear and let us love the living God.
And may we love each other with a sincere heart.

Where charity and love are, God is there.
As we are gathered into one body,
beware, lest we be divided in mind.

Let evil impulses stop, let controversy cease,
And may Christ our God be in our midst.

Where charity and love are, God is there.
And may we with the saints also,
see your face in glory, O Christ our God;

The joy that is immense and good,
unto the ages, through infinite ages.
Amen.

The Readings

Then the following Scriptures are read, or some other suitable Scripture, and each is followed by the prayer of a believer or by a suitable hymn:

Exodus 12:1–14
Psalm 78:14–25
1 Corinthians 11:23–26,27–34
John 13:1–15 or Luke 22:14–30

The Sermon

Then follows a brief sermon from one of the readings.

Communion

Communion is then celebrated using one of the Orders for Communion in this book, preferably the Order for Communion by Intinction, or according to the tradition of your local church.

If intinction is used, silence is kept throughout the communion service except when otherwise noted.

The Stripping of the Altar

After the last communion song is complete, there will be a brief pause.

Then a final song will begin, or the Stripping of the Altar may proceed in silence.

The ordained ministers will rise and go to the altar and consume all the remaining elements.

Then they will give the communion pieces and cloths to appointed children to put away.

Then, beginning closest to the baptistry, each piece of decoration will be put away, last of all the altar cloths. An appointed child may hold the Bible in an open position, until the remaining altar appointments are put away.

Then the pastor will take the Bible, stand in front of the congregation, close it, and will depart the sanctuary in silence, followed by deacons, ministers, and other families.

A final blessing or benediction is omitted.

The Great Vigil of Easter

About the Great Vigil of Easter

The celebration of a vigil on the evening before Easter Sunday is an ancient part of Christian life. As early as the middle of the third century AD (i.e. the mid 200's), a work called the *Didascalia Apostolorum* gives these instructions to Christian communities:

> "You shall come together and watch and keep vigil all the night with prayers and intercessions, and with reading of the Prophets, and with the Gospel and with Psalms, with fear and trembling and with earnest supplication... Especially incumbent on you therefore is the fast of the Friday and of the Sabbath; and likewise the vigil and watching of the Sabbath, and the reading of the Scriptures, and psalms, and prayer and intercession for them that have sinned, and the expectation and hope of the resurrection of our Lord Jesus, until the third hour in the night after the Sabbath. And then offer your oblations; and thereafter eat and make good cheer, and rejoice and be glad, because that the earnest of our resurrection, Christ, is risen." [25]

The antiquity of this vigil in Christian practice should engender a certain respect. But modern Christians, and Evangelicals in particular, should not celebrate the Easter Vigil simply because it is ancient. Most importantly of all, there are biblical grounds for the people of God keeping vigil to commemorate his deliverance (Exodus 12:42). And, there are also

---

[25] Connolly, Hugh, *Didascalia Apostolorum*. Oxford: Clarendon Press, 1929, XXI

important reasons for observance that arise from and speak directly to our own time and culture and to the contemporary witness of the Church.

The Apostle Paul said, "And if Christ has not been raised, your faith is futile; you are still in your sins" (1 Cor. 15:17 NIV). This is a bold claim! Behind it and under it are many other claims equally as bold. History has seen many remarkable people come and go. Every remarkable historical figure has a birth story (obviously!), sometimes even one clouded in mysterious circumstances. Many historical figures have even made remarkable sacrifices for the sake of others. Many of these people have even made the ultimate sacrifice. Even so, Christians believe only one of these people was truly God and truly man. Only one man gave his life to make reconciliation between God and humanity. Only this one man, the Lord Jesus Christ, was raised bodily from death by the power of God and will return in glory to judge the living and the dead. As the ancient confessions affirm, these are the core tenets of our faith. Each and every one is a staggeringly bold claim. Each and every one is a mystery. In 1 Corinthians, Paul affirmed that the resurrection is right at the heart of these doctrines and mysteries.

Unfortunately, the Church too often acts as though other occasions or holy days, such as Christmas, are the central act of our faith (and, perhaps even more troublingly, takes its cues in this from secular commercialization of the holiday). In fact, we sometimes put even more effort and planning into Halloween outreach events than we do into Christmas and certainly more than we do into Easter! To be clear, it is certainly right and fitting that the Church make a "big deal" out of Christmas! But it is simply not fitting for the church to treat Easter like "just another manic Sunday." It is not right for the Church to neglect Easter and the days leading up to it because they are the central and critical moments in the history of God's saving acts!

In fact, neglecting Easter is spiritually harmful because it can implicitly reinforce the idea that Christ is not still living, or worse still, even if he is, it is not all that important. Contrast such neglect with Paul's bottom line: the Christian faith is either an Easter Faith or it amounts to nothing! Apart from Easter, all preaching is in vain! With one voice the true Church has always proclaimed the good news of a living Christ, even as she proclaims the living Lord Christ as both the end and goal of all faith. Thus, the Great Vigil of Easter is fundamentally biblical because it unashamedly *makes a big deal out of Easter*. It is also fundamentally evangelical because it proclaims the good news of the *whole gospel in one occasion*. Observing the Great Vigil of Easter can gently and powerfully add appropriate emphasis to the Easter moment in the life of the local church.

The Apostle Paul also recalled in 1 Corinthians how he passed on what was "of first importance," "that Christ died for our sins in accordance with the Scriptures, that he was buried, that he was raised on the third day in accordance with the Scriptures." (1 Cor. 15:3–4 ESV). He was clear and unwavering in affirming these doctrines. And yet, this same Paul wrote in his letter to Timothy that "Great indeed, we confess, is the mystery of godliness:

He was manifested in the flesh,
   vindicated by the Spirit,
     seen by angels,
proclaimed among the nations,
  believed on in the world,
    taken up in glory" (1 Tim. 3:16 ESV).

Paul knew that there were limits to the human ability to explain and understand the saving acts of God in history. He knew that a truly Christian faith always holds right knowledge (doctrine) in tension with the limits of knowledge (mystery). At some point, we must simply confess in awe and gratitude what God has done in our midst, even if we cannot fully explain it.

Most people outside of the church know, down deep, that there is great mystery in life and in the world. To these people it only makes sense that there would be great mystery in religious devotion as well. Like all people, the people around us are hungry to hear a bold affirmation of the gospel, even while they are deeply skeptical of anyone that has a ready answer for every arcane theological question. In this, they are not far from the spirit of the gospel. Because it holds together these two important elements of the Christian faith — unwavering affirmation of truth and the reality (and atmosphere) of solemn mystery — the Great Vigil of Easter can also be deeply missional to an unbelieving culture. This type of celebration can make contact with deep longings that reside in the heart of all people: the longing for an organizing principle of life and the longing to be touched by a mystery, even the mystery of God himself.

Gathering

If there is no precipitation, the people should begin gathering outside the church about sunset, near a small firepit placed close to the front entrance of the sanctuary. The exact time will vary according to the date of Easter. If possible, the people should wait in reverent silence as others gather.

If there is precipitation, people should gather outside of the sanctuary and/or, if possible, under a churches gable or awning. Or, if there is no other place, people may gather in silence in the church, with a candle lit near the back of the church.

The pastor may choose to begin by greeting everyone warmly and then, if appropriate, give the following words of instruction:

1. This is a longer service than most are used to. Little ones may get a little restless, and that is okay! Please don't feel embarrassed if your little one cries or isn't perfectly behaved.

2. After the Paschal Candle is lit and the flame shared, the Pastor will lead a procession of congregants, behind the altar bible carried out on Maundy Thursday, into the darkened sanctuary. The Pastor and Ministers will ascend the chancel (or stage) to sit behind or near the pulpit. As congregants proceed into the sanctuary, they should maintain silent to the extent possible.

3. After everyone is seated, the pastor or ministers will say a brief invocation, and then each person will come up to the reading podium and help to lead the service in whatever way they have agreed; everyone should know their roll beforehand and the worship guide should make their roles clear.

4. The pattern for most of this worship service is to read a scripture, then responsively say a Psalm, then pray, (then repeat!). There's no need for anyone to wait for a cue; just follow along in the order of worship. When you read a scripture, you should begin it with one of these introductions:

> A reading from [a citation giving book and chapter].
>
> *Or:*
>
> Hear the word of the Lord from [a citation giving book and chapter].

When you have completed your reading, pause briefly, then say one of the following conclusions:

> *Reader:* The word of the Lord.
>
> *Or:*
>
> *Or the reader may say:* May God bless the reading of his word.

This method for introducing and concluding a reading is important not only because it is traditional, but because it reflects the pattern of worship God has revealed throughout the Bible: Call and Response (His Spirit calls through the word and our spirits respond in faith). Even more importantly, it affirms a high view of Holy Scripture, that it is indeed "the word of the Lord", and that it is precious gift for which we should give thanks!

When one person has completed their role and is seated, or when the congregation is finished responsively reading a psalm, the next person will perform their role; simply go up to the pulpit or lectern and read or pray. The pastor, or another minister will start each of the responsive Psalms by reading first. The congregation will respond.

The Service of Lights

Invocation

At the appropriate time, just after sundown, the pastor or another minister will begin with these words:

Brothers and sisters in Christ, on this holy night, when our Savior, Jesus, passed from death to life, we gather with the whole church in vigil and prayer. This is the Passover of Jesus Christ: through light and the Word we recall Jesus' death and resurrection, we share Christ's triumph over sin and death, and with inextinguishable hope, we await Christ's coming again!

A Light in the Darkness

Elder or deacon:

In the beginning was the Word, and the Word was with God, and the Word was God. In him was life; and the life was the light of men. And the light shineth in darkness; and the darkness comprehended it not. (John 1:1, 4–5, KJV)

The Passover Light

Pastor: The light of Christ rises in glory, overcoming the darkness of sin and death!

After the pastor says these words, he will take a long candle (The Paschal Candle), and will draw flame from the fire pit and pass it to the people, who share it until all candles are lit. After most or all of the candles are lit, the people will process into the sanctuary, which should be fully dark, and in which appropriate music for the situation may be playing softly.

The pastor, ministers or other helpers may light the candles on the altar, if any are used, place the altar Bible upon the altar and open it.

The Service of the Word

Invocation

Then the pastor or another minister will continue by reciting or singing the following prayer:

Let us pray.

Heavenly Father, it is truly right and good, always and everywhere, with our whole heart and mind and voice, to praise you, the invisible, almighty, and eternal God and your only-begotten Son, Jesus Christ our Lord; for he is the true Passover Lamb, who at the Feast of the Passover paid for us the debt of Adam's sin, and by his blood delivered your faithful people.

This is the night when you brought our fathers, the children of Israel, out of bondage in Egypt and led them through the Red Sea on dry land. This is the night when all who believe in Christ were delivered from the gloom of sin and are restored to grace and holiness of life. This is the night when Christ broke the bonds of death and hell and rose victorious from the grave.

How wonderful and beyond our knowing, O God, is your mercy and loving-kindness to us, that to redeem a slave, you gave a Son. How holy is this night, when wickedness is put to flight, and sin is washed away;

It restores innocence to the fallen and joy to those who mourn! It casts out pride and hatred and brings peace and concord!

How blessed is this night, when earth and heaven are joined and man is reconciled to God. Amen.

Then, after the prayer the pastor or minister will continue with these words:

Now, let us hear the record of God's saving deeds in history, how he saved his people in ages past, and let us pray that the Lord will bring and preserve each of us to the fullness of redemption.

The Story of Creation

Then a person assigned for the first reading will go to the pulpit or reading lectern and will read the following passage:

Genesis 1:1–2:2

1 In the beginning, God created the heavens and the earth. **2** The earth was formless and empty. Darkness was on the surface of the deep and God's Spirit was hovering over the surface of the waters.

3 God said, "Let there be light," and there was light. **4** God saw the light, and saw that it was good. God divided the light from the darkness. **5** God called the light "day", and the darkness he called "night". There was evening and there was morning, the first day.

6 God said, "Let there be an expanse in the middle of the waters, and let it divide the waters from the waters." **7** God made the expanse, and divided the waters which were under the expanse from the waters which were above the expanse; and it was so. **8** God called the expanse "sky". There was evening and there was morning, a second day.

9 God said, "Let the waters under the sky be gathered together to one place, and let the dry land appear;" and it was so. **10** God called the dry land "earth", and the gathering together of the waters he called "seas". God saw that it was good. **11** God said, "Let the earth yield grass, herbs yielding seeds, and fruit trees bearing fruit after their kind, with their seeds in it, on the earth;"

and it was so. ¹² The earth yielded grass, herbs yielding seed after their kind, and trees bearing fruit, with their seeds in it, after their kind; and God saw that it was good. ¹³ There was evening and there was morning, a third day.

¹⁴ God said, "Let there be lights in the expanse of the sky to divide the day from the night; and let them be for signs to mark seasons, days, and years; ¹⁵ and let them be for lights in the expanse of the sky to give light on the earth;" and it was so. ¹⁶ God made the two great lights: the greater light to rule the day, and the lesser light to rule the night. He also made the stars. ¹⁷ God set them in the expanse of the sky to give light to the earth, ¹⁸ and to rule over the day and over the night, and to divide the light from the darkness. God saw that it was good. ¹⁹ There was evening and there was morning, a fourth day.

²⁰ God said, "Let the waters abound with living creatures, and let birds fly above the earth in the open expanse of the sky." ²¹ God created the large sea creatures and every living creature that moves, with which the waters swarmed, after their kind, and every winged bird after its kind. God saw that it was good. ²² God blessed them, saying, "Be fruitful, and multiply, and fill the waters in the seas, and let birds multiply on the earth." ²³ There was evening and there was morning, a fifth day.

²⁴ God said, "Let the earth produce living creatures after their kind, livestock, creeping things, and animals of the earth after their kind;" and it was so. ²⁵ God made the animals of the earth after their kind, and the livestock after their kind, and everything that creeps on the ground after its kind. God saw that it was good.

²⁶ God said, "Let's make man in our image, after our likeness. Let them have dominion over the fish of the sea, and over the birds of the sky, and over the livestock, and over all the earth, and over every creeping thing that creeps on the earth." ²⁷ God created man in his own image. In God's image he created him;

male and female he created them. [28] God blessed them. God said to them, "Be fruitful, multiply, fill the earth, and subdue it. Have dominion over the fish of the sea, over the birds of the sky, and over every living thing that moves on the earth." [29] God said, "Behold, I have given you every herb yielding seed, which is on the surface of all the earth, and every tree, which bears fruit yielding seed. It will be your food. [30] To every animal of the earth, and to every bird of the sky, and to everything that creeps on the earth, in which there is life, I have given every green herb for food;" and it was so.

[31] God saw everything that he had made, and, behold, it was very good. There was evening and there was morning, a sixth day.

2 The heavens, the earth, and all their vast array were finished. [2] On the seventh day God finished his work which he had done; and he rested on the seventh day from all his work which he had done.

Reader: The word of the Lord.
Or the reader may say: May God bless the reading of his Word.

People: **Thanks be to God.**

Psalm 33:1–11

Then, after the scripture reading, the congregation will say the following Psalm responsively:

Rejoice in The LORD, you righteous!
Praise is fitting for the upright.
[2] Give thanks to The LORD with the lyre.
Sing praises to him with the harp of ten strings.
[3] Sing to him a new song.
Play skillfully with a shout of joy!
[4] For The LORD's word is right.
All his work is done in faithfulness.

⁵ He loves righteousness and justice.
   The earth is full of the loving kindness of The LORD.
⁶ By The LORD's word, the heavens were made:
   all their army by the breath of his mouth.
⁷ He gathers the waters of the sea together as a heap.
   He lays up the deeps in storehouses.
⁸ Let all the earth fear The LORD.
   Let all the inhabitants of the world stand in awe of him.
⁹ For he spoke, and it was done.
   He commanded, and it stood firm.
¹⁰ The LORD brings the counsel of the nations to nothing.
   He makes the thoughts of the peoples to be of no effect.
¹¹ **The counsel of The LORD stands fast forever,**
   the thoughts of his heart to all generations.

The Prayer

Then a member of the congregation will offer a prayer of thanksgiving for creation (or something else appropriate to the scriptures). The prayer may be read or said extemporaneously.

The Flood

Then the person assigned for the second reading will go to the pulpit or reading lectern and will read the following passage:

Genesis 7:1–5, 11–18; 8:6–19; 9:8–13

7 The L ORD said to Noah, "Come with all of your household into the ship, for I have seen your righteousness before me in this generation. **2** You shall take seven pairs of every clean animal with you, the male and his female. Of the animals that are not clean, take two, the male and his female. **3** Also of the birds of the sky, seven and seven, male and female, to keep seed alive on the surface of all the earth. **4** In seven days, I will cause it to rain on the earth for forty days and forty nights. I will destroy every living thing that I have made from the surface of the ground." **5** Noah did everything that The L ORD commanded him.

11 In the six hundredth year of Noah's life, in the second month, on the seventeenth day of the month, on that day all the fountains of the great deep burst open, and the sky's windows opened. **12** It rained on the earth forty days and forty nights.

13 In the same day Noah, and Shem, Ham, and Japheth—the sons of Noah—and Noah's wife and the three wives of his sons with them, entered into the ship— **14** they, and every animal after its kind, all the livestock after their kind, every creeping thing that creeps on the earth after its kind, and every bird after its kind, every bird of every sort. **15** Pairs from all flesh with the breath of life in them went into the ship to Noah. **16** Those who went in, went in male and female of all flesh, as God commanded him; then The L ORD shut him in. **17** The flood was forty days on the earth. The waters increased, and lifted up the ship, and it was lifted up above the earth. **18** The waters rose, and increased greatly on the earth; and the ship floated on the surface of the waters.

6 At the end of forty days, Noah opened the window of the ship which he had made, 7 and he sent out a raven. It went back and forth, until the waters were dried up from the earth. 8 He himself sent out a dove to see if the waters were abated from the surface of the ground, 9 but the dove found no place to rest her foot, and she returned into the ship to him, for the waters were on the surface of the whole earth. He put out his hand, and took her, and brought her to him into the ship. 10 He waited yet another seven days; and again he sent the dove out of the ship. 11 The dove came back to him at evening and, behold, in her mouth was a freshly plucked olive leaf. So Noah knew that the waters were abated from the earth. 12 He waited yet another seven days, and sent out the dove; and she didn't return to him any more.

13 In the six hundred first year, in the first month, the first day of the month, the waters were dried up from the earth. Noah removed the covering of the ship, and looked. He saw that the surface of the ground was dry. 14 In the second month, on the twenty-seventh day of the month, the earth was dry.

15 God spoke to Noah, saying, 16 "Go out of the ship, you, your wife, your sons, and your sons' wives with you. 17 Bring out with you every living thing that is with you of all flesh, including birds, livestock, and every creeping thing that creeps on the earth, that they may breed abundantly in the earth, and be fruitful, and multiply on the earth."

18 Noah went out, with his sons, his wife, and his sons' wives with him. 19 Every animal, every creeping thing, and every bird, whatever moves on the earth, after their families, went out of the ship.

8 God spoke to Noah and to his sons with him, saying, 9 "As for me, behold, I establish my covenant with you, and with your offspring after you, 10 and with every living creature that is with you: the birds, the livestock, and every animal of the earth with

you, of all that go out of the ship, even every animal of the earth. ¹¹ I will establish my covenant with you: All flesh will not be cut off any more by the waters of the flood. There will never again be a flood to destroy the earth." ¹² God said, "This is the token of the covenant which I make between me and you and every living creature that is with you, for perpetual generations: ¹³ I set my rainbow in the cloud, and it will be a sign of a covenant between me and the earth.

Reader: The word of the Lord.
Or the reader may say: May God bless the reading of his Word.

People: **Thanks be to God.**

Psalm 46

Then the congregation will say the following Psalm responsively:

God is our refuge and strength,
    a very present help in trouble.
² **Therefore we won't be afraid, though the earth changes,**
    though the mountains are shaken
    into the heart of the seas;
³ though its waters roar and are troubled,
    though the mountains tremble with their swelling.
⁴ **There is a river, the streams of which make the city of**
    God glad, the holy place of the tents of the Most High.
⁵ God is within her. She shall not be moved.
    God will help her at dawn.
⁶ **The nations raged. The kingdoms were moved.**
    He lifted his voice and the earth melted.
⁷ The LORD of Armies is with us.
    The God of Jacob is our refuge.
⁸ **Come, see The LORD's works,**
    what desolations he has made in the earth.
⁹ He makes wars cease to the end of the earth.
    He breaks the bow, and shatters the spear.

He burns the chariots in the fire.
10 "Be still, and know that I am God.
I will be exalted among the nations.
I will be exalted in the earth."
11 The LORD of Armies is with us.
The God of Jacob is our refuge.

The Prayer

Then a member of the congregation will offer a prayer of thanksgiving for God's provision of deliverance and promise of mercy (or something else appropriate to the scriptures). The prayer may be read or said extemporaneously.

Abraham's Sacrifice of Isaac

Then the person assigned for the third reading will go to the pulpit or reading lectern and will read the following passage:

Genesis 22:1–18

22 After these things, God tested Abraham, and said to him, "Abraham!"

He said, "Here I am."

2 He said, "Now take your son, your only son, Isaac, whom you love, and go into the land of Moriah. Offer him there as a burnt offering on one of the mountains which I will tell you of."

3 Abraham rose early in the morning, and saddled his donkey; and took two of his young men with him, and Isaac his son. He split the wood for the burnt offering, and rose up, and went to the place of which God had told him. **4** On the third day Abraham lifted up his eyes, and saw the place far off. **5** Abraham said to his young men, "Stay here with the donkey. The boy and I will go over there. We will worship, and come back to you." **6** Abraham took the wood of the burnt offering and laid it on Isaac his son. He took in his hand the fire and the knife. They both went together. **7** Isaac spoke to Abraham his father, and said, "My father?"

He said, "Here I am, my son."

He said, "Here is the fire and the wood, but where is the lamb for a burnt offering?"

8 Abraham said, "God will provide himself the lamb for a burnt offering, my son." So they both went together. **9** They came to the place which God had told him of. Abraham built the altar there, and laid the wood in order, bound Isaac his son, and laid him on the altar, on the wood. ¹⁰ Abraham stretched out his hand, and took the knife to kill his son.

¹¹ The LORD's angel called to him out of the sky, and said, "Abraham, Abraham!"

He said, "Here I am."

¹² He said, "Don't lay your hand on the boy or do anything to him. For now I know that you fear God, since you have not withheld your son, your only son, from me."

¹³ Abraham lifted up his eyes, and looked, and saw that behind him was a ram caught in the thicket by his horns. Abraham went and took the ram, and offered him up for a burnt offering instead of his son. ¹⁴ Abraham called the name of that place "The LORD Will Provide". As it is said to this day, "On The LORD's mountain, it will be provided."

¹⁵ The LORD's angel called to Abraham a second time out of the sky, ¹⁶ and said, "'I have sworn by myself,' says The LORD, 'because you have done this thing, and have not withheld your son, your only son, ¹⁷ that I will bless you greatly, and I will multiply your offspring greatly like the stars of the heavens, and like the sand which is on the seashore. Your offspring will possess the gate of his enemies. ¹⁸ All the nations of the earth will be blessed by your offspring, because you have obeyed my voice.'"

Reader: The word of the Lord.
Or the reader may say: May God bless the reading of his Word.

People: **Thanks be to God.**

496

Psalm 16

Then the congregation will say the following Psalm responsively:

16 Preserve me, God, for I take refuge in you.
² My soul, you have said to the LORD, "You are my Lord.
Apart from you I have no good thing."
³ As for the saints who are in the earth,
they are the excellent ones in whom is all my delight.
⁴ Their sorrows shall be multiplied
who give gifts to another god.
Their drink offerings of blood I will not offer,
nor take their names on my lips.
⁵ The LORD assigned my portion and my cup.
You made my lot secure.
⁶ The lines have fallen to me in pleasant places.
Yes, I have a good inheritance.
⁷ I will bless The LORD, who has given me counsel.
Yes, my heart instructs me in the night seasons.
⁸ I have set The LORD always before me.
Because he is at my right hand, I shall not be moved.
⁹ Therefore my heart is glad, and my tongue rejoices.
My body shall also dwell in safety.
¹⁰ For you will not leave my soul in Sheol,
neither will you allow your holy one to see corruption.
¹¹ You will show me the path of life.
In your presence is fullness of joy.
In your right hand there are pleasures forever more.

The Prayer

Then a member of the congregation will offer a prayer of thanksgiving for God's provision of a sacrifice for sin (or something else appropriate to the scriptures). The prayer may be read or said extemporaneously.

Israel's Deliverance at the Red Sea

Then the person assigned for the fourth reading will go to the pulpit or reading lectern and will read the following passage:

Exodus 12:29, 14:5-7, 9–31

12²⁹ At midnight, the LORD struck all the firstborn in the land of Egypt, from the firstborn of Pharaoh who sat on his throne to the firstborn of the captive who was in the dungeon, and all the firstborn of livestock. ³⁰ Pharaoh rose up in the night, he, and all his servants, and all the Egyptians; and there was a great cry in Egypt, for there was not a house where there was not one dead. ³¹ He called for Moses and Aaron by night, and said, "Rise up, get out from among my people, both you and the children of Israel; and go, serve the LORD, as you have said! ³² Take both your flocks and your herds, as you have said, and be gone; and bless me also!"

14⁵ The king of Egypt was told that the people had fled; and the heart of Pharaoh and of his servants was changed toward the people, and they said, "What is this we have done, that we have let Israel go from serving us?" ⁶ He prepared his chariot, and took his army with him; ⁷ and he took six hundred chosen chariots, and all the chariots of Egypt, with captains over all of them.

⁹ The Egyptians pursued them. All the horses and chariots of Pharaoh, his horsemen, and his army overtook them encamping by the sea, beside Pihahiroth, before Baal Zephon.

¹⁰ When Pharaoh came near, the children of Israel lifted up their eyes, and behold, the Egyptians were marching after them; and they were very afraid. The children of Israel cried out to the LORD. ¹¹ They said to Moses, "Because there were no graves in Egypt, have you taken us away to die in the wilderness? Why

have you treated us this way, to bring us out of Egypt? ¹² Isn't this the word that we spoke to you in Egypt, saying, 'Leave us alone, that we may serve the Egyptians?' For it would have been better for us to serve the Egyptians than to die in the wilderness."

¹³ Moses said to the people, "Don't be afraid. Stand still, and see the salvation of the LORD, which he will work for you today; for you will never again see the Egyptians whom you have seen today. ¹⁴ the LORD will fight for you, and you shall be still."

¹⁵ The LORD said to Moses, "Why do you cry to me? Speak to the children of Israel, that they go forward. ¹⁶ Lift up your rod, and stretch out your hand over the sea and divide it. Then the children of Israel shall go into the middle of the sea on dry ground. ¹⁷ Behold, I myself will harden the hearts of the Egyptians, and they will go in after them. I will get myself honor over Pharaoh, and over all his armies, over his chariots, and over his horsemen. ¹⁸ The Egyptians shall know that I am the LORD when I have gotten myself honor over Pharaoh, over his chariots, and over his horsemen." ¹⁹ The angel of God, who went before the camp of Israel, moved and went behind them; and the pillar of cloud moved from before them, and stood behind them. ²⁰ It came between the camp of Egypt and the camp of Israel. There was the cloud and the darkness, yet it gave light by night. One didn't come near the other all night.

²¹ Moses stretched out his hand over the sea, and the LORD caused the sea to go back by a strong east wind all night, and made the sea dry land, and the waters were divided. ²² The children of Israel went into the middle of the sea on the dry ground; and the waters were a wall to them on their right hand and on their left. ²³ The Egyptians pursued, and went in after them into the middle of the sea: all of Pharaoh's horses, his chariots, and his horsemen. ²⁴ In the morning watch, the LORD looked out on the Egyptian army through the pillar of fire and of cloud, and confused the Egyptian army. ²⁵ He took off their

chariot wheels, and they drove them heavily; so that the Egyptians said, "Let's flee from the face of Israel, for the LORD fights for them against the Egyptians!"

26 The LORD said to Moses, "Stretch out your hand over the sea, that the waters may come again on the Egyptians, on their chariots, and on their horsemen." 27 Moses stretched out his hand over the sea, and the sea returned to its strength when the morning appeared; and the Egyptians fled against it. The LORD overthrew the Egyptians in the middle of the sea. 28 The waters returned, and covered the chariots and the horsemen, even all Pharaoh's army that went in after them into the sea. There remained not so much as one of them. 29 But the children of Israel walked on dry land in the middle of the sea, and the waters were a wall to them on their right hand and on their left.

30 Thus The LORD saved Israel that day out of the hand of the Egyptians; and Israel saw the Egyptians dead on the seashore. 31 Israel saw the great work which The LORD did to the Egyptians, and the people feared The LORD; and they believed in The LORD and in his servant Moses.

Reader: The word of the Lord.
Or the reader may say: May God bless the reading of his Word.

People: **Thanks be to God.**

Exodus 15:11–18

Then the congregation will say the following scripture responsively:

11 Who is like you, LORD, among the gods?
Who is like you, glorious in holiness,
fearful in praises, doing wonders?
12 You stretched out your right hand.
The earth swallowed them.
13 "You, in your loving kindness, have led the people that you
   have redeemed.

You have guided them in your strength to your holy habitation.

14 The peoples have heard.

They tremble.

Pangs have taken hold of the inhabitants of Philistia.

15 Then the chiefs of Edom were dismayed.

Trembling takes hold of the mighty men of Moab.

All the inhabitants of Canaan have melted away.

16 Terror and dread falls on them.

By the greatness of your arm they are as still as a stone,

until your people pass over, LORD,

until the people you have purchased pass over.

17 You will bring them in, and plant them in the mountain of your inheritance,

the place, LORD, which you have made for yourself to dwell in;

the sanctuary, Lord, which your hands have established.

18 **The LORD will reign forever and ever."**

<u>The Prayer</u>

Then a member of the congregation will offer a prayer of thanksgiving for God's deliverance of his people (or something else appropriate to the scriptures). The prayer may be read or said extemporaneously.

Salvation Offered Freely to All

Then the person assigned for the fifth reading will go to the pulpit or reading lectern and will read the following passage:

Isaiah 55:1-11

55 Come, everyone who thirsts, to the waters!
    Come, he who has no money, buy, and eat!
    Yes, come, buy wine and milk without money
    and without price.
² Why do you spend money for that which is not bread,
    and your labor for that which doesn't satisfy?
Listen diligently to me, and eat that which is good,
    and let your soul delight itself in richness.
³ Turn your ear, and come to me.
    Hear, and your soul will live.
    I will make an everlasting covenant with you,
    even the sure mercies of David.
⁴ Behold, I have given him for a witness to the peoples,
    a leader and commander to the peoples.
⁵ Behold, you shall call a nation that you don't know;
    and a nation that didn't know you shall run to you,
    because of The LORD your God,
    and for the Holy One of Israel;
    for he has glorified you."
⁶ Seek The LORD while he may be found.
    Call on him while he is near.
⁷ Let the wicked forsake his way,
    and the unrighteous man his thoughts.
Let him return to the LORD, and he will have mercy on him,
    to our God, for he will freely pardon.
⁸ "For my thoughts are not your thoughts,
    and your ways are not my ways," says the LORD.
⁹ "For as the heavens are higher than the earth,
    so are my ways higher than your ways,
    and my thoughts than your thoughts.

[10] For as the rain comes down and the snow from the sky,
  and doesn't return there, but waters the earth,
  and makes it grow and bud,
  and gives seed to the sower and bread to the eater;
[11] so is my word that goes out of my mouth:
  it will not return to me void,
  but it will accomplish that which I please,
  and it will prosper in the thing I sent it to do.

> *Reader:* The word of the Lord.
> *Or the reader may say:* May God bless the reading of his Word.

> *People:* **Thanks be to God.**

Psalm 42:1-8

Then the congregation will say the following Psalm responsively:

> As the deer pants for brooks of water,
>   so my soul pants after you, God.
> [2] **My soul thirsts for God, for the living God.**
>   **When shall I come and appear before God?**
> [3] My tears have been my food day and night,
>   while they continually ask me, "Where is your God?"
> [4] **These things I remember,**
> **and pour out my soul within me,**
>   how I used to go with the crowd,
>   and led them to God's house,
>   **with the voice of joy and praise,**
>   **a multitude keeping a holy day.**
> [5] Why are you in despair, my soul?
>   Why are you disturbed within me?
>   **Hope in God!**
>   **For I shall still praise him**
>   **for the saving help of his presence.**
> [6] My God, my soul is in despair within me.
>   **Therefore I remember you from the land of the Jordan,**

the heights of Hermon, from the hill Mizar.

7 Deep calls to deep at the noise of your waterfalls.

All your waves and your billows have swept over me.

8 The LORD will command his loving kindness in the daytime.

In the night his song shall be with me:

a prayer to the God of my life.

9 I will ask God, my rock, "Why have you forgotten me?

Why do I go mourning because of the oppression of the enemy?"

10 As with a sword in my bones, my adversaries reproach me,

while they continually ask me, "Where is your God?"

11 **Why are you in despair, my soul?**

Why are you disturbed within me?

Hope in God! For I shall still praise him,

the saving help of my countenance, and my God.

The Prayer

Then a member of the congregation will offer a prayer of thanksgiving for God's universal offer of salvation (or something else appropriate to the scriptures). The prayer may be read or said extemporaneously.

A New Heart and a New Spirit

Then the person assigned for the sixth reading will go to the pulpit or reading lectern and will read the following passage:

Ezekiel 36:24–36

24 For I will take you from among the nations and gather you out of all the countries, and will bring you into your own land. **25** I will sprinkle clean water on you, and you will be clean. I will cleanse you from all your filthiness, and from all your idols. **26** I will also give you a new heart, and I will put a new spirit within you. I will take away the stony heart out of your flesh, and I will give you a heart of flesh. **27** I will put my Spirit within you, and cause you to walk in my statutes. You will keep my ordinances and do them. **28** You will dwell in the land that I gave to your fathers. You will be my people, and I will be your God. **29** I will save you from all your uncleanness. I will call for the grain, and will multiply it, and lay no famine on you. **30** I will multiply the fruit of the tree and the increase of the field, that you may receive no more the reproach of famine among the nations.

31 Then you will remember your evil ways, and your deeds that were not good; and you will loathe yourselves in your own sight for your iniquities and for your abominations. **32** I don't do this for your sake," says the Lord GOD. "Let it be known to you: be ashamed and confounded for your ways, house of Israel."

33 "'The Lord GOD says: "In the day that I cleanse you from all your iniquities, I will cause the cities to be inhabited and the waste places will be built. **34** The land that was desolate will be tilled instead of being a desolation in the sight of all who passed by. **35** They will say, 'This land that was desolate has become like the garden of Eden. The waste, desolate, and ruined cities are fortified and inhabited.' **36** Then the nations that are left around you will know that I, the LORD, have built the ruined places, and planted that which was desolate. I, the LORD, have spoken it, and I will do it."

Reader: The word of the Lord.
Or the reader may say: May God bless the reading of his Word.

People: **Thanks be to God.**

Isaiah 12:1–6

Then the congregation will say the following scripture responsively:

12 In that day you will say,
"I will give thanks to you, LORD;
  for though you were angry with me,
    your anger has turned away
  and you comfort me.
² Behold, God is my salvation.
  I will trust, and will not be afraid;
for the LORD himself, is my strength and song;
  and he has become my salvation."
³ Therefore with joy you will draw water
  out of the wells of salvation.
⁴ **In that day you will say,**
  "Give thanks to the LORD! Call on his name!
Declare his doings among the peoples!
  Proclaim that his name is exalted!
⁵ **Sing to the LORD, for he has done excellent things!**
  Let this be known in all the earth!
⁶ Cry aloud and shout, you inhabitant of Zion;
  for the Holy One of Israel is great among you!"

The Prayer

Then a member of the congregation will offer a prayer of thanksgiving for God's provision of a new heart and spirit through Christ (or something else appropriate to the scriptures). The prayer may be read or said extemporaneously.

The Valley of Dry Bones

Then the person assigned for the seventh reading will go to the pulpit or reading lectern and will read the following passage:

<u>Ezekiel 37:1–14</u>

37 The LORD hand was on me, and he brought me out in the LORD's Spirit, and set me down in the middle of the valley; and it was full of bones. ² He caused me to pass by them all around: and behold, there were very many in the open valley; and behold, they were very dry. ³ He said to me, "Son of man, can these bones live?"

I answered, "Oh, Lord GOD, you know."

⁴ Again he said to me, "Prophesy over these bones, and tell them, 'You dry bones, hear the word of The LORD. ⁵ The Lord GOD says to these bones: "Behold, I will cause breath to enter into you, and you will live. ⁶ I will lay sinews on you, and will bring up flesh on you, and cover you with skin, and put breath in you, and you will live. Then you will know that I am The LORD.""""

⁷ So I prophesied as I was commanded. As I prophesied, there was a noise, and behold, there was an earthquake. Then the bones came together, bone to its bone. ⁸ I saw, and, behold, there were sinews on them, and flesh came up, and skin covered them above; but there was no breath in them.

⁹ Then he said to me, "Prophesy to the wind, prophesy, son of man, and tell the wind, 'The Lord GOD says: "Come from the four winds, breath, and breathe on these slain, that they may live.""""

¹⁰ So I prophesied as he commanded me, and the breath came into them, and they lived, and stood up on their feet, an exceedingly great army.

¹¹ Then he said to me, "Son of man, these bones are the whole house of Israel. Behold, they say, 'Our bones are dried up, and our hope is lost. We are completely cut off.' ¹² Therefore prophesy, and tell them, 'The Lord GOD says: "Behold, I will open your graves, and cause you to come up out of your graves, my people; and I will bring you into the land of Israel. ¹³ You will know that I am The LORD, when I have opened your graves, and caused you to come up out of your graves, my people. ¹⁴ I will put my Spirit in you, and you will live. Then I will place you in your own land; and you will know that I, the LORD, have spoken it and performed it," says the LORD.'"

Reader: The word of the Lord.
Or the reader may say: May God bless the reading of his Word.

People: **Thanks be to God.**

Psalm 30

Then the congregation will say the following Psalm responsively:

I will extol you, LORD, for you have raised me up,
   and have not made my foes to rejoice over me.
² **LORD my God, I cried to you,**
   and you have healed me.
³ LORD, you have brought up my soul from Sheol.
   You have kept me alive,
   that I should not go down to the pit.
⁴ Sing praise to The LORD, you saints of his.
   Give thanks to his holy name.
⁵ For his anger is but for a moment.
   His favor is for a lifetime.
Weeping may stay for the night,

but joy comes in the morning.
⁶ As for me, I said in my prosperity,
"I shall never be moved."
⁷ You, LORD, when you favored me,
made my mountain stand strong;
but when you hid your face, I was troubled.
⁸ I cried to you, LORD.
I made supplication to the Lord:
⁹ "What profit is there in my destruction,
if I go down to the pit?
Shall the dust praise you?
Shall it declare your truth?
¹⁰ Hear, LORD, and have mercy on me.
LORD, be my helper."
¹¹ You have turned my mourning into dancing for me.
You have removed my sackcloth,
and clothed me with gladness,
¹² to the end that my heart may sing praise to you,
and not be silent.
LORD my God, I will give thanks to you forever!

The Prayer

Then a member of the congregation will offer a prayer of thanksgiving for God's provision of a new heart and spirit through Christ (or something else appropriate to the scriptures). The prayer may be read or said extemporaneously.

The Ministry of Jesus

Then the person assigned for the eighth reading will go to the pulpit or reading lectern and will read one of the following passages:

John 2:1–11

2 The third day, there was a wedding in Cana of Galilee. Jesus' mother was there. **2** Jesus also was invited, with his disciples, to the wedding.

3 When the wine ran out, Jesus' mother said to him, "They have no wine." **4** Jesus said to her, "Woman, what does that have to do with you and me? My hour has not yet come." **5** His mother said to the servants, "Whatever he says to you, do it."

6 Now there were six water pots of stone set there after the Jews' way of purifying, containing two or three metretes apiece. **7** Jesus said to them, "Fill the water pots with water." So they filled them up to the brim. **8** He said to them, "Now draw some out, and take it to the ruler of the feast." So they took it. **9** When the ruler of the feast tasted the water now become wine, and didn't know where it came from (but the servants who had drawn the water knew), the ruler of the feast called the bridegroom **10** and said to him, "Everyone serves the good wine first, and when the guests have drunk freely, then that which is worse. You have kept the good wine until now!" **11** This beginning of his signs Jesus did in Cana of Galilee, and revealed his glory; and his disciples believed in him.

Or this

Matthew 14:13-21 (WEB)

13 Now when Jesus heard this, he withdrew from there in a boat to a deserted place apart. When the multitudes heard it, they followed him on foot from the cities.

¹⁴ Jesus went out, and he saw a great multitude. He had compassion on them and healed their sick. ¹⁵ When evening had come, his disciples came to him, saying, "This place is deserted, and the hour is already late. Send the multitudes away, that they may go into the villages, and buy themselves food."

¹⁶ But Jesus said to them, "They don't need to go away. You give them something to eat."

¹⁷ They told him, "We only have here five loaves and two fish."

¹⁸ He said, "Bring them here to me." ¹⁹ He commanded the multitudes to sit down on the grass; and he took the five loaves and the two fish, and looking up to heaven, he blessed, broke and gave the loaves to the disciples; and the disciples gave to the multitudes. ²⁰ They all ate and were filled. They took up twelve baskets full of that which remained left over from the broken pieces. ²¹ Those who ate were about five thousand men, in addition to women and children.

Reader: The word of the Lord.
Or the reader may say: May God bless the reading of his Word.

People: **Thanks be to God.**

Psalm 40:7–10

Then the congregation will say the following Psalm responsively:

⁷ Then I said, "Behold, I have come.
It is written about me in the book in the scroll.
⁸ **I delight to do your will, my God.**
Yes, your law is within my heart."
⁹ I have proclaimed glad news of righteousness
in the great assembly.
Behold, I will not seal my lips, LORD, you know.

511

10 I have not hidden your righteousness within my heart.
I have declared your faithfulness and your salvation.
I have not concealed your loving kindness and your truth
from the great assembly.

Or, all will say the Lord's Prayer (Matt. 6:9–13 ESV) in unison:

9"Our Father in heaven,
hallowed be your name.
10 Your kingdom come,
your will be done,
**   on earth as it is in heaven.**
11 Give us this day our daily bread,
12 and forgive us our debts,
**   as we also have forgiven our debtors.**
13 And lead us not into temptation,
**   but deliver us from evil.**

For thine is the kingdom, and the power, and the glory,
for ever and ever. Amen[26]

The Prayer

Then a member of the congregation will offer a prayer of thanksgiving for
the life and ministry of Christ (or something else appropriate to the
scriptures). The prayer may be read or said extemporaneously.

---

[26] This postscript to the Lord's Prayer is drawn from the 1979 version of the Book of
Common Prayer. Most modern biblical scholars are in agreement that these words are not
an original part of the Lord's Prayer in Matthew's gospel account. The ending is included,
but set it apart, to be said as a theologically fitting praise to conclude the words that Jesus
gave his disciples.

The Last Supper

At this time, the established pattern of the service may continue, or the church may instead observe a service of communion. If communion is observed, then the church's Order for Communion takes the place of the reading, psalm, and prayer below.

If communion is not observed, the person assigned for the ninth reading will go to the pulpit or reading lectern and will read the following passage:

Luke 22:1–27 (WEB)

22 Now the feast of unleavened bread, which is called the Passover, was approaching. ² The chief priests and the scribes sought how they might put him to death, for they feared the people. ³ Satan entered into Judas, who was also called Iscariot, who was counted with the twelve. ⁴ He went away, and talked with the chief priests and captains about how he might deliver him to them. ⁵ They were glad, and agreed to give him money. ⁶ He consented, and sought an opportunity to deliver him to them in the absence of the multitude. ⁷ The day of unleavened bread came, on which the Passover must be sacrificed. ⁸ Jesus sent Peter and John, saying, "Go and prepare the Passover for us, that we may eat."

⁹ They said to him, "Where do you want us to prepare?" ¹⁰ He said to them, "Behold, when you have entered into the city, a man carrying a pitcher of water will meet you. Follow him into the house which he enters. ¹¹ Tell the master of the house, 'The Teacher says to you, "Where is the guest room, where I may eat the Passover with my disciples?"' ¹² He will show you a large, furnished upper room. Make preparations there."

¹³ They went, found things as Jesus had told them, and they prepared the Passover. ¹⁴ When the hour had come, he sat down with the twelve apostles. ¹⁵ He said to them, "I have earnestly

desired to eat this Passover with you before I suffer,[16] for I tell you, I will no longer by any means eat of it until it is fulfilled in God's Kingdom." [17] He received a cup, and when he had given thanks, he said, "Take this, and share it among yourselves, [18] for I tell you, I will not drink at all again from the fruit of the vine, until God's Kingdom comes."

[19] He took bread, and when he had given thanks, he broke, and gave it to them, saying, "This is my body which is given for you. Do this in memory of me."[20] Likewise, he took the cup after supper, saying, "This cup is the new covenant in my blood, which is poured out for you. [21] But behold, the hand of him who betrays me is with me on the table. [22] The Son of Man indeed goes, as it has been determined, but woe to that man through whom he is betrayed!"

[23] They began to question among themselves, which of them it was who would do this thing. [24] A dispute also arose among them, which of them was considered to be greatest. [25] He said to them, "The kings of the nations lord it over them, and those who have authority over them are called 'benefactors.' [26] But not so with you. But one who is the greater among you, let him become as the younger, and one who is governing, as one who serves. [27] For who is greater, one who sits at the table, or one who serves? Isn't it he who sits at the table? But I am among you as one who serves.

Reader: The word of the Lord.
Or the reader may say: May God bless the reading of his Word.

People: **Thanks be to God.**

Psalm 23

Then the congregation will say the following Psalm responsively:

The LORD is my shepherd:
    I shall lack nothing.
2 He makes me lie down in green pastures.
    He leads me beside still waters.
3 He restores my soul.
    He guides me in the paths of righteousness
    for his name's sake.
4 Even though I walk through the valley
    of the shadow of death,
    I will fear no evil, for you are with me.
Your rod and your staff,
    they comfort me.
5 You prepare a table before me
    in the presence of my enemies.
You anoint my head with oil.
    My cup runs over.
6 Surely goodness and loving kindness shall follow me
    all the days of my life,
    and I will dwell in The LORD's house forever.

The Prayer

Then a member of the congregation will offer a prayer of thanksgiving for
the atoning death of Christ (or something else appropriate to the scriptures).
The prayer may be read or said extemporaneously.

The Crucifixion

Then the person assigned for the tenth reading will go to the pulpit or reading lectern and will read one of the following passages If the Passage from Matthew's Gospel was used earlier, the passage from John's Gospel should now be read. If the passage from John's Gospel was read earlier, the passage from Matthew's Gospel should now be read.

<u>Matthew 27:32–53 (WEB)</u>

[27] Then the governor's soldiers took Jesus into the Praetorium, and gathered the whole garrison together against him. [28] They stripped him and put a scarlet robe on him. [29] They braided a crown of thorns and put it on his head, and a reed in his right hand; and they kneeled down before him and mocked him, saying, "Hail, King of the Jews!" [30] They spat on him, and took the reed and struck him on the head. [31] When they had mocked him, they took the robe off him, and put his clothes on him, and led him away to crucify him.

[32] As they came out, they found a man of Cyrene, Simon by name, and they compelled him to go with them, that he might carry his cross. [33] When they came to a place called "Golgotha", that is to say, "The place of a skull," [34] they gave him sour wine to drink mixed with gall. When he had tasted it, he would not drink. [35] When they had crucified him, they divided his clothing among them, casting lots, [36] and they sat and watched him there. [37] They set up over his head the accusation against him written, "THIS IS JESUS, THE KING OF THE JEWS."
[38] Then there were two robbers crucified with him, one on his right hand and one on the left.

[39] Those who passed by blasphemed him, wagging their heads [40] and saying, "You who destroy the temple and build it in three days, save yourself! If you are the Son of God, come down from the cross!"

⁴¹ Likewise the chief priests also mocking with the scribes, the Pharisees, and the elders, said, ⁴² "He saved others, but he can't save himself. If he is the King of Israel, let him come down from the cross now, and we will believe in him. ⁴³ He trusts in God. Let God deliver him now, if he wants him; for he said, 'I am the Son of God.'" ⁴⁴ The robbers also who were crucified with him cast on him the same reproach.

⁴⁵ Now from the sixth hour there was darkness over all the land until the ninth hour. ⁴⁶ About the ninth hour Jesus cried with a loud voice, saying, "Eli, Eli, lima sabachthani?" That is, "My God, my God, why have you forsaken me?"

⁴⁷ Some of them who stood there, when they heard it, said, "This man is calling Elijah."

⁴⁸ Immediately one of them ran and took a sponge, filled it with vinegar, put it on a reed, and gave him a drink. ⁴⁹ The rest said, "Let him be. Let's see whether Elijah comes to save him."

⁵⁰ Jesus cried again with a loud voice, and yielded up his spirit.

⁵¹ Behold, the veil of the temple was torn in two from the top to the bottom. The earth quaked and the rocks were split. ⁵² The tombs were opened, and many bodies of the saints who had fallen asleep were raised; ⁵³ and coming out of the tombs after his resurrection, they entered into the holy city and appeared to many.

Or this:

John 19:16b-30 (WEB)

So they took Jesus and led him away. ¹⁷ He went out, bearing his cross, to the place called "The Place of a Skull", which is called in Hebrew, "Golgotha", ¹⁸ where they crucified him, and with him two others, on either side one, and Jesus in the middle. ¹⁹ Pilate wrote a title also, and put it on the cross. There was written, "JESUS OF NAZARETH, THE KING OF THE

JEWS." **20** Therefore many of the Jews read this title, for the place where Jesus was crucified was near the city; and it was written in Hebrew, in Latin, and in Greek. **21** The chief priests of the Jews therefore said to Pilate, "Don't write, 'The King of the Jews,' but, 'he said, "I am King of the Jews."'"

22 Pilate answered, "What I have written, I have written."

23 Then the soldiers, when they had crucified Jesus, took his garments and made four parts, to every soldier a part; and also the coat. Now the coat was without seam, woven from the top throughout. **24** Then they said to one another, "Let's not tear it, but cast lots for it to decide whose it will be," that the Scripture might be fulfilled, which says,

> "They parted my garments among them.
> For my cloak they cast lots."

Therefore the soldiers did these things.

25 But standing by Jesus' cross were his mother, his mother's sister, Mary the wife of Clopas, and Mary Magdalene. **26** Therefore when Jesus saw his mother, and the disciple whom he loved standing there, he said to his mother, "Woman, behold, your son!" **27** Then he said to the disciple, "Behold, your mother!" From that hour, the disciple took her to his own home.

28 After this, Jesus, seeing that all things were now finished, that the Scripture might be fulfilled, said, "I am thirsty." **29** Now a vessel full of vinegar was set there; so they put a sponge full of the vinegar on hyssop, and held it at his mouth. **30** When Jesus therefore had received the vinegar, he said, "It is finished." Then he bowed his head, and gave up his spirit.

Reader: The word of the Lord.
Or the reader may say: May God bless the reading of his Word.

People: **Thanks be to God.**

After the reading is complete, all congregants will extinguish their candles and will sit in silence and darkness for a period of time.

The Resurrection

After a due passage of time, the person assigned for the tenth reading will go to the pulpit or reading lectern and will read the following passage:

Mark 16:1–8 (WEB)

16 When the Sabbath was past, Mary Magdalene, and Mary the mother of James, and Salome, bought spices, that they might come and anoint him. [2] Very early on the first day of the week, they came to the tomb when the sun had risen. [3] They were saying among themselves, "Who will roll away the stone from the door of the tomb for us?" [4] for it was very big. Looking up, they saw that the stone was rolled back.

[5] Entering into the tomb, they saw a young man sitting on the right side, dressed in a white robe, and they were amazed. [6] He said to them, "Don't be amazed. You seek Jesus, the Nazarene, who has been crucified. He has risen. He is not here. Behold, the place where they laid him! [7] But go, tell his disciples and Peter, 'He goes before you into Galilee. There you will see him, as he said to you.'"

[8] They went out, and fled from the tomb, for trembling and astonishment had come on them. They said nothing to anyone; for they were afraid.

If the congregation has sat in full darkness, after the reading the lights should be turned on in the sanctuary.

Then the pastor or another minister will rise and stand in front of the congregation and greet them with the traditional Paschal Greeting:

The Paschal Greeting

Speaker: Brothers and sisters, Christ is risen!
Congregation: **He is risen, indeed! Alleluia!**

Then all will stand and sing a traditional Easter hymn (for example: "Christ the Lord is Risen Today" or another similar hymn).

The Service of Baptism or Renewal

After the Paschal Greeting baptisms should occur, or a Service of Renewal of the Baptismal Covenant.

If there are to be baptisms, the pastor should go to the baptismal during the Easter hymn, together with the candidates for baptism. Or the pastor may wish to meet the candidates in front of the altar and process with them to the baptistry while the congregation sings.

After the baptism, or if there is no baptism, the pastor or another minister will come to stand in front of or near the baptistry. If there are choir seats in front of the baptistry, they should have been removed before the vigil!

Pastor: Let all who have been baptized as believers come forward and renew their dedication to Christ.

Then, after all have gathered, the pastor or other minister will continue.

Pastor: Upon what occasion did you first come to the baptismal waters?

People: **Upon repentance and a public profession of faith in Jesus Christ.**

Pastor: And how is it that you were brought to saving faith?

People: **We were brought to faith by God's free and sovereign grace.**

Pastor: And what do you believe about this God who has called you from darkness into light and life?

People: **We believe that he is our heavenly Father, that he is the Almighty One, the creator of heaven and earth.**

Pastor. What do you believe concerning Jesus of Nazareth, about whom you have declared your faith, and in whom you have trusted?

> *People:* **We believe that Jesus was the Christ, the only begotten Son of God, our Lord;**
> **that he was conceived by the power of the Holy Spirit**
> **and born of the Virgin Mary;**
> **that he suffered under Pontius Pilate,**
> **was crucified, died, and was buried;**
> **that he descended to the dead,**
> **but on the third day he rose again;**
> **that he has ascended into heaven,**
> **and is seated at the right hand of the Father;**
> **and that he will come again to judge the living and the dead.**

Pastor. And what do you believe about the Holy Spirit, his work on earth, and the consummation of all things?

> *People:* **We believe in the Holy Spirit,**
> **the one universal Church,**
> **the communion of saints,**
> **the forgiveness of sins,**
> **the resurrection of the body,**
> **and life everlasting.**

Pastor. Will you continue in the teaching and admonition of Scripture, in the spirit of fellowship, the breaking of bread, and in prayer?

> *People:* **We will, with God's help.**

Pastor. Will you live a life of continual repentance, proclaiming by word and example the good news of salvation through Christ?

> *People:* **We will, with God's help.**

Pastor: Will you show the love of Christ to all persons and so love your neighbor as yourself?

People: **We will, with God's help.**

Pastor: Amen and amen. Let us pray.

Then the pastor will say a prayer for the church and dismiss all gathered to their seats, and the service will conclude with a Benediction.

Benediction

Then the person assigned for the final reading will go to the pulpit or reading lectern and will read the following passages:

Revelation 21:1–7;

21 I saw a new heaven and a new earth: for the first heaven and the first earth have passed away, and the sea is no more. ²I saw the holy city, New Jerusalem, coming down out of heaven from God, prepared like a bride adorned for her husband.

³I heard a loud voice out of heaven saying, "Behold, God's dwelling is with people, and he will dwell with them, and they will be his people, and God himself will be with them as their God. ⁴He will wipe away every tear from their eyes. Death will be no more; neither will there be mourning, nor crying, nor pain, any more. The first things have passed away."

⁵He who sits on the throne said, "Behold, I am making all things new." He said, "Write, for these words of God are faithful and true." ⁶He said to me, "I am the Alpha and the Omega, the Beginning and the End. I will give freely to him who is thirsty from the spring of the water of life. ⁷He who overcomes, I will give him these things. I will be his God, and he will be my son.

Revelation 22:7,17,20,21

⁷"Behold, I come quickly. Blessed is he who keeps the words of the prophecy of this book."

¹⁷The Spirit and the bride say, "Come!" He who hears, let him say, "Come!" He who is thirsty, let him come. He who desires, let him take the water of life freely.

²⁰He who testifies these things says, "Yes, I come quickly."
Amen! Yes, come, Lord Jesus.
²¹The grace of the Lord Jesus Christ be with all the saints.
Amen.

After the Benediction, the congregants are dismissed to a celebration!

BENEDICTIONS

"The Lord bless you and keep you; the Lord make his face to shine upon you and be gracious to you; the Lord lift up his countenance upon you and give you peace." Amen. (Numbers 6:22–26 ESV)

"May the LORD increase you more and more, you and your children. Blessed are you by The LORD, who made heaven and earth." Amen. (Psalm 115:14-15, WEB)

"Neither death, nor life, nor angels, nor principalities, nor things present, nor things to come, nor powers, nor height, nor depth, nor any other created thing will be able to separate us from God's love which is in Christ Jesus our Lord." Amen. (Romans 8:38-39, WEB)

"Of him, and through him, and to him are all things. To him be the glory for ever! Amen." (Romans 11:36, WEB)

"Now the God of perseverance and of encouragement grant you to be of the same mind with one another according to Christ Jesus, that with one accord you may with one mouth glorify the God and Father of our Lord Jesus Christ." Amen. (Romans 15:5-6, WEB)

"Now may the God of hope fill you with all joy and peace in believing, that you may abound in hope, in the power of the Holy Spirit." Amen. (Romans 15:13)

"Beloved brothers, be steadfast, immovable, always abounding in the Lord's work, because you know that your labor is not in vain in the Lord." Amen. (1 Corinthians 15:58, WEB)

"Finally, brothers, rejoice! Be perfected. Be comforted. Be of the same mind. Live in peace, and the God of love and peace will be with you." Amen. (2 Corinthians 13:11, WEB)

"The grace of the Lord Jesus Christ, God's love, and the fellowship of the Holy Spirit be with you all." Amen. (2 Corinthians 13:14, WEB)

"The grace of our Lord Jesus Christ be with your spirit. Amen." (Galatians 6:18, WEB)

May Christ "dwell in your hearts through faith, to the end that you, being rooted and grounded in love, may be strengthened to comprehend with all the saints what is the width and length and height and depth, and to know Christ's love which surpasses knowledge, that you may be filled with all the fullness of God." Amen. (Ephesians 3:17-19, WEB)

"Peace be to the brothers, and love with faith, from God the Father and the Lord Jesus Christ. Grace be with all those who love our Lord Jesus Christ with incorruptible love." Amen. (Ephesians 6:23-24, WEB)

"The peace of God, which surpasses all understanding, will guard your hearts and your thoughts in Christ Jesus." Amen. (Philippians 4:7, WEB)

"Let the peace of God rule in your hearts, to which also you were called in one body, and be thankful." Amen. (Colossians 3:15, WEB)

"Let the word of Christ dwell in you richly; in all wisdom teaching and admonishing one another with psalms, hymns, and spiritual songs, singing with grace in your heart to the Lord. Whatever you do, in word or in deed, do all in the name of the Lord Jesus, giving thanks to God the Father, through him." Amen. (Colossians 3:16-17, WEB)

"May the Lord make you to increase and abound in love toward one another, and toward all men, even as we also do toward you, to the end he may establish your hearts blameless in holiness before our God and Father at the coming of our Lord Jesus with all his saints." Amen. (1 Thessalonians 3:12-13, WEB)

"May the God of peace himself sanctify you completely. May your whole spirit, soul, and body be preserved blameless at the coming of our Lord Jesus Christ. He who calls you is faithful, who will also do it." Amen. (1 Thessalonians 5:23-24, WEB)

"Now our Lord Jesus Christ himself, and God our Father, who loved us and gave us eternal comfort and good hope through grace, comfort your hearts and establish you in every good work and word." Amen. (2 Thessalonians 2:16-17, WEB)

"Now to the King eternal, immortal, invisible, to God who alone is wise, be honor and glory forever and ever. Amen." (1 Timothy 1:17, WEB)

"Follow after righteousness, godliness, faith, love, perseverance, and gentleness. Fight the good fight of faith. Take hold of the eternal life to which you were called, and you confessed the good confession in the sight of many witnesses." Amen. (1 Timothy 6:11-12, WEB)

"Now may the God of peace, who brought again from the dead the great shepherd of the sheep with the blood of an eternal covenant, our Lord Jesus, make you complete in every good work to do his will, working in you that which is well pleasing in his sight, through Jesus Christ, to whom be the glory forever and ever. Amen." (Hebrews 13:20-2, WEB)

"Grow in the grace and knowledge of our Lord and Savior Jesus Christ. To him be the glory both now and forever. Amen." (2 Peter 3:18, WEB)

"Grace, mercy, and peace will be with us, from God the Father, and from the Lord Jesus Christ, the Son of the Father, in truth and love." (2 John 3, WEB)

"Now to him who is able to keep you from stumbling and to present you blameless before the presence of his glory with great joy, to the only God, our Savior, through Jesus Christ our Lord, be glory, majesty, dominion, and authority, before all time and now and forever. Amen." (Jude 24-25, ESV)

" To him who loves us, and washed us from our sins by his blood— and he made us to be a Kingdom, priests to his God and Father— to him be the glory and the dominion forever and ever. Amen." (Revelation 1:5-6, WEB)

"To him who sits on the throne, and to the Lamb be the blessing, the honor, the glory, and the dominion, forever and ever! Amen!" (Revelation 5:13, WEB)

""Amen! Blessing, glory, wisdom, thanksgiving, honor, power, and might, be to our God forever and ever! Amen."" (Revelation 7:12, WEB)

"He who testifies these things says, "Yes, I come quickly." Amen! Yes, come, Lord Jesus. The grace of the Lord Jesus Christ be with all the saints. Amen." (Revelation 22:20-21, WEB)

SCHEDULE OF READINGS

Introduction to The Schedule

The schedule of scripture readings will take readers through the Old Testament once every four years, the book of Psalms twice every six months, and the New Testament once a year. Year One of the schedule is always a leap year (with readings omitted for February 29th). If anyone wishes to use the schedule for an annual reading plan, they should read all four of the daily readings from all of the four yearly Old Testament schedules each day (in other words, all four January 1 readings on January 1, etc.). Below is a chart for the next several years.

Year One: *2020, 2024, 2028, 2032, 2036, 2040, 2044, 2048, 2052, 2056, 2060, 2064, 2068*

Year Two: *2021, 2025, 2029, 2033, 2037, 2041, 2045, 2049, 2053, 2057, 2061, 2065, 2069*

Year Three: *2022, 2026, 2030, 2034, 2038, 2042, 2046, 2050, 2054, 2058, 2062, 2066, 2070*

Year Four: *2023, 2027, 2031, 2035, 2039, 2043, 2047, 2051, 2055, 2059, 2063, 2067, 2071*

Year 1

*2016, 2020, 2024, 2028, 2032, 2036, 2040, 2044, 2048, 2052, 2056,
2060, 2064, 2068*

Yr 1	Jan 1	Gen 1:1–19	Ps 1;2	Ps 78:32–39	Matt 1
Yr 1	Jan 2	Gen 1:20–2:3a	Ps 3;4	Ps 78:40–55	Matt 2
Yr 1	Jan 3	Gen 2:3b–25	Ps 5	Ps 78:56–64	Matt 3
Yr 1	Jan 4	Gen 3:1–19	Ps 6	Ps 78:65–72	Matt 4
Yr 1	Jan 5	Gen 3:20–24	Ps 7	Ps 79	Matt 5:1–20
Yr 1	Jan 6	Gen 4:1–16	Ps 8	Ps 80	Matt 5:21–37
Yr 1	Jan 7	Gen 4:17–26	Ps 9:1–10	Ps 81	Matt 5:38–6:4
Yr 1	Jan 8	Gen 5:1–16	Ps 9:11–20	Ps 82	Matt 6:5–34
Yr 1	Jan 9	Gen 5:17–32	Ps 10	Ps 83	Matt 7
Yr 1	Jan 10	Gen 6:1–8	Ps 11;12	Ps 84	Matt 8:1–22
Yr 1	Jan 11	Gen 6:9–22	Ps 13;14	Ps 85	Matt 8:23–34
Yr 1	Jan 12	Gen 7:1–10	Ps 15;16	Ps 86	Matt 9:1–17
Yr 1	Jan 13	Gen 7:11–24	Ps 17	Ps 87	Matt 9:18–38
Yr 1	Jan 14	Gen 8	Ps 18:1–15	Ps 88	Matt 10:1–23
Yr 1	Jan 15	Gen 9:1–17	Ps 18:16–29	Ps 89:1–14	Matt 10:24–42
Yr 1	Jan 16	Gen 9:18–29	Ps 18:30–45	Ps 89:15–37	Matt 11
Yr 1	Jan 17	Gen 10:1–20	Ps 18:46–50	Ps 89:38–52	Matt 12:1–21
Yr 1	Jan 18	Gen 10:21–32	Ps 19	Ps 90	Matt 12:22–50
Yr 1	Jan 19	Gen 11:1–8	Ps 20	Ps 91	Matt 13:1–23
Yr 1	Jan 20	Gen 11:10–26	Ps 21	Ps 92	Matt 13:24–43
Yr 1	Jan 21	Gen 11:27–32	Ps 22:1–24	Ps 93	Matt 13:44–58
Yr 1	Jan 22	Gen 12:1–9	Ps 22:25–31	Ps 94	Matt 14
Yr 1	Jan 23	Gen 12:10–20	Ps 23;24	Ps 95	Matt 15:1–20
Yr 1	Jan 24	Gen 13	Ps 25	Ps 96	Matt 15:21–39
Yr 1	Jan 25	Gen 14:1–16	Ps 26	Ps 97	Matt 16
Yr 1	Jan 26	Gen 14:17–24	Ps 27	Ps 98	Matt 17
Yr 1	Jan 27	Josh 1	Ps 28	Ps 99	Matt 18:1–20
Yr 1	Jan 28	Josh 2	Ps 29	Ps 100;101	Matt 18:21–35
Yr 1	Jan 29	Josh 3	Ps 30	Ps 102:1–17	Matt 19:1–15
Yr 1	Jan 30	Josh 4:1–14	Ps 31:1–8	Ps 102:18–28	Matt 19:16–30
Yr 1	Jan 31	Josh 4:15–5:1	Ps 31:9–24	Ps 103	Matt 20:1–16
Yr 1	Feb 1	Josh 5:2–15	Ps 32	Ps 104:1–18	Matt 20:17–34

Yr 1	Feb 2	Josh 6:1–14	Ps 33	Ps 104:19–35	Matt 21:1–22
Yr 1	Feb 3	Josh 6:15–27	Ps 34	Ps 105:1–15	Matt 21:23–46
Yr 1	Feb 4	Josh 7:1–15	Ps 35:1–10	Ps 105:16–25	Matt 22:1–33
Yr 1	Feb 5	Josh 7:16–26	Ps 35:11–28	Ps 105:26–45	Matt 22:34–46
Yr 1	Feb 6	Josh 8:1–17	Ps 36	Ps 106:1–11	Matt 23:1–24
Yr 1	Feb 7	Josh 8:18–29	Ps 37:1–7	Ps 106:12–27	Matt 23:25–39
Yr 1	Feb 8	Josh 8:30–35	Ps 37:8–19	Ps 106:28–39	Matt 24:1–31
Yr 1	Feb 9	Josh 9	Ps 37:20–33	Ps 106:40–48	Matt 24:32–25:13
Yr 1	Feb 10	Josh 10:1–15	Ps 37:34–40	Ps 107:1–16	Matt 25:14–30
Yr 1	Feb 11	Josh 10:16–27	Ps 38	Ps 107:17–32	Matt 25:31–46
Yr 1	Feb 12	Josh 10:28–43	Ps 39	Ps 107:33–43	Matt 26:1–16
Yr 1	Feb 13	Josh 11:1–15	Ps 40	Ps 108	Matt 26:17–46
Yr 1	Feb 14	Josh 11:16–23	Ps 41	Ps 109:1–19	Matt 26:47–75
Yr 1	Feb 15	Josh 12:1–6	Ps 42	Ps 109:20–31	Matt 27:1–26
Yr 1	Feb 16	Josh 12:7–24	Ps 43	Ps 110	Matt 27:27–56
Yr 1	Feb 17	Josh 13:1–14	Ps 44	Ps 111	Matt 27:57–66;28
Yr 1	Feb 18	Josh 13:15–33	Ps 45	Ps 112	Mk 1:1–20
Yr 1	Feb 19	Josh 14	Ps 46	Ps 113;114	Mk 1:21–45
Yr 1	Feb 20	Josh 15:1–12	Ps 47	Ps 115	Mk 2:1–17
Yr 1	Feb 21	Josh 15:13–19	Ps 48	Ps 116;117	Mk 2:18–28
Yr 1	Feb 22	Josh 15:20–44	Ps 49	Ps 118:1–18	Mk 3:1–19
Yr 1	Feb 23	Josh 15:45–63	Ps 50:1–6	Ps 118:19–29	Mk 3:20–35
Yr 1	Feb 24	Josh 16:1–10	Ps 50:7–23	Ps 119:1–16	Mk 4:1–20
Yr 1	Feb 25	Josh 17:1–6	Ps 51	Ps 119:17–32	Mk 4:21–41
Yr 1	Feb 26	Josh 17:7–13	Ps 52	Ps 119:33–40	Mk 5:1–20
Yr 1	Feb 27	Josh 17:14–18	Ps 53;54	Ps 119:41–48	Mk 5:21–43
Yr 1	Feb 28	Job 1	Ps 55	Ps 119:49–56	Mk 6:1–29
Yr 1	Feb 29	Job 2	——	Ps 119:65–80	——
Yr 1	Mar 1	Job 3:1–10	Ps 56	Ps 119:81–96	Mk 6:30–56
Yr 1	Mar 2	Job 3:11–26	Ps 57	Ps 119:97–104	Mk 7:1–23
Yr 1	Mar 3	Job 4:1–11	Ps 58	Ps 119:105–112	Mk 7:24–37
Yr 1	Mar 4	Job 4:12–21	Ps 59	Ps 119:113–128	Mk 8:1–26
Yr 1	Mar 5	Job 5:1–16	Ps 60	Ps 119:129–144	Mk 8:27–9:1
Yr 1	Mar 6	Job 5:17–27	Ps 61	Ps 119:145–152	Mk 9:2–29
Yr 1	Mar 7	Job 6:1–13	Ps 62	Ps 119:153–160	Mk 9:30–50
Yr 1	Mar 8	Job 6:14–30	Ps 63	Ps 119:161–176	Mk 10:1–16
Yr 1	Mar 9	Is 1:1–20	Ps 64	Ps 120;121	Mk 10:17–34
Yr 1	Mar 10	Is 1:21–31	Ps 65	Ps 122;123;124	Mk 10:35–52
Yr 1	Mar 11	Is 2	Ps 66	Ps 125;126;127	Mk 11
Yr 1	Mar 12	Is 3:1–15	Ps 67	Ps 128;129	Mk 12:1–27
Yr 1	Mar 13	Is 3:16–26	Ps 68:1–19	Ps 130;131	Mk 12:28–44
Yr 1	Mar 14	Is 4;5:1–7	Ps 68:20–35	Ps 132	Mk 13:1–25
Yr 1	Mar 15	Is 5:8–19	Ps 69:1–18	Ps 133;134	Mk 13:26–37
Yr 1	Mar 16	Is 5:20–30	Ps 69:19–36	Ps 135	Mk 14:1–26
Yr 1	Mar 17	Is 6	Ps 70	Ps 136:1–16	Mk 14:27–52
Yr 1	Mar 18	Is 7	Ps 71:1–16	Ps 137	Mk 14:53–72
Yr 1	Mar 19	Is 8:1–10	Ps 71:17–24	Ps 138	Mk 15:1–20
Yr 1	Mar 20	Is 8:11–22	Ps 72:1–11	Ps 139:1–12	Mk 15:21–47
Yr 1	Mar 21	Is 9:1–7	Ps 72:12–20	Ps 139:13–24	Mk 16:1–20*
Yr 1	Mar 22	Is 9:8–21	Ps 73:1–16	Ps 140	Lk 1:1–25
Yr 1	Mar 23	Is 10:1–19	Ps 73:17–28	Ps 141	Lk 1:26–45

Yr 1	Mar 24	Is 10:20–34	Ps 74:1–8	Ps 142	Lk 1:46–66
Yr 1	Mar 25	Is 11	Ps 74:9–23	Ps 143	Lk 1:67–80
Yr 1	Mar 26	Is 12;13:1–8	Ps 75	Ps 144	Lk 2:1–20
Yr 1	Mar 27	Is 13:9–22	Ps 76	Ps 145:1–13	Lk 2:21–52
Yr 1	Mar 28	Is 14:1–23	Ps 77	Ps 145:14–21	Lk 3:1–20
Yr 1	Mar 29	Is 14:24–32	Ps 78:1–16	Ps 146	Lk 3:21–38
Yr 1	Mar 30	Is 15	Ps 78:17–31	Ps 147	Lk 4:1–30
Yr 1	Mar 31	Is 16	Ps 78:32–39	Ps 148	Lk 4:31–44
Yr 1	Apr 1	Is 17	Ps 78:40–55	Ps 149;150	Lk 5:1–26
Yr 1	Apr 2	Gen 15	Ps 78:56–64	Ps 1;2	Lk 5:27–39
Yr 1	Apr 3	Gen 16	Ps 78:65–72	Ps 3;4	Lk 6:1–26
Yr 1	Apr 4	Gen 17:1–14	Ps 79	Ps 5	Lk 6:27–49
Yr 1	Apr 5	Gen 17:15–27	Ps 80	Ps 6	Lk 7:1–27
Yr 1	Apr 6	Gen 18:1–15	Ps 81	Ps 7	Lk 7:28–50
Yr 1	Apr 7	Gen 18:16–33	Ps 82	Ps 8	Lk 8:1–15
Yr 1	Apr 8	Gen 19:1–29	Ps 83	Ps 9:1–10	Lk 8:16–39
Yr 1	Apr 9	Gen 19:30–38	Ps 84	Ps 9:11–20	Lk 8:40–56
Yr 1	Apr 10	Gen 20	Ps 85	Ps 10	Lk 9:1–27
Yr 1	Apr 11	Gen 21:1–7	Ps 86	Ps 11;12	Lk 9:28–48
Yr 1	Apr 12	Gen 21:8–21	Ps 87	Ps 13;14	Lk 9:49–62
Yr 1	Apr 13	Gen 21:22–34	Ps 88	Ps 15;16	Lk 10:1–29
Yr 1	Apr 14	Gen 22:1–8	Ps 89:1–14	Ps 17	Lk 10:30–42
Yr 1	Apr 15	Gen 22:9–24	Ps 89:15–37	Ps 18:1–15	Lk 11:1–28
Yr 1	Apr 16	Gen 23	Ps 89:38–52	Ps 18:16–29	Lk 11:29–54
Yr 1	Apr 17	Gen 24:1–14	Ps 90	Ps 18:30–45	Lk 12:1–21
Yr 1	Apr 18	Gen 24:15–31	Ps 91	Ps 18:46–50	Lk 12:22–48
Yr 1	Apr 19	Gen 24:32–49	Ps 92	Ps 19	Lk 12:49–59
Yr 1	Apr 20	Gen 24:50–67	Ps 93	Ps 20	Lk 13:1–21
Yr 1	Apr 21	Gen 25:1–11	Ps 94	Ps 21	Lk 13:22–35
Yr 1	Apr 22	Gen 25:12–18	Ps 95	Ps 22:1–24	Lk 14
Yr 1	Apr 23	Gen 25:19–34	Ps 96	Ps 22:25–31	Lk 15:1–10
Yr 1	Apr 24	Gen 26:1–11	Ps 97	Ps 23;24	Lk 15:11–32
Yr 1	Apr 25	Gen 26:12–25	Ps 98	Ps 25	Lk 16
Yr 1	Apr 26	Gen 26:26–35	Ps 99	Ps 26	Lk 17
Yr 1	Apr 27	Gen 27:1–13	Ps 100;101	Ps 27	Lk 18:1–17
Yr 1	Apr 28	Gen 27:14–29	Ps 102:1–17	Ps 28	Lk 18:18–43
Yr 1	Apr 29	Gen 27:30–46	Ps 102:18–28	Ps 29	Lk 19:1–10
Yr 1	Apr 30	Josh 18:1–10	Ps 103	Ps 30	Lk 19:11–27
Yr 1	May 1	Josh 18:11–28	Ps 104:1–18	Ps 31:1–8	Lk 19:28–48
Yr 1	May 2	Josh 19:1–16	Ps 104:19–35	Ps 31:9–24	Lk 20:1–19
Yr 1	May 3	Josh 19:17–31	Ps 105:1–15	Ps 32	Lk 20:20–47
Yr 1	May 4	Josh 19:32–51	Ps 105:16–25	Ps 33	Lk 21:1–11
Yr 1	May 5	Josh 20	Ps 105:26–45	Ps 34	Lk 21:12–38
Yr 1	May 6	Josh 21:1–23	Ps 106:1–11	Ps 35:1–10	Lk 22:1–13
Yr 1	May 7	Josh 21:24–45	Ps 106:12–27	Ps 35:11–28	Lk 22:14–38
Yr 1	May 8	Josh 22:1–9	Ps 106:28–39	Ps 36	Lk 22:39–71
Yr 1	May 9	Josh 22:10–34	Ps 106:40–48	Ps 37:1–7	Lk 23:1–25
Yr 1	May 10	Josh 23	Ps 107:1–16	Ps 37:8–19	Lk 23:26–43
Yr 1	May 11	Josh 24:1–15	Ps 107:17–32	Ps 37:20–33	Lk 23:44–56
Yr 1	May 12	Josh 24:16–28	Ps 107:33–43	Ps 37:34–40	Lk 24:1–34
Yr 1	May 13	Josh 24:29–33	Ps 108	Ps 38	Lk 24:35–53

Yr 1	May 14	Judg 1:1–18	Ps 109:1–19	Ps 39	Jn 1:1–28
Yr 1	May 15	Judg 1:19–36	Ps 109:20–31	Ps 40	Jn 1:29–51
Yr 1	May 16	Judg 2:1–5	Ps 110	Ps 41	Jn 2:1–12
Yr 1	May 17	Judg 2:6–9	Ps 111	Ps 42	Jn 2:13–25
Yr 1	May 18	Judg 2:10–15	Ps 112	Ps 43	Jn 3:1–21
Yr 1	May 19	Judg 2:16–23	Ps 113;114	Ps 44	Jn 3:22–36
Yr 1	May 20	Judg 3:1–6	Ps 115	Ps 45	Jn 4:1–38
Yr 1	May 21	Judg 3:7–11	Ps 116;117	Ps 46	Jn 4:39–5:15
Yr 1	May 22	Judg 3:12–31	Ps 118:1–18	Ps 47	Jn 5:16–47
Yr 1	May 23	Judg 4	Ps 118:19–29	Ps 48	Jn 6:1–21
Yr 1	May 24	Judg 5	Ps 119:1–16	Ps 49	Jn 6:22–59
Yr 1	May 25	Judg 6:1–24	Ps 119:17–32	Ps 50:1–6	Jn 6:60–7:9
Yr 1	May 26	Judg 6:25–32	Ps 119:33–40	Ps 50:7–23	Jn 7:10–36
Yr 1	May 27	Judg 6:33–40	Ps 119:41–48	Ps 51	Jn 7:37–52
Yr 1	May 28	Judg 7	Ps 119:49–56	Ps 52	Jn 7:53–8:11
Yr 1	May 29	Judg 8:1–21	Ps 119:65–80	Ps 53;54	Jn 8:12–30
Yr 1	May 30	Judg 8:22–35	Ps 119:81–96	Ps 55	Jn 8:31–59
Yr 1	May 31	Job 7	Ps 119:97–104	Ps 56	Jn 9:1–34
Yr 1	June 1	Job 8:1–10	Ps 119:105–112	Ps 57	Jn 9:35–41
Yr 1	June 2	Job 8:11–22	Ps 119:113–128	Ps 58	Jn 10:1–21
Yr 1	June 3	Job 9:1–13	Ps 119:129–144	Ps 59	Jn 10:22–42
Yr 1	June 4	Job 9:14–24	Ps 119:145–152	Ps 60	Jn 11:1–29
Yr 1	June 5	Job 9:25–35	Ps 119:153–160	Ps 61	Jn 11:30–57
Yr 1	June 6	Job 10	Ps 119:161–176	Ps 62	Jn 12:1–19
Yr 1	June 7	Job 11:1–12	Ps 120;121	Ps 63	Jn 12:20–36
Yr 1	June 8	Job 11:13–20	Ps 122;123;124	Ps 64	Jn 12:37–50
Yr 1	June 9	Job 12	Ps 125;126;127	Ps 65	Jn 13:1–20
Yr 1	June 10	Is 18;19:1–4	Ps 128;129	Ps 66	Jn 13:21–38
Yr 1	June 11	Is 19:5–25;20	Ps 130;131	Ps 67	Jn 14
Yr 1	June 12	Is 21:1–10	Ps 132	Ps 68:1–19	Jn 15
Yr 1	June 13	Is 21:11–22:4	Ps 133;134	Ps 68:20–35	Jn 16:1–15
Yr 1	June 14	Is 22:5–25	Ps 135	Ps 69:1–18	Jn 16:16–33
Yr 1	June 15	Is 23	Ps 136:1–16	Ps 69:19–36	Jn 17
Yr 1	June 16	Is 24:1–5	Ps 137	Ps 70	Jn 18:1–24
Yr 1	June 17	Is 24:6–23	Ps 138	Ps 71:1–16	Jn 18:25–40
Yr 1	June 18	Is 25	Ps 139:1–12	Ps 71:17–24	Jn 19:1–27
Yr 1	June 19	Is 26:1–19	Ps 139:13–24	Ps 72:1–11	Jn 19:28–42
Yr 1	June 20	Is 26:20–21; 27	Ps 140	Ps 72:12–20	Jn 20:1–18
Yr 1	June 21	Is 28:1–10	Ps 141	Ps 73:1–16	Jn 20:19–31
Yr 1	June 22	Is 28:11–29	Ps 142	Ps 73:17–28	Jn 21
Yr 1	June 23	Is 29:1–10	Ps 143	Ps 74:1–8	Acts 1
Yr 1	June 24	Is 29:11–24	Ps 144	Ps 74:9–23	Acts 2:1–21
Yr 1	June 25	Is 30:1–17	Ps 145:1–13	Ps 75	Acts 2:22–47
Yr 1	June 26	Is 30:18–33	Ps 145:14–21	Ps 76	Acts 3:1–11
Yr 1	June 27	Is 31	Ps 146	Ps 77	Acts 3:12–26
Yr 1	June 28	Is 32	Ps 147	Ps 78:1–16	Acts 4:1–22
Yr 1	June 29	Is 33:1–9	Ps 148	Ps 78:17–31	Acts 4:23–37
Yr 1	June 30	Is 33:10–24	Ps 149;150	Ps 78:32–39	Acts 5:1–16
Yr 1	July 1	Is 34	Ps 1;2	Ps 78:40–55	Acts 5:17–42
Yr 1	July 2	Is 35	Ps 3;4	Ps 78:56–64	Acts 6; 7:1–10
Yr 1	July 3	Is 36	Ps 5	Ps 78:65–72	Acts 7:11–60

Yr 1	July 4	Gen 28:1–9	Ps 6	Ps 79	Acts 8:1–25
Yr 1	July 5	Gen 28:10–22	Ps 7	Ps 80	Acts 8:26–40
Yr 1	July 6	Gen 29:1–14a	Ps 8	Ps 81	Acts 9:1–19
Yr 1	July 7	Gen 29:14b–30	Ps 9:1–10	Ps 82	Acts 9:20–43
Yr 1	July 8	Gen 29:31–35	Ps 9:11–20	Ps 83	Acts 10:1–33
Yr 1	July 9	Gen 30:1–24	Ps 10	Ps 84	Acts 10:34–48
Yr 1	July 10	Gen 30:25–43	Ps 11;12	Ps 85	Acts 11:1–18
Yr 1	July 11	Gen: 31:1–21	Ps 13;14	Ps 86	Acts 11:19–30
Yr 1	July 12	Gen 31:22–32	Ps 15;16	Ps 87	Acts 12
Yr 1	July 13	Gen 31:33–42	Ps 17	Ps 88	Acts 13:1–12
Yr 1	July 14	Gen 31:43–32:2	Ps 18:1–15	Ps 89:1–14	Acts 13:13–43
Yr 1	July 15	Gen 32:3–21	Ps 18:16–29	Ps 89:15–37	Acts 13:44–14:7
Yr 1	July 16	Gen 32:22–32	Ps 18:30–45	Ps 89:38–52	Acts 14:8–28
Yr 1	July 17	Gen 33	Ps 18:46–50	Ps 90	Acts 15
Yr 1	July 18	Gen 34:1–17	Ps 19	Ps 91	Acts 16:1–21
Yr 1	July 19	Gen 34:18–31	Ps 20	Ps 92	Acts 16:22–40
Yr 1	July 20	Gen 35:1–15	Ps 21	Ps 93	Acts 17
Yr 1	July 21	Gen 35:16–29	Ps 22:1–24	Ps 94	Acts 18:1–23
Yr 1	July 22	Gen 36:1–8	Ps 22:25–31	Ps 95	Acts 18:24–19:7
Yr 1	July 23	Gen 36:9–19	Ps 23;24	Ps 96	Acts 19:8–22
Yr 1	July 24	Gen 36:20–30	Ps 25	Ps 97	Acts 19:23–41
Yr 1	July 25	Gen 36:31–43	Ps 26	Ps 98	Acts 20
Yr 1	July 26	Gen 37:1–17	Ps 27	Ps 99	Acts 21:1–25
Yr 1	July 27	Gen 37:18–36	Ps 28	Ps 100 101	Acts 21:26–40
Yr 1	July 28	Gen 38:1–11	Ps 29	Ps 102:1–17	Acts 22:1–23
Yr 1	July 29	Gen 38:12–30	Ps 30	Ps 102:18–28	Acts 22:24–23:11
Yr 1	July 30	Judg 9:1–6	Ps 31:1–8	Ps 103	Acts 23:12–35
Yr 1	July 31	Judg 9:7–21	Ps 31:9–24	Ps 104:1–18	Acts 24
Yr 1	Aug 1	Judg 9:22–41	Ps 32	Ps 104:19–35	Acts 25:1–12
Yr 1	Aug 2	Judg 9:42–57	Ps 33	Ps 105:1–15	Acts 25:13–27
Yr 1	Aug 3	Judg 10:1–5	Ps 34	Ps 105:16–25	Acts 26
Yr 1	Aug 4	Judg 10:6–18	Ps 35:1–10	Ps 105:26–45	Acts 27:1–26
Yr 1	Aug 5	Judg 11:1–28	Ps 35:11–28	Ps 106:1–11	Acts 27:27–44
Yr 1	Aug 6	Judg 11:29–40	Ps 36	Ps 106:12–27	Acts 28:1–16
Yr 1	Aug 7	Judg 12:1–7	Ps 37:1–7	Ps 106:28–39	Acts 28:17–31
Yr 1	Aug 8	Judg 12:8–15	Ps 37:8–19	Ps 106:40–48	Rom 1:1–17
Yr 1	Aug 9	Judg 13:1–8	Ps 37:20–33	Ps 107:1–16	Rom 1:18–32
Yr 1	Aug 10	Judg 13:9–25	Ps 37:34–40	Ps 107:17–32	Rom 2
Yr 1	Aug 11	Judg 14.	Ps 38	Ps 107:33–43	Rom 3:1–8
Yr 1	Aug 12	Judg 15	Ps 39	Ps 108	Rom 3:9–31
Yr 1	Aug 13	Judg 16:1–3	Ps 40	Ps 109:1–19	Rom 4
Yr 1	Aug 14	Judg 16:4–22	Ps 41	Ps 109:20–31	Rom 5
Yr 1	Aug 15	Judg 16:23–31	Ps 42	Ps 110	Rom 6
Yr 1	Aug 16	Judg 17	Ps 43	Ps 111	Rom 7
Yr 1	Aug 17	Judg 18	Ps 44	Ps 112	Rom 8:1–17
Yr 1	Aug 18	Judg 19:1–15	Ps 45	Ps 113;114	Rom 8:18–39
Yr 1	Aug 19	Judg 19:16–30	Ps 46	Ps 115	Rom 9:1–24
Yr 1	Aug 20	Judg 20:1–11	Ps 47	Ps 116;117	Rom 9:25–10:4
Yr 1	Aug 21	Judg 20:12–25	Ps 48	Ps 118:1–18	Rom 10:5–21
Yr 1	Aug 22	Judg 20:26–48	Ps 49	Ps 118:19–29	Rom 11
Yr 1	Aug 23	Judg 21:1–14	Ps 50:1–6	Ps 119:1–16	Rom 12

Yr 1	Aug 24	Judg 21:15–25	Ps 50:7–23	Ps 119:17–32	Rom 13
Yr 1	Aug 25	Ruth 1:1–5	Ps 51	Ps 119:33–40	Rom 14
Yr 1	Aug 26	Ruth 1:6–22	Ps 52	Ps 119:41–48	Rom 15:1–22
Yr 1	Aug 27	Ruth 2:1–16	Ps 53;54	Ps 119:49–56	Rom 15:23–16:16
Yr 1	Aug 28	Ruth 2:17–23	Ps 55	Ps 119:65–80	Rom 16:17–27
Yr 1	Aug 29	Ruth 3	Ps 56	Ps 119:81–96	1 Cor 1
Yr 1	Aug 30	Job 13:1–19	Ps 57	Ps 119:97–104	1 Cor 2
Yr 1	Aug 31	Job 13:20–28	Ps 58	Ps 119:105–112	1 Cor 3
Yr 1	Sept 1	Job 14:1–12	Ps 59	Ps 119:113–128	1 Cor 4
Yr 1	Sept 2	Job 14:13–22	Ps 60	Ps 119:129–144	1 Cor 5–6:11
Yr 1	Sept 3	Job 15:1–16	Ps 61	Ps 119:145–152	1 Cor 6:12–7:11
Yr 1	Sept 4	Job 15:17–35	Ps 62	Ps 119:153–160	1 Cor 7:12–40
Yr 1	Sept 5	Job 16:1–6	Ps 63	Ps 119:161–176	1 Cor 8
Yr 1	Sept 6	Job 16:7–22	Ps 64	Ps 120;121	1 Cor 9
Yr 1	Sept 7	Job 17	Ps 65	Ps 122;123;124	1 Cor 10
Yr 1	Sept 8	Job 18:1–10	Ps 66	Ps 125;126;127	1 Cor 11:1–16
Yr 1	Sept 9	Job 18:11–21	Ps 67	Ps 128;129	1 Cor 11:17–34
Yr 1	Sept 10	Is 37:1–20	Ps 68:1–19	Ps 130;131	1 Cor 12:1–26
Yr 1	Sept 11	Is 37:21–29	Ps 68:20–35	Ps 132	1 Cor 12:27–31;13
Yr 1	Sept 12	Is 37:30–38	Ps 69:1–18	Ps 133;134	1 Cor 14:1–25
Yr 1	Sept 13	Is 38:1–8	Ps 69:19–36	Ps 135	1 Cor 14:26–40
Yr 1	Sept 14	Is 38:9–22	Ps 70	Ps 136:1–16	1 Cor 15:1–34
Yr 1	Sept 15	Is 39	Ps 71:1–16	Ps 136:17–26	1 Cor 15:35–58
Yr 1	Sept 16	Is 40:1–11	Ps 71:17–24	Ps 137	1 Cor 16
Yr 1	Sept 17	Is 40:12–31	Ps 72:1–11	Ps 138	2 Cor 1
Yr 1	Sept 18	Is 41:1–20	Ps 72:12–20	Ps 139:1–12	2 Cor 2
Yr 1	Sept 19	Is 41:21–29	Ps 73:1–16	Ps 139:13–24	2 Cor 3
Yr 1	Sept 20	Is 42:1–9	Ps 73:17–28	Ps 140	2 Cor 4
Yr 1	Sept 21	Is 42:10–25	Ps 74:1–8	Ps 141	2 Cor 5:1–6:2
Yr 1	Sept 22	Is 43:1–13	Ps 74:9–23	Ps 142	2 Cor 6:3–7:4
Yr 1	Sept 23	Is 43:14–28	Ps 75	Ps 143	2 Cor 7:5–8:15
Yr 1	Sept 24	Is 44:1–20	Ps 76	Ps 144	2 Cor 8:16–9:15
Yr 1	Sept 25	Is 44:21–28	Ps 77	Ps 145:1–13	2 Cor 10
Yr 1	Sept 26	Is 45:1–13	Ps 78:1–16	Ps 145:14–21	2 Cor 11
Yr 1	Sept 27	Is 45:14–25	Ps 78:17–31	Ps 146	2 Cor 12
Yr 1	Sept 28	Is 46	Ps 78:32–39	Ps 147	2 Cor 13
Yr 1	Sept 29	Is 47	Ps 78:40–55	Ps 148	Gal 1
Yr 1	Sept 30	Is 48	Ps 78:56–64	Ps 147	Gal 2
Yr 1	Oct 1	Is 49:1–12	Ps 78:65–72	Ps 148	Gal 3:1–14
Yr 1	Oct 2	Is 49:13–26	Ps 79	Ps 149;150	Gal 3:15–29
Yr 1	Oct 3	Is 50	Ps 80	Ps 1;2	Gal 4
Yr 1	Oct 4	Gen 39:1–18	Ps 81	Ps 3;4	Gal 5
Yr 1	Oct 5	Gen 39:19–23	Ps 82	Ps 5	Gal 6
Yr 1	Oct 6	Gen 40	Ps 83	Ps 6	Eph 1
Yr 1	Oct 7	Gen 41:1–13	Ps 84	Ps 7	Eph 2
Yr 1	Oct 8	Gen 41:14–24	Ps 85	Ps 8	Eph 3
Yr 1	Oct 9	Gen 41:25–36	Ps 86	Ps 9:1–10	Eph 4:1–16
Yr 1	Oct 10	Gen 41:37–49	Ps 87	Ps 9:11–20	Eph 4:17–5:14
Yr 1	Oct 11	Gen 41:50–57	Ps 88	Ps 10	Eph 5:15–33
Yr 1	Oct 12	Gen 42:1–24	Ps 89:1–14	Ps 11;12	Eph 6
Yr 1	Oct 13	Gen 42:25–38	Ps 89:15–37	Ps 13;14	Phil 1:1–19

Yr 1	Oct 14	Gen 43:1–18	Ps 89:38–52	Ps 15;16	Phil 1:20–2:11
Yr 1	Oct 15	Gen 43:19–34	Ps 90	Ps 17	Phil 2:12–30
Yr 1	Oct 16	Gen 44:1–17	Ps 91	Ps 18:1–15	Phil 3
Yr 1	Oct 17	Gen 44:18–34	Ps 92	Ps 18:16–29	Phil 4
Yr 1	Oct 18	Gen 45:1–15	Ps 93	Ps 18:30–45	Col 1:1–23
Yr 1	Oct 19	Gen 45:16–28	Ps 94	Ps 18:46–50	Col 1:24–2:23
Yr 1	Oct 20	Gen 46:1–7	Ps 95	Ps 19	Col 3
Yr 1	Oct 21	Gen 46:8–14	Ps 96	Ps 20	Col 4
Yr 1	Oct 22	Gen 46:15–27	Ps 97	Ps 21	1 Thes 1
Yr 1	Oct 23	Gen 46:28–34	Ps 98	Ps 22:1–24	1 Thes 2
Yr 1	Oct 24	Gen 47:1–12	Ps 99	Ps 22:25–31	1 Thes 3 4
Yr 1	Oct 25	Gen 47:13–31	Ps 100;101	Ps 23;24	1 Thes 5
Yr 1	Oct 26	Gen 48	Ps 102:1–17	Ps 25	2 Thes 1
Yr 1	Oct 27	Ruth 4:1–12	Ps 102:18–28	Ps 26	2 Thes 2
Yr 1	Oct 28	Ruth 4:13–22	Ps 103	Ps 27	2 Thes 3
Yr 1	Oct 29	1 Sam 1:1–8	Ps 104:1–18	Ps 28	1 Tim 1
Yr 1	Oct 30	1 Sam 1:9–18	Ps 104:19–35	Ps 29	1 Tim 2;3
Yr 1	Oct 31	1 Sam 1:19–28	Ps 105:1–15	Ps 30	1 Tim 4
Yr 1	Nov 1	1 Sam 2:1–11	Ps 105:16–25	Ps 31:1–8	1 Tim 5:1–6:2
Yr 1	Nov 2	1 Sam 2:12–26	Ps 105:26–45	Ps 31:9–24	1 Tim 6:3–21
Yr 1	Nov 3	1 Sam 2:27–36	Ps 106:1–11	Ps 32	2 Tim 1
Yr 1	Nov 4	1 Sam 3:1–14	Ps 106:12–27	Ps 33	2 Tim 2
Yr 1	Nov 5	1 Sam 3:15–4:1	Ps 106:28–39	Ps 34	2 Tim 3
Yr 1	Nov 6	1 Sam 4:1–11	Ps 106:40–48	Ps 35:1–10	2 Tim 4
Yr 1	Nov 7	1 Sam 4:12–22	Ps 107:1–16	Ps 35:11–28	Titus 1 2
Yr 1	Nov 8	1 Sam 5	Ps 107:17–32	Ps 36	Titus 3
Yr 1	Nov 9	1 Sam 6	Ps 107:33–43	Ps 37:1–7	Philemon
Yr 1	Nov 10	1 Sam 7	Ps 108	Ps 37:8–19	Heb 1
Yr 1	Nov 11	1 Sam 8	Ps 109:1–19	Ps 37:20–33	Heb 2
Yr 1	Nov 12	1 Sam 9	Ps 109:20–31	Ps 37:34–40	Heb 3 4
Yr 1	Nov 13	1 Sam 10:1–8	Ps 110	Ps 38	Heb 5:1–6:12
Yr 1	Nov 14	1 Sam 10:9–16	Ps 111	Ps 39	Heb 6:13–7:14
Yr 1	Nov 15	1 Sam 10:17–27	Ps 112	Ps 40	Heb 7:15–28
Yr 1	Nov 16	1 Sam 11	Ps 113;114	Ps 41	Heb 8:1–9:10
Yr 1	Nov 17	1 Sam 12	Ps 115	Ps 42	Heb 9:11–10:10
Yr 1	Nov 18	1 Sam 13:1–7a	Ps 116;117	Ps 43	Heb 10:11–39
Yr 1	Nov 19	1 Sam 13:7b–23	Ps 118:1–18	Ps 44	Heb 11:1–12
Yr 1	Nov 20	1 Sam 14:1–15	Ps 118:19–29	Ps 45	Heb 11:13–40
Yr 1	Nov 21	1 Sam 14:16–23	Ps 119:1–16	Ps 46	Heb 12:1–13
Yr 1	Nov 22	1 Sam 14:24–46	Ps 119:17–32	Ps 47	Heb 12:14–29
Yr 1	Nov 23	1 Sam 14:47–52	Ps 119:33–40	Ps 48	Heb 13
Yr 1	Nov 24	1 Sam 15:1–9	Ps 119:41–48	Ps 49	Jas 1
Yr 1	Nov 25	1 Sam 15:10–23	Ps 119:49–56	Ps 50:1–6	Jas 2
Yr 1	Nov 26	1 Sam 15:24–35	Ps 119:57–80	Ps 50:7–23	Jas 3
Yr 1	Nov 27	Job 19:1–12	Ps 119:81–96	Ps 51	Jas 4
Yr 1	Nov 28	Job 19:13–29	Ps 119:97–104	Ps 52	Jas 5
Yr 1	Nov 29	Job 20:1–11	Ps 119:105–112	Ps 53;54	1 Pet 1
Yr 1	Nov 30	Job 20:12–29	Ps 119:113–128	Ps 55	1 Pet 2
Yr 1	Dec 1	Job 21:1–18	Ps 119:129–144	Ps 56	1 Pet 3
Yr 1	Dec 2	Job 21:19–34	Ps 119:145–152	Ps 57	1 Pet 4
Yr 1	Dec 3	Job 22:1–14	Ps 119:153–160	Ps 58	1 Pet 5

Yr 1	Dec 4	Job 22:15–30	Ps 119:161–176	Ps 59	2 Pet 1
Yr 1	Dec 5	Job 23	Ps 120;121	Ps 60	2 Pet 2
Yr 1	Dec 6	Job 24:1–12	Ps 122;123;124	Ps 61	2 Pet 3
Yr 1	Dec 7	Job 24:13–25	Ps 125;126;127	Ps 62 1	1 Jn 1;2:1–2:27
Yr 1	Dec 8	Is 51	Ps 128;129	Ps 63 1	1 Jn 2:28–3:24
Yr 1	Dec 9	Is 52	Ps 130;131	Ps 64 1	1 Jn 4
Yr 1	Dec 10	Is 53	Ps 132	Ps 65 1	1 Jn 5
Yr 1	Dec 11	Is 54	Ps 133;134	Ps 66 2	2 Jn
Yr 1	Dec 12	Is 55	Ps 135	Ps 67 3	3 Jn
Yr 1	Dec 13	Is 56	Ps 136:1–16	Ps 68:1–19	Jude
Yr 1	Dec 14	Is 57	Ps 136:17–26	Ps 68:20–35	Rev 1:1–2:11
Yr 1	Dec 15	Is 58	Ps 137	Ps 69:1–18	Rev 2:12–3:6
Yr 1	Dec 16	Is 59:1–8	Ps 138	Ps 69:19–36	Rev 3:7–22
Yr 1	Dec 17	Is 59:9–21	Ps 139:1–12	Ps 70	Rev 4 5
Yr 1	Dec 18	Is 60:1–14	Ps 139:13–24	Ps 71:1–16	Rev 6
Yr 1	Dec 19	Is 60:15–22	Ps 140	Ps 71:17–24	Rev 7
Yr 1	Dec 20	Is 61	Ps 141	Ps 72:1–11	Rev 8:1–9:12
Yr 1	Dec 21	Is 62	Ps 142	Ps 72:12–20	Rev 9:13–10:11
Yr 1	Dec 22	Is 63	Ps 143	Ps 73:1–16	Rev 11;12
Yr 1	Dec 23	Is 64	Ps 144	Ps 73:17–28	Rev 13
Yr 1	Dec 24	Is 65	Ps 145:1–13	Ps 74:1–8	Rev 14
Yr 1	Dec 25	Is 66:1–13	Ps 145:14–21	Ps 74:9–23	Rev 15;16
Yr 1	Dec 26	Is 66:14–24	Ps 146	Ps 75	Rev 17
Yr 1	Dec 27	Jer 1	Ps 147	Ps 76	Rev 18
Yr 1	Dec 28	Jer 2:1–13	Ps 148	Ps 77	Rev 19
Yr 1	Dec 29	Jer 2:14–37	Ps 147	Ps 78:1–16	Rev 20
Yr 1	Dec 30	Jer 3:1–10	Ps 148	Ps 78:17–31	Rev 21
Yr 1	Dec 31	Jer 3:11–25	Ps 149;150	Ps 78:32–39	Rev 22

Year 2

2017, 2021, 2025, 2029, 2033, 2037, 2041, 2045, 2049, 2053, 2057, 2061, 2065, 2069

Yr 2 Jan 1	Gen 49:1–12	Ps 1; 2	Ps 78:40–55	Matt 1
Yr 2 Jan 2	Gen 49:13–21	Ps 3; 4	Ps 78:56–64	Matt 2
Yr 2 Jan 3	Gen 49:22–28	Ps 5	Ps 78:65–72	Matt 3
Yr 2 Jan 4	Gen 49:29–50:13	Ps 6	Ps 79	Matt 4
Yr 2 Jan 5	Gen 50:14–26	Ps 7	Ps 80	Matt 5:1–20
Yr 2 Jan 6	Ex 1:1–14	Ps 8	Ps 81	Matt 5:21–37
Yr 2 Jan 7	Ex 1:15–22	Ps 9:1–10	Ps 82	Matt 5:38–6:4
Yr 2 Jan 8	Ex 2:1–10	Ps 9:11–20	Ps 83	Matt 6:5–34
Yr 2 Jan 9	Ex 2:11–25	Ps 10	Ps 84	Matt 7
Yr 2 Jan 10	Ex 3	Ps 11; 12	Ps 85	Matt 8:1–22
Yr 2 Jan 11	Ex 4:1–17	Ps 13; 14	Ps 86	Matt 8:23–34
Yr 2 Jan 12	Ex 4:18–31	Ps 15; 16	Ps 87	Matt 9:1–17
Yr 2 Jan 13	Ex 5:1–5	Ps 17	Ps 88	Matt 9:18–38
Yr 2 Jan 14	Ex 5:6–23	Ps 18:1–15	Ps 89:1–14	Matt 10:1–23
Yr 2 Jan 15	Ex 6:1–13	Ps 18:16–29	Ps 89:15–37	Matt 10:24–42
Yr 2 Jan 16	Ex 6:14–19	Ps 18:30–45	Ps 89:38–52	Matt 11
Yr 2 Jan 17	Ex 6:20–30	Ps 18:46–50	Ps 90	Matt 12:1–21
Yr 2 Jan 18	Ex 7:1–13	Ps 19	Ps 91	Matt 12:22–50
Yr 2 Jan 19	Ex 7:14–25	Ps 20	Ps 92	Matt 13:1–23
Yr 2 Jan 20	Ex 8:1–15	Ps 21	Ps 93	Matt 13:24–43
Yr 2 Jan 21	Ex 8:16–19	Ps 22:1–24	Ps 94	Matt 13:44–58
Yr 2 Jan 22	Ex 8:20–32	Ps 22:25–31	Ps 95	Matt 14
Yr 2 Jan 23	Ex 9:1–12	Ps 23; 24	Ps 96	Matt 15:1–20
Yr 2 Jan 24	Ex 9:13–35	Ps 25	Ps 97	Matt 15:21–39
Yr 2 Jan 25	Ex 10:1–20	Ps 26	Ps 98	Matt 16
Yr 2 Jan 26	Ex 10:21–29	Ps 27	Ps 99	Matt 17
Yr 2 Jan 27	1 Sam 16:1–13	Ps 28	Ps 100; 101	Matt 18:1–20
Yr 2 Jan 28	1 Sam 16:14–23	Ps 29	Ps 102:1–17	Matt 18:21–35
Yr 2 Jan 29	1 Sam 17:1–11	Ps 30	Ps 102:18–28	Matt 19:1–15
Yr 2 Jan 30	1 Sam 17:12–31	Ps 31:1–8	Ps 103	Matt 19:16–30
Yr 2 Jan 31	1 Sam 17:32–51a	Ps 31:9–24	Ps 104:1–18	Matt 20:1–16
Yr 2 Feb 1	1 Sam 17:51b–58	Ps 32	Ps 104:19–35	Matt 20:17–34
Yr 2 Feb 2	1 Sam 18:1–16	Ps 33	Ps 105:1–15	Matt 21:1–22

Yr 2	Feb 3	1 Sam 18:17–30	Ps 34	Ps 105:16–25	Matt 21:23–46
Yr 2	Feb 4	1 Sam 19	Ps 35:1–10	Ps 105:26–45	Matt 22:1–33
Yr 2	Feb 5	1 Sam 20:1–23	Ps 35:11–28	Ps 106:1–11	Matt 22:34–46
Yr 2	Feb 6	1 Sam 20:24–42	Ps 36	Ps 106:12–27	Matt 23:1–24
Yr 2	Feb 7	1 Sam 21	Ps 37:1–7	Ps 106:28–39	Matt 23:25–39
Yr 2	Feb 8	1 Sam 22:1–10	Ps 37:8–19	Ps 106:40–48	Matt 24:1–31
Yr 2	Feb 9	1 Sam 22:11–23	Ps 37:20–33	Ps 107:1–16	Matt 24:32–25:13
Yr 2	Feb 10	1 Sam 23:1–12	Ps 37:34–40	Ps 107:17–32	Matt 25:14–30
Yr 2	Feb 11	1 Sam 23:13–29	Ps 38	Ps 107:33–43	Matt 25:31–46
Yr 2	Feb 12	1 Sam 24	Ps 39	Ps 108	Matt 26:1–16
Yr 2	Feb 13	1 Sam 25:1–22	Ps 40	Ps 109:1–19	Matt 26:17–46
Yr 2	Feb 14	1 Sam 25:23–35	Ps 41	Ps 109:20–31	Matt 26:47–75
Yr 2	Feb 15	1 Sam 25:36–44	Ps 42	Ps 110	Matt 27:1–26
Yr 2	Feb 16	1 Sam 26	Ps 43	Ps 111	Matt 27:27–56
Yr 2	Feb 17	1 Sam 27	Ps 44	Ps 112	Matt 27:57–66:28
Yr 2	Feb 18	1 Sam 28	Ps 45	Ps 113; 114	Mk 1:1–20
Yr 2	Feb 19	1 Sam 29	Ps 46	Ps 115	Mk 1:21–45
Yr 2	Feb 20	1 Sam 30:1–8	Ps 47	Ps 116; 117	Mk 2:1–17
Yr 2	Feb 21	1 Sam 30:9–20	Ps 48	Ps 118:1–18	Mk 2:18–28
Yr 2	Feb 22	1 Sam 30:21–31	Ps 49	Ps 118:19–29	Mk 3:1–19
Yr 2	Feb 23	1 Sam 31	Ps 50:1–6	Ps 119:1–16	Mk 3:20–35
Yr 2	Feb 24	2 Sam 1:1–16	Ps 50:7–23	Ps 119:17–32	Mk 4:1–20
Yr 2	Feb 25	2 Sam 1:17–27	Ps 51	Ps 119:33–40	Mk 4:21–41
Yr 2	Feb 26	Job 25; 26	Ps 52	Ps 119:41–48	Mk 5:1–20
Yr 2	Feb 27	Job 27:1–15	Ps 53; 54	Ps 119:49–56	Mk 5:21–43
Yr 2	Feb 28	Job 27:16–23	Ps 55	Ps 119:65–80	Mk 6:1–29
Yr 2	Mar 1	Job 28:1–19	Ps 56	Ps 119:81–96	Mk 6:30–56
Yr 2	Mar 2	Job 28:20–28	Ps 57	Ps 119:97–104	Mk 7:1–23
Yr 2	Mar 3	Job 29:1–10	Ps 58	Ps 119:105–112	Mk 7:24–37
Yr 2	Mar 4	Job 29:11–25	Ps 59	Ps 119:113–128	Mk 8:1–26
Yr 2	Mar 5	Job 30:1–15	Ps 60	Ps 119:129–144	Mk 8:27–9:1
Yr 2	Mar 6	Job 30:16–31	Ps 61	Ps 119:145–152	Mk 9:2–29
Yr 2	Mar 7	Job 31:1–12	Ps 62	Ps 119:153–160	Mk 9:30–50
Yr 2	Mar 8	Job 31:13–28	Ps 63	Ps 119:161–176	Mk 10:1–16
Yr 2	Mar 9	Job 31:29–40	Ps 64	Ps 120; 121	Mk 10:17–34
Yr 2	Mar 10	Jer 4:1–18	Ps 65	Ps 122; 123; 124	Mk 10:35–52
Yr 2	Mar 11	Jer 4:19–22	Ps 66	Ps 125; 126; 127	Mk 11
Yr 2	Mar 12	Jer 4:23–31	Ps 67	Ps 128; 129	Mk 12:1–27
Yr 2	Mar 13	Jer 5:1–19	Ps 68:1–19	Ps 130; 131	Mk 12:28–44
Yr 2	Mar 14	Jer 5:20–31	Ps 68:20–35	Ps 132	Mk 13:1–25
Yr 2	Mar 15	Jer 6:1–15	Ps 69:1–18	Ps 133; 134	Mk 13:26–37
Yr 2	Mar 16	Jer 6:16–30	Ps 69:19–36	Ps 135	Mk 14:1–26
Yr 2	Mar 17	Jer 7:1–15	Ps 70	Ps 136:1–16	Mk 14:27–52
Yr 2	Mar 18	Jer 7:16–34	Ps 71:1–16	Ps 136:17–26	Mk 14:53–72
Yr 2	Mar 19	Jer 8:1–17	Ps 71:17–24	Ps 137	Mk 15:1–20
Yr 2	Mar 20	Jer 8:18–22	Ps 72:1–11	Ps 138	Mk 15:21–47
Yr 2	Mar 21	Jer 9:1–16	Ps 72:12–20	Ps 139:1–12	Mk 16:1–20*
Yr 2	Mar 22	Jer 9:17–26	Ps 73:1–16	Ps 139:13–24	Lk 1:1–25
Yr 2	Mar 23	Jer 10:1–16	Ps 73:17–28	Ps 140	Lk 1:26–45
Yr 2	Mar 24	Jer 10:17–25	Ps 74:1–8	Ps 141	Lk 1:46–66
Yr 2	Mar 25	Jer 11	Ps 74:9–23	Ps 142	Lk 1:67–80

Yr 2	Mar 26	Jer 12:1–13	Ps 75	Ps 143	Lk 2:1–20
Yr 2	Mar 27	Jer 12:14–13:14	Ps 76	Ps 144	Lk 2:21–52
Yr 2	Mar 28	Jer 13:15–27	Ps 77	Ps 145:1–13	Lk 3:1–20
Yr 2	Mar 29	Jer 14:1–10	Ps 78:1–16	Ps 145:14–21	Lk 3:21–38
Yr 2	Mar 30	Jer 14:11–22	Ps 78:17–31	Ps 146	Lk 4:1–30
Yr 2	Mar 31	Jer 15	Ps 78:32–39	Ps 147	Lk 4:31–44
Yr 2	Apr 1	Jer 16:1–13	Ps 78:40–55	Ps 148	Lk 5:1–26
Yr 2	Apr 2	Jer 16:14–21	Ps 78:56–64	Ps 149	Lk 5:27–39
Yr 2	Apr 3	Ex 11	Ps 78:65–72	Ps 150	Lk 6:1–26
Yr 2	Apr 4	Ex 12:1–20	Ps 79	Ps 1; 2	Lk 6:27–49
Yr 2	Apr 5	Ex 12:21–30	Ps 80	Ps 3; 4	Lk 7:1–27
Yr 2	Apr 6	Ex 12:31–42	Ps 81	Ps 5	Lk 7:28–50
Yr 2	Apr 7	Ex 12:43–51	Ps 82	Ps 6	Lk 8:1–15
Yr 2	Apr 8	Ex 13:1–16	Ps 83	Ps 7	Lk 8:16–39
Yr 2	Apr 9	Ex 13:17–22	Ps 84	Ps 8	Lk 8:40–56
Yr 2	Apr 10	Ex 14:1–14	Ps 85	Ps 9:1–10	Lk 9:1–27
Yr 2	Apr 11	Ex 14:15–31	Ps 86	Ps 9:11–20	Lk 9:28–48
Yr 2	Apr 12	Ex 15:1–21	Ps 87	Ps 10	Lk 9:49–62
Yr 2	Apr 13	Ex 15:22–27	Ps 88	Ps 11; 12	Lk 10:1–29
Yr 2	Apr 14	Ex 16:1–20	Ps 89:1–14	Ps 13; 14	Lk 10:30–42
Yr 2	Apr 15	Ex 16:21–36	Ps 89:15–37	Ps 15; 16	Lk 11:1–28
Yr 2	Apr 16	Ex 17	Ps 89:38–52	Ps 17	Lk 11:29–54
Yr 2	Apr 17	Ex 18:1–12	Ps 90	Ps 18:1–15	Lk 12:1–21
Yr 2	Apr 18	Ex 18:13–27	Ps 91	Ps 18:16–29	Lk 12:22–48
Yr 2	Apr 19	Ex 18:1–15	Ps 92	Ps 18:30–45	Lk 12:49–59
Yr 2	Apr 20	Ex 18:16–25	Ps 93	Ps 18:46–50	Lk 13:1–21
Yr 2	Apr 21	Ex 20:1–26	Ps 94	Ps 19	Lk 13:22–35
Yr 2	Apr 22	Ex 21:1–11	Ps 95	Ps 20	Lk 14
Yr 2	Apr 23	Ex 21:12–21	Ps 96	Ps 21	Lk 15:1–10
Yr 2	Apr 24	Ex 21:22–36	Ps 97	Ps 22:1–24	Lk 15:11–32
Yr 2	Apr 25	Ex 22:1–15	Ps 98	Ps 22:25–31	Lk 16
Yr 2	Apr 26	Ex 22:16–31	Ps 99	Ps 23; 24	Lk 17
Yr 2	Apr 27	Ex 23:1–13	Ps 100; 101	Ps 25	Lk 18:1–17
Yr 2	Apr 28	Ex 23:14–19	Ps 102:1–17	Ps 26	Lk 18:18–43
Yr 2	Apr 29	Ex 23:20–33	Ps 102:18–28	Ps 27	Lk 19:1–10
Yr 2	Apr 30	2 Sam 2:1–11	Ps 103	Ps 28	Lk 19:11–27
Yr 2	May 1	2 Sam 2:12–17	Ps 104:1–18	Ps 29	Lk 19:28–48
Yr 2	May 2	2 Sam 2:18–32	Ps 104:19–35	Ps 30	Lk 20:1–19
Yr 2	May 3	2 Sam 3:1–21	Ps 105:1–15	Ps 31:1–8	Lk 20:20–47
Yr 2	May 4	2 Sam 3:22–30	Ps 105:16–25	Ps 31:9–24	Lk 21:1–11
Yr 2	May 5	2 Sam 3:31–39	Ps 105:26–45	Ps 32	Lk 21:12–38
Yr 2	May 6	2 Sam 4	Ps 106:1–11	Ps 33	Lk 22:1–13
Yr 2	May 7	2 Sam 5:1–16	Ps 106:12–27	Ps 34	Lk 22:14–38
Yr 2	May 8	2 Sam 5:17–25	Ps 106:28–39	Ps 35:1–10	Lk 22:39–71
Yr 2	May 9	2 Sam 6:1–15	Ps 106:40–48	Ps 35:11–28	Lk 23:1–25
Yr 2	May 10	2 Sam 6:16–23	Ps 107:1–16	Ps 36	Lk 23:26–43
Yr 2	May 11	2 Sam 7:1–17	Ps 107:17–32	Ps 37:1–7	Lk 23:44–56
Yr 2	May 12	2 Sam 7:18–29	Ps 107:33–43	Ps 37:8–19	Lk 24:1–34
Yr 2	May 13	2 Sam 8	Ps 108	Ps 37:20–33	Lk 24:35–53
Yr 2	May 14	2 Sam 9	Ps 109:1–19	Ps 37:34–40	Jn 1:1–28
Yr 2	May 15	2 Sam 10	Ps 109:20–31	Ps 38	Jn 1:29–51

Yr 2	May 16	2 Sam 11:1–13	Ps 110	Ps 39	Jn 2:1–12
Yr 2	May 17	2 Sam 11:14–27	Ps 111	Ps 40	Jn 2:13–25
Yr 2	May 18	2 Sam 12:1–11	Ps 112	Ps 41	Jn 3:1–21
Yr 2	May 19	2 Sam 12:12–31	Ps 113; 114	Ps 42	Jn 3:22–36
Yr 2	May 20	2 Sam 13:1–22	Ps 115	Ps 43	Jn 4:1–38
Yr 2	May 21	2 Sam 13:23–39	Ps 116; 117	Ps 44	Jn 4:39–5:15
Yr 2	May 22	2 Sam 14:1–24	Ps 118:1–18	Ps 45	Jn 5:16–47
Yr 2	May 23	2 Sam 14:25–33	Ps 118:19–29	Ps 46	Jn 6:1–21
Yr 2	May 24	2 Sam 15:1–12	Ps 119:1–16	Ps 47	Jn 6:22–59
Yr 2	May 25	2 Sam 15:13–37	Ps 119:17–32	Ps 48	Jn 6:60–7:9
Yr 2	May 26	2 Sam 16:1–14	Ps 119:33–40	Ps 49	Jn 7:10–36
Yr 2	May 27	2 Sam 16:15–17:4	Ps 119:41–48	Ps 50:1–6	Jn 7:37–52
Yr 2	May 28	2 Sam 17:5–14	Ps 119:49–56	Ps 50:7–23	Jn 7:53–8:11
Yr 2	May 29	2 Sam 17:15–29	Ps 119:65–80	Ps 51	Jn 8:12–30
Yr 2	May 30	2 Sam 18:1–18	Ps 119:81–96	Ps 52	Jn 8:31–59
Yr 2	May 31	2 Sam 18:19–33	Ps 119:97–104	Ps 53; 54	Jn 9:1–34
Yr 2	June 1	Job 32	Ps 119:105–112	Ps 55	Jn 9:35–41
Yr 2	June 2	Job 33:1–18	Ps 119:113–128	Ps 56	Jn 10:1–21
Yr 2	June 3	Job 33:19–33	Ps 119:129–144	Ps 57	Jn 10:22–42
Yr 2	June 4	Job 34:1–15	Ps 119:145–152	Ps 58	Jn 11:1–29
Yr 2	June 5	Job 34:16–30	Ps 119:153–160	Ps 59	Jn 11:30–57
Yr 2	June 6	Job 34:31–37	Ps 119:161–176	Ps 60	Jn 12:1–19
Yr 2	June 7	Job 35	Ps 120; 121	Ps 61	Jn 12:20–36
Yr 2	June 8	Job 36:1–21	Ps 122; 123; 124	Ps 62	Jn 12:37–50
Yr 2	June 9	Job 36:22–33	Ps 125; 126; 127	Ps 63	Jn 13:1–20
Yr 2	June 10	Job 37:1–13	Ps 128; 129	Ps 64	Jn 13:21–38
Yr 2	June 11	Job 37:14–24	Ps 130; 131	Ps 65	Jn 14
Yr 2	June 12	Jer 17:1–18	Ps 132	Ps 66	Jn 15
Yr 2	June 13	Jer 17:19–27	Ps 133; 134	Ps 67	Jn 16:1–15
Yr 2	June 14	Jer 18	Ps 135	Ps 68:1–19	Jn 16:16–33
Yr 2	June 15	Jer 19	Ps 136:1–16	Ps 68:20–35	Jn 17
Yr 2	June 16	Jer 20	Ps 136:17–26	Ps 69:1–18	Jn 18:1–24
Yr 2	June 17	Jer 21	Ps 137	Ps 69:19–36	Jn 18:25–40
Yr 2	June 18	Jer 22:1–9	Ps 138	Ps 70	Jn 19:1–27
Yr 2	June 19	Jer 22:10–23	Ps 139:1–12	Ps 71:1–16	Jn 19:28–42
Yr 2	June 20	Jer 22:24–23:8	Ps 139:13–24	Ps 71:17–24	Jn 20:1–18
Yr 2	June 21	Jer 23:9–24	Ps 140	Ps 72:1–11	Jn 20:19–31
Yr 2	June 22	Jer 23:25–40	Ps 141	Ps 72:12–20	Jn 21
Yr 2	June 23	Jer 24	Ps 142	Ps 73:1–16	Acts 1
Yr 2	June 24	Jer 25:1–14	Ps 143	Ps 73:17–28	Acts 2:1–21
Yr 2	June 25	Jer 25:15–38	Ps 144	Ps 74:1–8	Acts 2:22–47
Yr 2	June 26	Jer 26:1–9	Ps 145:1–13	Ps 74:9–23	Acts 3:1–11
Yr 2	June 27	Jer 26:10–16	Ps 145:14–21	Ps 75	Acts 3:12–26
Yr 2	June 28	Jer 26:17–24	Ps 146	Ps 76	Acts 4:1–22
Yr 2	June 29	Jer 27	Ps 147	Ps 77	Acts 4:23–37
Yr 2	June 30	Jer 28	Ps 148	Ps 78:1–16	Acts 5:1–16
Yr 2	July 1	Jer 29:1–23	Ps 149	Ps 78:17–31	Acts 5:17–42
Yr 2	July 2	Jer 29:24–32	Ps 150	Ps 78:32–39	Acts 6; 7:1–10
Yr 2	July 3	Jer 30:1–9	Ps 1; 2	Ps 78:40–55	Acts 7:11–60
Yr 2	July 4	Jer 30:10–24	Ps 3; 4	Ps 78:56–64	Acts 8:1–25
Yr 2	July 5	Ex 24	Ps 5	Ps 78:65–72	Acts 8:26–40

Yr 2	July 6	Ex 25:1–22	Ps 6	Ps 79	Acts 9:1–19
Yr 2	July 7	Ex 25:23–40	Ps 7	Ps 80	Acts 9:20–43
Yr 2	July 8	Ex 26:1–14	Ps 8	Ps 81	Acts 10:1–33
Yr 2	July 9	Ex 26:15–37	Ps 9:1–10	Ps 82	Acts 10:34–48
Yr 2	July 10	Ex 27:1–8	Ps 9:11–20	Ps 83	Acts 11:1–18
Yr 2	July 11	Ex 27:9–21	Ps 10	Ps 84	Acts 11:19–30
Yr 2	July 12	Ex 28:1–14	Ps 11; 12	Ps 85	Acts 12
Yr 2	July 13	Ex 28:15–30	Ps 13; 14	Ps 86	Acts 13:1–12
Yr 2	July 14	Ex 28:31–43	Ps 15; 16	Ps 87	Acts 13:13–43
Yr 2	July 15	Ex 29:1–14	Ps 17	Ps 88	Acts 13:44–14:7
Yr 2	July 16	Ex 29:15–30	Ps 18:1–15	Ps 89:1–14	Acts 14:8–28
Yr 2	July 17	Ex 29:31–46	Ps 18:16–29	Ps 89:15–37	Acts 15
Yr 2	July 18	Ex 30:1–10	Ps 18:30–45	Ps 89:38–52	Acts 16:1–21
Yr 2	July 19	Ex 30:11–21	Ps 18:46–50	Ps 90	Acts 16:22–40
Yr 2	July 20	Ex 30:22–38	Ps 19	Ps 91	Acts 17
Yr 2	July 21	Ex 31	Ps 20	Ps 92	Acts 18:1–23
Yr 2	July 22	Ex 32:1–14	Ps 21	Ps 93	Acts 18:24–19:7
Yr 2	July 23	Ex 32:15–29	Ps 22:1–24	Ps 94	Acts 19:8–22
Yr 2	July 24	Ex 32:30–35	Ps 22:25–31	Ps 95	Acts 19:23–41
Yr 2	July 25	Ex 33	Ps 23; 24	Ps 96	Acts 20
Yr 2	July 26	Ex 34:1–18	Ps 25	Ps 97	Acts 21:1–25
Yr 2	July 27	Ex 34:19–35	Ps 26	Ps 98	Acts 21:26–40
Yr 2	July 28	Ex 35:1–19	Ps 27	Ps 99	Acts 22:1–23
Yr 2	July 29	Ex 35:20–35	Ps 28	Ps 100; 101	Acts 22:24–23:11
Yr 2	July 30	2 Sam 19:1–14	Ps 29	Ps 102:1–17	Acts 23:12–35
Yr 2	July 31	2 Sam 19:15–22	Ps 30	Ps 102:18–28	Acts 24
Yr 2	Aug 1	2 Sam 19:23–30	Ps 31:1–8	Ps 103	Acts 25:1–12
Yr 2	Aug 2	2 Sam 19:31–43	Ps 31:9–24	Ps 104:1–18	Acts 25:13–27
Yr 2	Aug 3	2 Sam 20	Ps 32	Ps 104:19–35	Acts 26
Yr 2	Aug 4	2 Sam 21:1–14	Ps 33	Ps 105:1–15	Acts 27:1–26
Yr 2	Aug 5	2 Sam 21:15–22	Ps 34	Ps 105:16–25	Acts 27:27–44
Yr 2	Aug 6	2 Sam 22:1–16	Ps 35:1–10	Ps 105:26–45	Acts 28:1–16
Yr 2	Aug 7	2 Sam 22:17–30	Ps 35:11–28	Ps 106:1–11	Acts 28:17–31
Yr 2	Aug 8	2 Sam 22:31–43	Ps 36	Ps 106:12–27	Rom 1:1–17
Yr 2	Aug 9	2 Sam 22:44–51	Ps 37:1–7	Ps 106:28–39	Rom 1:18–32
Yr 2	Aug 10	2 Sam 23:1–17	Ps 37:8–19	Ps 106:40–48	Rom 2
Yr 2	Aug 11	2 Sam 23:18–39	Ps 37:20–33	Ps 107:1–16	Rom 3:1–8
Yr 2	Aug 12	2 Sam 24:1–17	Ps 37:34–40	Ps 107:17–32	Rom 3:9–31
Yr 2	Aug 13	2 Sam 24:18–25	Ps 38	Ps 107:33–43	Rom 4
Yr 2	Aug 14	1 Kgs 1:1–14	Ps 39	Ps 108	Rom 5
Yr 2	Aug 15	1 Kgs 1:15–27	Ps 40	Ps 109:1–19	Rom 6
Yr 2	Aug 16	1 Kgs 1:28–53	Ps 41	Ps 109:20–31	Rom 7
Yr 2	Aug 17	1 Kgs 2:1–12	Ps 42	Ps 110	Rom 8:1–17
Yr 2	Aug 18	1 Kgs 2:13–33	Ps 43	Ps 111	Rom 8:18–39
Yr 2	Aug 19	1 Kgs 2:34–46	Ps 44	Ps 112	Rom 9:1–24
Yr 2	Aug 20	1 Kgs 3:1–15	Ps 45	Ps 113; 114	Rom 9:25–10:4
Yr 2	Aug 21	1 Kgs 3:16–28	Ps 46	Ps 115	Rom 10:5–21
Yr 2	Aug 22	1 Kgs 4:1–19	Ps 47	Ps 116; 117	Rom 11
Yr 2	Aug 23	1 Kgs 4:20–34	Ps 48	Ps 118:1–18	Rom 12
Yr 2	Aug 24	1 Kgs 5	Ps 49	Ps 118:19–29	Rom 13
Yr 2	Aug 25	1 Kgs 6:1–13	Ps 50:1–6	Ps 119:1–16	Rom 14

Yr 2 Aug 26	1 Kgs 6:14–30	Ps 50:7–23	Ps 119:17–32	Rom 15:1–22
Yr 2 Aug 27	1 Kgs 6:31–38	Ps 51	Ps 119:33–40	Rom 15:23–16:16
Yr 2 Aug 28	Job 38:1–15	Ps 52	Ps 119:41–48	Rom 16:17–27
Yr 2 Aug 29	Job 38:16–30	Ps 53; 54	Ps 119:49–56	1 Cor 1
Yr 2 Aug 30	Job 38:31–41	Ps 55	Ps 119:65–80	1 Cor 2
Yr 2 Aug 31	Job 39:1–12	Ps 56	Ps 119:81–96	1 Cor 3
Yr 2 Sept 1	Job 39:13–30	Ps 57	Ps 119:97–104	1 Cor 4
Yr 2 Sept 2	Job 40:1–14	Ps 58	Ps 119:105–112	1 Cor 5–6:11
Yr 2 Sept 3	Job 40:15–24	Ps 59	Ps 119:113–128	1 Cor 6:12–7:11
Yr 2 Sept 4	Job 41:1–11	Ps 60	Ps 119:129–144	1 Cor 7:12–40
Yr 2 Sept 5	Job 41:12–21	Ps 61	Ps 119:145–152	1 Cor 8
Yr 2 Sept 6	Job 41:22–34	Ps 62	Ps 119:153–160	1 Cor 9
Yr 2 Sept 7	Job 42	Ps 63	Ps 119:161–176	1 Cor 10
Yr 2 Sept 8	Jer 31:1–14	Ps 64	Ps 120; 121	1 Cor 11:1–16
Yr 2 Sept 9	Jer 31:15–30	Ps 65	Ps 122; 123; 124	1 Cor 11:17–34
Yr 2 Sept 10	Jer 31:31–40	Ps 66	Ps 125; 126; 127	1 Cor 12:1–26
Yr 2 Sept 11	Jer 32:1–15	Ps 67	Ps 128; 129	1 Cor 12:27–31; 13
Yr 2 Sept 12	Jer 32:16–25	Ps 68:1–19	Ps 130;131	1 Cor 14:1–25
Yr 2 Sept 13	Jer 32:26–44	Ps 68:20–35	Ps 132	1 Cor 14:26–40
Yr 2 Sept 14	Jer 33:1–11	Ps 69:1–18	Ps 133; 134	1 Cor 15:1–34
Yr 2 Sept 15	Jer 33:12–26	Ps 69:19–36	Ps 135	1 Cor 15:35–58
Yr 2 Sept 16	Jer 34:1–7	Ps 70	Ps 136:1–16	1 Cor 16
Yr 2 Sept 17	Jer 34:8–22	Ps 71:1–16	Ps 136:17–26	2 Cor 1
Yr 2 Sept 18	Jer 35	Ps 71:17–24	Ps 137	2 Cor 2
Yr 2 Sept 19	Jer 36:1–20	Ps 72:1–11	Ps 138	2 Cor 3
Yr 2 Sept 20	Jer 36:21–32	Ps 72:12–20	Ps 139:1–12	2 Cor 4
Yr 2 Sept 21	Jer 37:1–10	Ps 73:1–16	Ps 139:13–24	2 Cor 5:1–6:2
Yr 2 Sept 22	Jer 37:11–21	Ps 73:17–28	Ps 140	2 Cor 6:3–7:4
Yr 2 Sept 23	Jer 38:1–13	Ps 74:1–8	Ps 141	2 Cor 7:5–8:15
Yr 2 Sept 24	Jer 38:14–28	Ps 74:9–23	Ps 142	2 Cor 8:16–9:15
Yr 2 Sept 25	Jer 39	Ps 75	Ps 143	2 Cor 10
Yr 2 Sept 26	Jer 40	Ps 76	Ps 144	2 Cor 11
Yr 2 Sept 27	Jer 41	Ps 77	Ps 145:1–13	2 Cor 12
Yr 2 Sept 28	Jer 42:1–17	Ps 78:1–16	Ps 145:14–21	2 Cor 13
Yr 2 Sept 29	Jer 42:18–22	Ps 78:17–31	Ps 146	Gal 1
Yr 2 Sept 30	Jer 43	Ps 78:32–39	Ps 147	Gal 2
Yr 2 Oct 1	Jer 44:1–14	Ps 78:40–55	Ps 148	Gal 3:1–14
Yr 2 Oct 2	Jer 44:15–30	Ps 78:56–64	Ps 149; 150	Gal 3:15–29
Yr 2 Oct 3	Ex 36:1–7	Ps 78:65–72	Ps 1; 2	Gal 4
Yr 2 Oct 4	Ex 36:8–19	Ps 79	Ps 3; 4	Gal 5
Yr 2 Oct 5	Ex 36:20–38	Ps 80	Ps 5	Gal 6
Yr 2 Oct 6	Ex 37:1–9	Ps 81	Ps 6	Eph 1
Yr 2 Oct 7	Ex 37:10–24	Ps 82	Ps 7	Eph 2
Yr 2 Oct 8	Ex 37:25–29	Ps 83	Ps 8	Eph 3
Yr 2 Oct 9	Ex 38:1–8	Ps 84	Ps 9:1–10	Eph 4:1–16
Yr 2 Oct 10	Ex 38:9–20	Ps 85	Ps 9:11–20	Eph 4:17–5:14
Yr 2 Oct 11	Ex 38:21–31	Ps 86	Ps 10	Eph 5:15–33
Yr 2 Oct 12	Ex 39:1–21	Ps 87	Ps 11; 12	Eph 6
Yr 2 Oct 13	Ex 39:22–43	Ps 88	Ps 13; 14	Phil 1:1–19
Yr 2 Oct 14	Ex 40:1–15	Ps 89:1–14	Ps 15; 16	Phil 1:20–2:11
Yr 2 Oct 15	Ex 40:16–33	Ps 89:15–37	Ps 17	Phil 2:12–30

Yr 2	Oct 16	Ex 40:34–38	Ps 89:38–52	Ps 18:1–15	Phil 3
Yr 2	Oct 17	Lev 1	Ps 90	Ps 18:16–29	Phil 4
Yr 2	Oct 18	Lev 2	Ps 91	Ps 18:30–45	Col 1:1–23
Yr 2	Oct 19	Lev 3	Ps 92	Ps 18:46–50	Col 1:24–2:23
Yr 2	Oct 20	Lev 4:1–12	Ps 93	Ps 19	Col 3
Yr 2	Oct 21	Lev 4:13–26	Ps 94	Ps 20	Col 4
Yr 2	Oct 22	Lev 4:27–35	Ps 95	Ps 21	1 Thes 1
Yr 2	Oct 23	Lev 5:1–13	Ps 96	Ps 22:1–24	1 Thes 2
Yr 2	Oct 24	Lev 5:14–19	Ps 97	Ps 22:25–31	1 Thes 3; 4
Yr 2	Oct 25	Lev 6:1–13	Ps 98	Ps 23; 24	1 Thes 5
Yr 2	Oct 26	Lev 6:14–30	Ps 99	Ps 25	2 Thes 1
Yr 2	Oct 27	Lev 7:1–21	Ps 100; 101	Ps 26	2 Thes 2
Yr 2	Oct 28	Lev 7:22–38	Ps 102:1–17	Ps 27	2 Thes 3
Yr 2	Oct 29	1 Kgs 7:1–12	Ps 102:18–28	Ps 28	1 Tim 1
Yr 2	Oct 30	1 Kgs 7:13–22	Ps 103	Ps 29	1 Tim 2; 3
Yr 2	Oct 31	1 Kgs 7:23–37	Ps 104:1–18	Ps 30	1 Tim 4
Yr 2	Nov 1	1 Kgs 7:38–51	Ps 104:19–35	Ps 31:1–8	1 Tim 5:1–6:2
Yr 2	Nov 2	1 Kgs 8:1–11	Ps 105:1–15	Ps 31:9–24	1 Tim 6:3–21
Yr 2	Nov 3	1 Kgs 8:12–21	Ps 105:16–25	Ps 32	2 Tim 1
Yr 2	Nov 4	1 Kgs 8:22–40	Ps 105:26–45	Ps 33	2 Tim 2
Yr 2	Nov 5	1 Kgs 8:41–53	Ps 106:1–11	Ps 34	2 Tim 3
Yr 2	Nov 6	1 Kgs 8:54–66	Ps 106:12–27	Ps 35:1–10	2 Tim 4
Yr 2	Nov 7	1 Kgs 9:1–14	Ps 106:28–39	Ps 35:11–28	Titus 1; 2
Yr 2	Nov 8	1 Kgs 9:15–28	Ps 106:40–48	Ps 36	Titus 3
Yr 2	Nov 9	1 Kgs 10:1–13	Ps 107:1–16	Ps 37:1–7	Philemon
Yr 2	Nov 10	1 Kgs 10:14–29	Ps 107:17–32	Ps 37:8–19	Heb 1
Yr 2	Nov 11	1 Kgs 11:1–13	Ps 107:33–43	Ps 37:20–33	Heb 2
Yr 2	Nov 12	1 Kgs 11:14–25	Ps 108	Ps 37:34–40	Heb 3; 4
Yr 2	Nov 13	1 Kgs 11:26–43	Ps 109:1–19	Ps 38	Heb 5:1–6:12
Yr 2	Nov 14	1 Kgs 12:1–20	Ps 109:20–31	Ps 39	Heb 6:13–7:14
Yr 2	Nov 15	1 Kgs 12:21–24	Ps 110	Ps 40	Heb 7:15–28
Yr 2	Nov 16	1 Kgs 12:25–33	Ps 111	Ps 41	Heb 8:1–9:10
Yr 2	Nov 17	1 Kgs 13:1–10	Ps 112	Ps 42	Heb 9:11–10:10
Yr 2	Nov 18	1 Kgs 13:11–34	Ps 113; 114	Ps 43	Heb 10:11–39
Yr 2	Nov 19	1 Kgs 14:1–20	Ps 115	Ps 44	Heb 11:1–12
Yr 2	Nov 20	1 Kgs 14:21–31	Ps 116; 117	Ps 45	Heb 11:13–40
Yr 2	Nov 21	1 Kgs 15:1–8	Ps 118:1–18	Ps 46	Heb 12:1–13
Yr 2	Nov 22	1 Kgs 15:9–24	Ps 118:19–29	Ps 47	Heb 12:14–29
Yr 2	Nov 23	1 Kgs 15:25–34	Ps 119:1–16	Ps 48	Heb 13
Yr 2	Nov 24	1 Kgs 16:1–14	Ps 119:17–32	Ps 49	Jas 1
Yr 2	Nov 25	1 Kgs 16:15–28	Ps 119:33–40	Ps 50:1–6	Jas 2
Yr 2	Nov 26	1 Kgs 16:29–34	Ps 119:41–48	Ps 50:7–23	Jas 3
Yr 2	Nov 27	1 Kgs 17:1–7	Ps 119:49–56	Ps 51	Jas 4
Yr 2	Nov 28	1 Kgs 17:8–24	Ps 119:65–80	Ps 52	Jas 5
Yr 2	Nov 29	Prov 1:1–19	Ps 119:81–96	Ps 53; 54	1 Pet 1
Yr 2	Nov 30	Prov 1:20–33	Ps 119:97–104	Ps 55	1 Pet 2
Yr 2	Dec 1	Prov 2:1–11	Ps 119:105–112	Ps 56	1 Pet 3
Yr 2	Dec 2	Prov 2:12–22	Ps 119:113–128	Ps 57	1 Pet 4
Yr 2	Dec 3	Prov 3:1–20	Ps 119:129–144	Ps 58	1 Pet 5
Yr 2	Dec 4	Prov 3:21–35	Ps 119:145–152	Ps 59	2 Pet 1
Yr 2	Dec 5	Prov 4:1–9	Ps 119:153–160	Ps 60	2 Pet 2

Yr 2	Dec 6	Prov 4:10–27	Ps 119:161–176	Ps 61	2 Pet 3
Yr 2	Dec 7	Prov 5:1–14	Ps 120; 121	Ps 62; 1	1 Jn 1; 2:1–2:27
Yr 2	Dec 8	Prov 5:15–23	Ps 122; 123; 124	Ps 63; 1	1 Jn 2:28–3:24
Yr 2	Dec 9	Jer 45; 46:1–12	Ps 125; 126; 127	Ps 64; 1	1 Jn 4
Yr 2	Dec 10	Jer 46:13–28	Ps 128; 129	Ps 65; 1	1 Jn 5
Yr 2	Dec 11	Jer 47	Ps 130; 131	Ps 66; 2	2 Jn
Yr 2	Dec 12	Jer 48:1–17	Ps 132	Ps 67; 3	3 Jn
Yr 2	Dec 13	Jer 48:18–33	Ps 133; 134	Ps 68:1–19	Jude
Yr 2	Dec 14	Jer 48:34–47	Ps 135	Ps 68:20–35	Rev 1:1–2:11
Yr 2	Dec 15	Jer 49:1–22	Ps 136:1–16	Ps 69:1–18	Rev 2:12–3:6
Yr 2	Dec 16	Jer 49:23–33	Ps 136:17–26	Ps 69:19–36	Rev 3:7–22
Yr 2	Dec 17	Jer 49:34–50:3	Ps 137	Ps 70	Rev 4; 5
Yr 2	Dec 18	Jer 50:4–20	Ps 138	Ps 71:1–16	Rev 6
Yr 2	Dec 19	Jer 50:21–34	Ps 139:1–12	Ps 71:17–24	Rev 7
Yr 2	Dec 20	Jer 50:35–46	Ps 139:13–24	Ps 72:1–11	Rev 8:1–9:12
Yr 2	Dec 21	Jer 51:1–14	Ps 140	Ps 72:12–20	Rev 9:13–10:11
Yr 2	Dec 22	Jer 51:15–35	Ps 141	Ps 73:1–16	Rev 11; 12
Yr 2	Dec 23	Jer 51:36–44	Ps 142	Ps 73:17–28	Rev 13
Yr 2	Dec 24	Jer 51:45–64	Ps 143	Ps 74:1–8	Rev 14
Yr 2	Dec 25	Jer 52:1–11	Ps 144	Ps 74:9–23	Rev 15; 16
Yr 2	Dec 26	Jer 52:12–34	Ps 145:1–13	Ps 75	Rev 17
Yr 2	Dec 27	Lam 1:1–5	Ps 145:14–21	Ps 76	Rev 18
Yr 2	Dec 28	Lam 1:6–22	Ps 146	Ps 77	Rev 19
Yr 2	Dec 29	Lam 2:1–12	Ps 147	Ps 78:1–16	Rev 20
Yr 2	Dec 30	Lam 2:13–22	Ps 148	Ps 78:17–31	Rev 21
Yr 2	Dec 31	Lev 8:1–13	Ps 149; 150	Ps 78:32–39	Rev 22

Year 3

2018, 2022, 2026, 2030, 2034, 2038, 2042, 2046, 2050, 2054, 2058,
2062, 2066, 2070

Yr 3 Jan 1	Lev 8:14–36	Ps 1; 2	Ps 78:40–55	Matt 1
Yr 3 Jan 2	Lev 9	Ps 3; 4	Ps 78:56–64	Matt 2
Yr 3 Jan 3	Lev 10:1–7	Ps 5	Ps 78:65–72	Matt 3
Yr 3 Jan 4	Lev 10:8–20	Ps 6	Ps 79	Matt 4
Yr 3 Jan 5	Lev 11:1–12	Ps 7	Ps 80	Matt 5:1–20
Yr 3 Jan 6	Lev 11:13–23	Ps 8	Ps 81	Matt 5:21–37
Yr 3 Jan 7	Lev 11:24–38	Ps 9:1–10	Ps 82	Matt 5:38–6:4
Yr 3 Jan 8	Lev 11:39–47	Ps 9:11–20	Ps 83	Matt 6:5–34
Yr 3 Jan 9	Lev 12	Ps 10	Ps 84	Matt 7
Yr 3 Jan 10	Lev 13:1–23	Ps 11; 12	Ps 85	Matt 8:1–22
Yr 3 Jan 11	Lev 13:24–37	Ps 13; 14	Ps 86	Matt 8:23–34
Yr 3 Jan 12	Lev 13:38–46	Ps 15; 16	Ps 87	Matt 9:1–17
Yr 3 Jan 13	Lev 13:47–59	Ps 17	Ps 88	Matt 9:18–38
Yr 3 Jan 14	Lev 14:1–20	Ps 18:1–15	Ps 89:1–14	Matt 10:1–23
Yr 3 Jan 15	Lev 14:21–32	Ps 18:16–29	Ps 89:15–37	Matt 10:24–42
Yr 3 Jan 16	Lev 14:33–57	Ps 18:30–45	Ps 89:38–52	Matt 11
Yr 3 Jan 17	Lev 15:1–18	Ps 18:46–50	Ps 90	Matt 12:1–21
Yr 3 Jan 18	Lev 15:19–33	Ps 19	Ps 91	Matt 12:22–50
Yr 3 Jan 19	Lev 16:1–19	Ps 20	Ps 92	Matt 13:1–23
Yr 3 Jan 20	Lev 16:20–34	Ps 21	Ps 93	Matt 13:24–43
Yr 3 Jan 21	Lev 17	Ps 22:1–24	Ps 94	Matt 13:44–58
Yr 3 Jan 22	Lev 18:1–17	Ps 22:25–31	Ps 95	Matt 14
Yr 3 Jan 23	Lev 24:18–30	Ps 23; 24	Ps 96	Matt 15:1–20
Yr 3 Jan 24	Lev 19:1–10	Ps 25	Ps 97	Matt 15:21–39
Yr 3 Jan 25	Lev 19:11–22	Ps 26	Ps 98	Matt 16
Yr 3 Jan 26	Lev 19:23–37	Ps 27	Ps 99	Matt 17
Yr 3 Jan 27	1 Kgs 18:1–19	Ps 28	Ps 100; 101	Matt 18:1–20
Yr 3 Jan 28	1 Kgs 18:20–40	Ps 29	Ps 102:1–17	Matt 18:21–35
Yr 3 Jan 29	1 Kgs 18:41–46	Ps 30	Ps 102:18–28	Matt 19:1–15
Yr 3 Jan 30	1 Kgs 19:1–9a	Ps 31:1–8	Ps 103	Matt 19:16–30
Yr 3 Jan 31	1 Kgs 19:9b–21	Ps 31:9–24	Ps 104:1–18	Matt 20:1–16
Yr 3 Feb 1	1 Kgs 20:1–12	Ps 32	Ps 104:19–35	Matt 20:17–34
Yr 3 Feb 2	1 Kgs 20:13–22	Ps 33	Ps 105:1–15	Matt 21:1–22

Yr 3	Feb 3	1 Kgs 20:23–34	Ps 34	Ps 105:16–25	Matt 21:23–46
Yr 3	Feb 4	1 Kgs 20:35–43	Ps 35:1–10	Ps 105:26–45	Matt 22:1–33
Yr 3	Feb 5	1 Kgs 21:1–29	Ps 35:11–28	Ps 106:1–11	Matt 22:34–46
Yr 3	Feb 6	1 Kgs 22:1–9	Ps 36	Ps 106:12–27	Matt 23:1–24
Yr 3	Feb 7	1 Kgs 22:10–28	Ps 37:1–7	Ps 106:28–39	Matt 23:25–39
Yr 3	Feb 8	1 Kgs 22:29–40	Ps 37:8–19	Ps 106:40–48	Matt 24:1–31
Yr 3	Feb 9	1 Kgs 22:41–53	Ps 37:20–33	Ps 107:1–16	Matt 24:32–25:13
Yr 3	Feb 10	2 Kgs 1:1–18	Ps 37:34–40	Ps 107:17–32	Matt 25:14–30
Yr 3	Feb 11	2 Kgs 2:1–18	Ps 38	Ps 107:33–43	Matt 25:31–46
Yr 3	Feb 12	2 Kgs 2:19–25	Ps 39	Ps 108	Matt 26:1–16
Yr 3	Feb 13	2 Kgs 3	Ps 40	Ps 109:1–19	Matt 26:17–46
Yr 3	Feb 14	2 Kgs 4:1–7	Ps 41	Ps 109:20–31	Matt 26:47–75
Yr 3	Feb 15	2 Kgs 4:8–17	Ps 42	Ps 110	Matt 27:1–26
Yr 3	Feb 16	2 Kgs 4:18–37	Ps 43	Ps 111	Matt 27:27–56
Yr 3	Feb 17	2 Kgs 4:38–44	Ps 44	Ps 112	Matt 27:57–66;28
Yr 3	Feb 18	2 Kgs 5:1–19	Ps 45	Ps 113; 114	Mk 1:1–20
Yr 3	Feb 19	2 Kgs 5:20–27	Ps 46	Ps 115	Mk 1:21–45
Yr 3	Feb 20	2 Kgs 6:1–7	Ps 47	Ps 116; 117	Mk 2:1–17
Yr 3	Feb 21	2 Kgs 6:8–23	Ps 48	Ps 118:1–18	Mk 2:18–28
Yr 3	Feb 22	2 Kgs 6:24–7:2	Ps 49	Ps 118:19–29	Mk 3:1–19
Yr 3	Feb 23	2 Kgs 7:3–20	Ps 50:1–6	Ps 119:1–16	Mk 3:20–35
Yr 3	Feb 24	2 Kgs 8:1–15	Ps 50:7–23	Ps 119:17–32	Mk 4:1–20
Yr 3	Feb 25	2 Kgs 8:16–29	Ps 51	Ps 119:33–40	Mk 4:21–41
Yr 3	Feb 26	Prov 6:1–15	Ps 52	Ps 119:41–48	Mk 5:1–20
Yr 3	Feb 27	Prov 6:16–35	Ps 53; 54	Ps 119:49–56	Mk 5:21–43
Yr 3	Feb 28	Prov 7:1–5	Ps 55	Ps 119:65–80	Mk 6:1–29
Yr 3	Mar 1	Prov 7:6–27	Ps 56	Ps 119:81–96	Mk 6:30–56
Yr 3	Mar 2	Prov 8:1–11	Ps 57	Ps 119:97–104	Mk 7:1–23
Yr 3	Mar 3	Prov 8:12–21	Ps 58	Ps 119:105–112	Mk 7:24–37
Yr 3	Mar 4	Prov 8:22–36	Ps 59	Ps 119:113–128	Mk 8:1–26
Yr 3	Mar 5	Prov 9	Ps 60	Ps 119:129–144	Mk 8:27–9:1
Yr 3	Mar 6	Prov 10:1–14	Ps 61	Ps 119:145–152	Mk 9:2–29
Yr 3	Mar 7	Prov 10:15–32	Ps 62	Ps 119:153–160	Mk 9:30–50
Yr 3	Mar 8	Prov 11:1–13	Ps 63	Ps 119:161–176	Mk 10:1–16
Yr 3	Mar 9	Prov 11:14–31	Ps 64	Ps 120; 121	Mk 10:17–34
Yr 3	Mar 10	Lam 3:1–12	Ps 65	Ps 122; 123; 124	Mk 10:35–52
Yr 3	Mar 11	Lam 3:13–30	Ps 66	Ps 125; 126; 127	Mk 11
Yr 3	Mar 12	Lam 3:31–42	Ps 67	Ps 128; 129	Mk 12:1–27
Yr 3	Mar 13	Lam 3:43–66	Ps 68:1–19	Ps 130; 131	Mk 12:28–44
Yr 3	Mar 14	Lam 4:1–5	Ps 68:20–35	Ps 132	Mk 13:1–25
Yr 3	Mar 15	Lam 4:6–22	Ps 69:1–18	Ps 133; 134	Mk 13:26–37
Yr 3	Mar 16	Lam 5:1–7	Ps 69:19–36	Ps 135	Mk 14:1–26
Yr 3	Mar 17	Lam 5:8–22	Ps 70	Ps 136:1–16	Mk 14:27–52
Yr 3	Mar 18	Ez 1:1–14	Ps 71:1–16	Ps 136:17–26	Mk 14:53–72
Yr 3	Mar 19	Ez 1:15–28	Ps 71:17–24	Ps 137	Mk 15:1–20
Yr 3	Mar 20	Ez 2	Ps 72:1–11	Ps 138	Mk 15:21–47
Yr 3	Mar 21	Ez 3	Ps 72:12–20	Ps 139:1–12	Mk 16:1–20*
Yr 3	Mar 22	Ez 4:1–8	Ps 73:1–16	Ps 139:13–24	Lk 1:1–25
Yr 3	Mar 23	Ez 4:9–17	Ps 73:17–28	Ps 140	Lk 1:26–45
Yr 3	Mar 24	Ez 5	Ps 74:1–8	Ps 141	Lk 1:46–66
Yr 3	Mar 25	Ez 6	Ps 74:9–23	Ps 142	Lk 1:67–80

Yr 3	Mar 26	Ez 7:1–13	Ps 75	Ps 143	Lk 2:1–20
Yr 3	Mar 27	Ez 7:14–27	Ps 76	Ps 144	Lk 2:21–52
Yr 3	Mar 28	Ez 8	Ps 77	Ps 145:1–13	Lk 3:1–20
Yr 3	Mar 29	Ez 9	Ps 78:1–16	Ps 145:14–21	Lk 3:21–38
Yr 3	Mar 30	Ez 10	Ps 78:17–31	Ps 146	Lk 4:1–30
Yr 3	Mar 31	Ez 11:1–13	Ps 78:32–39	Ps 147	Lk 4:31–44
Yr 3	Apr 1	Ez 11:14–25	Ps 78:40–55	Ps 148	Lk 5:1–26
Yr 3	Apr 2	Ez 12:1–20	Ps 78:56–64	Ps 149	Lk 5:27–39
Yr 3	Apr 3	Ez 12:21–28	Ps 78:65–72	Ps 150	Lk 6:1–26
Yr 3	Apr 4	Lev 20:1–8	Ps 79	Ps 1; 2	Lk 6:27–49
Yr 3	Apr 5	Lev 20:9–21	Ps 80	Ps 3; 4	Lk 7:1–27
Yr 3	Apr 6	Lev 20:22–27	Ps 81	Ps 5	Lk 7:28–50
Yr 3	Apr 7	Lev 21	Ps 82	Ps 6	Lk 8:1–15
Yr 3	Apr 8	Lev 22:1–16	Ps 83	Ps 7	Lk 8:16–39
Yr 3	Apr 9	Lev 22:17–33	Ps 84	Ps 8	Lk 8:40–56
Yr 3	Apr 10	Lev 23:1–8	Ps 85	Ps 9:1–10	Lk 9:1–27
Yr 3	Apr 11	Lev 23:9–14	Ps 86	Ps 9:11–20	Lk 9:28–48
Yr 3	Apr 12	Lev 23:15–22	Ps 87	Ps 10	Lk 9:49–62
Yr 3	Apr 13	Lev 23:23–32	Ps 88	Ps 11; 12	Lk 10:1–29
Yr 3	Apr 14	Lev 23:33–44	Ps 89:1–14	Ps 13; 14	Lk 10:30–42
Yr 3	Apr 15	Lev 24:1–9	Ps 89:15–37	Ps 15; 16	Lk 11:1–28
Yr 3	Apr 16	Lev 24:10–23	Ps 89:38–52	Ps 17	Lk 11:29–54
Yr 3	Apr 17	Lev 25:1–22	Ps 90	Ps 18:1–15	Lk 12:1–21
Yr 3	Apr 18	Lev 25:23–34	Ps 91	Ps 18:16–29	Lk 12:22–48
Yr 3	Apr 19	Lev 25:35–55	Ps 92	Ps 18:30–45	Lk 12:49–59
Yr 3	Apr 20	Lev 26:1–13	Ps 93	Ps 18:46–50	Lk 13:1–21
Yr 3	Apr 21	Lev 26:14–39	Ps 94	Ps 19	Lk 13:22–35
Yr 3	Apr 22	Lev 26:40–46	Ps 95	Ps 20	Lk 14
Yr 3	Apr 23	Lev 27:1–13	Ps 96	Ps 21	Lk 15:1–10
Yr 3	Apr 24	Lev 27:14–34	Ps 97	Ps 22:1–24	Lk 15:11–32
Yr 3	Apr 25	Num 1:1–15	Ps 98	Ps 22:25–31	Lk 16
Yr 3	Apr 26	Num 1:16–43	Ps 99	Ps 23; 24	Lk 17
Yr 3	Apr 27	Num 1:44–54	Ps 100; 101	Ps 25	Lk 18:1–17
Yr 3	Apr 28	2 Kgs 9:1–13	Ps 102:1–17	Ps 26	Lk 18:18–43
Yr 3	Apr 29	2 Kgs 9:14–29	Ps 102:18–28	Ps 27	Lk 19:1–10
Yr 3	Apr 30	2 Kgs 9:30–37	Ps 103	Ps 28	Lk 19:11–27
Yr 3	May 1	2 Kgs 10:1–17	Ps 104:1–18	Ps 29	Lk 19:28–48
Yr 3	May 2	2 Kgs 10:18–36	Ps 104:19–35	Ps 30	Lk 20:1–19
Yr 3	May 3	2 Kgs 11	Ps 105:1–15	Ps 31:1–8	Lk 20:20–47
Yr 3	May 4	2 Kgs 12	Ps 105:16–25	Ps 31:9–24	Lk 21:1–11
Yr 3	May 5	2 Kgs 13	Ps 105:26–45	Ps 32	Lk 21:12–38
Yr 3	May 6	2 Kgs 14:1–22	Ps 106:1–11	Ps 33	Lk 22:1–13
Yr 3	May 7	2 Kgs 14:23–29	Ps 106:12–27	Ps 34	Lk 22:14–38
Yr 3	May 8	2 Kgs 15:1–12	Ps 106:28–39	Ps 35:1–10	Lk 22:39–71
Yr 3	May 9	2 Kgs 15:13–26	Ps 106:40–48	Ps 35:11–28	Lk 23:1–25
Yr 3	May 10	2 Kgs 15:27–38	Ps 107:1–16	Ps 36	Lk 23:26–43
Yr 3	May 11	2 Kgs 16	Ps 107:17–32	Ps 37:1–7	Lk 23:44–56
Yr 3	May 12	2 Kgs 17:1–23	Ps 107:33–43	Ps 37:8–19	Lk 24:1–34
Yr 3	May 13	2 Kgs 17:24–41	Ps 108	Ps 37:20–33	Lk 24:35–53
Yr 3	May 14	2 Kgs 18:1–12	Ps 109:1–19	Ps 37:34–40	Jn 1:1–28
Yr 3	May 15	2 Kgs 18:13–17	Ps 109:20–31	Ps 38	Jn 1:29–51

553

Yr 3	May 16	2 Kgs 18:19–37	Ps 110	Ps 39	Jn 2:1–12
Yr 3	May 17	2 Kgs 19:1–19	Ps 111	Ps 40	Jn 2:13–25
Yr 3	May 18	2 Kgs 19:20–37	Ps 112	Ps 41	Jn 3:1–21
Yr 3	May 19	2 Kgs 20:1–11	Ps 113; 114	Ps 42	Jn 3:22–36
Yr 3	May 20	2 Kgs 20:12–21	Ps 115	Ps 43	Jn 4:1–38
Yr 3	May 21	2 Kgs 21:1–18	Ps 116; 117	Ps 44	Jn 4:39–5:15
Yr 3	May 22	2 Kgs 21:19–26	Ps 118:1–18	Ps 45	Jn 5:16–47
Yr 3	May 23	2 Kgs 22:1–7	Ps 118:19–29	Ps 46	Jn 6:1–21
Yr 3	May 24	2 Kgs 22:8–20	Ps 119:1–16	Ps 47	Jn 6:22–59
Yr 3	May 25	2 Kgs 23:1–20	Ps 119:17–32	Ps 48	Jn 6:60–7:9
Yr 3	May 26	2 Kgs 23:21–30	Ps 119:33–40	Ps 49	Jn 7:10–36
Yr 3	May 27	2 Kgs 23:31–37	Ps 119:41–48	Ps 50:1–6	Jn 7:37–52
Yr 3	May 28	2 Kgs 24	Ps 119:49–56	Ps 50:7–23	Jn 7:53–8:11
Yr 3	May 29	Prov 12:1–12	Ps 119:65–80	Ps 51	Jn 8:12–30
Yr 3	May 30	Prov 12:13–28	Ps 119:81–96	Ps 52	Jn 8:31–59
Yr 3	May 31	Prov 13:1–9	Ps 119:97–104	Ps 53; 54	Jn 9:1–34
Yr 3	June 1	Prov 13:10–25	Ps 119:105–112	Ps 55	Jn 9:35–41
Yr 3	June 2	Prov 14:1–12	Ps 119:113–128	Ps 56	Jn 10:1–21
Yr 3	June 3	Prov 14:13–22	Ps 119:129–144	Ps 57	Jn 10:22–42
Yr 3	June 4	Prov 14:23–35	Ps 119:145–152	Ps 58	Jn 11:1–29
Yr 3	June 5	Prov 15:1–16	Ps 119:153–160	Ps 59	Jn 11:30–57
Yr 3	June 6	Prov 15:16–33	Ps 119:161–176	Ps 60	Jn 12:1–19
Yr 3	June 7	Prov 16:1–15	Ps 120; 121	Ps 61	Jn 12:20–36
Yr 3	June 8	Prov 16:16–33	Ps 122; 123; 124	Ps 62	Jn 12:37–50
Yr 3	June 9	Ez 13:1–16	Ps 125; 126; 127	Ps 63	Jn 13:1–20
Yr 3	June 10	Ez 13:17–23	Ps 128; 129	Ps 64	Jn 13:21–38
Yr 3	June 11	Ez 14	Ps 130; 131	Ps 65	Jn 14
Yr 3	June 12	Ez 15; 16:1–8	Ps 132	Ps 66	Jn 15
Yr 3	June 13	Ez 16:9–19	Ps 133; 134	Ps 67	Jn 16:1–15
Yr 3	June 14	Ez 16:20–34	Ps 135	Ps 68:1–19	Jn 16:16–33
Yr 3	June 15	Ez 16:35–45	Ps 136:1–16	Ps 68:20–35	Jn 17
Yr 3	June 16	Ez 16:46–63	Ps 136:17–26	Ps 69:1–18	Jn 18:1–24
Yr 3	June 17	Ez 17:1–10	Ps 137	Ps 69:19–36	Jn 18:25–40
Yr 3	June 18	Ez 17:11–24	Ps 138	Ps 70	Jn 19:1–27
Yr 3	June 19	Ez 18:1–13	Ps 139:1–12	Ps 71:1–16	Jn 19:28–42
Yr 3	June 20	Ez 18:14–32	Ps 139:13–24	Ps 71:17–24	Jn 20:1–18
Yr 3	June 21	Ez 19	Ps 140	Ps 72:1–11	Jn 20:19–31
Yr 3	June 22	Ez 20:1–12	Ps 141	Ps 72:12–20	Jn 21
Yr 3	June 23	Ez 20:13–26	Ps 142	Ps 73:1–16	Acts 1
Yr 3	June 24	Ez 20:27–44	Ps 143	Ps 73:17–28	Acts 2:1–21
Yr 3	June 25	Ez 20:45–21:1–7	Ps 144	Ps 74:1–8	Acts 2:22–47
Yr 3	June 26	Ez 21:8–17	Ps 145:1–13	Ps 74:9–23	Acts 3:1–11
Yr 3	June 27	Ez 21:18–32	Ps 145:14–21	Ps 75	Acts 3:12–26
Yr 3	June 28	Ez 22:1–16	Ps 146	Ps 76	Acts 4:1–22
Yr 3	June 29	Ez 22:17–31	Ps 147	Ps 77	Acts 4:23–37
Yr 3	June 30	Ez 23:1–10	Ps 148	Ps 78:1–16	Acts 5:1–16
Yr 3	July 1	Ez 23:11–27	Ps 149	Ps 78:17–31	Acts 5:17–42
Yr 3	July 2	Ez 23:28–35	Ps 150	Ps 78:32–39	Acts 6; 7:1–10
Yr 3	July 3	Ez 23:36–49	Ps 1; 2	Ps 78:40–55	Acts 7:11–60
Yr 3	July 4	Num 2:1–9	Ps 3; 4	Ps 78:56–64	Acts 8:1–25
Yr 3	July 5	Num 2:10–24	Ps 5	Ps 78:65–72	Acts 8:26–40

Yr 3	July 6	Num 2:25–34	Ps 6	Ps 79	Acts 9:1–19
Yr 3	July 7	Num 3:1–13	Ps 7	Ps 80	Acts 9:20–43
Yr 3	July 8	Num 3:14–26	Ps 8	Ps 81	Acts 10:1–33
Yr 3	July 9	Num 3:27–39	Ps 9:1–10	Ps 82	Acts 10:34–48
Yr 3	July 10	Num 3:40–51	Ps 9:11–20	Ps 83	Acts 11:1–18
Yr 3	July 11	Num 4:1–20	Ps 10	Ps 84	Acts 11:19–30
Yr 3	July 12	Num 4:21–33	Ps 11; 12	Ps 85	Acts 12
Yr 3	July 13	Num 4:34–49	Ps 13; 14	Ps 86	Acts 13:1–12
Yr 3	July 14	Num 5:1–10	Ps 15; 16	Ps 87	Acts 13:13–43
Yr 3	July 15	Num 5:11–31	Ps 17	Ps 88	Acts 13:44–14:7
Yr 3	July 16	Num 6:1–21	Ps 18:1–15	Ps 89:1–14	Acts 14:8–28
Yr 3	July 17	Num 6:22–27	Ps 18:16–29	Ps 89:15–37	Acts 15
Yr 3	July 18	Num 7:1–11	Ps 18:30–45	Ps 89:38–52	Acts 16:1–21
Yr 3	July 19	Num 7:12–23	Ps 18:46–50	Ps 90	Acts 16:22–40
Yr 3	July 20	Num 7:24–35	Ps 19	Ps 91	Acts 17
Yr 3	July 21	Num 7:36–47	Ps 20	Ps 92	Acts 18:1–23
Yr 3	July 22	Num 7:48–59	Ps 21	Ps 93	Acts 18:24–19:7
Yr 3	July 23	Num 7:60–71	Ps 22:1–24	Ps 94	Acts 19:8–22
Yr 3	July 24	Num 7:72–83	Ps 22:25–31	Ps 95	Acts 19:23–41
Yr 3	July 25	Num 7:84–89	Ps 23; 24	Ps 96	Acts 20
Yr 3	July 26	Num 8	Ps 25	Ps 97	Acts 21:1–25
Yr 3	July 27	Num 9:1–14	Ps 26	Ps 98	Acts 21:26–40
Yr 3	July 28	Num 9:15–23	Ps 27	Ps 99	Acts 22:1–23
Yr 3	July 29	Num 10:1–10	Ps 28	Ps 100; 101	Acts 22:24–23:11
Yr 3	July 30	Num 10:11–36	Ps 29	Ps 102:1–17	Acts 23:12–35
Yr 3	July 31	2 Kgs 25:1–21	Ps 30	Ps 102:18–28	Acts 24
Yr 3	Aug 1	2 Kgs 25:22–30	Ps 31:1–8	Ps 103	Acts 25:1–12
Yr 3	Aug 2	1 Chr 1:1–16	Ps 31:9–24	Ps 104:1–18	Acts 25:13–27
Yr 3	Aug 3	1 Chr 1:17–27	Ps 32	Ps 104:19–35	Acts 26
Yr 3	Aug 4	1 Chr 1:28–42	Ps 33	Ps 105:1–15	Acts 27:1–26
Yr 3	Aug 5	1 Chr 1:43–54	Ps 34	Ps 105:16–25	Acts 27:27–44
Yr 3	Aug 6	1 Chr 2:1–17	Ps 35:1–10	Ps 105:26–45	Acts 28:1–16
Yr 3	Aug 7	1 Chr 2:18–24	Ps 35:11–28	Ps 106:1–11	Acts 28:17–31
Yr 3	Aug 8	1 Chr 2:25–41	Ps 36	Ps 106:12–27	Rom 1:1–17
Yr 3	Aug 9	1 Chr 2:42–55	Ps 37:1–7	Ps 106:28–39	Rom 1:18–32
Yr 3	Aug 10	1 Chr 3:1–9	Ps 37:8–19	Ps 106:40–48	Rom 2
Yr 3	Aug 11	1 Chr 3:10–24	Ps 37:20–33	Ps 107:1–16	Rom 3:1–8
Yr 3	Aug 12	1 Chr 4:1–20	Ps 37:34–40	Ps 107:17–32	Rom 3:9–31
Yr 3	Aug 13	1 Chr 4:21–37	Ps 38	Ps 107:33–43	Rom 4
Yr 3	Aug 14	1 Chr 4:38–43	Ps 39	Ps 108	Rom 5
Yr 3	Aug 15	1 Chr 5:1–10	Ps 40	Ps 109:1–19	Rom 6
Yr 3	Aug 16	1 Chr 5:11–26	Ps 41	Ps 109:20–31	Rom 7
Yr 3	Aug 17	1 Chr 6:1–15	Ps 42	Ps 110	Rom 8:1–17
Yr 3	Aug 18	1 Chr 6:16–30	Ps 43	Ps 111	Rom 8:18–39
Yr 3	Aug 19	1 Chr 6:31–48	Ps 44	Ps 112	Rom 9:1–24
Yr 3	Aug 20	1 Chr 6:49–65	Ps 45	Ps 113; 114	Rom 9:25–10:4
Yr 3	Aug 21	1 Chr 6:66–81	Ps 46	Ps 115	Rom 10:5–21
Yr 3	Aug 22	1 Chr 7:1–12	Ps 47	Ps 116; 117	Rom 11
Yr 3	Aug 23	1 Chr 7:13–29	Ps 48	Ps 118:1–18	Rom 12
Yr 3	Aug 24	1 Chr 7:30–40	Ps 49	Ps 118:19–29	Rom 13
Yr 3	Aug 25	1 Chr 8:1–28	Ps 50:1–6	Ps 119:1–16	Rom 14

Yr 3	Aug 26	1 Chr 8:29–40	Ps 50:7–23	Ps 119:17–32	Rom 15:1–22
Yr 3	Aug 27	1 Chr 9:1–13	Ps 51	Ps 119:33–40	Rom 15:23–16:16
Yr 3	Aug 28	1 Chr 9:14–34	Ps 52	Ps 119:41–48	Rom 16:17–27
Yr 3	Aug 29	1 Chr 9:35–44	Ps 53; 54	Ps 119:49–56	1 Cor 1
Yr 3	Aug 30	1 Chr 10	Ps 55	Ps 119:65–80	1 Cor 2
Yr 3	Aug 31	Prov 17:1–13	Ps 56	Ps 119:81–96	1 Cor 3
Yr 3	Sept 1	Prov 17:14–28	Ps 57	Ps 119:97–104	1 Cor 4
Yr 3	Sept 2	Prov 18:1–10	Ps 58	Ps 119:105–112	1 Cor 5–6:11
Yr 3	Sept 3	Prov 18:11–24	Ps 59	Ps 119:113–128	1 Cor 6:12–7:11
Yr 3	Sept 4	Prov 19:1–14	Ps 60	Ps 119:129–144	1 Cor 7:12–40
Yr 3	Sept 5	Prov 19:15–29	Ps 61	Ps 119:145–152	1 Cor 8
Yr 3	Sept 6	Prov 20:1–14	Ps 62	Ps 119:153–160	1 Cor 9
Yr 3	Sept 7	Prov 20:15–30	Ps 63	Ps 119:161–176	1 Cor 10
Yr 3	Sept 8	Prov 21:1–15	Ps 64	Ps 120; 121	1 Cor 11:1–16
Yr 3	Sept 9	Prov 21:16–31	Ps 65	Ps 122; 123; 124	1 Cor 11:17–34
Yr 3	Sept 10	Prov 22:1–16	Ps 66	Ps 125; 126; 127	1 Cor 12:1–26
Yr 3	Sept 11	Prov 22:17–29	Ps 67	Ps 128; 129	1 Cor 12:27–31;13
Yr 3	Sept 12	Ez 24:1–14	Ps 68:1–19	Ps 130; 131	1 Cor 14:1–25
Yr 3	Sept 13	Ez 24:15–27	Ps 68:20–35	Ps 132	1 Cor 14:26–40
Yr 3	Sept 14	Ez 25	Ps 69:1–18	Ps 133; 134	1 Cor 15:1–34
Yr 3	Sept 15	Ez 26	Ps 69:19–36	Ps 135	1 Cor 15:35–58
Yr 3	Sept 16	Ez 27:1–9	Ps 70	Ps 136:1–16	1 Cor 16
Yr 3	Sept 17	Ez 27:10–25	Ps 71:1–16	Ps 136:17–26	2 Cor 1
Yr 3	Sept 18	Ez 27:26–36	Ps 71:17–24	Ps 137	2 Cor 2
Yr 3	Sept 19	Ez 28:1–19	Ps 72:1–11	Ps 138	2 Cor 3
Yr 3	Sept 20	Ez 28:20–26	Ps 72:12–20	Ps 139:1–12	2 Cor 4
Yr 3	Sept 21	Ez 29	Ps 73:1–16	Ps 139:13–24	2 Cor 5:1–6:2
Yr 3	Sept 22	Ez 30:1–12	Ps 73:17–28	Ps 140	2 Cor 6:3–7:4
Yr 3	Sept 23	Ez 30:13–26	Ps 74:1–8	Ps 141	2 Cor 7:5–8:15
Yr 3	Sept 24	Ez 31	Ps 74:9–23	Ps 142	2 Cor 8:16–9:15
Yr 3	Sept 25	Ez 32:1–16	Ps 75	Ps 143	2 Cor 10
Yr 3	Sept 26	Ez 32:17–32	Ps 76	Ps 144	2 Cor 11
Yr 3	Sept 27	Ez 33:1–9	Ps 77	Ps 145:1–13	2 Cor 12
Yr 3	Sept 28	Ez 33:10–20	Ps 78:1–16	Ps 145:14–21	2 Cor 13
Yr 3	Sept 29	Ez 33:21–33	Ps 78:17–31	Ps 146	Gal 1
Yr 3	Sept 30	Ez 34:1–10	Ps 78:32–39	Ps 147	Gal 2
Yr 3	Oct 1	Ez 34:11–31	Ps 78:40–55	Ps 148	Gal 3:1–14
Yr 3	Oct 2	Ez 35	Ps 78:56–64	Ps 149; 150	Gal 3:15–29
Yr 3	Oct 3	Ez 36:1–15	Ps 78:65–72	Ps 1; 2	Gal 4
Yr 3	Oct 4	Ez 36:16–27	Ps 79	Ps 3; 4	Gal 5
Yr 3	Oct 5	Ez 36:28–38	Ps 80	Ps 5	Gal 6
Yr 3	Oct 6	Num 11:1–15	Ps 81	Ps 6	Eph 1
Yr 3	Oct 7	Num 11:16–29	Ps 82	Ps 7	Eph 2
Yr 3	Oct 8	Num 11:31–35	Ps 83	Ps 8	Eph 3
Yr 3	Oct 9	Num 12	Ps 84	Ps 9:1–10	Eph 4:1–16
Yr 3	Oct 10	Num 13:1–24	Ps 85	Ps 9:11–20	Eph 4:17–5:14
Yr 3	Oct 11	Num 13:25–33	Ps 86	Ps 10	Eph 5:15–33
Yr 3	Oct 12	Num 14:1–12	Ps 87	Ps 11; 12	Eph 6
Yr 3	Oct 13	Num 14:13–25	Ps 88	Ps 13; 14	Phil 1:1–19
Yr 3	Oct 14	Num 14:26–45	Ps 89:1–14	Ps 15; 16	Phil 1:20–2:11
Yr 3	Oct 15	Num 15:1–16	Ps 89:15–37	Ps 17	Phil 2:12–30

Yr 3	Oct 16	Num 15:17–31	Ps 89:38–52	Ps 18:1–15	Phil 3
Yr 3	Oct 17	Num 15:32–41	Ps 90	Ps 18:16–29	Phil 4
Yr 3	Oct 18	Num 16:1–35	Ps 91	Ps 18:30–45	Col 1:1–23
Yr 3	Oct 19	Num 16:36–50	Ps 92	Ps 18:46–50	Col 1:24–2:23
Yr 3	Oct 20	Num 17	Ps 93	Ps 19	Col 3
Yr 3	Oct 21	Num 18:1–7	Ps 94	Ps 20	Col 4
Yr 3	Oct 22	Num 18:8–13	Ps 95	Ps 21	1 Thes 1
Yr 3	Oct 23	Num 18:14–19	Ps 96	Ps 22:1–24	1 Thes 2
Yr 3	Oct 24	Num 18:20–32	Ps 97	Ps 22:25–31	1 Thes 3; 4
Yr 3	Oct 25	Num 19:1–10	Ps 98	Ps 23; 24	1 Thes 5
Yr 3	Oct 26	Num 19:11–22	Ps 99	Ps 25	2 Thes 1
Yr 3	Oct 27	Num 20:1–13	Ps 100; 101	Ps 26	2 Thes 2
Yr 3	Oct 28	Num 20:14–29	Ps 102:1–17	Ps 27	2 Thes 3
Yr 3	Oct 29	Num 21:1–20	Ps 102:18–28	Ps 28	1 Tim 1
Yr 3	Oct 30	Num 21:21–35	Ps 103	Ps 29	1 Tim 2; 3
Yr 3	Oct 31	1 Chr 11:1–9	Ps 104:1–18	Ps 30	1 Tim 4
Yr 3	Nov 1	1 Chr 11:10–19	Ps 104:19–35	Ps 31:1–8	1 Tim 5:1–6:2
Yr 3	Nov 2	1 Chr 11:20–25	Ps 105:1–15	Ps 31:9–24	1 Tim 6:3–21
Yr 3	Nov 3	1 Chr 11:26–47	Ps 105:16–25	Ps 32	2 Tim 1
Yr 3	Nov 4	1 Chr 12:1–7	Ps 105:26–45	Ps 33	2 Tim 2
Yr 3	Nov 5	1 Chr 12:8–22	Ps 106:1–11	Ps 34	2 Tim 3
Yr 3	Nov 6	1 Chr 12:23–40	Ps 106:12–27	Ps 35:1–10	2 Tim 4
Yr 3	Nov 7	1 Chr 13	Ps 106:28–39	Ps 35:11–28	Titus 1; 2
Yr 3	Nov 8	1 Chr 14	Ps 106:40–48	Ps 36	Titus 3
Yr 3	Nov 9	1 Chr 15:1–24	Ps 107:1–16	Ps 37:1–7	Philemon
Yr 3	Nov 10	1 Chr 15:25–29	Ps 107:17–32	Ps 37:8–19	Heb 1
Yr 3	Nov 11	1 Chr 6:1–6	Ps 107:33–43	Ps 37:20–33	Heb 2
Yr 3	Nov 12	1 Chr 6:7–22	Ps 108	Ps 37:34–40	Heb 3; 4
Yr 3	Nov 13	1 Chr 6:23–36	Ps 109:1–19	Ps 38	Heb 5:1–6:12
Yr 3	Nov 14	1 Chr 6:37–43	Ps 109:20–31	Ps 39	Heb 6:13–7:14
Yr 3	Nov 15	1 Chr 17:1–15	Ps 110	Ps 40	Heb 7:15–28
Yr 3	Nov 16	1 Chr 17:16–27	Ps 111	Ps 41	Heb 8:1–9:10
Yr 3	Nov 17	1 Chr 18	Ps 112	Ps 42	Heb 9:11–10:10
Yr 3	Nov 18	1 Chr 19	Ps 113; 114	Ps 43	Heb 10:11–39
Yr 3	Nov 19	1 Chr 20	Ps 115	Ps 44	Heb 11:1–12
Yr 3	Nov 20	1 Chr 21:1–17	Ps 116; 117	Ps 45	Heb 11:13–40
Yr 3	Nov 21	1 Chr 21:18–30	Ps 118:1–18	Ps 46	Heb 12:1–13
Yr 3	Nov 22	1 Chr 22	Ps 118:19–29	Ps 47	Heb 12:14–29
Yr 3	Nov 23	1 Chr 23:1–11	Ps 119:1–16	Ps 48	Heb 13
Yr 3	Nov 24	1 Chr 23:12–20	Ps 119:17–32	Ps 49	Jas 1
Yr 3	Nov 25	1 Chr 23:21–32	Ps 119:33–40	Ps 50:1–6	Jas 2
Yr 3	Nov 26	1 Chr 24:1–19	Ps 119:41–48	Ps 50:7–23	Jas 3
Yr 3	Nov 27	1 Chr 24:20–31	Ps 119:49–56	Ps 51	Jas 4
Yr 3	Nov 28	1 Chr 25:1–7	Ps 119:65–80	Ps 52	Jas 5
Yr 3	Nov 29	1 Chr 25:8–31	Ps 119:81–96	Ps 53; 54	1 Pet 1
Yr 3	Nov 30	Prov 23:1–9	Ps 119:97–104	Ps 55	1 Pet 2
Yr 3	Dec 1	Prov 23:10–25	Ps 119:105–112	Ps 56	1 Pet 3
Yr 3	Dec 2	Prov 23:26–35	Ps 119:113–128	Ps 57	1 Pet 4
Yr 3	Dec 3	Prov 24:1–22	Ps 119:129–144	Ps 58	1 Pet 5
Yr 3	Dec 4	Prov 24:23–34	Ps 119:145–152	Ps 59	2 Pet 1
Yr 3	Dec 5	Prov 25:1–15	Ps 119:153–160	Ps 60	2 Pet 2

557

Yr 3	Dec 6	Prov 25:16–28	Ps 119:161–176	Ps 61	2 Pet 3
Yr 3	Dec 7	Prov 26:1–12	Ps 120; 121	Ps 62; 1	1 Jn 1; 2:1–2:27
Yr 3	Dec 8	Prov 26:13–28	Ps 122; 123; 124	Ps 63; 1	1 Jn 2:28–3:24
Yr 3	Dec 9	Prov 27:1–10	Ps 125; 126; 127	Ps 64; 1	1 Jn 4
Yr 3	Dec 10	Prov 27:11–27	Ps 128; 129	Ps 65; 1	1 Jn 5
Yr 3	Dec 11	Ez 37:1–14	Ps 130; 131	Ps 66; 2	2 Jn
Yr 3	Dec 12	Ez 37:15–28	Ps 132	Ps 67; 3	3 Jn
Yr 3	Dec 13	Ez 38	Ps 133; 134	Ps 68:1–19	Jude
Yr 3	Dec 14	Ez 39:1–8	Ps 135	Ps 68:20–35	Rev 1:1–2:11
Yr 3	Dec 15	Ez 39:9–24	Ps 136:1–16	Ps 69:1–18	Rev 2:12–3:6
Yr 3	Dec 16	Ez 39:25–40:4	Ps 136:17–26	Ps 69:19–36	Rev 3:7–22
Yr 3	Dec 17	Ez 40:5–23	Ps 137	Ps 70	Rev 4; 5
Yr 3	Dec 18	Ez 40:24–37	Ps 138	Ps 71:1–16	Rev 6
Yr 3	Dec 19	Ez 40:38–49	Ps 139:1–12	Ps 71:17–24	Rev 7
Yr 3	Dec 20	Ez 41:1–15	Ps 139:13–24	Ps 72:1–11	Rev 8:1–9:12
Yr 3	Dec 21	Ez 41:16–26	Ps 140	Ps 72:12–20	Rev 9:13–10:11
Yr 3	Dec 22	Ez 42	Ps 141	Ps 73:1–16	Rev 11; 12
Yr 3	Dec 23	Ez 43:1–12	Ps 142	Ps 73:17–28	Rev 13
Yr 3	Dec 24	Ez 43:13–27	Ps 143	Ps 74:1–8	Rev 14
Yr 3	Dec 25	Ez 44:1–14	Ps 144	Ps 74:9–23	Rev 15; 16
Yr 3	Dec 26	Ez 44:15–31	Ps 145:1–13	Ps 75	Rev 17
Yr 3	Dec 27	Ez 45:1–12	Ps 145:14–21	Ps 76	Rev 18
Yr 3	Dec 28	Ez 45:13–25	Ps 146	Ps 77	Rev 19
Yr 3	Dec 29	Ez 46:1–18	Ps 147	Ps 78:1–16	Rev 20
Yr 3	Dec 30	Ez 46:19– 47:12	Ps 148	Ps 78:17–31	Rev 21
Yr 3	Dec 31	Ez 47:13–23	Ps 149; 150	Ps 78:32–39	Rev 22

Year 4

2019, 2023, 2027, 2031, 2035, 2039, 2043, 2047, 2051, 2055, 2059, 2063, 2067, 2071

Yr 4 Jan 1	Ez 48:1–20	Ps 1; 2	Ps 78:40–55	Matt 1
Yr 4 Jan 2	Ez 48:21–35	Ps 3; 4	Ps 78:56–64	Matt 2
Yr 4 Jan 3	Num 22:1–20	Ps 5	Ps 78:65–72	Matt 3
Yr 4 Jan 4	Num 22:21–41	Ps 6	Ps 79	Matt 4
Yr 4 Jan 5	Num 23:1–12	Ps 7	Ps 80	Matt 5:1–20
Yr 4 Jan 6	Num 23:13–30	Ps 8	Ps 81	Matt 5:21–37
Yr 4 Jan 7	Num 24:1–14	Ps 9:1–10	Ps 82	Matt 5:38–6:4
Yr 4 Jan 8	Num 24:15–25	Ps 9:11–20	Ps 83	Matt 6:5–34
Yr 4 Jan 9	Num 25	Ps 10	Ps 84	Matt 7
Yr 4 Jan 10	Num 26:1–11	Ps 11; 12	Ps 85	Matt 8:1–22
Yr 4 Jan 11	Num 26:12–22	Ps 13; 14	Ps 86	Matt 8:23–34
Yr 4 Jan 12	Num 26:23–34	Ps 15; 16	Ps 87	Matt 9:1–17
Yr 4 Jan 13	Num 26:35–41	Ps 17	Ps 88	Matt 9:18–38
Yr 4 Jan 14	Num 26:42–56	Ps 18:1–15	Ps 89:1–14	Matt 10:1–23
Yr 4 Jan 15	Num 26:57–65	Ps 18:16–29	Ps 89:15–37	Matt 10:24–42
Yr 4 Jan 16	Num 27:1–11	Ps 18:30–45	Ps 89:38–52	Matt 11
Yr 4 Jan 17	Num 27:12–23	Ps 18:46–50	Ps 90	Matt 12:1–21
Yr 4 Jan 18	Num 28:1–15	Ps 19	Ps 91	Matt 12:22–50
Yr 4 Jan 19	Num 28:16–31	Ps 20	Ps 92	Matt 13:1–23
Yr 4 Jan 20	Num 29:1–11	Ps 21	Ps 93	Matt 13:24–43
Yr 4 Jan 21	Num 29:12–40	Ps 22:1–24	Ps 94	Matt 13:44–58
Yr 4 Jan 22	Num 30	Ps 22:25–31	Ps 95	Matt 14
Yr 4 Jan 23	Num 31:1–24	Ps 23; 24	Ps 96	Matt 15:1–20
Yr 4 Jan 24	Num 31:25–47	Ps 25	Ps 97	Matt 15:21–39
Yr 4 Jan 25	Num 31:48–54	Ps 26	Ps 98	Matt 16
Yr 4 Jan 26	Num 32:1–24	Ps 27	Ps 99	Matt 17
Yr 4 Jan 27	Num 32:25–32	Ps 28	Ps 100; 101	Matt 18:1–20
Yr 4 Jan 28	Num 32:33–42	Ps 29	Ps 102:1–17	Matt 18:21–35
Yr 4 Jan 29	1 Chr 26:1–19	Ps 30	Ps 102:18–28	Matt 19:1–15
Yr 4 Jan 30	1 Chr 26:20–32	Ps 31:1–8	Ps 103	Matt 19:16–30
Yr 4 Jan 31	1 Chr 27:1–15	Ps 31:9–24	Ps 104:1–18	Matt 20:1–16
Yr 4 Feb 1	1 Chr 27:16–34	Ps 32	Ps 104:19–35	Matt 20:17–34
Yr 4 Feb 2	1 Chr 28:1–10	Ps 33	Ps 105:1–15	Matt 21:1–22

Yr 4	Feb 3	1 Chr 28:11–21	Ps 34	Ps 105:16–25	Matt 21:23–46
Yr 4	Feb 4	1 Chr 29:1–9	Ps 35:1–10	Ps 105:26–45	Matt 22:1–33
Yr 4	Feb 5	1 Chr 29:10–20	Ps 35:11–28	Ps 106:1–11	Matt 22:34–46
Yr 4	Feb 6	1 Chr 29:21–30	Ps 36	Ps 106:12–27	Matt 23:1–24
Yr 4	Feb 7	2 Chr 1	Ps 37:1–7	Ps 106:28–39	Matt 23:25–39
Yr 4	Feb 8	2 Chr 2	Ps 37:8–19	Ps 106:40–48	Matt 24:1–31
Yr 4	Feb 9	2 Chr 3	Ps 37:20–33	Ps 107:1–16	Matt 24:32–25:13
Yr 4	Feb 10	2 Chr 4	Ps 37:34–40	Ps 107:17–32	Matt 25:14–30
Yr 4	Feb 11	2 Chr 5	Ps 38	Ps 107:33–43	Matt 25:31–46
Yr 4	Feb 12	2 Chr 6:1–11	Ps 39	Ps 108	Matt 26:1–16
Yr 4	Feb 13	2 Chr 6:12–42	Ps 40	Ps 109:1–19	Matt 26:17–46
Yr 4	Feb 14	2 Chr 7:1–10	Ps 41	Ps 109:20–31	Matt 26:47–75
Yr 4	Feb 15	2 Chr 7:11–22	Ps 42	Ps 110	Matt 27:1–26
Yr 4	Feb 16	2 Chr 8	Ps 43	Ps 111	Matt 27:27–56
Yr 4	Feb 17	2 Chr 9:1–12	Ps 44	Ps 112	Matt 27:57–66;28
Yr 4	Feb 18	2 Chr 9:13–31	Ps 45	Ps 113; 114	Mk 1:1–20
Yr 4	Feb 19	2 Chr 10	Ps 46	Ps 115	Mk 1:21–45
Yr 4	Feb 20	2 Chr 11	Ps 47	Ps 116; 117	Mk 2:1–17
Yr 4	Feb 21	2 Chr 12	Ps 48	Ps 118:1–18	Mk 2:18–28
Yr 4	Feb 22	2 Chr 13:1–12	Ps 49	Ps 118:19–29	Mk 3:1–19
Yr 4	Feb 23	2 Chr 13:13–22	Ps 50:1–6	Ps 119:1–16	Mk 3:20–35
Yr 4	Feb 24	2 Chr 14	Ps 50:7–23	Ps 119:17–32	Mk 4:1–20
Yr 4	Feb 25	2 Chr 15:1–8	Ps 51	Ps 119:33–40	Mk 4:21–41
Yr 4	Feb 26	2 Chr15:9–19	Ps 52	Ps 119:41–48	Mk 5:1–20
Yr 4	Feb 27	2 Chr 16	Ps 53; 54	Ps 119:49–56	Mk 5:21–43
Yr 4	Feb 28	2 Chr 17	Ps 55	Ps 119:65–80	Mk 6:1–29
Yr 4	Mar 1	Prov 28:1–13	Ps 56	Ps 119:81–96	Mk 6:30–56
Yr 4	Mar 2	Prov 28:14–28	Ps 57	Ps 119:97–104	Mk 7:1–23
Yr 4	Mar 3	Prov 29:1–13	Ps 58	Ps 119:105–112	Mk 7:24–37
Yr 4	Mar 4	Prov 29:14–27	Ps 59	Ps 119:113–128	Mk 8:1–26
Yr 4	Mar 5	Prov 30:1–16	Ps 60	Ps 119:129–144	Mk 8:27–9:1
Yr 4	Mar 6	Prov 30:17–33	Ps 61	Ps 119:145–152	Mk 9:2–29
Yr 4	Mar 7	Prov 31:1–9	Ps 62	Ps 119:153–160	Mk 9:30–50
Yr 4	Mar 8	Prov 31:10–31	Ps 63	Ps 119:161–176	Mk 10:1–16
Yr 4	Mar 9	Eccl 1:1–11	Ps 64	Ps 120; 121	Mk 10:17–34
Yr 4	Mar 10	Eccl 1:12–18	Ps 65	Ps 122; 123; 124	Mk 10:35–52
Yr 4	Mar 11	Dan 1:1–21	Ps 66	Ps 125; 126; 127	Mk 11
Yr 4	Mar 12	Dan 2:1–23	Ps 67	Ps 128; 129	Mk 12:1–27
Yr 4	Mar 13	Dan 1:24–45	Ps 68:1–19	Ps 130; 131	Mk 12:28–44
Yr 4	Mar 14	Dan 1:46–49	Ps 68:20–35	Ps 132	Mk 13:1–25
Yr 4	Mar 15	Dan 3:1–18	Ps 69:1–18	Ps 133; 134	Mk 13:26–37
Yr 4	Mar 16	Dan 3:19–30	Ps 69:19–36	Ps 135	Mk 14:1–26
Yr 4	Mar 17	Dan 4:1–18	Ps 70	Ps 136:1–16	Mk 14:27–52
Yr 4	Mar 18	Dan 4:19–27	Ps 71:1–16	Ps 136:17–26	Mk 14:53–72
Yr 4	Mar 19	Dan 4:28–33	Ps 71:17–24	Ps 137	Mk 15:1–20
Yr 4	Mar 20	Dan 4:34–37	Ps 72:1–11	Ps 138	Mk 15:21–47
Yr 4	Mar 21	Dan 5:1–12	Ps 72:12–20	Ps 139:1–12	Mk 16:1–20*
Yr 4	Mar 22	Dan 5:13–31	Ps 73:1–16	Ps 139:13–24	Lk 1:1–25
Yr 4	Mar 23	Dan 6:1–18	Ps 73:17–28	Ps 140	Lk 1:26–45
Yr 4	Mar 24	Dan 6:19–28	Ps 74:1–8	Ps 141	Lk 1:46–66
Yr 4	Mar 25	Dan 7:1–14	Ps 74:9–23	Ps 142	Lk 1:67–80

Yr 4	Mar 26	Dan 7:15–28	Ps 75	Ps 143	Lk 2:1–20
Yr 4	Mar 27	Dan 8:1–14	Ps 76	Ps 144	Lk 2:21–52
Yr 4	Mar 28	Dan 8:15–27	Ps 77	Ps 145:1–13	Lk 3:1–20
Yr 4	Mar 29	Dan 9:1–19	Ps 78:1–16	Ps 145:14–21	Lk 3:21–38
Yr 4	Mar 30	Dan 9:20–27	Ps 78:17–31	Ps 146	Lk 4:1–30
Yr 4	Mar 31	Dan 10	Ps 78:32–39	Ps 147	Lk 4:31–44
Yr 4	Apr 1	Dan 11:1–12	Ps 78:40–55	Ps 148	Lk 5:1–26
Yr 4	Apr 2	Dan 11:13–28	Ps 78:56–64	Ps 149	Lk 5:27–39
Yr 4	Apr 3	Dan 11:29–45	Ps 78:65–72	Ps 150	Lk 6:1–26
Yr 4	Apr 4	Num 33:1–15	Ps 79	Ps 1; 2	Lk 6:27–49
Yr 4	Apr 5	Num 33:16–36	Ps 80	Ps 3; 4	Lk 7:1–27
Yr 4	Apr 6	Num 33:37–49	Ps 81	Ps 5	Lk 7:28–50
Yr 4	Apr 7	Num 33:50–56	Ps 82	Ps 6	Lk 8:1–15
Yr 4	Apr 8	Num 34:1–15	Ps 83	Ps 7	Lk 8:16–39
Yr 4	Apr 9	Num 34:16–29	Ps 84	Ps 8	Lk 8:40–56
Yr 4	Apr 10	Num 35:1–8	Ps 85	Ps 9:1–10	Lk 9:1–27
Yr 4	Apr 11	Num 35:9–34	Ps 86	Ps 9:11–20	Lk 9:28–48
Yr 4	Apr 12	Num 36	Ps 87	Ps 10	Lk 9:49–62
Yr 4	Apr 13	Deut 1:1–8	Ps 88	Ps 11; 12	Lk 10:1–29
Yr 4	Apr 14	Deut 1:9–18	Ps 89:1–14	Ps 13; 14	Lk 10:30–42
Yr 4	Apr 15	Deut 1:19–25	Ps 89:15–37	Ps 15; 16	Lk 11:1–28
Yr 4	Apr 16	Deut 1:26–46	Ps 89:38–52	Ps 17	Lk 11:29–54
Yr 4	Apr 17	Deut 2:1–15	Ps 90	Ps 18:1–15	Lk 12:1–21
Yr 4	Apr 18	Deut 2:16–25	Ps 91	Ps 18:16–29	Lk 12:22–48
Yr 4	Apr 19	Deut 2:26–37	Ps 92	Ps 18:30–45	Lk 12:49–59
Yr 4	Apr 20	Deut 3:1–11	Ps 93	Ps 18:46–50	Lk 13:1–21
Yr 4	Apr 21	Deut 3:12–20	Ps 94	Ps 19	Lk 13:22–35
Yr 4	Apr 22	Deut 3:21–29	Ps 95	Ps 20	Lk 14
Yr 4	Apr 23	Deut 4:1–14	Ps 96	Ps 21	Lk 15:1–10
Yr 4	Apr 24	Deut 4:15–31	Ps 97	Ps 22:1–24	Lk 15:11–32
Yr 4	Apr 25	Deut 4:32–43	Ps 98	Ps 22:25–31	Lk 16
Yr 4	Apr 26	Deut 4:44–49	Ps 99	Ps 23; 24	Lk 17
Yr 4	Apr 27	Deut 5:1–21	Ps 100; 101	Ps 25	Lk 18:1–17
Yr 4	Apr 28	Deut 5:22–33	Ps 102:1–17	Ps 26	Lk 18:18–43
Yr 4	Apr 29	Deut 6	Ps 102:18–28	Ps 27	Lk 19:1–10
Yr 4	Apr 30	2 Chr 18:1–8	Ps 103	Ps 28	Lk 19:11–27
Yr 4	May 1	2 Chr 18:9–27	Ps 104:1–18	Ps 29	Lk 19:28–48
Yr 4	May 2	2 Chr 18:28–34	Ps 104:19–35	Ps 30	Lk 20:1–19
Yr 4	May 3	2 Chr 19	Ps 105:1–15	Ps 31:1–8	Lk 20:20–47
Yr 4	May 4	2 Chr 20:1–12	Ps 105:16–25	Ps 31:9–24	Lk 21:1–11
Yr 4	May 5	2 Chr 20:13–30	Ps 105:26–45	Ps 32	Lk 21:12–38
Yr 4	May 6	2 Chr 20:31–37	Ps 106:1–11	Ps 33	Lk 22:1–13
Yr 4	May 7	2 Chr 21	Ps 106:12–27	Ps 34	Lk 22:14–38
Yr 4	May 8	2 Chr 22	Ps 106:28–39	Ps 35:1–10	Lk 22:39–71
Yr 4	May 9	2 Chr 23:1–11	Ps 106:40–48	Ps 35:11–28	Lk 23:1–25
Yr 4	May 10	2 Chr 23:12–21	Ps 107:1–16	Ps 36	Lk 23:26–43
Yr 4	May 11	2 Chr 24:1–16	Ps 107:17–32	Ps 37:1–7	Lk 23:44–56
Yr 4	May 12	2 Chr 24:17–27	Ps 107:33–43	Ps 37:8–19	Lk 24:1–34
Yr 4	May 13	2 Chr 25:1–12	Ps 108	Ps 37:20–33	Lk 24:35–53
Yr 4	May 14	2 Chr 25:13–28	Ps 109:1–19	Ps 37:34–40	Jn 1:1–28
Yr 4	May 15	2 Chr 26:1–15	Ps 109:20–31	Ps 38	Jn 1:29–51

561

Yr 4 May 16	2 Chr 26:16–23	Ps 110	Ps 39	Jn 2:1–12
Yr 4 May 17	2 Chr 27	Ps 111	Ps 40	Jn 2:13–25
Yr 4 May 18	2 Chr 28	Ps 112	Ps 41	Jn 3:1–21
Yr 4 May 19	2 Chr 29:1–17	Ps 113; 114	Ps 42	Jn 3:22–36
Yr 4 May 20	2 Chr 29:18–36	Ps 115	Ps 43	Jn 4:1–38
Yr 4 May 21	2 Chr 30:1–9	Ps 116; 117	Ps 44	Jn 4:39–5:15
Yr 4 May 22	2 Chr 30:10–27	Ps 118:1–18	Ps 45	Jn 5:16–47
Yr 4 May 23	2 Chr 31	Ps 118:19–29	Ps 46	Jn 6:1–21
Yr 4 May 24	2 Chr 32:1–8	Ps 119:1–16	Ps 47	Jn 6:22–59
Yr 4 May 25	2 Chr 32:9–23	Ps 119:17–32	Ps 48	Jn 6:60–7:9
Yr 4 May 26	2 Chr 32:24–33	Ps 119:33–40	Ps 49	Jn 7:10–36
Yr 4 May 27	2 Chr 33:1–13	Ps 119:41–48	Ps 50:1–6	Jn 7:37–52
Yr 4 May 28	2 Chr 33:14–25	Ps 119:49–56	Ps 50:7–23	Jn 7:53–8:11
Yr 4 May 29	2 Chr 34:1–13	Ps 119:65–80	Ps 51	Jn 8:12–30
Yr 4 May 30	2 Chr 34:14–33	Ps 119:81–96	Ps 52	Jn 8:31–59
Yr 4 May 31	Eccl 2:1–17	Ps 119:97–104	Ps 53; 54	Jn 9:1–34
Yr 4 June 1	Eccl 2:18–26	Ps 119:105–112	Ps 55	Jn 9:35–41
Yr 4 June 2	Eccl 3	Ps 119:113–128	Ps 56	Jn 10:1–21
Yr 4 June 3	Eccl 4	Ps 119:129–144	Ps 57	Jn 10:22–42
Yr 4 June 4	Eccl 5:1–7	Ps 119:145–152	Ps 58	Jn 11:1–29
Yr 4 June 5	Eccl 5:8–20	Ps 119:153–160	Ps 59	Jn 11:30–57
Yr 4 June 6	Eccl 6	Ps 119:161–176	Ps 60	Jn 12:1–19
Yr 4 June 7	Eccl 7:1–14	Ps 120; 121	Ps 61	Jn 12:20–36
Yr 4 June 8	Eccl 7:15–29	Ps 122; 123; 124	Ps 62	Jn 12:37–50
Yr 4 June 9	Eccl 8	Ps 125; 126; 127	Ps 63	Jn 13:1–20
Yr 4 June 10	Eccl 9	Ps 128; 129	Ps 64	Jn 13:21–38
Yr 4 June 11	Dan 12	Ps 130; 131	Ps 65	Jn 14
Yr 4 June 12	Hos 1–2:1	Ps 132	Ps 66	Jn 15
Yr 4 June 13	Hos 2:2–13	Ps 133; 134	Ps 67	Jn 16:1–15
Yr 4 June 14	Hos 2:14–23	Ps 135	Ps 68:1–19	Jn 16:16–33
Yr 4 June 15	Hos 3	Ps 136:1–16	Ps 68:20–35	Jn 17
Yr 4 June 16	Hos 4	Ps 136:17–26	Ps 69:1–18	Jn 18:1–24
Yr 4 June 17	Hos 5	Ps 137	Ps 69:19–36	Jn 18:25–40
Yr 4 June 18	Hos 6	Ps 138	Ps 70	Jn 19:1–27
Yr 4 June 19	Hos 7	Ps 139:1–12	Ps 71:1–16	Jn 19:28–42
Yr 4 June 20	Hos 8	Ps 139:13–24	Ps 71:17–24	Jn 20:1–18
Yr 4 June 21	Hos 9	Ps 140	Ps 72:1–11	Jn 20:19–31
Yr 4 June 22	Hos 10	Ps 141	Ps 72:12–20	Jn 21
Yr 4 June 23	Hos 11	Ps 142	Ps 73:1–16	Acts 1
Yr 4 June 24	Hos 12	Ps 143	Ps 73:17–28	Acts 2:1–21
Yr 4 June 25	Hos 13	Ps 144	Ps 74:1–8	Acts 2:22–47
Yr 4 June 26	Hos 14	Ps 145:1–13	Ps 74:9–23	Acts 3:1–11
Yr 4 June 27	Joel 1	Ps 145:14–21	Ps 75	Acts 3:12–26
Yr 4 June 28	Joel 2:1–11	Ps 146	Ps 76	Acts 4:1–22
Yr 4 June 29	Joel 2:12–17	Ps 147	Ps 77	Acts 4:23–37
Yr 4 June 30	Joel 2:18–32	Ps 148	Ps 78:1–16	Acts 5:1–16
Yr 4 July 1	Joel 3	Ps 149	Ps 78:17–31	Acts 5:17–42
Yr 4 July 2	Amos 1	Ps 150	Ps 78:32–39	Acts 6; 7:1–10
Yr 4 July 3	Amos 2	Ps 1; 2	Ps 78:40–55	Acts 7:11–60
Yr 4 July 4	Amos 3	Ps 3; 4	Ps 78:56–64	Acts 8:1–25
Yr 4 July 5	Deut 7:1–15	Ps 5	Ps 78:65–72	Acts 8:26–40

Yr 4	July 6	Deut 7:16–26	Ps 6	Ps 79	Acts 9:1–19
Yr 4	July 7	Deut 8	Ps 7	Ps 80	Acts 9:20–43
Yr 4	July 8	Deut 9:1–6	Ps 8	Ps 81	Acts 10:1–33
Yr 4	July 9	Deut 9:7–29	Ps 9:1–10	Ps 82	Acts 10:34–48
Yr 4	July 10	Deut 10:1–11	Ps 9:11–20	Ps 83	Acts 11:1–18
Yr 4	July 11	Deut 10:12–22	Ps 10	Ps 84	Acts 11:19–30
Yr 4	July 12	Deut 11:1–7	Ps 11; 12	Ps 85	Acts 12
Yr 4	July 13	Deut 11:8–32	Ps 13; 14	Ps 86	Acts 13:1–12
Yr 4	July 14	Deut 12:1–19	Ps 15; 16	Ps 87	Acts 13:13–43
Yr 4	July 15	Deut 12:20–32	Ps 17	Ps 88	Acts 13:44–14:7
Yr 4	July 16	Deut 13	Ps 18:1–15	Ps 89:1–14	Acts 14:8–28
Yr 4	July 17	Deut 14:1–21	Ps 18:16–29	Ps 89:15–37	Acts 15
Yr 4	July 18	Deut 14:22–29	Ps 18:30–45	Ps 89:38–52	Acts 16:1–21
Yr 4	July 19	Deut 15:1–11	Ps 18:46–50	Ps 90	Acts 16:22–40
Yr 4	July 20	Deut 15:12–23	Ps 19	Ps 91	Acts 17
Yr 4	July 21	Deut 16:1–8	Ps 20	Ps 92	Acts 18:1–23
Yr 4	July 22	Deut 16:9–22	Ps 21	Ps 93	Acts 18:24–19:7
Yr 4	July 23	Deut 17	Ps 22:1–24	Ps 94	Acts 19:8–22
Yr 4	July 24	Deut 18	Ps 22:25–31	Ps 95	Acts 19:23–41
Yr 4	July 25	Deut 19	Ps 23; 24	Ps 96	Acts 20
Yr 4	July 26	Deut 20	Ps 25	Ps 97	Acts 21:1–25
Yr 4	July 27	Deut 21:1–14	Ps 26	Ps 98	Acts 21:26–40
Yr 4	July 28	Deut 21:15–23	Ps 27	Ps 99	Acts 22:1–23
Yr 4	July 29	Deut 22:1–12	Ps 28	Ps 100; 101	Acts 22:24–23:11
Yr 4	July 30	Deut 22:13–30	Ps 29	Ps 102:1–17	Acts 23:12–35
Yr 4	July 31	2 Chr 35:1–19	Ps 30	Ps 102:18–28	Acts 24
Yr 4	Aug 1	2 Chr 35:20–27	Ps 31:1–8	Ps 103	Acts 25:1–12
Yr 4	Aug 2	2 Chr 36	Ps 31:9–24	Ps 104:1–18	Acts 25:13–27
Yr 4	Aug 3	Ezra 1	Ps 32	Ps 104:19–35	Acts 26
Yr 4	Aug 4	Ezra 2:1–15	Ps 33	Ps 105:1–15	Acts 27:1–26
Yr 4	Aug 5	Ezra 2:16–30	Ps 34	Ps 105:16–25	Acts 27:27–44
Yr 4	Aug 6	Ezra 2:31–42	Ps 35:1–10	Ps 105:26–45	Acts 28:1–16
Yr 4	Aug 7	Ezra 2:43–58	Ps 35:11–28	Ps 106:1–11	Acts 28:17–31
Yr 4	Aug 8	Ezra 2:59–70	Ps 36	Ps 106:12–27	Rom 1:1–17
Yr 4	Aug 9	Ezra 3	Ps 37:1–7	Ps 106:28–39	Rom 1:18–32
Yr 4	Aug 10	Ezra 4:1–16	Ps 37:8–19	Ps 106:40–48	Rom 2
Yr 4	Aug 11	Ezra 4:17–24	Ps 37:20–33	Ps 107:1–16	Rom 3:1–8
Yr 4	Aug 12	Ezra 5	Ps 37:34–40	Ps 107:17–32	Rom 3:9–31
Yr 4	Aug 13	Ezra 6:1–12	Ps 38	Ps 107:33–43	Rom 4
Yr 4	Aug 14	Ezra 6:13–22	Ps 39	Ps 108	Rom 5
Yr 4	Aug 15	Ezra 7:1–10	Ps 40	Ps 109:1–19	Rom 6
Yr 4	Aug 16	Ezra 7:11–28	Ps 41	Ps 109:20–31	Rom 7
Yr 4	Aug 17	Ezra 8:1–14	Ps 42	Ps 110	Rom 8:1–17
Yr 4	Aug 18	Ezra 8:15–36	Ps 43	Ps 111	Rom 8:18–39
Yr 4	Aug 19	Ezra 9	Ps 44	Ps 112	Rom 9:1–24
Yr 4	Aug 20	Ezra 10:1–17	Ps 45	Ps 113; 114	Rom 9:25–10:4
Yr 4	Aug 21	Ezra 10:18–44	Ps 46	Ps 115	Rom 10:5–21
Yr 4	Aug 22	Neh 1	Ps 47	Ps 116; 117	Rom 11
Yr 4	Aug 23	Neh 2:1–10	Ps 48	Ps 118:1–18	Rom 12
Yr 4	Aug 24	Neh 2:11–20	Ps 49	Ps 118:19–29	Rom 13
Yr 4	Aug 25	Neh 3:1–14	Ps 50:1–6	Ps 119:1–16	Rom 14

Yr 4	Aug 26	Neh 3:15–32	Ps 50:7–23	Ps 119:17–32	Rom 15:1–22
Yr 4	Aug 27	Neh 4:1–13	Ps 51	Ps 119:33–40	Rom 15:23–16:16
Yr 4	Aug 28	Neh 4:14–23	Ps 52	Ps 119:41–48	Rom 16:17–27
Yr 4	Aug 29	Neh 5:1–13	Ps 53; 54	Ps 119:49–56	1 Cor 1
Yr 4	Aug 30	Neh 5:14–19	Ps 55	Ps 119:65–80	1 Cor 2
Yr 4	Aug 31	Eccl 10:1–10	Ps 56	Ps 119:81–96	1 Cor 3
Yr 4	Sept 1	Eccl 10:11–20	Ps 57	Ps 119:97–104	1 Cor 4
Yr 4	Sept 2	Eccl 11	Ps 58	Ps 119:105–112	1 Cor 5–6:11
Yr 4	Sept 3	Eccl 12	Ps 59	Ps 119:113–128	1 Cor 6:12–7:11
Yr 4	Sept 4	Amos 4	Ps 60	Ps 119:129–144	1 Cor 7:12–40
Yr 4	Sept 5	Amos 5:1–17	Ps 61	Ps 119:145–152	1 Cor 8
Yr 4	Sept 6	Amos 5:18–27	Ps 62	Ps 119:153–160	1 Cor 9
Yr 4	Sept 7	Amos 6	Ps 63	Ps 119:161–176	1 Cor 10
Yr 4	Sept 8	Amos 7	Ps 64	Ps 120; 121	1 Cor 11:1–16
Yr 4	Sept 9	Amos 8	Ps 65	Ps 122; 123; 124	1 Cor 11:17–34
Yr 4	Sept 10	Amos 9	Ps 66	Ps 125; 126; 127	1 Cor 12:1–26
Yr 4	Sept 11	Obad 1:1–14	Ps 67	Ps 128; 129	1 Cor 12:27–31;13
Yr 4	Sept 12	Obad 1:15–21	Ps 68:1–19	Ps 130; 131	1 Cor 14:1–25
Yr 4	Sept 13	Jonah 1	Ps 68:20–35	Ps 132	1 Cor 14:26–40
Yr 4	Sept 14	Jonah 2	Ps 69:1–18	Ps 133; 134	1 Cor 15:1–34
Yr 4	Sept 15	Jonah 3	Ps 69:19–36	Ps 135	1 Cor 15:35–58
Yr 4	Sept 16	Jonah 4	Ps 70	Ps 136:1–16	1 Cor 16
Yr 4	Sept 17	Micah 1	Ps 71:1–16	Ps 136:17–26	2 Cor 1
Yr 4	Sept 18	Micah 2	Ps 71:17–24	Ps 137	2 Cor 2
Yr 4	Sept 19	Micah 3	Ps 72:1–11	Ps 138	2 Cor 3
Yr 4	Sept 20	Micah 4	Ps 72:12–20	Ps 139:1–12	2 Cor 4
Yr 4	Sept 21	Micah 5	Ps 73:1–16	Ps 139:13–24	2 Cor 5:1–6:2
Yr 4	Sept 22	Micah 6	Ps 73:17–28	Ps 140	2 Cor 6:3–7:4
Yr 4	Sept 23	Micah 7:1–13	Ps 74:1–8	Ps 141	2 Cor 7:5–8:15
Yr 4	Sept 24	Micah 7:14–20	Ps 74:9–23	Ps 142	2 Cor 8:16–9:15
Yr 4	Sept 25	Nah 1	Ps 75	Ps 143	2 Cor 10
Yr 4	Sept 26	Nah 2	Ps 76	Ps 144	2 Cor 11
Yr 4	Sept 27	Nah 3	Ps 77	Ps 145:1–13	2 Cor 12
Yr 4	Sept 28	Deut 23:1–8	Ps 78:1–16	Ps 145:14–21	2 Cor 13
Yr 4	Sept 29	Deut 23:9–25	Ps 78:17–31	Ps 146	Gal 1
Yr 4	Sept 30	Deut 24:1–9	Ps 78:32–39	Ps 147	Gal 2
Yr 4	Oct 1	Deut 24:10–22	Ps 78:40–55	Ps 148	Gal 3:1–14
Yr 4	Oct 2	Deut 25:1–19	Ps 78:56–64	Ps 149; 150	Gal 3:15–29
Yr 4	Oct 3	Deut 26:1–15	Ps 78:65–72	Ps 1; 2	Gal 4
Yr 4	Oct 4	Deut 26:16–19	Ps 79	Ps 3; 4	Gal 5
Yr 4	Oct 5	Deut 27:1–10	Ps 80	Ps 5	Gal 6
Yr 4	Oct 6	Deut 27:11–26	Ps 81	Ps 6	Eph 1
Yr 4	Oct 7	Deut 28:1–14	Ps 82	Ps 7	Eph 2
Yr 4	Oct 8	Deut 28:15–46	Ps 83	Ps 8	Eph 3
Yr 4	Oct 9	Deut 28:47–57	Ps 84	Ps 9:1–10	Eph 4:1–16
Yr 4	Oct 10	Deut 28:58–29:1	Ps 85	Ps 9:11–20	Eph 4:17–5:14
Yr 4	Oct 11	Deut 29:2–15	Ps 86	Ps 10	Eph 5:15–33
Yr 4	Oct 12	Deut 29:16–29	Ps 87	Ps 11; 12	Eph 6
Yr 4	Oct 13	Deut 30:1–10	Ps 88	Ps 13; 14	Phil 1:1–19
Yr 4	Oct 14	Deut 30:11–20	Ps 89:1–14	Ps 15; 16	Phil 1:20–2:11
Yr 4	Oct 15	Deut 31:1–13	Ps 89:15–37	Ps 17	Phil 2:12–30

Yr 4	Oct 16	Deut 31:14–29	Ps 89:38–52	Ps 18:1–15	Phil 3
Yr 4	Oct 17	Deut 31:30–32:10	Ps 90	Ps 18:16–29	Phil 4
Yr 4	Oct 18	Deut 32:11–27	Ps 91	Ps 18:30–45	Col 1:1–23
Yr 4	Oct 19	Deut 32:28–47	Ps 92	Ps 18:46–50	Col 1:24–2:23
Yr 4	Oct 20	Deut 32:48–52	Ps 93	Ps 19	Col 3
Yr 4	Oct 21	Deut 33:1–11	Ps 94	Ps 20	Col 4
Yr 4	Oct 22	Deut 33:12–29	Ps 95	Ps 21	1 Thes 1
Yr 4	Oct 23	Deut 34	Ps 96	Ps 22:1–24	1 Thes 2
Yr 4	Oct 24	Neh 6	Ps 97	Ps 22:25–31	1 Thes 3; 4
Yr 4	Oct 25	Neh 7:1–18	Ps 98	Ps 23; 24	1 Thes 5
Yr 4	Oct 26	Neh 7:19–38	Ps 99	Ps 25; 2	2 Thes 1
Yr 4	Oct 27	Neh 7:39–60	Ps 100; 101	Ps 26; 2	2 Thes 2
Yr 4	Oct 28	Neh 7:61–73	Ps 102:1–17	Ps 27; 2	2 Thes 3
Yr 4	Oct 29	Neh 8:1–6	Ps 102:18–28	Ps 28	1 Tim 1
Yr 4	Oct 30	Neh 8:7–18	Ps 103	Ps 29	1 Tim 2; 3
Yr 4	Oct 31	Neh 9:1–12	Ps 104:1–18	Ps 30	1 Tim 4
Yr 4	Nov 1	Neh 9:13–26	Ps 104:19–35	Ps 31:1–8	1 Tim 5:1–6:2
Yr 4	Nov 2	Neh 9:27–37	Ps 105:1–15	Ps 31:9–24	1 Tim 6:3–21
Yr 4	Nov 3	Neh 9:38–10:13	Ps 105:16–25	Ps 32	2 Tim 1
Yr 4	Nov 4	Neh 10:14–29	Ps 105:26–45	Ps 33	2 Tim 2
Yr 4	Nov 5	Neh 10:30–39	Ps 106:1–11	Ps 34	2 Tim 3
Yr 4	Nov 6	Neh 11:1–14	Ps 106:12–27	Ps 35:1–10	2 Tim 4
Yr 4	Nov 7	Neh 11:15–36	Ps 106:28–39	Ps 35:11–28	Titus 1; 2
Yr 4	Nov 8	Neh 12:1–11	Ps 106:40–48	Ps 36	Titus 3
Yr 4	Nov 9	Neh 12:12–21	Ps 107:1–16	Ps 37:1–7	Philemon
Yr 4	Nov 10	Neh 12:22–26	Ps 107:17–32	Ps 37:8–19	Heb 1
Yr 4	Nov 11	Neh 12:27–47	Ps 107:33–43	Ps 37:20–33	Heb 2
Yr 4	Nov 12	Neh 13:1–9	Ps 108	Ps 37:34–40	Heb 3; 4
Yr 4	Nov 13	Neh 13:10–22	Ps 109:1–19	Ps 38	Heb 5:1–6:12
Yr 4	Nov 14	Neh 13:23–31	Ps 109:20–31	Ps 39	Heb 6:13–7:14
Yr 4	Nov 15	Esth 1:1–9	Ps 110	Ps 40	Heb 7:15–28
Yr 4	Nov 16	Esth 1:10–22	Ps 111	Ps 41	Heb 8:1–9:10
Yr 4	Nov 17	Esth 2	Ps 112	Ps 42	Heb 9:11–10:10
Yr 4	Nov 18	Esth 3	Ps 113; 114	Ps 43	Heb 10:11–39
Yr 4	Nov 19	Esth 4	Ps 115	Ps 44	Heb 11:1–12
Yr 4	Nov 20	Esth 5	Ps 116; 117	Ps 45	Heb 11:13–40
Yr 4	Nov 21	Esth 6	Ps 118:1–18	Ps 46	Heb 12:1–13
Yr 4	Nov 22	Esth 7	Ps 118:19–29	Ps 47	Heb 12:14–29
Yr 4	Nov 23	Esth 8	Ps 119:1–16	Ps 48	Heb 13
Yr 4	Nov 24	Esth 9:1–19	Ps 119:17–32	Ps 49	Jas 1
Yr 4	Nov 25	Esth 9:20–10:3	Ps 119:33–40	Ps 50:1–6	Jas 2
Yr 4	Nov 26	Song 1	Ps 119:41–48	Ps 50:7–23	Jas 3
Yr 4	Nov 27	Song 2	Ps 119:49–56	Ps 51	Jas 4
Yr 4	Nov 28	Song 3	Ps 119:65–80	Ps 52	Jas 5
Yr 4	Nov 29	Song 4	Ps 119:81–96	Ps 53; 54	1 Pet 1
Yr 4	Nov 30	Song 5	Ps 119:97–104	Ps 55	1 Pet 2
Yr 4	Dec 1	Song 6	Ps 119:105–112	———	1 Pet 3
Yr 4	Dec 2	Song 7	Ps 119:113–128	Ps 56	1 Pet 4
Yr 4	Dec 3	Song 8	Ps 119:129–144	Ps 57	1 Pet 5
Yr 4	Dec 4	Hab 1	Ps 119:145–152	Ps 58	2 Pet 1
Yr 4	Dec 5	Hab 2	Ps 119:153–160	Ps 59	2 Pet 2

Yr 4	Dec 6	Hab 3	Ps 119:161–176	Ps 60	2 Pet 3
Yr 4	Dec 7	Zeph 1	Ps 120; 121	Ps 61; 1	1 Jn 1; 2:1–2:27
Yr 4	Dec 8	Zeph 2	Ps 122; 123; 124	Ps 62; 1	1 Jn 2:28–3:24
Yr 4	Dec 9	Zeph 3:1–13	Ps 125; 126; 127	Ps 63; 1	1 Jn 4
Yr 4	Dec 10	Zeph 3:14–20	Ps 128; 129	Ps 64; 1	1 Jn 5
Yr 4	Dec 11	Hag 1	Ps 130; 131	Ps 65; 2	2 Jn
Yr 4	Dec 12	Hag 2	Ps 132	Ps 66; 3	3 Jn
Yr 4	Dec 13	Zech 1	Ps 133; 134	Ps 67	Jude
Yr 4	Dec 14	Zech 2	Ps 135	Ps 68:1–19	Rev 1:1–2:11
Yr 4	Dec 15	Zech 3	Ps 136:1–16	Ps 68:20–35	Rev 2:12–3:6
Yr 4	Dec 16	Zech 4	Ps 136:17–26	Ps 69:1–18	Rev 3:7–22
Yr 4	Dec 17	Zech 5	Ps 137	Ps 69:19–36	Rev 4; 5
Yr 4	Dec 18	Zech 6	Ps 138	Ps 70	Rev 6
Yr 4	Dec 19	Zech 7	Ps 139:1–12	Ps 71:1–16	Rev 7
Yr 4	Dec 20	Zech 8	Ps 139:13–24	Ps 71:17–24	Rev 8:1–9:12
Yr 4	Dec 21	Zech 9:1–8	Ps 140	Ps 72:1–11	Rev 9:13–10:11
Yr 4	Dec 22	Zech 9:9–17	Ps 141	Ps 72:12–20	Rev 11; 12
Yr 4	Dec 23	Zech 10	Ps 142	Ps 73:1–16	Rev 13
Yr 4	Dec 24	Zech 11	Ps 143	Ps 73:17–28	Rev 14
Yr 4	Dec 25	Zech 12	Ps 144	Ps 74:1–8	Rev 15; 16
Yr 4	Dec 26	Zech 13	Ps 145:1–13	Ps 74:9–23	Rev 17
Yr 4	Dec 27	Zech 14	Ps 145:14–21	Ps 75	Rev 18
Yr 4	Dec 28	Mal 1	Ps 146	Ps 76	Rev 19
Yr 4	Dec 29	Mal 2	Ps 147	Ps 77	Rev 20
Yr 4	Dec 30	Mal 3	Ps 148	Ps 78:1–16	Rev 21
Yr 4	Dec 31	Mal 4	Ps 149; 150	Ps 78:17–31	Rev 22

A Rule of Life
for
Christian Communities

1. Do not worship, or permit the community to worship any person, ideology, aim, or anything whatsoever except the triune God alone.

2. Do not love anything you have fashioned, built or curated more than the Lord.

3. Do not use the name of God casually, or give false assurances, or tolerate gossip or any other form of abusive language.

4. Let all members of the community honor their father and mother, fatherhood and motherhood, and those who have mentored them as fathers and mothers in the faith.

5. Do not nurse anger or be easily angered with those in the community.

6. Work to mend broken relationships, especially with those in the community.

7. Insist on the practice of biblical sexuality by all members of the community, however attracted, whether married or celibate.

8. Do not steal from others or from the community, whether time, talent, or treasure.

9. Practice disciplined rest in the community by avoiding unnecessary busyness; insist on sufficient rest for leaders of the community.

10. Do not covet anything that belongs to others, whether people or things.

11. Practice intentional patience with the community, both as individuals and as a whole.

12. Practice intentional kindness to the whole community, and especially to the difficult.

13. Search for ways that the community can work together to protect the vulnerable: unborn, born, young, old, poor, transient, and sick.

14. Break bread together with others in the community at least once per week, and whenever possible as an act of hospitality in the home.

15. Work hard together, both physically and spiritually.

16. Honor all rulers; the secular, whether or not you agree with them politically, and the spiritual that have been called to serve the community as overseers, elders, and deacons.

17. Do not hold grudges against anyone, forgive quickly even as you have been forgiven.

18. Do not seek your own good or advantage first, but in all things seek first the glory of Christ and the flourishing of the community.

19. Actively work to build trust with others, especially those in the community.

20. Whenever possible, believe the best about others, especially those in the community.

21. Give generously, especially to those who have need in the community and to support the vocation of the community.

22. Do not divide the community according to mortal or worldly classifications, except when absolutely necessary for human development or spiritual formation.

23. Worship as a community at least once a week, on the Lord's Day.

24. Read Holy Scripture in community at least twice per week: once on the Lords Day, and once between Lord's Days.

25. Celebrate holy communion as often as the life and unity of the community will permit.

26. Only baptize those who claim a new birth, can articulate an orthodox profession of the faith, and have shown fruits of conversion.

27. Pray in community at least once per week, in addition to the Lord's day, and midweek gathering, with both discipline and fervor.

28. Learn to love the truth of Holy Scripture and allow it alone to chasten your spirit and form the doctrine of the community.

29. Do not presume to teach those you are unwilling to love.

30. Do not presume to preach unless you love the community that will sit under your preaching.

31. Do not presume that your faith is genuine unless you truly love the community of faith.

32. Never permit foolish controversies to divide the community.

33. Study well the whole tradition of the church, and allow the wisdom of whatever is not forbidden by scripture to season your common life and worship.

34. Rejoice when truth triumphs, especially in conversions.

35. Rejoice whenever possible by organizing community wide celebrations.

36. Be firm when necessary, but gentle always.

37. Believe passionately, but practice humility; do not allow pride to infect your heart.

38. God has made your body and the earth; he has redeemed them both, and will remake them both for eternity: therefore, tend both as a holy obligation.

39. Do not allow anyone to remain in the community who pridefully, willfully, and repeatedly continues to ignore these scriptural precepts, even after loving and godly correction.

40. Do not lose hope or grow weary in doing good.

ACKNOWLEDGMENTS

by Patrick Morrow

I am deeply grateful to all the people who helped me appreciate this way of praying. In particular, I am thankful for the theological influence and personal friendship of Dr. Brian Brewer, my Historical Theology professor in seminary (and boss for several years!). Dr. Brewer helped me discern a specifically pastoral calling and instilled in me a great appreciation for the formative potential of common prayer and for liturgy in general. I am thankful to my mentor, Fr. Lee Nelson, for his wisdom as I learned the craft and calling of ministry through his patient tutelage.

I am also grateful to David Stone for his friendship, his sense of humor, his patience with my personality, and, of course, his partnership in this work. He understands our native Baptist tongue as well as anyone I know, and his wisdom in helping our translation work has been simply irreplaceable.

I am, of course, deeply indebted to my parents, Greg and Ila Morrow, my sister, Valarie Moseley, and my brother, James Morrow. All of them are formidable theologians in their own right and each have contributed in unique and irreplaceable ways to my own thinking and formation. Without them I would have never even graduated from elementary school (literally), much less seminary.

I am deeply grateful to my wife, Amy, for her love, unwavering support, and long suffering while I worked and worried my way through seminary and this project. More than any person I know, her hard work and sacrifice have made this work and our ministry together possible. I must also thank both my daughters, Caitlin and Rhiannon, for the many hours they spent formatting and proofreading early versions of this text.

Above all, I am grateful to the Lord; apart from His grace, no blessing at all is possible. He who causes the sun to shine on the crops of both the wicked and the righteous has caused His light to shine into the hearts of those who cast all their cares on Him. He is indeed the Faithful One, in whom all hope holds together. With a heart full of gratitude, I commend this work to Him in the hope that it will glorify Christ Jesus and help to grow His kingdom.

Amen.

by David Stone

I am constantly amazed at how God has placed people in my life to help me become the man I am today. It's even more amazing when those same influential people come back into my life, often after many years. The Christian life and discipleship are all about relationships.

Some of my earliest memories happened at 525 South Avenue in downtown Springfield, Missouri, at First Baptist Church. I am grateful for all the teachers and youth sponsors that showed me and my friends in the youth group how to serve others and live for Jesus. It is amazing how God has brought me back "home" to First Baptist to serve her people.

I want to thank Michael Haynes, the Director of Missions for Greene County Baptist Association, for my first exposure to the Daily Office. He has been taking groups of pastors to Assumption Abbey near Ava, Missouri, for years. I am grateful for my time with the monks which planted a seed in my heart for these spiritual disciplines.

I am grateful to my partner in this project, Patrick Morrow. Thank you for teaching me the finer points of the Daily Office for our "tribe." Thank you for your patience during morning prayer when I couldn't find my place in the midst of all the pages. You have blessed me so much by inviting me to be a part of the vision the Lord gave you for this book while at Baylor. Your passion for the Church, missional living, and faithfulness to Christian orthodoxy is absolutely amazing! I am so glad the Lord brought us back together after all these years.

I am thankful my parents, Bill and Betty Stone, for raising me in a Christian home. They were always there for me to taxi me to church events, band competitions, and Bears football games to watch me march. They have been extremely supportive of my call to ministry, even though they worry way too much—especially dad!

I am so proud to be the father to two wonderful young men, Taylor and Tucker. Mom and I are so grateful that you are growing up to become amazing men that love Jesus and love other people, especially the underdog.

And to Jenny, I am so thankful that we never remember meeting at First Baptist Church, that "I was always around, like a bad habit." Throughout this journey together in ministry, I can't think of another person beside whom I would rather serve! You truly are the best part of me, and I'm so grateful that you can "translate" for me. I love you with all my heart!

Finally, I am eternally grateful to Jesus, who has been chasing me my entire life... I just didn't realize it until I was twelve years old at that Leighton Ford Crusade. I am so thankful that you continue to send people into my life (and sometimes *back* into my life) to grow my faith. Thank you for always hearing my prayers, especially when I don't even know what to say!

"Now to him who is able to do far more abundantly than all that we ask or think, according to the power at work within us, to him be glory in the church and in Christ Jesus throughout all generations, forever and ever. Amen." (Eph. 3:20–21 ESV).

PRAYER JOURNAL

Praise or Concern   Date

_____ _____
_____ _____
_____ _____
_____ _____
_____ _____
_____ _____
_____ _____
_____ _____
_____ _____
_____ _____
_____ _____
_____ _____
_____ _____
_____ _____
_____ _____
_____ _____
_____ _____
_____ _____
_____ _____
_____ _____
_____ _____

Praise or Concern

Date

Praise or Concern

Date

Praise or Concern

Date

Praise or Concern   Date

_____   _____

_____   _____

_____   _____

_____   _____

_____   _____

_____   _____

_____   _____

_____   _____

_____   _____

_____   _____

_____   _____

_____   _____

_____   _____

_____   _____

_____   _____

_____   _____

_____   _____

_____   _____

_____   _____

_____   _____

_____   _____

_____   _____

_____   _____

_____   _____

Praise or Concern   Date

_____   _____

_____   _____

_____   _____

_____   _____

_____   _____

_____   _____

_____   _____

_____   _____

_____   _____

_____   _____

_____   _____

_____   _____

_____   _____

_____   _____

_____   _____

_____   _____

_____   _____

_____   _____

_____   _____

_____   _____

_____   _____

_____   _____

_____   _____

_____   _____

_____   _____

Praise or Concern

Date

Praise or Concern   Date

_____   _____
_____   _____
_____   _____
_____   _____
_____   _____
_____   _____
_____   _____
_____   _____
_____   _____
_____   _____
_____   _____
_____   _____
_____   _____
_____   _____
_____   _____
_____   _____
_____   _____
_____   _____
_____   _____
_____   _____
_____   _____
_____   _____
_____   _____
_____   _____
_____   _____
_____   _____

Praise or Concern

Date

Praise or Concern

Date

Praise or Concern   Date

_____   _____

_____   _____

_____   _____

_____   _____

_____   _____

_____   _____

_____   _____

_____   _____

_____   _____

_____   _____

_____   _____

_____   _____

_____   _____

_____   _____

_____   _____

_____   _____

_____   _____

_____   _____

_____   _____

_____   _____

_____   _____

_____   _____

_____   _____

_____   _____

_____   _____

_____   _____

_____   _____

_____   _____

Praise or Concern   Date

_____   _____
_____   _____
_____   _____
_____   _____
_____   _____
_____   _____
_____   _____
_____   _____
_____   _____
_____   _____
_____   _____
_____   _____
_____   _____
_____   _____
_____   _____
_____   _____
_____   _____
_____   _____
_____   _____
_____   _____
_____   _____
_____   _____
_____   _____
_____   _____